Commemorating Peterloo

Edinburgh Critical Studies in Romanticism
Series Editors: Ian Duncan and Penny Fielding

Available Titles
A Feminine Enlightenment: British Women Writers and the Philosophy of Progress, 1759–1820
JoEllen DeLucia
Reinventing Liberty: Nation, Commerce and the Historical Novel from Walpole to Scott
Fiona Price
The Politics of Romanticism: The Social Contract and Literature
Zoe Beenstock
Radical Romantics: Prophets, Pirates, and the Space Beyond Nation
Talissa J. Ford
Literature and Medicine in the Nineteenth-Century Periodical Press: Blackwood's Edinburgh Magazine, *1817–1858*
Megan Coyer
Discovering the Footsteps of Time: Geological Travel Writing in Scotland, 1700–1820
Tom Furniss
The Dissolution of Character in Late Romanticism, 1820–1839
Jonas Cope
Commemorating Peterloo: Violence, Resilience and Claim-making during the Romantic Era
Michael Demson and Regina Hewitt

Forthcoming Titles
Dialectics of Improvement: Scottish Romanticism, 1786–1829
Gerard Lee McKeever

Visit our website at: www.edinburghuniversitypress.com/series/edinburgh-critical-studies-in-romanticism

Commemorating Peterloo

Violence, Resilience and Claim-making during the Romantic Era

Edited by Michael Demson and Regina Hewitt

EDINBURGH
University Press

Edinburgh University Press is one of the leading university presses in the UK. We publish academic books and journals in our selected subject areas across the humanities and social sciences, combining cutting-edge scholarship with high editorial and production values to produce academic works of lasting importance. For more information visit our website: edinburghuniversitypress.com

Edinburgh University Press Ltd
The Tun – Holyrood Road
12(2f) Jackson's Entry
Edinburgh EH8 8PJ

First published in hardback by Edinburgh University Press 2019

Typeset in 11/14 Adobe Sabon by
IDSUK (DataConnection) Ltd

A CIP record for this book is available from the British Library

ISBN 978 1 4744 2856 9 (hardback)
ISBN 978 1 4744 2857 6 (paperback)
ISBN 978 1 4744 2858 3 (webready PDF)
ISBN 978 1 4744 2859 0 (epub)

Contents

List of Illustrations

Acknowledgements

The co-editors would like to thank Ian Duncan and Penny Fielding, the editors of the Edinburgh University Press series to which this volume now belongs, for welcoming our proposal, challenging us to bring out its potential and guiding our efforts to make it a timely and relevant study. We are grateful also to Michelle Houston and her team at the Press for their patient and thorough answers to our questions and the work they put into making this project a book. Our research was facilitated by Robert Poole (University of Lancashire) and Craig Horner and Michala Hulme (Manchester Centre for Public History and Heritage, Manchester Metropolitan University), who kindly corresponded with us and helped us obtain copies of their landmark issues of the *Manchester Region History Review* on Peterloo, but the volume could not have advanced without the eager and insightful responses of our contributors. We thank all of these colleagues for their scholarship and generosity. Finally, Michael would like to thank his wife, Audrey Murfin, to whom he dedicates his work, and Regina would like to thank her brother, Bill Hewitt, for his interest and encouragement.

Notes on Contributors

Stephen C. Behrendt (University of Nebraska) is University Professor and George Holmes Distinguished Professor. In addition to numerous articles, he has authored ten books, including *British Women Poets and the Romantic Writing Community* (Johns Hopkins University Press, 2009) and *Royal Mourning and Regency Culture: Elegies and Memorials of Princess Charlotte* (Macmillan/St. Martin's, 1997).

Frederick Burwick (University of California, Los Angeles), Research Professor at the University of California Los Angeles, is author and editor of thirty-three books and 150 essays. He is editor of the *Coleridge's Biographia Literaria: Text and Meaning* (Ohio State University Press, 1989) and *The Oxford Handbook of Coleridge* (Oxford University Press, 2009). Recent monographs include *Romanticism: Keywords* (Blackwell, 2015), *British Pirates in Print and Performance* (Palgrave, 2015) and *British Drama of the Industrial Revolution* (Cambridge University Press, 2015). Burwick has been named Distinguished Scholar by the British Academy (1992) and by the Keats-Shelley Association (1998). The International Conference on Romanticism has presented him with their Lifetime Achievement Award (2013).

Gerard Carruthers (University of Glasgow) is the Francis Hutcheson Professor of Scottish Literature and Co-Director of the Centre for Robert Burns Studies. He is the General Editor of the Oxford University Press edition of the *Works of Robert Burns* and Editor of the *Scottish Literary Review*. His recent books include *Scottish Literature* (2009), part of the Edinburgh University Press Critical Guides to Literature Series, and *Robert Burns* (Northcote House, 2005). Among his current projects is the Carnegie Trust funded, 'The People's Voice: Poetry, Song & the Franchise in Scotland, 1832–1918' on which he is co-investigator with Catriona Macdonald and Kirstie Blair.

Katey Castellano (James Madison University) has published articles in *European Romantic Review*, *SubStance: A Review of Theory and Literary Criticism* and *Romanticism on the Net*, among others, and her book, *The Ecology of British Romantic Conservatism, 1790–1837*, part of the Palgrave Series on the Enlightenment, Romanticism and Cultures of Print, was published in 2013.

Michael Demson (Sam Houston State University) has published articles in *European Romantic Review*, *Romanticism* and *Romantic Circles Praxis*, among others. He is currently completing a monograph on agrarian radicalism and Romanticism, a project supported by an American Council of Learned Societies Fellowship, and his non-fiction graphic novel, *Masks of Anarchy: From Percy Shelley to the Triangle Shirtwaist Factory Fire*, was published by Verso Books in 2013.

Michelle Faubert (University of Manitoba) is an Associate Professor at the University of Manitoba and Visiting Fellow at the University of Northumbria. She has been awarded both a Social Sciences and Humanities Research Council award and a Gerda Henkel Stiftung Research Scholarship. She has authored the monographs *Rhyming Reason: The Poetry of Romantic-Era Psychologists* (Pickering & Chatto 2009) and *Granville Sharpe's Uncovered Letter and the Zong Massacre* (Palgrave, 2018). She has also published two critical editions with Broadview Press, Mary Shelley's *Mathilda* (2017) and Mary Wollstonecraft's *The Wrongs of Woman and Mary* (2012), and she has edited both essay collections and special issues of journals, including *Literary Compass* and the *European Romantic Review*.

John Gardner (Anglia Ruskin University) is Professor of English Literature at Anglia Ruskin University. He has published articles in an array of journals, including *The Wordsworth Circle*, *Romanticism* and *The Keats-Shelley Journal*, among others, and his monograph, *Poetry and Popular Protest: Peterloo, Cato Street and the Queen Caroline Controversy*, was published by Palgrave in 2011.

Ian Haywood (University of Roehampton) focuses his research on the literature, radical politics and visual culture of the eighteenth and nineteenth centuries. In 2011–12 he received a Leverhulme Fellowship to complete *Romanticism and Caricature* (Cambridge University Press, 2013). His other recent books include *The Gordon Riots: Politics, Culture and Insurrection in Late Eighteenth-Century Britain*, co-edited with John Seed (Cambridge University Press, 2012), *Bloody Romanticism: Spectacular Violence and the Politics of Representation 1776–1832* (Palgrave, 2006) and *The Revolution in Popular Literature: Print, Politics and the People 1790–1860* (Cambridge University Press, 2004). He was elected President of the British Association of Romantic Studies (BARS) in 2015.

Regina Hewitt (University of South Florida) is Professor of English and Consulting Editor (formerly Co-Editor) of the *European Romantic Review*. She has edited a volume of essays titled *John Galt: Observations and Conjectures on Literature, History, and Society* (Bucknell University Press, 2012) and published essays on Maria Edgeworth in *Studies in the Novel* (2014) and on Joanna Baillie in the *Scottish Literary Review* (2009) and in *Romantic Circles Praxis* (2008). Her earlier books include *Symbolic Interactions: Social Problems and Literary Interventions in the Works of Baillie, Scott, and Landor* (Bucknell University Press, 2006) and *The Possibilities of Society: Wordsworth, Coleridge, and the Sociological Viewpoint of English Romanticism* (State University of New York Press, 1997).

James Kelly (University of Exeter, Cornwall Campus) is the author of *Charles Maturin: Authorship, Authenticity, and the Nation* (Four Courts Press, 2011) and edited the collection of essays *Ireland and Romanticism: Publics, Nations, and Scenes of Cultural Production* (Palgrave, 2011). He has written extensively on Irish literature in the Romantic period, with articles for the forthcoming *Oxford Handbook of Romanticism* and *A History of Modern Irish Women's Writing* joining similar entries for *The Blackwell Encyclopedia of Romanticism* and *The Gothic World*. Kelly's journal articles have covered the connection between popular culture and national identity, the influence of Robert Burns on nineteenth-century Irish nationalism, and links between rhetorical theory in the Romantic period and Irish literature.

Victoria Myers (Pepperdine University) is Professor Emerita of English and former editor of *Pacific Coast Philology*, the journal of the west coast Modern Language Association (1999–2007). She has published extensively on Romanticism: her essays on Romantic-era law and literature have appeared in *Studies in Romanticism* (2001, 2013), *The Wordsworth Circle* (2004), *European Romantic Review* (2007), *Spheres of Action* (ed. Angela Esterhammer and

Alex Dick, 2009), *Blackwell Encyclopedia of Romanticism: Drama* (ed. Frederick Burwick, 2011), and the *Oxford Handbook of British Romanticism* (ed. David Duff, 2018). Her edited collection, *Godwinian Moments: From Enlightenment to Romanticism*, co-edited with Robert Maniquis, was published by the University of Toronto Press in 2011, and she has been a chief editor on the *William Godwin's Diary* project, which was the recipient of the 2012 annual award for digital editions by the British Society for Eighteenth-Century Studies.

Murray Pittock (University of Glasgow) is Bradley Professor of English Literature and is a Fellow of the Royal Society of Edinburgh, the English Association, the Royal Historical Society, the Royal Society of Arts and the Society of Antiquaries of Scotland among other bodies. His most recent books include *Culloden* (Oxford University Press, 2016), *Material Culture and Sedition* (Palgrave, 2013), *The Edinburgh Companion to Scottish Romanticism* (Edinburgh University Press, 2011), *The Myth of the Jacobite Clans: The Jacobite Army in 1745* (Edinburgh University Press, 2009) and *Scottish and Irish Romanticism* (Oxford University Press, 2008).

Michael Scrivener (Wayne State University) is a Distinguished Professor at Wayne State and has received both a Guggenheim Fellowship and a Keats-Shelley Distinguished Scholar Award. He has published extensively on Romanticism, including his books *Jewish Representation in British Literature 1780–1840: After Shylock* (Palgrave Macmillan, 2011), *Seditious Allegories: John Thelwall and Jacobin Writing* (Pennsylvania State University Press, 2001) and *Radical Shelley: The Philosophical Anarchism and Utopian Thought of Percy Bysshe Shelley* (Princeton University Press, 1982).

Philip Shaw (University of Leicester) concentrates his research on the intersection of martial and literary culture. His books are *Suffering and Sentiment in Romantic Military Art* (Ashgate, 2013), *The Sublime* (Routledge, 2006), *Waterloo and the Romantic Imagination* (Palgrave, 2002) and *Romantic Wars: Studies in Culture and Conflict, 1789–1822* (Ashgate, 2000).

Introduction

Michael Demson and Regina Hewitt

The historical event that furnishes the occasion for this volume, the massacre of protestors in St Peter's Field in Manchester, England, on 16 August 1819, is well known in its physical details. Earlier in the month of that year, Joseph Johnson, who founded the *Manchester Observer* and the Manchester Patriotic Union, began organising for a mass public meeting in St Peter's Field, inviting the prominent radical agitator Henry Hunt to be the event's principal speaker. Their aim was to make peaceful demand for parliamentary reform and repeal of the Corn Laws, but the local magistrates, under the chairmanship of William Hulton, were anxious of riot, and sought to block the protest. When the meeting was eventually held on 16 August despite his efforts, the frustrated Hulton once again attempted to halt the event, this time by having the organisers and Hunt arrested. The assembled crowds, however, were too large – by modest estimation, some 50,000 people had come from across the surrounding areas – and they obstructed the constables from closing on the hustings where the principals had gathered. Hulton then called for Deputy Constable Joseph Nadin, and then both the Manchester and Salford Yeomanry and the 15th Hussars, who had been stationed on a street nearby, to assist in the arrests. They responded promptly and tragically: they charged the crowd with drawn sabres and, in the ensuing panic, trampled and slashed protestors haphazardly. In the end, the mayhem of the inexperienced and unskilled yeomanry left, according to Michael Bush's study of infirmary records, at least seventeen dead and more than 600 injured.[1]

Two hundred years later, the massacre is being commemorated not only by this volume but also by many other exhibits, lectures, conferences and publications. Such interest in observing the bicentennial raises the question of what is being commemorated – surely not the propensity of governments to reply with self-protective violence to any questioning of established ways of doing things, though such a violent response is the most searingly memorable feature of 'Peterloo', as it was wryly dubbed in 1819 by James Wroe the then-editor of the *Manchester Observer*. Rather, what most of us want to remember, and then analyse and understand, is the ultimate triumph of the people over repressive violence. Though terrible in its short-term effects, state violence at Peterloo was ineffective in the long term in suppressing protest and reinforcing authority. State violence mobilised protesters and supporters to identify themselves as civic participants, to renew their claims on the government and to make their voices heard. Indeed, the violence of Peterloo precipitated the Great Reform Act of 1832. It is this human resilience that we commemorate, and how it operates in a culture of violence that we investigate.

We take Peterloo to be a crucial episode in two parallel narratives of cultural history. One track – explored by Anthony Jarrells, Charles Tilly and James Chandler, among others[2] – tells a story of diminishing violence in Britain from the Glorious Revolution onwards. In this narrative, negotiation replaces confrontation as the means of effecting socio-political change. People rely on words to make claims on each other, and they aspire to non-violent identities; even if they do not always live up to their aspirations, this preference informs their attitudes towards violence, making them place it outside of cultural norms and acceptable practices.[3] According to Mark Doyle's account of conflicts in later colonial affairs, Peterloo set a precedent for 'the sort of popular outcry' against 'state violence . . . that Britain's rulers thought it wise to avoid'.[4] The capacity to be shocked by violence – the dominant reaction in accounts of Peterloo – illustrates this sensibility. This narrative encourages satisfaction with advances in civil rights gained since Peterloo and confidence in continuing progress towards a more just society, even if that progress suffers violent setbacks along the way. Troublingly, this narrative can also lead us to turn a blind eye to the more subtle kinds of violence in everyday life which deny the claims of many individuals and groups. This hidden violence – theorised and exposed by Judith Butler, Slavoj Žižek and Rob Nixon[5] – forms the plot of the parallel narrative. On that track, violence has not been diminished so much as emulsified – monumental confrontations dispersed in smaller and pervasive practices of oppression that are harder to recognise and resist. This narrative is illustrated by the capacity to justify unequal gains in rights and protections, being satisfied that claim-making is effective as long as it is effective for elite segments of society. Peterloo figures in this narrative too as an episode requiring continuing interpretation. Instead of fostering complacency about the negotiated social order, Peterloo symbolises the need to uncover the oppressive practices in normative assumptions and routines and to resist their limiting effects.

In the remainder of this Introduction, we outline these two narratives, offering them as contexts in which to reconsider the meaning(s) of Peterloo and Romantic-era violence. We pay particular attention to the ways in which violent interactions involve perceptions of selves and others and thus we argue for the importance of supplementing documentary histories of Peterloo with literature and art, for those cultural resources show us the images of selves and others that motivate particular interactions; they make interpretation of documentary evidence possible, and they open ways for perceptions to be evaluated and revised. In the chapters that follow, our contributors join in these reinterpretive aims. As we point out more fully below, they examine the cultural experience of Peterloo, analysing how claims were articulated, identities were constructed, behaviours were scripted, and gestures were interpreted through art and artefacts, words, sounds and rituals. And they examine too how different cultural positions – particularly in Scotland, Ireland or America – conditioned responses to Peterloo. On the whole, we see resilience as the central value in each narrative. Conceived as the ability to spring back from injury or restriction, resilience is evident in the commitment to claim-making that links Peterloo with the eventual passage of reform, and it is necessary for the continuing resistance to violence in all its forms. Before embarking on the two narratives, we offer a brief overview of landmark historical accounts of Peterloo that raise the questions our narratives explore.

Historical Accounts and Cultural Narratives

Historical accounts centre on the problem of assigning responsibility for the violence of Peterloo. This process does not consist in choosing between the yeomen and the demonstrators: consensus holds that the demonstrators were peaceful. Rather, the process consists of determining the degree of responsibility the government bears in the encounter and the levels of government approving of the use of force. Two special issues of the *Manchester Region History Review* (*MRHR*) have considered the matter of assigning responsibility and the empirical evidence available for doing so.[6]

In the first issue, Neville Kirk assessed the treatments in what perhaps remain the three most significant historical accounts of Peterloo: Donald Read's *Peterloo: 'The Massacre' and its Background* (1958, reprinted 1973), E. P. Thompson's reading, presented in 'God and King and Law' (*New Reasoner*, 3, 1957–8) and *The Making of the English Working Class* (1963), and Robert Walmsley's *Peterloo: The Case Reopened* (1969). To recap briefly, Read indicted the Manchester magistrates, whose inexperience and anxiety, inflamed by radical rhetoric, prompted them to rash and unfortunate actions and cleared the national government of any responsibility; Thompson, who set Peterloo in the national context of the growing radical movement, unequivocally indicted the reactionary and repressive government, of whom the local magistrates were only an extension; and, Walmsley, attempting to overturn Thompson's argument, asserted that there were agitating militants in the crowds, who provoked the violence, and the violence of the yeomanry was carried out in self-defence. Kirk found, and subsequent historians have largely agreed, that Read provides the best factual account, but that his conclusions remain unsatisfactory, that Thompson's account – the only one that places Peterloo in a larger socio-historical context – remains the most compelling, and that Walmsley's evidence, though extensive, does not ultimately support his assertions.[7] Indeed, of the three, Thompson's thesis has proven the most enduring, and could well be said to inform most studies of Peterloo, from the next special issue of the *MRHR* to our own volume.[8] To Thompson's contextualisation of Peterloo in national history, essays in this collection add awareness of Scottish and Irish responses.

In the second *MRHR* special issue, Robert Poole returns to Kirk's question remarking, 'It is strange that there should have been so much to dispute about Peterloo since some 300 eye-witness accounts survive, making it one of the best-documented events of the nineteenth century'.[9] After he surveys the eye-witness accounts, most of which were given as testimony at one of the three Peterloo trials (the 1819 inquest into the death of John Lees, the 1820 trial of Henry Hunt and other radicals, and the 1822 civil action of Redford *vs* Birley), he draws two significant conclusions. First, 'the question of who started the violence on the day was [and remains] a propaganda sideshow', meant to distract us from the more urgent question of why the violence occurred at all. Second, 'the core of the magistrates' case [in 1822] was not that they had responded to actual violence but that they had acted to pre-empt *expected* violence' (emphasis added).[10] If the response was at least partly to an expectation of how an imagined scenario might unfold, then more fully accounting for it must go beyond sense data to mental images – a move made by Jan Mieszkowski in his study of 'war stories' from the Napoleonic Age onwards. According to Mieszkowski, 'ideals, prejudices . . . [and] expectations' about how battles should be conducted are as 'reliable' in reports of combat as observed details: witnessing is done not only with the eyes but with the 'creative faculties' of the mind.[11] Surely Mieszkowski's hypothesis about the value-laden witnessing of war applies to the witnessing of Peterloo as well. Studies of the evidence must look for the values, motives, emotions underlying the documented actions and decisions. The cultural resources of literature and art can help us identify these intangible factors. As Jeffrey Cox argues in *Romanticism in the Shadow of War*, 'art is political' because it helps us figure out and reconfigure 'human community'.[12]

Historians themselves have been turning to more culturally integrated approaches to studying Peterloo. Poole's editorial preface points out that this second special issue makes more use of literary sources and pays more attention to conceptualisations of 'loyalism and radicalism' than the first special issue.[13] Elaborating in his Introduction on what remains puzzling about Peterloo, Poole raises questions that go beyond the documentary record. We know, he indicates, that the magistrates prepared evidence in advance that local residents were fearful about the projected gathering at St Peter's Field so that they could either prevent the meeting or justify themselves if they did use force against it, but we do not know 'why they were so set upon confrontation' (10–15); similarly, 'we do not really know what the radicals thought they were doing at Peterloo', i.e., what effects they expected from the process and practice of assembling, or why women participated so prominently when they were not included in the proposed expansion of the franchise.[14]

To answer these questions, historians in that issue enlist a variety of sources – songs, poems, proclamations, prints, caricatures, banners, newspapers, and reports and records of different kinds of civic organisations – to suggest that official aggression may have been motivated by patriotic feelings about the military or that women hoped for improvements in household and family security if working-class men were more involved in political affairs.[15] Furthering this turn towards culturally integrated explorations, the literary scholars in our collection look at an even greater range of expressive sources to reflect on how Peterloo was shaped by and in turn shaped attitudes towards the use of conflict in society and who is entitled to contend with whom over public policies and practices.

To gain a broader perspective on Peterloo, we turn to Charles Tilly's and James Chandler's ground-breaking studies of claim-making during, respectively, the long eighteenth century and the year 1819. While they come from the disparate fields of sociology and literature, they are compatible in their broadly cultural investigations of conflict within their time frames and their willingness to cross over into other fields: Tilly couches his analysis in terms of stories, performances and repertoires evocative of literary studies, though he maintains some disciplinary distinctions;[16] Chandler deliberately brings literature and history together, looking at 'writings that seek to state *the case of the nation*' and in the process 'to alter its case'.[17] Together, Tilly and Chandler form the basis for what we call a narrative of diminishing violence, a narrative in which the violence of Peterloo is shockingly aberrant.

Cultural Narrative I: Diminishing Violence

In *Popular Contention in Great Britain 1758–1834*, Tilly shows widespread efforts among reformers to adopt the procedures and routines of law-abiding institutions in stating their causes and assembling their supporters. Examining newspaper and periodical accounts of more than 8,000 gatherings within the given time frame for words that would depict them as disruptive or orderly, Tilly discerns a pattern of increased planning and decreased outbursts. He argues that the pattern displays in advance the successful broadening of political participation institutionalised by the 1832 Reform Act and related legislation. When people were able to organise and be recognised as having legitimate claims on government, they tended to cultivate peaceful means of stating their cases and to avoid combative behaviour. When unable to organise or be treated as legitimate claimants, they expressed their frustration in violent gestures. Over all, Tilly concludes that the reform of Parliament reflects a change in the evaluation of conflict in society: violence came to be perceived as aberrant while non-violent contention – the process of making claims on government – became the popular expectation.

Mindful of the tension between this conclusion and the undeniable outbreaks of violence in the nineteenth century through to our own time, Tilly's later work supplements the progress narrative with a more episodic model. In *Regimes and Repertoires*, Tilly concentrates on the correspondence between opportunities for claim-making in political systems and the strategies ('repertoires') that people use to make their claims. Relatively democratic, republican or constitutional systems afford opportunities for effective petitioning or litigating that make it unnecessary and counter-productive to take violence as a first course of action. Absolutist systems and dictatorships offer few or no opportunities for claim-making; in such systems, violence may seem to be the only means available to express dissent and force change. Tilly treats the development of repertoires and the choice of strategies to implement from among them 'improvisational': people draw on valued and accepted behaviours in their cultures and on successful precedents from their history to figure out how to identify themselves and their wishes as worthy of attention in their societies.[18] This process of repertoire formation might be compared to the 'border raids' on genre that Jeffrey Cox describes in *Romanticism in the Shadow of War*. Cox sees the Romantic era as a time of 'almost constant war' but war carried out in episodic skirmishes. He argues that the poets of the era mirrored this pattern in writing that sought to use literature as a way to cope with conflict: they 'raided' traditional genres and adapted them for contemporary purposes.[19] To return to Tilly's vocabulary, such accounts of the use of cultural resources allow for multiple, situational narratives or dramas of diminishing violence to come into play as people test various ways to make their claims on society. A narrative of diminishing violence might be said to predominate in a society when confidence in non-violent strategies predominates.

Scholars of Romantic-era literature will recognise in Tilly's valorising of contention a parallel valorising of claim-making in Chandler's *England in 1819*. For Chandler, the literature of 1819, including accounts of Peterloo, is most distinguished for practising, and inviting readers to practise, 'casuistry'. As a process of deliberating the relative merits of a case,[20] casuistry, like contention, is an alternative to violence. It manages conflict in constructive ways, helping people see and reflect on the competing moral and legal values (or 'structure[s] of feeling', to borrow Raymond Williams' term, as does Chandler himself).[21] By deliberating, people gain insight into how claims are represented as well as into how they might be represented differently: the process generates 'a rival normative framework in which the hegemony of the central system comes in for challenge and possible modification'.[22] Chandler argues that the habit of casuistry evident in the writing and reading of 1819 – whether in accounts of Peterloo that were 'told and retold' by journalists or in novels and treatises that examined political power and social stratification without direct reference to Peterloo – contributed to a rethinking of the 'modes and means of national self-representation' necessary for parliamentary reform. In treating accounts of Peterloo, he stresses the 'outrage' at the use of official violence against the crowd expressed by Samuel Bamford, the radical poet who had participated in organising the protest, and most other witnesses.[23] This emotional reaction – which is also noted by Tilly, and more recently by Mary Fairclough[24] – depends on believing that claim-making assemblies are normative and that the attack therefore betrayed the trust in government citizens were demonstrating. Interpreting Peterloo reinforced the identity of citizens as claimants on government, the identity eventually institutionalised by parliamentary reform.

Tilly and Chandler open up new possibilities for studying Peterloo and other Romantic-era conflicts at the level of value enquiry. While value consciousness has informed investigations of Peterloo since Thompson located it within a narrative of working-class struggles, a broader approach to contention allows for a broader examination of Peterloo and its surrounding conflicts as about the perceived and aspirational identities of participants and observers. Such an examination elaborates not only on Chandler and Tilly but joins in the affectual investigations growing in Romantic-era scholarship since John Barrell pointed out the imaginary basis for the real consequences of treason during this period.[25] We consider this investigation a culturally integrated approach, with culture defined in terms adapted from John Jasper's *Art of Moral Protest*: culture consists of 'beliefs, images, feelings, values and categories' that exist in 'mental worlds and their physical embodiments'.[26] For Jasper, protest is as much a means of discovering and asserting 'who I am' or 'who we are' (and 'who I am/who we are *not*') as a means of obtaining a specific goal; indeed protest can fulfil the intangible, identity forming goal even when fulfilling the tangible goal is unlikely.[27] While achieving parliamentary reform was a plausible goal in 1819, something less tangible was at stake in the gathering at St Peter's Field, the attack on the participants and the interpretations of the encounter that followed. For protestors and officials alike, the stake was the right to determine the identity of 'the people' and the nature of the claims they were entitled to make.

Historically, attitudes towards who can participate in government are linked with definitions of 'the people' that stretch back to the Glorious Revolution and its celebrated achievement of a non-violent change in monarchical succession and an increase in parliamentary powers. While 'the people' are often credited with this achievement, the identity of 'the people' behind this accomplishment and their role, if any, in subsequent political affairs have been construed in different ways. In a study of renewed controversies over 'the people' during the Romantic era, Georgina Green shows that debate centred on whether violence was, paradoxically, a component of 'the people's' identity.[28] As Green explains the conundrum, the constituent power of the people places them outside of the law, and if they are outside of the law they are beyond any restraint on the havoc they might wreak in the process of destroying an old order and creating a new. Only extremists like Robespierre valorised the destructive side. Conservatives feared and denounced it, using the possibility of uncontrolled popular violence to reassert an older view of the role of 'the people': 'the people' were not to make claims on government but to behave like obedient children, grateful for any care they received in a paternalistic system. More moderate radicals and reformers, such as John Thelwall, tried to make the creative capacity prevail in the consciousness and conceptualisation of 'the people', and, for Green, William Wordsworth succeeded in limiting the destructive capacity of 'the people' by interpreting them as always subject to a universal moral law even if outside of the laws of any states.[29] Though not addressing Peterloo, Green's detailed analysis of the fears and hopes invested in 'the people' sheds light on the identities being formed and challenged in that later event.

At the level of values and identity formation, the goal of the gathering at St Peter's Field was to constitute 'the people' as a civic assembly capable of interaction in the non-violently contentious ways characteristic of official political organisations, including Parliament itself. Its procedures followed precedents that Green analyses, such as the meetings Thelwall staged, which aimed to make 'the people' visible and audible to those who did not want to see or hear them but also to the members of the group itself so that they would self-consciously experience their collective identity. Under Thelwall's direction, meeting places became 'counter-sphere[s] that challenged the dominant ideology' about 'the people's' ability to govern themselves.[30] The significance of claiming a right to meet in a given space is examined more closely by Katrina Navickas. Pointing out that control over physical spaces and over the meaning of cultural places is control over who belongs in 'the body politic', Navickas argues that 'middle- and working-class political groups struggled for inclusion' in that body from which elite officials were determined to exclude them.[31] Excluded groups could assert claims by meeting in 'liminal spaces' at a city's limits or in open areas within towns where ownership was not clearly defined, giving the demonstrators the opportunity to define them 'as their own'. St Peter's Field was one such area, and demonstrations had begun to be held there in 1816.[32]

Crucial for the success of non-elite claims was the dissociation of 'the people' from violence, for it was their potentially destructive force that officials most feared. The need to show that 'the people' are not inherently violent or brutish, not incapable of thinking or controlling their emotions, accounts for the 'repertoire' of peacefully contentious strategies, such as speech-making, debating, processioning and assembling to make claims, on which studies of Peterloo and other reformist meetings of the era often remark, calling attention to the resemblance between the methods of reformist demonstrations and the methods of established government. What was demonstrated was the ability of 'the people' to carry out normative contention. What differed was the content of the claims: instead of representing elite interests, reformers represented a broader range of needs and wants.

Maintaining a non-violent identity may have been even more important to reformers in Scotland than in England. According to Gordon Pentland's account of Scottish reform activity in the years leading up to the crucial passage of the 1832 acts, organisers idealised the peaceful demonstration at Thrushgrove in 1816 and ignored the 'Radical War' of 1820, thus 'remov[ing] . . . physical force from the[ir] agenda'.[33] Pentland explains the Scottish commitment to non-violence as partly influenced by the valorisation of commerce in Scottish Enlightenment conjectural histories, which traced the progress of society from hunter-gatherer subsistence to commercial prosperity. For conjectural historians, commerce deters war because war interferes with trade. Pentland sees Whig reformers like Francis Jeffrey wanting Scotland's commercial modernisation to be followed by political modernisation, and he quotes Jeffrey's advice that reformers must stay 'quiet and orderly and . . . adhere to . . . all firm and lawful ways' even if a draft bill is rejected because 'a physically violent response' would be self-defeating; it would invite repression, lose the ground they had already gained and retard their progress.[34] Jeffrey's rejection of force fits the pattern of repertoire selection theorised by Tilly. Jeffrey and other pro-Union Scots believed that the given political system, however flawed, offered effective means of protest and could eventually be changed.

Scottish confidence in change through the system stands out in contrast to the 'anti-state *mentalité*' that James Patterson finds prevalent in Ireland.[35] Patterson details how the United Irishmen and their sympathisers turned increasingly from 'moral and popular persuasion' to 'force' in their efforts to gain parliamentary reform and Catholic Emancipation when war between Britain and France arrested the progress they had made towards those goals earlier in the 1790s and when the 1798 uprising was brutally put down, but Patterson also recognises the routinisation of violence in other aspects of Irish experience, such as agrarian unrest and smuggling enterprises, as well.[36] The link between political violence during the 1790s and agrarian violence well into the nineteenth century is pursued in James Donnelly's study of Captain Rock, which quotes Rockite wishes as including an 'Irish Parliament and kings crowned in Ireland as they were before'.[37] The long history of British domination in Ireland makes it unsurprising that reformers would take violence as the most available means of protest. What is surprising, perhaps, and certainly inspiring is the turn from violence taken by Daniel O'Connell in 1823 when he charged the Catholic Association with the mission of demonstrating lawfully and peacefully for Catholic Emancipation. Christine Kinealy's study of O'Connell suggests several factors that may have motivated him to seek alternatives to force; these factors include a keen historical imagination of the gains that might have been made if legislative reforms from the 1780s had not been curtailed by war and first-hand observation of the self-defeating nature of violence in France, where he studied during the revolutionary years.[38] A widespread scholarly consensus credits O'Connell with helping popular protest to recover the energy it lost after Peterloo and with making its massive and non-violent approach the favoured means towards many political and moral goals, including the abolition of slavery, into our own time.

While demonstrations enacted political identity, journalism, essays, poetry, novels and other forms of literature scripted it. As Chandler emphasises, literary deliberation was itself a part of the 'contest' over 'national self-representation' surrounding Peterloo.[39] In addition to the cases that Chandler examines, two kinds of examples considered by Fairclough and Green show how literary representation helped to constitute 'the people'. For Fairclough, the radical press, as a 'network of communication', generated the solidarity that enabled reformers to feel united with all those who shared their cause whether physically present or distant. Further, in its transcriptions of speeches, sometimes including interjections, it reproduced the collective voice, showing that it speaks reasonably and considerately and not in primitive cries and growls.[40] In contrast to Fairclough's emphasis on the collective voice as representative, Green singles out individual writers as representative for their influential conceptualisations of 'the people'. Wordsworth emerges as the ideal representative because of the moral responsibility he makes essential to the concept, but Green moves beyond the individual to conceptualise poetic representation itself: it is the 'voice of the poet' that articulates 'the deeper wisdom of "the people"'.[41]

Despite their opposite approaches to literary representation, Green and Fairclough both treat it as a means of containing violence. It inspires ethical behaviour and solidarity, and its reasonable words make claims without threats – or almost without threats, for Fairclough indicates that the radical texts do not entirely restrain the 'unruly energy of the crowd', which might break through the 'fragility of order' if its claims are indefinitely ignored.[42] If we 'read' Peterloo in the context of a long line of scripts describing, prescribing and proscribing the roles of the populace and their governors, we can more fully understand how it turned violent. Textualised and conditioned experience formed a composite image of 'the people' in the perceptions of its participants and witnesses. Magistrates and yeomen saw an image of the people influenced by many more scripts than the peaceful one the demonstrators were staging before their eyes; they responded to a preconditioned perception of 'the people' as essentially violent, irrespective of how the persons present behaved. The attack was directed at a symbol, but its consequences were horrifically real.

The violence of Peterloo sent shock waves throughout the Atlantic world. Gruesome eye-witness descriptions and graphic renditions spread at record speeds. Radicals, reformers and moderates condemned the use of force while such holders of power as the Prince Regent and Lords Castlereagh, Liverpool and Eldon approved of even violent means to keep order. What was urgently needed after Peterloo was a revaluation of the ways in which those who identified with power and privilege perceived those outside of this elite tier, but the polarising effect of Peterloo impeded progress towards altered views of social relations in the months, and even years, to come – particularly because the government responded to the crisis with legislation designed to repress all reformist efforts. The notorious Six Acts, passed six months after Peterloo, banned meetings of more than fifty people or of any number organising to train for marches, and imposed a tax on otherwise inexpensive editorials and sentences of fourteen years transportation for seditious libel. The latter, wielded as a weapon in the campaign of Lord Sidmouth, then Home Secretary, against liberal publishers, had a particularly chilling effect on reform. Those prosecuted included not only James Wroe, the Manchester newspaper editor who had coined the phrase 'Peterloo', but London-based printers Thomas Dolby and John Cahuac.[43] Dolby, who published proceedings of the trial of Henry Hunt in 1820 as well as at least twenty-eight satires of the king after Peterloo, was dogged by the Constitutional Association – an archly conservative, non-governmental organisation whose sole aim was, in James Sacks' words, 'to ferret out and then prevent by prosecution, if necessary, the publishing and circulation of objectionable books, pamphlets, and newspapers'.[44] They broke Dolby's spirit, and after two violent arrests he backed away from political publications entirely.[45] Less fortunate still, John Cahuac, who had self-published a scathing pamphlet on Peterloo with caricatures by Thomas Rowlandson, was transported to Australia for fourteen years on dubious evidence of criminal activity, which effectively silenced him forever.[46] Even the work that became the most famous denunciation of Peterloo – Shelley's *The Mask of Anarchy* – was affected by the repressive legislation because Leigh Hunt, to whom Shelley sent the manuscript, postponed its publication for fear of suffering Cahuac's fate.

Repressive legislation, however, proved futile against the spirit of reform and the aspirationally non-violent identity of the people. Despite prosecutions, the works of Dolby, Cahuac and others had appeared in print, and not all trials resulted in convictions. Reformers also found creative ways to circumvent the ban on meetings and marches by organising themselves as supporters of Queen Caroline, whose trial for adultery began the year after Peterloo. By defending the queen, reformers could associate themselves with traditional forms of government while also protesting abuses of power exemplified by the king's use of the trial to fulfil his personal wish for a divorce.[47] Organising became easier after the Seditious Meetings Act expired, and, as we have noted above, popular protest began to thrive again under the leadership of Daniel O'Connell. The resilience of 'the people' made it hard to maintain an image of them as a thoughtless mob in need of paternalistic control. Though delayed for some time after Peterloo, revaluation of the images representing social relations did occur.

That such revaluation included not only recognition of 'the people' as organised and competent but doubt about the judgement of the ruling class is evident in the reception of Walter Scott's pamphlet *The Visionary*. Published soon after Peterloo with the goal of supporting the magistrates and spreading anti-reformist sympathy, the pamphlet presents a conservative's caricatures of 'the people', including their representatives – the duplicitous orator Bob Bubblegoose and the bludgeon-wielding Tom Ten Acres. While it unintentionally epitomises the worst of conservative visions, it also reveals the blinding emotional investment that Scott had in the idea that government should be in the hands of those 'educated' to manage 'wealth and power' instead of 'adventurers' who will use them self-servingly.[48] That this pamphlet now seems an embarrassment to those who value the more complex and insightful view of social relations in Scott's novels further evidences the normative function of contention and the use of literature in practising it. Compared to the unifying 'outrage' at the violence of Peterloo spread by accounts of what happened, criticisms of the protesters and defences of the magistrates aroused much less sympathy.[49] For more and more readers, the conservative image drawn on Scott's pages represented 'who we are not'.

With the obsolescence of Scott's pamphlet we reach the end of the narrative of diminishing violence – or at least the end of the segment that runs through this portion of history. But the consequences of perceiving others through imposed caricatures of their identities remain. To investigate this subtle violence in Romantic-era culture – and resistance to it in Romantic-era writing – we turn to the narrative of dispersing violence.

Cultural Narrative II: Dispersing Violence

In her recent studies of state violence, Judith Butler warns that literature can work deliberately to obscure violence, to frame the lives of others in ways that blind us to the violence done by our perception. She reminds us to heed how frames, 'through which we apprehend, or indeed, fail to apprehend' violence, are 'politically saturated'. We all object when violence is perpetrated upon another person, she argues, but whom we recognise as 'another person' is politically conditioned: 'norms operate to produce certain subjects as "recognizable" persons and to make others decidedly more difficult to recognize'.[50] We are 'given over to others, to norms, to social and political organizations that have developed historically in order to maximize precariousness for some and minimize precariousness for others', with the result that we have become accustomed to neglecting violence that maintains our perspective on social order. To counter this, Butler urges, we must attend to 'a new bodily ontology' that comprehends a concern for 'precariousness, vulnerability, injurability, interdependency, exposure, bodily persistence, desire, work and the claims of language and social belonging'.[51] In other words, it is not enough to reject the confrontational violence like the yeomen's attack on the demonstrators at Peterloo or even the violence carried out by one individual on another. In this narrative, we must attend to the violence committed upon people who live in conditions neglected and obscure.

To bring Romantic-era texts into dialogue with theories of hidden violence, we elaborate on two exemplary poems – Percy Shelley's *The Mask of Anarchy* and John Keats' 'To Autumn' – which directly and indirectly bear witness to the impact of Peterloo.

The Mask of Anarchy deplores not only the overt violence of the attack on the crowd but the cultural authority that licensed such an attack. Further, its criticism of authoritarian attitudes extends beyond Peterloo to the institutions of imperialism and slavery that compromise human freedom. The depth of Shelley's insights can be newly appreciated by reading them in terms borrowed from Žižek, terms that explain how violence can be 'systemic' and 'objective'. In his study of violence, Žižek distinguishes between 'subjective' and 'objective' forms: the former is the 'obvious' kind of confrontation 'performed by a clearly identifiable agent' while the latter has no immediately identifiable perpetrators. Žižek further sorts 'objective' violence into two categories: 'symbolic' violence, which includes 'the relations of social domination reproduced in our habitual speech forms', and 'systemic' violence, which entails 'the often catastrophic consequences of the smooth functioning of our economic and political systems'.[52]

Here Žižek's work builds upon Michel Foucault's discussion of the violence of the ubiquitous 'carceral system' by which states and 'society in general' use internalised norms to effect discipline: 'The carceral system combines in a single figure discourses and architectures, coercive regulations and scientific propositions, real social effects and invincible utopias, programmes for correcting delinquents and mechanisms that reinforce delinquency'.[53] For both Foucault and Žižek, then, society suffers from a low-level but constant regulatory violence, the effectiveness of which is entirely dependent upon the invisibility of its agents.

Complementing Shelley's attention to menacing systems in *The Mask* is Keats' attention to threatening environments in 'To Autumn'. The implied links between nature and culture gain credibility in light of Rob Nixon's theories of the 'slow violence' of environmental degradation that affects both human and non-human life and of Timothy Morton's genealogies of 'hyperobjects'. Morton tracks the kind of ecological violence of which Nixon speaks back to the Romantic era by identifying James Watt's invention of the steam engine in 1784 as not only an historical moment but also 'a geological one': the invention opened the 'Anthropocene' era, 'when carbon from coal-fired industries began to be deposited worldwide', transforming the planet and initiating global warming, which Morton likens to 'an ultra slow motion nuclear bomb' – 'murder-suicide at a planetary level'.[54] If there is something awesome about humanity's collective ability to transform the very geology of the planet, to perpetrate such mass violence, that violence also exposes human 'fragility'. 'Industrial violence' destabilises our sense of life – we no longer 'live', but merely 'live on' in an eerie, unnatural ontological state he calls 'spectrality'; 'to exist is to be disabled' by our collective violence against the planet and ourselves.[55] It is in Wordsworth's poetry, Morton offers, that we can discover an early awareness of the ontological destabilisations that are the consequence of slow violence.[56] But, returning to Keats and Shelley, we find in 'To Autumn' and *The Mask of Anarchy* resilient images that offer hope for more trustworthy relations in the future.

Shelley's awareness of these more subtle forms of violence is most evident in his depiction of the 'maniac maid' in *The Mask*. Arising at the fall of Anarchy to inspire hope among the many, the maid repeatedly defines 'Freedom' as distinct from 'slavery':

> 'What is Freedom? – ye can tell
> That which slavery is, too well –
> For its very name has grown
> To an echo of your own. (ll. 156–9)[57]

The maid identifies the hardships of the lower classes with the violence of subjugation – the systematic brutalisation of labour – and indicts by implication the government as criminal slavers, involved in a trade that had been outlawed since 1807. The effect of Shelley's analogy with slavery is not to bridge the political divide in 1819 but to widen it, to alienate the 'few' from the 'many' in order to unmask them as perpetrators of great violence. The analogy to slavery could appeal to radicals and reformers because it implied that the harsh conditions in which the English worked were not natural; they were created by people who profited from them and who could be opposed by conscientious objectors.

Shelley was not alone in moving from Peterloo to other examples of socially systemic violence. Sydney Owenson's response to Peterloo – an incendiary book-length satirical poem somewhat misleadingly entitled *The Mohawks*, published in London in 1822 – displays similar manoeuvring.[58] The principal target of her satire was the conservative press in Scotland, with whom she had been battling for years – those 'hirelings' who 'on Peterloo's blood-letting fondly gloat'.[59] The process of exposing the hirelings as wholly dependent on the 'corruption', which 'serves in the national machine as grease', the poem becomes nothing less than a litany of radical, post-Peterloo complaints revealing the dispersal of violence across the 'English system'.[60] *The Mohawks* is comprehensive in its charges: it recounts the history of English repressive violence in Ireland, India and America, it critiques the British-European diplomacy of Metternich and Castlereagh that returned Europe to a system of violent subordination, and, by linking Peterloo, the Cato Street Conspiracy, and the Queen Caroline Affair, it exposes the government's intense campaign of violent domestic repression. When recourse to bribery and physical violence failed, Owenson argues, the government paid writers, including Southey and Scott, and journalists, including those who wrote for *The Quarterly Review*, *Blackwood's*, *John Bull*, and elsewhere, to 'write the State's opponents black and blue', underscoring their willingness to invade homes and abuse women.[61] In the pages of those journals, Owenson quarrels, 'stand in view / Reflected, all the vices of the faction' in power, 'The Irish hanging, picketings, and hewings, / And Manchester's too famed, and murd'rous doings'.[62] The government tasked conservative authors with maligning and suppressing radical authors, whom Owenson cleverly celebrates:

> Be sure you suffer nobody to name
> Such *naughty* books as those by Percy Shelley,
> Paine, Byron, Bentham, Burdon, Ensor, Hone,
> Volney, Voltaire, or Chenier – no not one.[63]

Privileging Shelley in this list is apt: Owenson's indictment of the defamation and calumny perpetrated by the conservative press, and specifically of *The Quarterly Review*, on authors, and particularly authors who are women, echoes Shelley's accusation in his 1821 preface to 'Adonais', that *The Quarterly Review* killed Keats.[64]

While the spread of violence throughout many areas of Romantic-era culture is remarkable, its concentration in some aspects – especially the institutions of slavery and patriarchy – is equally important to notice. Scholarship on Romantic-era abolitionism points out that after Peterloo liberal authors repeatedly drew analogies between the violent conditions in which the English working classes lived and laboured, and the institution of colonial slavery.[65] Further, Daniel O'Connell saw exact parallels between the mistreatment of the Irish under British rule and the mistreatment of slaves in the West Indies, North America and colonies around the world. O'Connell lent his eloquence to the cause of abolitionism, linking it with the cause of Catholic Emancipation and continuing to support it long after Catholic Emancipation was won.[66] Abolitionism also became a concern for Scottish reformers during the 1820s, and Scottish immigrants to America were often disturbed by the inconsistency of the principles of the Declaration of Independence with the practice of slavery.[67] Elizabeth Bohls' analysis of slavery sheds light on its damaging effects in all these contexts. Treating it in terms comparable to Žižek's 'objective' violence, Bohls writes: 'Slavery's profound harm is best understood not by studying incidents of overt, shocking violence but instead through everyday interactions', what might be called 'quotidian violence'.[68] Similarly, although she arose in the wake of the dramatic procession of the 'Mask' – that is, after the spectacular horror of Peterloo – the maiden's most important demand is that her auditors see beyond incidences of violence to patterns of violence too quotidian to cause alarm. For a quarter of a century, feminist and queer theorists of Romanticism have been doing the same: calling attention to patterns of violence intentionally neglected. The year 1993 saw the publication of both Butler's *Bodies that Matter* and Anne Mellor's *Romanticism & Gender*; subsequent studies, such as those by Daniel Watkins, Jacqueline Labbe, Adriana Craciun and more recently Gillian Russell, have addressed directly that pervasive normative violence that aims to regulate and punish both gender and sexual deviation in order to counter its influence.[69]

Patterns of violence are also of concern in Keats' 'To Autumn', but they are patterns of 'attrition' and erosion that 'gradually' take their toll on the beings subject to them – patterns theorised by Rob Nixon to account for sickness and suffering occasioned by environmental degradation. According to Nixon, this 'slow violence' is

> a violence that occurs gradually and out of sight, a violence of delayed destruction that is dispersed across time and space, an attritional violence that is typically not viewed as violence at all . . . a violence that is neither spectacular nor instantaneous, but rather incremental and accretive, its calamitous repercussions playing out across a range of temporal scales.[70]

We see the effects of a poisoned environment in the suspicions aroused in the poet's mind as he tries to identify Autumn as a visible agent responsible for the harvesting and cider-pressing.[71] This search for a lurking figure has been read by Nicholas Roe as a sign of the 'conspiracy theories' filling the air in the month after Peterloo when Keats wrote this poem – and put the term 'conspiring' into the first stanza.[72] Roe further identifies the missing figure as Justice, the goal sought by anyone who would distribute a harvest fairly as well as the goal sought by those who brought 'banners . . . emblazoned with the figure of Justice holding her scales' to St Peter's Field. By seeking this figure, the poem shows sympathy for those who have been 'unjustly excluded from their due share' of the country's goods and implies a criticism of officials who have denied popular claims.[73] Though Roe is most concerned with the acute awareness of distrust occasioned by Peterloo, other studies that remark on the government's use of spies from the 1790s onwards as well as on the repression of meetings and expression that drove reformers to subterfuge show that an 'atmosphere of suspicion' had been building up for some time.[74] We need only recall that the Manchester magistrates prepared in advance to close down the meeting in St Peter's Field on the supposition that it was making residents fearful to recognise the symptoms of a toxic political environment.

Attending to larger contexts of colonial and national affairs, Alan Bewell and Jonathan Bate have read 'To Autumn' as concerned with what constitutes a healthy environment for individuals and for the nation as a whole. For Bewell, its final stanza offers hope for a 'balance of extremes' that might provide a climate in which people can live peacefully, quietly and healthfully.[75] While compatible, Bate's interpretation is more cautionary, pointing out that the image of the 'gathering swallows' is reassuring for readers who can assume the return of spring but troubling for those who worry that the birds may be '"twitter[ing] in the skies" for the last time'.[76] A fear of an unnatural interruption of a life cycle would easily be aroused in readers familiar with John Cahuac's pamphlet *Who Killed Cock Robin?* which caricatures Peterloo as a callous mass slaughtering of robins, that other celebrated bird of spring.[77] Perhaps the ambiguity of the scene represented in 'To Autumn' allows it to provoke the rethinking of violence that Nixon calls for, making it 'dramatic enough to rouse public sentiment and warrant political intervention';[78] ultimately, 'To Autumn' holds out hope for resilience even in a climate of invisible threats.

Images of Violence

Though we have considered Peterloo in narrative terms, we wish to call attention to a striking image of violence – J. M. W. Turner's *Death on a Pale Horse* – recently interpreted not only as a response to Peterloo but specifically as a visualisation of Shelley's *The Mask of Anarchy.*[79] Dating the unfinished painting as a work of 1833–4, Sam Smiles argues that the central figure, a mutilated corpse of a crowned monarch pitched backwards over a ghastly nightmare, is a visual rendition of Shelley's allegorical monarch, Anarchy, who falls from a horse in Shelley's poem. Smiles even suggests that the painting be renamed *The Fall of Anarchy*. What seems most significant to us is the reversal of class violence in Smiles' interpretation: the body of the king has suffered the fate of non-elite bodies at Peterloo and, after Peterloo, of pauper bodies under the Anatomy Act of 1832, a measure that let surgeons use for their own purposes the bodies of people who could not afford burial.[80] In Smiles' words:

> If Turner is indeed depicting Anarchy here, the cadaver that he has represented is one that has had meted out to it what the Anatomy Act reserved for the poor. The mangled body of this fallen ruler constitutes an especially apt development of Shelley's deliberate inversion of values in 'The Masque of Anarchy'. It is as though Turner has adopted the anti-hierarchical principles of the reformers to extend the workings of the Anatomy Act to the highest ranks of society.[81]

Read in this way, the painting becomes a meditation on the horror of violence, almost overwhelming viewers with the ghastly allure of the aestheticised image but also enabling them to reflect on the subtle political ironies it represents and to long for a counter image of a 'great Assembly' operating in a world that has removed force from its repertoire of interactions.

Commemorative Claims

The chapters in this volume commemorate Peterloo in a variety of dynamic ways. They revisit the historical events, offering new ways to understand the conflicts, claims, symbols, images and accounts surrounding the events in St Peter's Field. Because each essay engages with multiple aspects of the topic and is potentially in dialogue with all the others, we have not partitioned them into separate sections. Instead, we have arranged them in a sequence that begins with Stephen Behrendt's chapter foregrounding the 'moral ambiguity' of interpretations and uses of the words, images and artefacts generated by efforts to understand Peterloo. The following chapters analyse and illustrate many processes of interpretation, and while none alludes to the narratives of diminishing and dispersing violence, those patterns do appear in their examinations.

Diminishing violence is most evident in Chapters 2 to 4, which explore how sounds, symbols and historical dramas allowed protestors and supporters to express claims and identities without resorting to violent assertion. Concentrating on the sounds emanating from St Peter's Field – from songs to speeches to cheers to, chillingly, cries and clanging sabres – Ian Haywood considers how protesters struggled to elevate 'the voice of the people' to the register of 'the sublime'. Turning from aural to visual displays, Murray Pittock analyses the symbolic significance of the white hat Orator Hunt habitually wore, which encoded not only contemporary manners but historical affinities, allowing him and his supporters to stake their claims through clothing rather than through force. Historical interpretations take centre stage in Frederick Burwick's chapter on the use of Guy Fawkes to insinuate radical ideas and bypass censorship in dramas performed after Peterloo.

The following four chapters pay particular attention to identity formation and claim-making outside of England – specifically in

Scotland, Ireland and the United States. Gerard Carruthers surveys literary responses to Peterloo and related demonstrations from a range of Scottish authors as well as commemorations of Peterloo held in Scotland to show an underlying consistency of conservative reactions and liberal sympathies across national boundaries even when the sentiments evoked Scottish culture. In contrast, James Kelly finds the mutual distrust between Ireland and England reinforced by Peterloo, but, more surprisingly, he discovers a swell of interest in oratory following in its wake. Kelly's chapter explores how this prominent element in Irish literary tradition became the focus of debates on the extent to which rhetoric influences – or should influence – an audience's thoughts and actions. Perceptions of Irish identity figure also in Michelle Faubert's chapter about the suicide of Lord Castlereagh. Faubert considers how his taking his own life posed an interpretive crisis for reformers and radicals who valorised self-sacrifice for a cause and did not want an oppressor of Ireland to have any claim on public sympathy. Generalising beyond the individual case, Faubert argues that Peterloo exhibited suicidal traits on a national scale, as officials attacked members of their own body politic. Violence against the body politic and valorisation of a deceased leader are the topics of Katey Castellano's chapter on the unusual response to Peterloo of William Cobbett from his new printing base in America. As Castellano details, Cobbett planned, literally and figuratively, to 'resurrect' Thomas Paine and have his bones enshrined in England, creating a monument that could serve as a gathering point for reformers and a means of strengthening their solidarity.

The last four chapters in the volume scrutinise conditions that we have called 'dispersed' violence – i.e., acts and forms of oppression that operate through institutional practices and prevailing norms. Taking the willingness of the clergy to authorise the attack on the protestors at St Peter's Field as indicative of a deeper hostility of the Established Church towards reformers, John Gardner revisits radical criticism of clerical behaviour as a displaced protest of the conspiracy of church and state against the people ostensibly in their care. 'Systemic violence', especially as effected through the legal system, is the topic of Victoria Myers' investigation of Jeremy Bentham's *Plan of Parliamentary Reform*. Myers reveals how prescient Bentham was, two years before Peterloo, in discerning the regular practices that enable a ruling class to dominate 'the people' and in positing corrections that would shift the balance of power. Perhaps there would have been no Peterloo had Bentham's ideas been heeded. Tensions between the 'constitutional violence' of politics and the peace of nature are the focus of Philip Shaw's chapter on *The River Duddon* and other poems Wordsworth published the year after Peterloo. Shaw addresses how Wordsworth complicates this simple dichotomy in his poems and moves beyond it towards spiritual resolution. In the final chapter, Michael Scrivener posits that *The Mask of Anarchy*, along with many of Shelley's other major poems, illustrates a process of rising above violence, of acting in ways consistent with the imagined and desired just world that could fill the space made free for it by the attrition of patriarchal norms. By concluding the volume with attention to the most iconic of literary responses to Peterloo, we call to mind the cover image of Turner's painting and commemorate the resilience of all efforts to end the rule of violence, oppression and exclusion.

Notes

1. Michael Bush, *The Casualities of Peterloo* (Manchester: Carnegie Publishing Ltd, 2006).
2. Anthony Jarrells, *Britain's Bloodless Revolutions: 1688 and the Romantic Reform of Literature* (Basingstoke: Palgrave Macmillan, 2005); Charles Tilly, *Popular Contention in Great Britain, 1758–1834* (Cambridge, MA: Harvard University Press, 1995); James Chandler, *England in 1819: The Politics of Literary Culture and the Case of Romantic Historicism* (Chicago: University of Chicago Press, 1998).
3. A similar thesis about attitudes towards war is developed by Mary Favret, *War at a Distance: Romanticism and the Making of Modern Warfare* (Princeton: Princeton University Press, 2009) and by Neil Ramsey and Gillian Russell in their 'Introduction', in *Tracing War in Enlightenment and Romantic Culture*, ed. Ramsey and Russell (New York: Palgrave Macmillan, 2015), pp. 1–15. In their assessment, post-Enlightenment attitudes towards war placed it outside of the normal order of things; instead of being merely, albeit deplorably, the usual means of territorial control, it came to be perceived as a breakdown in civil society that should not happen, p. 2.
4. Mark Doyle, *Communal Violence in the British Empire: Disturbing the Pax* (London: Bloomsbury Academic, 2016), p. 135.
5. Judith Butler, *Frames of War: When is Life Grievable?* (New York: Verso, 2009); Slavoj Žižek, *Violence: Six Sideways Reflections* (New

York: Picador, 2008); Rob Nixon, *Slow Violence and the Environmentalism of the Poor* (Cambridge, MA: Harvard University Press, 2011).

6. *Peterloo Special Edition, Manchester Region History Review* [*MRHR*] 3:1 (1989); *Return to Peterloo*, ed. Robert Poole, Special Issue of *MRHR* 23 ([2012] 2014).
7. Neville Kirk, 'Commonsense, Commitment and Objectivity: Themes in the Recent Historiography of Peterloo', *MRHR* 3:1 (1989), pp. 61–5.
8. For an example in another context, Thompson's influence is evident in Robert Poole's conclusion to '"By the Law or the Sword": Peterloo Revisited', *History* 91:302 (2006), pp. 254–76, which asserts that 'Peterloo was not a clumsy exercise in crowd control. It was the enthusiastic revenge of Manchester loyalists on the radicals who threatened to overwhelm them' (p. 276).
9. Robert Poole, 'What Don't We Know about Peterloo?' in Poole (ed.), *Return*, p. 2.
10. Ibid. p. 14.
11. Jan Mieszkowski, *Watching War* (Stanford: Stanford University Press, 2012), p. 5.
12. Jeffrey Cox, *Romanticism in the Shadow of War: Literary Culture in the Napoleonic War Years* (Cambridge: Cambridge University Press, 2014), p. 6.
13. Poole, 'Editorial', in Poole (ed.), *Return*, p. vi.
14. Poole, 'What Don't We Know', pp. 10–15.
15. Katrina Navickas, 'Lancashire Britishness: Patriotism in the Manchester Region During the Napoleonic Wars', in Poole (ed.), *Return*, pp. 33–48, esp. p. 35; Ruth Mather, 'These Lancashire Women Are Witches in Politics: Female Reform Societies and the Theatre of Radicalism, 1819–1820', in Poole (ed.), *Return*, pp. 49–64. The involvement of women in the demonstration at St Peter's Field and in reform activity more broadly has been a subject of ongoing investigation. See, for example, Katrina Navickas, *Protest and the Politics of Space and Place, 1789–1848* (Manchester: Manchester University Press, 2015), pp. 76–9.
16. As we explain in more detail below, Tilly's *Popular Contention* is based on the compilation of much data from newspaper accounts and expresses reservations about less grounded attention to 'discourse' and 'culture', pp. 38–41. Its quantitative emphasis and its tendency to generalise about Britain based on occurrences in southern England has been criticised by Navickas in *Protest*, pp. 6–7. Tilly's later work, however, especially *Regimes and Repertoires* (Chicago: University of Chicago Press, 2006) offers a more qualified treatment of the dynamics of popular protest and gives narrative and drama wider explanatory

scope. On Tilly's methods, including his use of 'stories', see Ernesto Casteñeda and Cathy Lisa Schneider, 'Introduction', in *Collective Violence, Contentious Politics, and Social Change: A Charles Tilly Reader*, ed. Casteñeda and Schneider (New York: Routledge, 2017), pp. 5–6, 18.

17. Chandler, *England in 1819*, p. 6.
18. Tilly, *Regimes*, pp. 30–59.
19. Cox, *Romanticism*, pp. 1–4, 7.
20. Chandler, *England in 1819*, p. 198.
21. Ibid. p. 75.
22. Ibid. p. 308.
23. Ibid. pp. 16–17.
24. Cf. Tilly, *Popular Contention*, p. 260 and Mary Fairclough, *The Romantic Crowd: Sympathy, Controversy and Print Culture* (Cambridge: Cambridge University Press, 2013), p. 160. We consider Fairclough's work in more detail later in this Introduction.
25. John Barrell, *Imagining the King's Death: Figurative Treason, Fantasies of Regicide 1793–1796* (Oxford: Oxford University Press, 2000). Additionally relevant are Thomas Pfau, *Romantic Moods: Paranoia, Trauma, and Melancholy, 1790–1840* (Baltimore: Johns Hopkins University Press, 2005), which diagnosed as 'paranoid' Jacobin fears during this period, and Fairclough's *Romantic Crowd*, which addresses theories of emotional 'contagion' as factors in fears of public gatherings, including Peterloo. For attention to the new prominence of emotion in Romantic-era studies, see *Romanticism and the Emotions*, ed. Joel Faflak and Richard C. Sha (Cambridge: Cambridge University Press, 2014).
26. James M. Jasper, *The Art of Moral Protest: Culture, Biography, and Creativity in Social Movements* (Chicago: University of Chicago Press, 1997), p. 12.
27. Ibid. pp. 69–99.
28. Georgina Green, *The Majesty of the People: Popular Sovereignty and the Role of the Writer in the 1790s* (Oxford: Oxford University Press, 2014).
29. This summary condenses a good deal of Green's argument; for the key points, see especially, pp. 8–10, 42–62, 172–200; on fear of 'the people's' destructive power, cf. Fairclough, *Romantic Crowd*, pp. 150, 162.
30. Green, *Majesty*, p. 57; cf. Chandler's 'rival normative framework[s]', quoted above.
31. Navickas, *Protest*, pp. 9–10.
32. Ibid. pp. 65–8.

33. Gordon Pentland, *Radicalism, Reform and National Identity in Scotland, 1820–1833* (Woodbridge, Suffolk: Boydell Press, 2008), p. 8. For more about Scottish reformers, see the chapter by Gerard Carruthers in this volume.
34. Pentland, *Radicalism*, pp. 95–7, 114–15.
35. James Patterson, *In the Wake of the Great Rebellion: Republicanism, Agrarianism and Banditry in Ireland after 1798* (Manchester: Manchester University Press, 2008), p. 11.
36. Ibid. pp. 3, 11. For more about expectations of violence in Ireland, see the chapter by James Kelly in this volume.
37. James S. Donnelly, Jr., *Captain Rock: Irish Agrarian Rebellion, 1821–1824* (Madison: University of Wisconsin Press, 2009). p. 23.
38. Christine Kinealy, *Daniel O'Connell and the Anti-Slavery Movement: 'The Saddest People the Sun Sees'* (London: Pickering and Chatto, 2011; rpt Routledge, 2016), p. 17.
39. Chandler, *England in 1819*, p. 19
40. Fairclough, *Romantic Crowd*, pp. 149–62.
41. Green, *Majesty*, pp. 199–200.
42. Fairclough, *Romantic Crowd*, pp. 157–8.
43. For more on the network of English Radical publishers in 1819, see David Worrall, '*Mab* and Mob: The Radical Press Community in Regency England', in *Romanticism, Radicalism, and the Press*, ed. Stephen Behrendt (Detroit: Wayne State University Press, 1997), pp. 137–56.
44. On Dolby, see Vic Gatrell, *City of Laughter: Sex and Satire in Eighteenth-Century London* (New York: Walker & Co., 2006), n. 21, p. 654. On the Constitutional Association, see James Sack, *From Jacobite to Conservative: Reaction and Orthodoxy in Britain, c. 1760–1832* (Cambridge: Cambridge University Press, 1993), pp. 104–7.
45. Thomas Dolby, *Memoirs of Thomas Dolby* (London: Hunt & Clarke, 1827).
46. Michael Demson, 'Remembering John Cahuac: Post-Peterloo Repression and the Fate of Radical-Romantic Satire', in *The Politics of Shelley: History, Theory, Form*, ed. Matthew Borushko, Romantic Circles Praxis Series (September 2015) <https://www.rc.umd.edu/praxis/shelley_politics/praxis.2015.shelley_politics.demson.html> (last accessed 17 August 2017).
47. On the multiple uses of the Queen Caroline Affair, see John Gardner, *Poetry and Popular Protest: Peterloo, Cato Street, and the Queen Caroline Controversy* (London: Palgrave Macmillan, 2011), pp. 159–217, and Navickas, *Protest*, pp. 102–4.
48. Walter Scott, *The Visionary*, edited with an Introduction by Peter Garside (Cardiff: University College of Cardiff Press, 1984), p. 42. The

pamphlet collects the three letters, first published in the *Edinburgh Weekly Journal*, to which Gerard Carruthers alludes in his chapter in this volume.

49. In his Introduction to *The Visionary*, Garside comments that Scott 'underestimated the extent to which opinion was daily shifting to the Whigs and moderate reform', p. ix. On the uses of sympathy in writing about Peterloo, see Poole, 'What Don't We Know', p. 3; Gardner, *Poetry*, p. 86; Fairclough, *Romantic Crowd*, pp. 149–66; and the chapter by Michael Scrivener in this volume.
50. Butler, *Frames*, pp. 1–6.
51. Ibid. p. 2.
52. Žižek, *Violence*, pp. 1–3.
53. Michel Foucault, *Discipline and Punish: The Birth of the Prison*, trans. Alan Sheridan, 2nd edn (New York: Vintage Books, 1995), p. 271.
54. Timothy Morton, *Hyperobjects: Philosophy and Ecology after the End of the World* (Minneapolis: University of Minnesota Press, 2013), pp. 4–7 and *Humankind: Solidarity with Non-Human People* (London: Verso, 2017), p. 146.
55. Morton, *Humankind*, p. 44.
56. Morton, *Hyperobjects*, p. 179. Cf. the view of Wordsworth and the consequences of violence in nature in Philip Shaw's chapter in this volume.
57. *Shelley's Poetry and Prose*, ed. Donald H. Reiman and Neil Fraistat (New York: Norton, 2002), pp. 315–26 (320).
58. Sydney Owenson, *The Mohawks; A Satirical Poem with Notes* (London: Henry Colburn and Co., 1822). The title does not refer to the Iroquoian tribe but to the 'Mohocks', a criminal fraternity of dissolute aristocrats that terrorised London in the early eighteenth century.
59. Ibid. pp. 91, 103.
60. Ibid. p. 43. In note 43, anticipating Žižek's 'objective violence', Owenson stresses the systemic nature of English corruption explicitly: 'Please to observe, reader, that corruption here applies to the system, and not personally to the individual', p. 142. For summary discussion of Owenson's ongoing conflicts with Scottish journals and with Scott, see Julie Donovan's *Sydney Owenson, Lady Morgan, and the Politics of Style* (Palo Alto: Academica, 2009), pp. 81–6.
61. Owenson, *The Mohawks*, p. 107.
62. Ibid, p. 79.
63. Ibid, p. 53. In linking these domestic events, Owenson anticipates John Gardner's radical history detailed in *Poetry*.
64. Owenson, *The Mohawks*, p. 72. For Owenson's denunciation of *ad hominem* attacks, see p. 70; for her association of defamation and murder, see p. 94.

65. Marcus Wood, 'William Cobbett, John Thelwall, Radicalism, Racism and Slavery: A Study of Burkean Parodics', in *Romantic Parody*, ed. John Strachan, *Romanticism on the Net* 15 (August 1999) <https://www.erudit.org/en/journals/ron/1999-n15-ron427/005873ar/> (last accessed 22 April 2017). Debbie Lee, *Slavery and the Romantic Imagination* (Philadelphia: University of Philadelphia Press, 2002), pp. 9–15. Elizabeth A. Bohls, *Slavery and the Politics of Place: Representing the Colonial Caribbean, 1770–1833* (Cambridge: Cambridge University Press, 2010), pp. 1–15, 108.
66. Kinealy's study (*Daniel O'Connell)* examines O'Connell's involvement with and influence on this matter in depth and throughout his career; for the parallel with Ireland, we draw particularly on pp. 3–7.
67. On Scottish abolitionism, see Pentland, *Radicalism*, pp. 28–9. Navickas ('Lancashire Britishness', pp. 44–6) calls attention to the perspective of Scottish immigrants; according to Kinealy, the perspective of Irish immigrants was complicated by a fear that they would lose their slender social and economic advantage if there were no enslaved population beneath them, *Daniel O'Connell*, p. 7.
68. Bohls, *Slavery*, p. 108.
69. Judith Butler, *Bodies that Matter: On the Discursive Limits of 'Sex'* (New York: Routledge, 1993); Anne Mellor, *Romanticism & Gender* (New York: Routledge, 1993); Daniel P. Watkins, *Sexual Power in British Romantic Poetry* (Gainesville: University Press of Florida, 1996); Jacqueline M. Labbe, *The Romantic Paradox: Love, Violence, and the Uses of Romance, 1760–1830* (New York: Palgrave Macmillan, 2000); Adriana Craciun, *Fatal Women of Romanticism* (Cambridge: Cambridge University Press, 2003); Gillian Russell, *Women, Sociability and Theatre in Georgian London* (Cambridge: Cambridge University Press, 2007). See also the chapter by Michael Scrivener in this volume.
70. Nixon, *Slow Violence*, p. 2.
71. *John Keats: Complete Poems*, ed. Jack Stillinger (Cambridge, MA: Belknap, 1978), pp. 360–1.
72. Nicholas Roe, *John Keats and the Culture of Dissent* (Oxford University Press, 1997), pp. 254–7. More recently, Richard Margraff Turley, in 'Objects of Suspicion: Keats, "To Autumn" and the Psychology of Romantic Surveillance', in *Keats and the Medical Imagination*, ed. Nicholas Roe (Cham, Switzerland: Springer for Palgrave Macmillan, 2017) has argued that 'To Autumn' 'internalizes' the 'surveillance culture' that prevailed after Peterloo, pp. 173–205 (174).
73. Roe, *John Keats*, pp. 260–5. Chandler also contextualises "To Autumn" with respect to Keats' awareness of Peterloo, but he is more concerned with how the poem opposes belief in a human ability to transcend nature (*England in 1819*, pp. 425–32).

74. In the first chapter of *Protest*, Navickas analyses how spies crossed lines between public and private spaces, making reformers and their sympathisers feel threatened in any situation (pp. 24–50); the phrase ‘atmosphere of suspicion’ recurs on pp. 26, 38, and 312. Cf. recurrent references to ‘surveillance’ throughout Turley’s article, ‘Objects of Suspicion’.
75. Alan Bewell, *Romanticism and Colonial Disease* (Baltimore: Johns Hopkins University Press, 1999), p. 176.
76. Bate, *Romantic Ecology: Wordsworth and the Environmental Tradition* (London: Routledge, 1991; rpt 2014), p. 2. See also Bate’s *Song of the Earth* (Cambridge: Harvard University Press, 2000), p. 104, for concerns about health relevant to ‘To Autumn’.
77. John Cahuac, *Who Killed Cock Robin? A Satirical Tragedy, or Hieroglyphic Prophecy on the Manchester Blot!* (London: John Cahuac, 1819).
78. Nixon, *Slow Violence*, p. 3.
79. Sam Smiles, ‘The Fall of Anarchy: Politics and Anatomy in an Enigmatic Painting by J.M.W. Turner’, *Tate Papers* 25 (Spring 2016) <http://www.tate.org.uk/research/publications/tate-papers/25/fall-of-anarchy-politics-anatomy-turner> (last accessed 17 May 2018).
80. Navickas considers how the Act was perceived as a further means to rule the poor out of the body politic, which occasioned some violent protests (*Protest*, pp. 133–5).
81. Smiles, ‘The Fall of Anarchy’, para. 28.

Chapter 1

Peterloo, Ambivalence and Commemorative Culture

Stephen C. Behrendt

Despite two centuries of discussion of the 'Peterloo massacre' of 16 August 1819 (including a 1989 special issue of *Manchester Region History Review*),[1] little has been written about extra-literary responses like caricature prints and commodity items (commemorative pottery, textiles, metalwork, and so on). Yet Diana Donald claims that 'the engravings have ultimately had the greater influence in creating a mental picture of "the Peterloo massacre"'.[2] Contemporary artefacts reveal unexpected ambivalence about the violence perpetrated upon the organisers and victims of the meeting in St Peter's Field and about legitimate responses to that violence. Perceived public need for commensurate responses to extraordinary events is often surprisingly brief, perhaps because such events are themselves often brief (the whole attack in St Peter's Field took only about half an hour[3]), and because options for commemorations with equivalent impact are limited.

The moral ambiguity evident in the Peterloo records reflects the Romantic period's uncertainty about appropriate individual and collective responses to government (or other institutional) despotism, especially concerning state intransigence about parliamentary reform (a key factor in the Manchester meeting), increased suffrage, labour issues (like Luddite unrest), and other simmering social and economic conflicts. The Peterloo artefacts intimate their differing moral, epistemological and aesthetic motives. The verbal records tend to suggest circumspection, the visual ones supply cautionary messages, and the commodity goods expose disjunctions between commemoration and acquiescence. These divergent attitudes and prescriptions illustrate

James Jasper's assertion that 'events with symbolic implications that go far beyond merely signaling the likelihood of repression' are 'the most common form of moral shock' and therefore elicit complex and often widely differing responses.[4]

John Milton argued in 1651 that 'no subjection is commanded, nor is any due' to any king who violates God's laws, 'nor are the people forbidden to resist such authority; for in so doing they do not resist the power nor the magistracy . . . but they resist a robber, a tyrant, an enemy'.[5] William Blackstone reiterated the 'law of redress against public oppression', asserting the community's right to even the 'extraordinary' action of revolution when the sovereign violates his compact with the citizens.[6] Was an appropriate response to Peterloo, then, the retributive confrontation urged by incendiary activists in the 'Stanzas Occasioned by the Manchester Massacre' that declared 'Let vengeance, bright flashes illume', and in 'The Appeal of Blood': 'Your children, friends, your husbands, wives, / Are sabred; some have lost their lives; / To you they call; avenge their woes'[7]? Or was non-violent resistance better, as epitomised in the ideologically charged Prometheus, the mythic resister *sine qua non* lionised by Goethe, Byron and (soon) Shelley? Or was peaceful legal recourse preferable?

> Remember! Britons, not Reform
>   Can e'er our country bless,
> Till we by safe and humble means
>   Obtain thy wish'd redress.[8]

Or perhaps a traditionally Christian alternative predicated upon anticipated eternal rebalancing of the scales of justice? 'The Meeting at Peterloo' beseeches, 'O God look down upon us for thou art just and true, / And those that can no mercy shew thy vengeance is now their due'.[9] So, too, counsels 'The Sword King': a fleeing mother admonishes her frightened child to 'let the murderers come' for 'there is vengeance in heaven for the base who strike home!'.[10] That even T. J. Wooler's vengeance-hungry *The Black Dwarf* included this uncharacteristic nod to the levelling nature of eternal justice suggests that the conviction of the inevitability of temporal justice (or retribution) was largely rhetorical. Given the unreasonable violence perpetrated upon a peaceful and reasoned assembly, what the citizens regarded as their bounden duty and how they proposed to discharge it bore immediately pragmatic and potentially lethal consequences. Their options turned on the nature of resistance and on the forms that it should take. For as Jasper writes, 'strategic calculations about success are also relevant [in social protest movements], in that few are willing to die for their cause, especially when their death will have no effect'.[11]

The Manchester crowd was 'probably at the time the largest mass peaceful demonstration ever assembled'.[12] The event, which E. P. Thompson called 'without question a formative experience in British social and political history', partly owing to its 'sheer *size*', John Belchem characterised as 'an early exercise in the politics of modern collective violence'.[13] The seeming contradiction evident in calling Peterloo either a 'mass peaceful demonstration' or an exercise in 'collective violence' informs this chapter. In reality it was both, and the moral ambivalence of the divergent responses has been overshadowed by the anger and pathos that shaped much post-Peterloo discourse. Ambivalence was entirely natural, though, given how events unfolded, were immediately reported, and subsequently reconfigured in the contemporary press, the legal proceedings (including their published records) and the broader public culture. This last category included relatively immediate literary responses like Percy Shelley's fierce *The Mask of Anarchy* and 'England in 1819' and later, forgettable works like Isabella Banks' 1876 novel, *The Manchester Man*. It also included nonce publications from broadside verses to mixed-media works like Hone's and Cruikshank's *Political House that Jack Built* to letters, petitions, 'accounts' and the like. But it also included eloquent extra-literary materials: caricature prints, ceramics, pottery, textiles and other commemorative artefacts like the well-known Peterloo medallion.

V. I. Tomlinson observed in 1989 that:

> the most difficult task in attempting to determine details of what actually happened at Peterloo is to reconcile the conflicting accounts provided by participants and spectators . . . [Even in] the sworn evidence of witnesses in court . . . contradictory versions are as marked as elsewhere . . .[14]

Witnesses are notoriously inconsistent, because 'seeing' is socially and culturally conditioned. Perception, cognition and interpretation entail complex interrelated personal, social, political, economic, religious and cultural schemata derived from every citizen's individual and collective experiences. How that collective public experience unfolds – or is shaped and manipulated – may often be as important as the event itself, as the extra-literary Peterloo materials demonstrate.

Verbal Records

James Jasper observes that 'social movements are conscious, concerted, and relatively sustained efforts by organised groups of ordinary people . . . to change some aspect of society by using extrainstitutional means', most of which involve 'protest: explicit criticism of people, organisations, and the things they believe or do'. When people cannot substantively alter what they oppose, they nevertheless 'express their contempt and outrage over existing practices'.[15] Protest movements aim to provide a moral voice and *force* for the aggrieved parties for whom they claim to speak and act. But this voice, like any collective voice, is inevitably a conditioned construct because 'most of our emotions are shaped by the understandings and responses of those around us'. Consequently, 'our institutions constantly promote certain moral beliefs and suppress others'.[16] Jasper's paradigm is useful because both the organisers and participants and its institutional opponents and their apologists cast Peterloo – before and afterwards – in calculatedly moral terms.

Contemporary title pages are illustrative. The complete title of one 'Account of the Dreadful Attack of the Military upon the Reformers' concludes with 'the treatment of Mr. Hunt, Mr. Johnson, &c. &c., and of the horrid barbarity to a number of females'.[17] Not to be outdone, the radical London publisher John Fairburn published John Wade's sensational forty-eight-page polemic: *Manchester Massacre!! An Authentic Narrative of the Magisterial and Yeomanry Massacre, at Manchester, with Remarks on the Illegal Conduct of the Magistrates in Suppressing the Meeting, and their Proceedings towards Mr. Hunt*. The title continues, but this part suggests the whole, which, significantly, concludes by advocating 'the Necessity of the Reformers PERSISTING in the Exercise of their undoubted Right to assemble and deliberate on the best Mode of redressing their Grievances'.[18]

The alternative view informs the title of Francis Philips' *Exposure of the Calumnies Circulated by the Enemies of Social Order, and Reiterated by their Abettors, against the Magistrates and Yeomanry Cavalry of Manchester and Salford*.[19] What George Canning cannily called 'the reign of terror at Manchester' appears in the anonymous *Letter to Earl Fitzwilliam*: 'The object of the great Manchester Meeting was "Universal Suffrage, or Death" – that is – the Overthrow of the British Constitution, and the Attainment of Universal Suffrage, by force and violence'.[20] Thus did political evangelists preach to their respective choirs.

Accounts of two contemporary observers illustrate the dilemma. Rev. James Scholefield (1790–1855), a young reform-minded minister of the Bible Christian Church from the grim Manchester suburb of Ancoats, was present, signed the *Declaration of Protest* that appeared in the *Manchester Observer* (11 September 1819), initiated a subscription fund to aid victims, and testified for the defence at the State Trial of Henry 'Orator' Hunt in March 1820. Thirty-one-year-old William Hulton (1787–1864), appointed Chairman of the Lancashire and Cheshire Manchester Magistrates in July 1819, ordered the dispersal of the crowd in Manchester less than two months later. As the prosecution's chief witness at Hunt's trial,[21] he testified that the meeting 'did undoubtedly inspire terror in the minds of the inhabitants', while Scholefield swore that he did not 'hear any persons express alarm at the meeting'. Hulton claimed that when the yeomanry arrived 'the crowd . . . groaned and hissed'; Scholefield 'perceived no opposition to have been manifested toward them'. Hulton insisted that 'those men who had sticks shook them in the air . . . in a menacing manner', Scholefield 'saw nothing held up except the hats of the people'. According to Hulton, 'stones and brickbats [were] flying in all directions', while Scholefield swore that 'there were no brick-bats, stones or sticks hurled'.[22] Similar contradictions fill the records of Peterloo, including details about injuries itemised in lists like the 'Accurate Alphabetical List of the Names and Residence of those who were Killed, Wounded, and Maimed by the sabre or otherwise; with an account of the nature of the Injuries sustained' (*Manchester Observer*, 18 December). Government entities like the Metropolitan and Central Committee (London) published their own lists, as did local philanthropic associations like the Manchester Relief Committee.[23]

Visual Records

Some of the most dramatic accounts of Peterloo were prints that appeared immediately afterward. *A View of St Peter's place and manner in which the Manchester Reform meeting was dispersed by civil and military power, August 16th 1819* (Figure 1.1), attributed by Margaret Leighton and Dorothy George to J. Wroe, the radical reformist editor of the *Manchester Observer*, but 'based on a cabinet picture by John Slack',[24] presents an oddly static panorama, despite the charging Yeomanry Cavalry.

The enormous crowd begins to break and flee, victims at lower right toppling beneath their attackers. At centre foreground a woman faces the viewer, her light-coloured dress drawing the eye and underscoring the considerable numbers of women present, including the woman on the hustings who is undoubtedly Mary Fildes, President of the Manchester Female Reform Society (who, like their counterparts

Figure 1.1 *A View of St Peter's place and manner in which the Manchester Reform meeting was dispersed by civil and military power, August 16th 1819* by J. Slack (© People's History Museum, Manchester)

from Royton, were 'dressed all in white'[25]), wounded when she was dragged from the hustings. What strikes one is the sheer immensity of the relatively well-dressed crowd crammed into the enclosed space from which speedy escape is clearly impossible.

This print emphasises the meeting's peaceful, orderly nature; despite the growing chaos, we see not violent resistance but only gestures indicating flight or self-defence. Indeed, most demonstrators – including women and children – were clean and neatly dressed, many in their 'Sunday best' clothes,[26] attesting to their peaceable intentions. Participants had been strictly enjoined to exhibit 'Cleanliness, Sobriety, Order and Peace', the organisers explicitly prohibiting 'all weapons of offence or defence'.[27] Hunt, the demonstration's organiser, prescribed strictly legal, orderly proceedings; his associates carefully kept their statements within the letter of the law, stipulating that only against unequivocally 'unconstitutional' or 'tyrannical' actions by the government and its representatives might physical force be entertained.[28] This print probably informs the commemorative handkerchiefs that subsequently appeared, bearing a banner at the top reading 'A Representation of the Manchester Reform Meeting Dispersed by the Civil and Military Power, Aug. 16 1819',[29] and repeating Slack's details, including the respectably-dressed crowd (virtually every man wears a hat and tailored coat, every woman a bonnet) being summarily routed. The scene's horror is compounded by the handkerchief's claustrophobic arrangement: the darkened sky, the surrounding border and the banner at the top. The unoccupied lower foreground depicts the tumbling protesters; interestingly, Slack's standing woman at lower centre is replaced here by the face-down, sprawled figure of a fallen man.[30]

Best known is the print that Richard Carlile published immediately following Peterloo; its full inscription reads: 'To Henry Hunt, Esqr. as Chairman of the meeting assembled on St Peter's Field, Manchester, on the 16th of August 1819, and to the Female Reformers of Manchester and the adjacent Towns who were exposed to and suffered from THE WANTON AND FURIOUS ATTACK MADE ON THEM BY THAT BRUTAL ARMED FORCE THE MANCHESTER AND CHESHIRE YEOMAN CAVALRY' (Figure 1.2).[31]

This epitomising print juxtaposes the tableau of violence and suffering (lower foreground) with the ineffective gestures of those on the hustings (again including Mary Fildes, holding her group's colours).

Figure 1.2 *To Henry Hunt, Esqr. [The Peterloo Massacre, 16th August 1819]* by George Cruikshank (Manchester Art Gallery, UK/Bridgeman Images)

Relative restraint is replaced here by suffering women and children, including the very young children (right of centre and lower right), and the infant conspicuously lifted towards the slashing sword of the mounted yeoman (centre). Gone, too, is the emphasis on the peaceful *and well-dressed* crowd; the few reasonably well-attired men are the minority. Diana Donald observes that prints published in London, like Carlile's and those of Cruikshank and Marks (to which I shall turn), typically portray the victims as a 'ragged and poverty-stricken' crowd that included 'women with their children' in greater numbers than the documentary evidence substantiates.[32] Although prints from London circulated widely in the country, the comparative restraint evident in visual materials from the immediate Manchester area suggests both their publishers' understandable caution and a local ambivalence about the Peterloo affair.

Propagandists exaggerated both the numbers and the nature of the injuries. The Carlile print, for example, emphasises the ferocity of the

Yeomanry Cavalry's attack, showing no fewer than a dozen sabres, against which the defenceless citizens raise only the liberty capped staves bearing their colours and banners, including one raised by the distressed man at lower right menaced by his pursuer's raised sabre. The symbolism is inescapable: the armed violence of the state and its military and civic representatives is levelled against an aggrieved citizenry armed only with the banners that claim their rights as 'free-born Englishmen' (and women) under the auspices of republican liberty. The iconography of this print bears out Belchem's claim that in summer 1819 'radicals managed to appropriate the legitimising language *and symbols* of the loyalist establishment', casting themselves 'in heroic guise as the true loyalists, upholding the rights of the freeborn Englishman, the constitution which had been won by the valor and cemented by the blood of our ancestors' (emphasis added). Moreover, women's participation infused the reform movement with the culturally revered image of 'motherhood and domestic responsibility'.[33] Against this 'natural' (that is, conventional[34]) order of human affairs the state and its legal and military representatives repeatedly deployed their forces.

When the militaristic state repression rendered further mass violence logistically impractical – even impossible – legal force was deployed in the form of repressive measures like the Liverpool ministry's Six Acts (December 1819) that labelled any meeting called to promote reform an overt act of treasonable conspiracy. Defeated in the streets, the radical reformers were in turn defeated in the courts. That the trials of Hunt and others arrested at Manchester dragged on irresolutely for months before guilty verdicts were delivered in March 1820 and sentences commenced distanced the actual event of Peterloo further still from its participants and the vehicles available to them for pursuing redress. National rebellion – civil war – on whose brink the nation teetered in late 1819 was averted, aided by the dissociating effects of legal and parliamentary wrangling.

The Carlile print's mixing of iconography, melodramatic staging and historical fact render the propagandistic visual polemic ambivalent. The classically inflected print, apparently based on a drawing by George Cruikshank, visually echoes two widely known subjects from grand style history painting. While Poussin's and Rubens' *Rape of the Sabines* arguably influenced contemporary depictions of Peterloo, their depictions of the *Massacre of the Innocents* have greater resonance.

Their paintings (both artists created multiple images) inevitably underscore the pathos of the situation: contorted vortices of action feature brutal attacks by sword-wielding warriors, dead and dying infants and wounded mothers fruitlessly attempting to protect them. While comparable images often figure in portrayals of military or civic warfare, Cruikshank and others expected at least some of their viewers to appreciate the immediate relevance of the biblical tale of the slaughter of 'innocents' (and the trauma to their mothers or families) as part of a state-sponsored campaign of assassination aimed at eliminating a promised redeemer. The innocent, the powerless, the disenfranchised, the implied argument reminds the viewer, suffer most when any unreasonable and intransigent state entity exerts its power to quash opposition and retain its dominance. The denouement of the biblical precedent bears contemporary relevance too: the Redeemer, who survived the state-inflicted carnage, became the agent of that state's eventual overthrow. Just so, images like Cruikshank's imply, on at least one level, the sacrifice of the innocent victims at Peterloo may become the enabling mechanism for the 'redemption' promised by the radical reformers, even if it is delayed rather than immediate.

We should remember, too, another, more recent image: Luke Clennell's prize-winning 1816 exhibition sketch, *The Decisive Charge of the Life Guards at Waterloo*, available in a variety of prints.[35] In Clennell's famous panoramic image, the French are routed by the timely arrival of the Life Guards, who charge dramatically towards the viewer, the central figure (on a rearing white horse) brandishing his sabre. French survivors flee while their dead and dying countrymen sprawl across the lower foreground, an array that eerily prefigures the foreground of the Carlile print and others in which post-Peterloo artists signalled the horrible parody – the tragic travesty – of that decisive action.

Probably the best known of these parodic satires is *Manchester Heroes* (Figure 1.3), usually attributed to George Cruikshank.[36] The Yeomanry Cavalry charge in from the left: one waves his sabre above his head, shouting 'Cut him down. Cut him down', a phrase that appears repeatedly in angry pamphlets like John Cam Hobhouse's *Supplicatory Letter* to Castlereagh: 'The soldiers have cut the people to pieces – you have shewn . . . that you care as little for them, as you do for the meanest of the rabble'.[37] To the right another attacker prepares to drive his sabre into the breast of a collapsing well-dressed

Figure 1.3 *Manchester Heroes* by George Cruikshank (Library of Congress, Prints & Photographs Division, Washington, DC, LC-DIG-ds-10154)

woman[38] supported by a comparably attired man, presumably her husband; before her a small boy clutches her scarf in his right hand and lifts his left defensively, crying, 'Oh pray Sir, don't Kill Mammy, she only came to see Mr. Hunt'. Meanwhile, her attacker ironically declares, 'None but the brave deserve the Fair'.[39] At upper left appears the disembodied head of the Prince Regent, the beam of the scales of justice balanced atop his head, the heavier scale inscribed 'Peculators' (indicating the government servants) and the lighter 'Reformers'. The Regent encourages the attackers, promising thanks, rewards and eternal fame 'in a Song, or second Chivey Chace'.[40]

Less well known is *The Massacre of Peterloo! or a Specimen of English Liberty. August 16th 1819* by John Lewis Marks (c. 1796–1855), published in London (Figure 1.4).[41] Marks' print is dark and claustrophobic, its large figures crammed into the foreground and Hunt's group on the hustings relegated to an inconspicuous rectangle in the upper left background. The cavalry is uglier here than in other prints, and three of the six sabres visible are bloody. At the far left one sabres a well-dressed elderly man supported by his

Figure 1.4 *The Massacre of Peterloo! or a Specimen of English Liberty. August 16th 1819* by John Lewis Marks (Library of Congress, Prints & Photographs Division, Washington, DC, LC-USZ62-138639)

decently attired son who raises an ineffectual hand, crying '"Oh! stay that lifted blade That brandish'd darts a crimson gleam". Oh! spare my Father'.[42] To his left, a bonneted woman holding a young child topples onto a fallen man while trying to ward off the blow of a fat cavalryman at the centre whose narrow pig eye is turned upon her. His right hand grasps his gory sabre while his left holds a trumpet that he is sounding. The *Manchester Massacre!!* states that when the Yeomanry Cavalry 'rode into the mob . . . [a] bugle-man went at their head'.[43] From the trumpet's bell rises a speech balloon that reads: 'Raise up the Trumpet in high cheerful Strain! / Fill the goblets of <u>rum</u>, to the <u>Loyal Yeomen</u>! / How Glorious our Ardour to lay down the Lives / Of defenceless Children, Husbands & Wives'. Beneath, in tiny print, appears the unattached word 'meagre', perhaps imputing the artist's opinion of the bully's egotistical bravado or the officer's slight regard for his victims. The first line of his speech darkly parodies the trumpet and joyful noise of Psalm 81's beginning.

The several youths and woman with an insensible infant at right may reference one Peterloo '*warrior*, [who] by fiercely brandishing his sabre, actually frightened to death a child in its mother's arms!'[44] Before her, a man's throat is clutched by an extraordinarily ugly, cudgel-wielding constable who cries 'What a Glorious Day, this is our Waterloo'. This figure epitomises the brutal Manchester constables and may identify Deputy Constable Joseph Nadin, who arrested Hunt at Peterloo. Samuel Bamford remembered Nadin as a man of 'uncommon breadth and solidity of frame' whose 'features were broad and non-intellectual, his voice loud, his language coarse and illiterate, and his manner rude and overbearing to equals or inferiors'.[45] Characterised by their 'savage spirit', the constables, *The Times* reported, were seen 'beating with their staves those who had been trodden or cut down; and one of them, in the drunken delirium of his triumph, brandished his staff, and exclaimed, in the hearing of the terrified inhabitants of Windmill-street, "*Here is our field of Waterloo!*"'[46]

The topical reference to Waterloo was as irresistible as the differences were patently clear. The elaborations in *Manchester Massacre!!* carefully distinguish between the perpetrators of indiscriminate violence and 'the regular soldiers', whom he reports tried to avoid causing injury because 'they did not want to flesh their maiden sword in the bodies of their countrymen, but on the bodies of their country's enemies'. This author declares bitterly that the 'magnanimity and valour' that produced such carnage was 'only to be found in the *assassins* of Peterloo, not in the *Heroes* of Waterloo', the latter of whom, according to multiple witnesses, berated the constables and Yeomanry Cavalry as 'cowardly scoundrels' and worse.[47] The contemporary theatre had flourished for years with 'victories to be triumphantly staged';[48] when the post-Waterloo peace drove such nationalistic pageants from the stage, Peterloo effectively transferred them to St Peter's Field. Likewise, caricaturists transformed Waterloo's heroic chaos, as portrayed by artists like Clennell, into the brutal and shameful chaos of Peterloo's battlefield. Waterloo's defeated French 'enemies' are hideously morphed in these prints into peaceful, domestic *British* casualties whom the government and its agents insidiously trope as enemies of the country and upon whom their agents perpetrate their violent attacks.

The depths of this depravity, and the calculated extremity to which the government pushes its 'legal' authority, is indicated in Marks' print by the presence in the upper right corner of a bewigged magistrate leaning out of a window, clutching a bottle and cup and shouting to the cavalrymen below, 'Cut away Lads! the Riot Act is being read up in the corner – ' while behind him another magistrate, facing the room's *interior*, reads from the Riot Act. For action against demonstrators to be legal, the Riot Act needed to be read in a prescribed fashion:

> Was this done? There has been no proof that proclamation was made at all; but IF it were made, thousands, and tens of thousands can testify, that it was not made 'OPENLY *and with loud voice*', nor among the '*rioters*', or as near them as the magistrates might '*safely come*'. [Therefore,] two points are clearly established: first, there is no proof that the Riot Act was read; second, there is abundant proof, that, if read, it was not read in the manner prescribed by law; therefore the Riot Act affords not the slightest justification for the subsequent dispersion and massacre of the meeting.[49]

The government apologist Rev. Melville Horne disagreed vehemently, claiming that many witnesses heard it being read – and 'with a *stentrophonic voice*' no less![50] The point is probably moot, given the government's notorious use of spies and agents provocateurs like Oliver the Spy, not to mention just plain paid liars.

Material Records

Following Peterloo, Carlile suggested (the *Manchester Massacre!!* reported) that the Yeomanry Cavalry be commemorated with a medallion, 'on one side of which should be inscribed THE SLAUGHTERMEN OF MANCHESTER, and a reverse bearing a description of their slaughter of defenceless men, women, and children, unprovoked and unnecessary'.[51] In fact, an oppositional medallion (modelled on Clennell's picture) was actually struck: Cavalrymen rush forward, sabres drawn, towards a man (seen from the rear) holding aloft a liberty cap on a staff while around him women, children, and at least one additional man fall or lie. The obverse side paraphrases Psalms 37:14: 'The wicked have drawn out the sword. They have cut down the poor and needy and such as be of upright conversation.'

Other commodity objects soon appeared: commemorative ceramic jugs, mugs and plates. The transfer-printed jugs, produced by Herculaneum Pottery (Liverpool), typically depict a single charging cavalryman, sabre raised, advancing on a fallen woman holding aloft a flag inscribed 'Liberty or Death'. Usually an inscription above the cavalryman reads 'Murderd [*sic*] on the Plains of Peterloo'. The obverse usually offers a vignette of Henry Hunt surrounded by an inscription reading 'Henry Hunt Esqr. The Preserving Advocate of the People's Rights'.[52] One fancier blue ewer with a gilt band around the top shows a mounted dragoon trampling fallen figures and a shield inscribed 'Justice'; an inscription beneath reads 'May the cause of distress be soon banished from the British Empire'.[53] There are also drinking mugs, like the Staffordshire earthenware piece that depicts the dragoon and fallen woman with her flag together with scrolls inscribed 'No Corn Laws' and 'Hunt & Liberty',[54] as well as a small circular transfer-printed Staffordshire plaque showing a horseman trampling fallen victims and a banner inscribed 'Liberty', with an incomplete inscription at the bottom.[55]

None of these commodity goods were without ambivalence, either. Like all commemorative touchstones, such items remind citizens (sympathisers in particular) of the events being commemorated and thereby keep the participants (*victims* in particular) 'alive' in the collective public memory. The *perpetrators*, on the other hand, gradually recede into the emotional distance that time provides even as the victims live on in the ongoing public culture. Rev. John Davison noted this tendency before 1819 ended, observing that public feeling 'has already made a large change in its direction': from 'condemnation', it 'has advanced a step backwards', moving from 'abhorrence and indignation' to 'the anterior process'.[56] We see this retrogression also in visual work, where Peterloo and its victims become mere passing references or background details in service to other, only tangentially related, ideological agendas, as in 'These are the People' from Hone and Cruikshank's *Political House that Jack Built* (1819), reappropriated in their 1820 *Political Alphabet* ('P'), or Rowlandson's 'The Manchester Sparrows' from *Who Killed Cock Robin?* (1819). *As physical artefacts*, commemorative objects help to diffuse immediate public anger into and throughout the wider public consciousness at the same time as they also de-fuse that anger (and especially the spontaneous desire for retributive vengeance), replacing the events themselves with their symbolic representations. But because those representations take the form of physical goods – utilitarian objects whose commemorative inscriptions and iconography privilege them above mere utilitarian status – they become the objects of a different sort of perception (and interaction) than the persons and events they represent: talismanic secular relics.

Following Peterloo numerous commemorative songs appeared, many printed as broadsheets like the *Tribute to the Immortal Memory of the Reformers* (some copies of which include hand colouring) and the broadly satirical *Renowned Atchievements* [*sic*] *of Peter-loo*, attributed to 'Sir Hugo Burlo Furioso DiMulo, Bart., M. V. C., and A. S. S.' with 'The Music composed by the celebrated Dr. Horsefood'.[57] Another broadsheet bears two poems, each titled 'New Song', one noted as following the tune of 'Parker's Widow' and beginning with 'Rise Britons, rise now from your slumber, / Rise and hail the glorious day'. The lines are eerily prescient of the words of Percy Shelley's rousing language in *The Mask of Anarchy*, composed in Italy upon learning about Peterloo on 5 September in a letter from Thomas Love Peacock.[58] The visionary voice that concludes Shelley's poem calls:

> Rise like Lions after slumber
> In unvanquishable number[;]
> Shake your chains to Earth like dew
> Which in sleep had fallen on you
> Ye are many – they are few. (ll. 151–5, 368–72)[59]

And yet Shelley's poem, too, is ambivalent. After the glorious phantom recounts seeing 'the Tyrant's crew / Ride over your wives and you' so that 'Blood is on the grass like dew', she suggests that it is understandable 'to feel revenge / Fiercely thirsting to exchange / Blood for blood—and wrong for wrong'. But, she cautions: 'Do not thus when ye are strong' (ll. 190–6). It seems a contradiction: battered and bloodied, they are 'strong'. Shelley's point, however, is that in their victimhood lies their strength, a strength that they are admonished not to squander by resorting to the unreasoned brutishness of their oppressors. A grievous moral error, he contends, vengeance constitutes an ethical compromise because, by using the same physical means as the oppressor, the victim is reduced to the same degraded moral level. Find strength, rather, Shelley's phantom counsels, in heroic passive resistance: 'Let them ride among you there, / Slash, and stab, and maim, and hew,– / What they like, that let them do' (ll. 341–3). Eventually overcome by guilt, they will be shunned and shamed by all,

> And the bold, true warriors
> Who have hugged Danger in wars
> Will turn to those who would be free,
> Ashamed of such base company. (ll. 356–9)

These 'true warriors' are of course both the veterans of the Napoleonic Wars and the restrained regulars at Manchester who disdained Yeomanry Cavalry and constables alike.

Interestingly, Bamford recounted that amid the post-Peterloo thirst for revenge a philosophical friend in nearby Royton counselled restraint, observing that 'our oppressors are already wretched' in their own shame: 'Those men would, even now, shrink out of existence, if they were only assured of getting to heaven quietly. They are already invoking that obliviousness which will never come to their relief.' Therefore, he continued, 'we had best remain as we were [because] the least outrage on our [part] would only strengthen the aggressors, and create that plea of justification which alone could mitigate their remorse'.[60] Writing a quarter of a century later, Thomas Carlyle likewise praised the forbearance of the victims for eschewing 'violence done[,] which is always sure to be injustice done, for violence does even justice unjustly'. Any insurrection that definitively exposes 'the disease' without exacting bloody vengeance, he writes, 'has attained the highest success possible for it'.[61]

Shelley could comfortably prescribe passive resistance: safe in Italy, he was not on the front lines. Bamford and his associates *were*, though, and like Leigh Hunt, who cautiously shelved Shelley's incendiary *Mask*, they appreciated the physical, institutional and legal forces marshalled by the repressive establishment. In other post-Peterloo poems like 'Song to the Men of England' and the fragmentary 'To the People of England' Shelley agrees that the oppressors are already wretched. But the brutalised victims must recognise, as a prerequisite to their liberation, that their acquiescence has ironically made them complicit in their oppression. Because real change will involve many such steps, it must necessarily be gradual, not cataclysmic. Thus, the ending of 'England in 1819' is left rhetorically (and politically) ambivalent: the arrival of the 'glorious Phantom' is *conditional*, not certain: it '*may*' burst 'to illumine our tempestuous day' – or it may not. Nevertheless, in *A Philosophical View of Reform* (1819–20), Shelley observes that while some 'system of gradual reform' might have been possible 'two years ago', present aggravated circumstances militate against gradualism: 'the petition of a million of men' having been 'rejected with disdain', the oppressed 'have become more universally aware of the true sources of their misery. It is [therefore] possible that the period of conciliation is past'.[62] It is difficult to choose the right course, in other words, amid uncertain circumstances.

So too with prints and other artefacts. Their graphic depictions of violence and suffering notwithstanding, images like those published by Carlile, Cruikshank and Marks were simultaneously inflammatory and cautionary. The prints afforded the unarmed ordinary citizens who are attacked, beaten, cut down and trampled no *means* of physical redress, even when the images unsparingly delineate their ready *motive*. Not just immediate resistance, the prints imply, but also future physical retaliation is largely pointless, counter-productive and likely even fatal, a brutal reality documented by the remarkable account book of the Peterloo Relief Fund.[63] The other side has all the weapons, all the sanction of state and (often) church. To retaliate, in such circumstances, is to engage in an unequal combat whose outcome the prints ominously foreshadow. The alternative impulse – trust to time and heaven for eventual redress – may not be capitulation after all, but rather a more heroic and visionary resistance. As John Cahuac put it in *Who Killed Cock Robin?*:

> These vile SPARROWS
> [W]ho kill ROBINS so callous,
> Will, sooner or later,
> Take their *swing* from a *Gallows!*
>
> . . .
>
> For sooner or later
> Some REFORM must take place. (pp. 6, 19)[64]

It is worth remembering Shelley's words to William Godwin already in 1812: 'I will look to events in which it will be impossible that I can share, and make myself the cause of an effect which will take place ages after I shall have mouldered into dust.'[65] Mary Shelley reiterated his sentiment in her note to Shelley's poems of 1816, writing that although Shelley had earlier tried to take his 'political doctrines' directly to the people, 'he had now begun to feel that the time was not ripe in England, and that the pen was the only instrument wherewith to prepare the way for better things'.[66]

One final pair of images marks the 'afterlife' of Peterloo. In 1821 William Hone released *A Slap at Slop*, his satirical parody of *The Times* under John Stoddart's editorship, the 'First Edition' of which included Cruikshank's designs for a Peterloo memorial and commemorative medallion (Figure 1.5).[67] The monument shows a single sabre-wielding cavalryman on a rearing horse trampling defenceless, fallen victims. Below, an altar-like structure is bordered with skulls; from a crown at its centre daggers radiate towards the skulls. Executed some two years after the event it commemorates, Cruikshank's image underscores the deadly odds stacked against the reformers. Crowded into a page that also lampoons a 'Royal Cuckoo Clock', 'Warren's Black-Bat Blacking' and 'Blackguard's Edinburgh Magazine', however, the image also inevitably trivialises the event and its deadly gravity.

Beneath the 'monument' appears the design for the proposed commemorative medallion that unmistakably recalls Wedgewood's famous 1786–7 abolitionist emblem, its pleading slave replaced by a ragged kneeling spinner,[68] arms raised futilely against the blow aimed by an axe-wielding uniformed officer behind whom lies a senseless woman. The design is ringed by skulls and crossbones. Beneath, a caption reads: 'Q. "Am I not a man and a brother?" / A. "No!—you are a poor weaver"'. This image does more than merely repurpose the familiar image. It reminds its viewer that the Manchester crowd included mostly weavers (who represented some 63 per cent of participants' occupations), augmented by spinners, carders and others associated with the weaving trade, making it apparent that 'support among other groups, particularly from factory workers, was very limited'.[69] In fact, Peterloo must be viewed through the lens of an emerging class warfare in which the 'middling classes' were more actively separating themselves from the labouring class and its anxieties about subsistence issues like proportional representation, a central plank in the reformers' platform. This division informs Salford's Rev. Horne's declaration that 'where great danger exists, while wisdom dissembles whatever can increase that danger, the Higher and Middle Classes

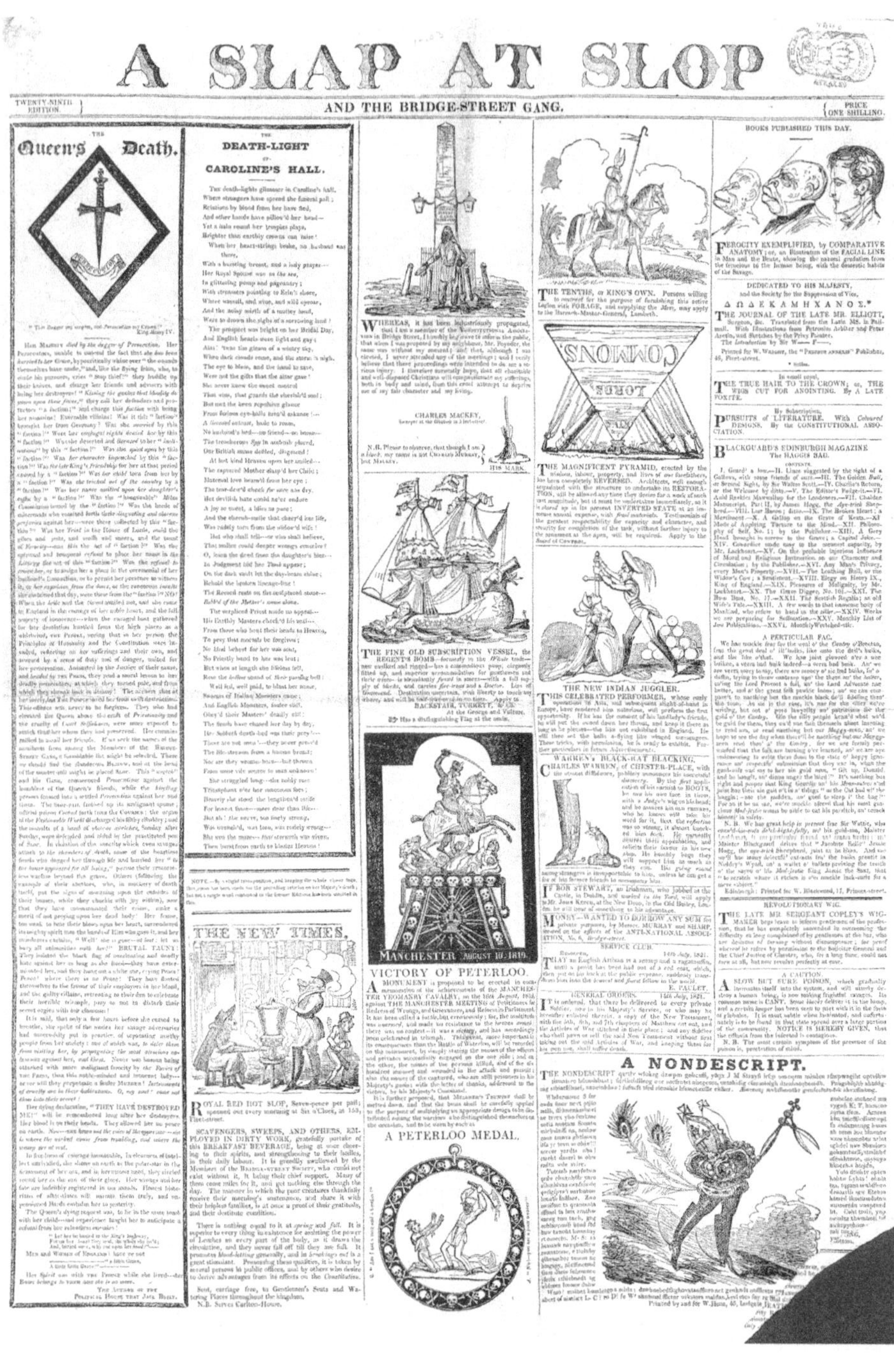

A SLAP AT SLOP

TWENTY-NINTH EDITION.

AND THE BRIDGE-STREET GANG.

PRICE ONE SHILLING.

THE Queen's Death.

THE DEATH-LIGHT OF CAROLINE'S HALL.

THE NEW TIMES.

MANCHESTER AUGUST 16. 1819.

VICTORY OF PETERLOO.

A PETERLOO MEDAL.

THE NEW INDIAN JUGGLER.

BOOKS PUBLISHED THIS DAY.

A NONDESCRIPT.

Figure 1.5 *A Slap at Slop* by William Hone and George Cruikshank (© The University of Manchester, Manchester)

should be made to feel the *necessity* of Union, courage and exertion' against the 'enemies . . . of our own household' among 'the Town [that] is all Manufacture, or Trade'.[70] The granular documentary data suggest that the public outcry over Peterloo was rooted more in outrage over the gross transgression of order and decency by the government and its agents and instruments than in genuine human sympathy for the individual victims, a distinction that reflected later Regency society's increasing distaste for the labouring classes.

The revolutionary flashpoint that was Peterloo did not in fact lead to revolution, for a variety of reasons including the simple absence of a charismatic leader who might have transformed the ardent reformers into an actual army of armed revolutionaries. Hobhouse tellingly reminded Castlereagh of Lord (William) Russell's statement at his trial in the Rye House Plot of 1683: 'A rebellion cannot be made now as in a former day: we have few great men now.'[71] Ultimately, the sort of violent revenge that the most radical spokespersons advocated was rejected for what is now called a 'wait and see' attitude. The *Manchester Massacre!!* was prescient: 'Justice, truth, and humanity, though now in abeyance, must ultimately resume their empire. Time will at length vindicate the motives of Reformers, and unmask the vile artifices, unceasing calumnies, and barbarity of their enemies.'[72] Humanistic, Christian forbearance, in other words, and a conviction that time sets all inequities (and iniquities) right. 'Meaningful morality is often hard to come by', Jasper observes in *The Art of Moral Protest*.[73] If Milton's Satan was read politically (as he frequently *was*) as the figure who epitomises the inherent *duty* and *obligation* to resist tyranny, it bears remembering that he was for his pains booted from heaven, damned to hell and demoted finally to the status of a narrow fellow in the (Edenic) grass. That grim paradigm surely gave pause to many politically and humanistically committed Romantic-era activists both before and after Peterloo.

Notes

1. *Manchester Region History Review* 3:1 (Spring/Summer 1989); hereafter *MRHR*.
2. Diana Donald, 'The Power of Print: Graphic Images of Peterloo', *MRHR*, pp. 21–30 (21).

3. Joyce Marlow, 'The Day of Peterloo', *MRHR*, p. 6.
4. James M. Jasper, *The Art of Moral Protest: Culture, Biography, and Creativity in Social Movements* (Chicago: University of Chicago Press, 1997), p. 324.
5. John Milton, *Defence of the People of England, in Answer to Salmasius's Defence of the King* (*Defensio pro Populo Anglicano*) (1651; English trans., 1692), pp. 68–9.
6. William Blackstone, *Commentaries on the Laws of England*, 4 vols (Oxford, 1765–9), vol. 1, pp. 238, 243.
7. *The Black Dwarf* 1:4 (16 October 1819), p. 564; *The Briton* 3:34 (25 August 1819), n.p.
8. Philo Peter Pindar [pseud.], *The Field of Peter-loo, an Heroic Poem, in Two Cantos, to which is added, An Address to Liberty* (London: W. Benbow, 1820), p. 8.
9. 'The Meeting at Peterloo'. Reproduced in Marlow, *MRHR*, pp. 3–7, 6.
10. *The Black Dwarf* 3:38 (22 September 1819), p. 628.
11. Jasper, *Art of Moral Protest*, p. 325.
12. James Chandler, 'On Peterloo, 16 August 1819', *BRANCH: Britain, Representation, and Nineteenth-Century History* <http://www.branchcollective.org/?ps_articles=james-chandler-on-peterloo-16-august-1819> (last accessed 20 February 2017). See also Chandler's *England in 1819: The Politics of Literary Culture and the Case of Romantic Historicism* (Chicago: University of Chicago Press, 1998).
13. E. P. Thompson, *The Making of the English Working Class* [1963] (New York: Vintage, 1966), p. 687; John Belchem, 'Manchester, Peterloo and the Radical Challenge', *MRHR*, pp. 9–14 (12).
14. V. I. Tomlinson, 'Postscript to Peterloo', *MRHR*, pp. 51–9 (51).
15. Jasper, *Art of Moral Protest*, p. 5.
16. Ibid. p. 10.
17. [John Wade], *Manchester Meeting. An Account of the Dreadful Attack of the Military upon the Reformers* (Birmingham, 1819).
18. [John Wade], *Manchester Massacre!!* By the Editor of 'The Black Book' (London, 1820); identified on the title pages of both books as printer and publisher, Fairburn published John Wade's controversial two-volume *Black Book* (1820), which identified all recipients of pensions and other payments from public funds.
19. Francis Philips, *An Exposure of the Calumnies . . .* (London, 1819).
20. *Speech of the Rt. Hon. George Canning . . . March 18, 1820* (London: P. Kelleher, 1820), p. 16; 'A Member of No Party', *A Letter to Earl Fitzwilliam* (London: F. C. and J. Rivington, 1819), p. 11; the author attacks Fitzwilliam for appearing on the same platform as T. J. Wooler to demand an investigation of Peterloo.

21. Tomlinson, *MRHR*, p. 51; see also Paul A. Pickering and Alex Tyrrell. '"In the Thickest of the Fight": The Reverend James Scholefield (1790–1855) and the Bible Christians of Manchester and Salford', *Albion: A Quarterly Journal Concerned with British Studies* 26:3 (Autumn 1994), pp. 461–82.
22. Tomlinson, *MRHR*, p. 51.
23. *Report of the Metropolitan and Central Committee Appointed for the Relief of the Manchester Sufferers* (London, 1820). The MCC consulted with the Manchester agency in November and compiled a unique account book detailing 318 casualties <http://luna.manchester.ac.uk/luna/servlet/detail/Manchester~91~1~14940~144478> (last accessed 20 February 2017).
24. Coloured print (8 x 6 inches), Manchester City Council, Manchester Local Image Collection 942.73 C5; identifier m07591. Margaret E. Leighton, 'Drawn and etched by J, Wroe, Manchester' *Peterloo, Monday, 16th August 1819: A Bibliography* (Manchester: Manchester Libraries Committee, 1969), p. 26. M. Dorothy George, *Catalogue of Political and Personal Satires Preserved in the Department of Prints and Drawings in the British Museum*, vol. IX (London: British Museum, 1949), pp. 920–1 (no. 13262). According to *T. P.'s Weekly*, J. Wroe 'was present at the onslaught' (3:63 [22 January 1904], p.124). For the attribution to Slack (quoted), see <http://www.wisconsinhistory.org/Content.aspx?dsNav=N:4294963828-4294955414&dsRecord> (last accessed 20 February 2017). John and James Slack were 'Engravers to Calico-Printers' in Salford and Manchester respectively (*London Gazette* No. 18590, 3 July 1829, p. xiii [1290]).
25. Marlow, 'Day of Peterloo', p. 4.
26. Edmund Frow and Ruth Frow, *Radical Salford: Episodes in Labour History* (Manchester: Neil Richardson, 1984), p. 7.
27. N. J. Frangopulo, *Tradition in Action: The Historical Evolution of the Greater Manchester County* (Wakefield: EP Publishing, 1977), p. 31.
28. John Belchem, *'Orator' Hunt: Henry Hunt and English Working-Class Radicalism* (Oxford: Clarendon Press,1985), pp. 4–5.
29. One such cotton handkerchief (20.5 x 24 inches) includes a laurel border inscribed with reformist slogans; six surrounding buildings are identified in a key. Manchester Art Gallery, accession number 1969.160. Another is at the Wisconsin Historical Society, Image 85166, format number 5–1363.
30. He seems to clutch a cane or curved-headed walking stick; two men to his immediate left also hold walking sticks, as do several men deeper among the crowd. One, slightly above centre foreground, raises his stick to ward off the sabre blow of the mounted yeoman

confronting him. Beside him another hatted man (or boy) brandishes what clearly appears to be a club. This print implies that walking sticks were employed only for self-defence. That only one 'club' is visible among the massive crowd emphasises how few participants came prepared for violence.

31. Published by Richard Carlile, London, 1 October 1819 (16.5 x 20 inches). Monochrome version, British Library; shelfmark 1871,0812.5310. Colored version, New York Public Library, Catalogue number b19815986. The image *may* be by George Cruikshank; see A. S. W. Rosenbach. *A Catalogue of the Works Illustrated by George Cruikshank and Isaac and Robert Cruikshank* (Philadelphia: privately printed, 1918), p. 180. George, *Catalogue*, p. 921 (no. 13263).
32. Donald, *MRHR*, p. 25. Malcolm Bee and Walter Bee hold the Yeomanry Cavalry responsible for a relatively low percentage of the injuries to women and children (noting that 'few children seem to have been present at the meeting'), while branding the rampaging constables wholly indiscriminate about gender or age in what *The Times* called their 'savage spirit of malice and revenge' ('The Casualties of Waterloo', *MRHR*, pp. 43–50 [45–6]). See also Michael Bush, 'The Women at Peterloo: The Impact of Female Reform on the Manchester Meeting of 16 August 1819', *History* 89:2 (April 2004), pp. 209–32.
33. Belchem, *MRHR*, p. 11.
34. The contested nature of this word and its variants is evident in its frequent recurrence throughout the later Enlightenment and Romantic periods to denote both an orthodox, conservative (even reactionary) hierarchical Christian world view that seemingly encompassed everything from physical science to civic, socio-economic, racial, religious and gender relations as well as contrary egalitarian scientific, social and philosophical cosmologies.
35. Clennell's sketch (never rendered as a painting) was awarded a premium at the British Institution's 1816 competition for finished sketches treating British victories in France, Spain and Portugal. Prints, in formats including the image alone, with printed 'keys', and with decorative borders, were executed by William Bromley and others and published by John Britton and others.
36. George attributed the unsigned print to the younger Cruikshank (*Catalogue*, pp. 922–3, no. 13266).
37. John C[am] Hobhouse, *A Supplicatory Letter to Lord Viscount Castlereagh* (London: Robert Stodart, 1819), p. 33.
38. She may be Margaret Downes, who was fatally sabred. Michael Bush, *The Casualties of Peterloo* (Manchester: Manchester Centre for Regional History, 2005), p. 90.

39. The line quotes Dryden's 'Alexander's Feast' (lines 15, 19) and refers to Alexander the Great and his Athenian courtesan Thaïs.
40. Referring to the bloody battle in 1388 between the victorious Scots, led by James, Earl of Douglas, and the English led by Harry 'Hotspur' Percy.
41. This print exists in both monochrome and aquatint.
42. The embedded quote is from Thomas Townshend's 'Ode to War' (*Poems*, London, 1796, p. 58).
43. *Manchester Massacre!!*, p. 10. The author claims to be quoting 'the *Times Reporter* [*sic*], who was on the hustings'. The author of *The Manchester Tragedy, the Suppressed Narrative of the Courier Reporter* (London, 1819) likewise remarks that 'I heard the bugle sound', p. 9.
44. Ibid. p. 14.
45. Samuel Bamford, *Passages in the Life of a Radical*, ed. Tim Hilton (Oxford: Oxford University Press, 1984), p. 66. Bamford had encountered Nadin in Spring 1817 when he was arrested for joining Lancashire weavers known as 'Blanketeers' in protesting suspension of the Habeas Corpus Act. George identifies the figure as 'evidently Joseph Nadin' (*Catalogue*, p. 920).
46. *Manchester Massacre!!*, p. 13.
47. Ibid. p. 14.
48. Gillian Russell, *The Theatres of War: Performance, Politics, and Society, 1793–1815* (Oxford: Clarendon Press, 1995), p. 179.
49. *Manchester Massacre!!*, p. 17.
50. Rev. Melville Horne, *The Moral and Political Crisis of England* (London: Hatchard, 1820), p. 16.
51. Quoted in *Manchester Massacre!!*, p. 12.
52. Two are in the Manchester City Galleries.
53. People's History Museum, Manchester; catalogue number NMLH.1995.91.3. The reference to 'the British Empire' may suggest a somewhat later date than 1819.
54. *Catalogue of a Collection of Pottery and Porcelain Illustrating Popular British History* (London: Her Majesty's Stationery Office, 1899), p. 42.
55. British Museum catalogue number 2009,8022.1. The inscription resembles that on the blue ewer, but the plaque's smaller scale failed to accommodate the words 'banished' and 'Empire'.
56. John Davison, *A Letter to John Ralph Fenwick Esq.*, 3rd edn (Newcastle, 1819), p. 6.
57. The former is in the 'Manchester Archives +' broadsides collection, catalogue number GB127.Broadsides/F1819.2.CC; the latter is in the Manchester Public Libraries, catalogue number f1819/2/B & B.R.942.730731 P95/12.

58. *The Letters of Percy Bysshe Shelley*, ed. Frederick L. Jones, 2 vols (Oxford: Clarendon Press, 1964), vol. 2, p. 119 (9 September 1819).
59. *Shelley's Poetry and Prose*, ed. Donald H. Reiman and Neil Fraistat, 2nd edn (New York: W. W. Norton, 2002), pp. 320, 326.
60. Bamford, *Passages*, pp. 159–60.
61. Thomas Carlyle, *Past and Present* (London: Chapman and Hall, 1843), pp. 21–2.
62. *A Philosophical View of Reform*, in *The Complete Works of Percy Bysshe Shelley*, ed. Roger Ingpen and Walter E. Peck, 10 vols (London: Ernest Benn, 1926–8), vol. 7, pp. 45–6.
63. Available online <http://luna.manchester.ac.uk/luna/servlet/detail/Manchester~91~1~14940~144478> (last accessed 20 February 2017).
64. See Michael Demson, 'Remembering John Cahuac: Post-Peterloo Repression and the Fate of Radical-Romantic Satire', in *The Politics of Shelley*, ed. Matthew Borushko, Romantic Circles Praxis Series, September 2015 <https://www.rc.umd.edu/print/praxis/shelley_politics/praxis.2015.shelley_politics.demson.html> (last accessed 20 February 2017).
65. *Letters*, vol. 1, p. 277 (18 March 1812).
66. Mary Shelley, 'Note on the Early Poems', in *Shelley: Poetical Works*, ed. Thomas Hutchinson (Oxford: Oxford University Press, 1983), p. 528.
67. British Library, shelfmark 806.k.1.(124).
68. He is so identified by Colin Brown, *The Scum of the Earth: What Happened to the Real British Heroes of Waterloo* (Stroud, Gloucestershire: The History Press, 2015), ebook section 10.
69. Bee and Bee, 'Casualties', p. 46.
70. Horne, *Moral and Political Crisis*, pp. 36, 16.
71. Hobhouse, *Supplicatory*, p. 7.
72. *Manchester Massacre!!*, pp. 47–8.
73. Jasper, *Art of Moral Protest*, p. xii.

Chapter 2

The Sounds of Peterloo

Ian Haywood

In his influential book *The Soundscape* (1994), Murray Shafer argues that artificial sound operates between two extremes.[1] At its loudest and most dominant, it is often associated with institutions of state power such as the military or (in the past) the church; Shafer calls this 'sacred' or 'imperialistic' noise. At the other pole is either silence or the unruly 'nuisance noise' of the common people. Though Shafer does not make this move, his terms map quite neatly onto the aesthetic and political 'soundscape' of radicalism in the eighteenth and nineteenth centuries. 'Imperialistic' or spectacular noise is reminiscent of the sublime, while 'nuisance noise' evokes the struggle for democracy, free speech and freedom of expression which came to a tragic head in the Peterloo massacre. To its detractors, the large-scale, open-air political rally – the 'monster meeting' – was the antitype or menacing version of a state-sponsored public ritual such as a military parade or coronation. Acoustically, it was a kind of bad sublime, a notion I have borrowed from Markman Ellis to evoke an emphatically negative application of an eighteenth-century cultural concept which postulated terror as both a stimulant for and marker of the mind's capacity for grandiose sensation.[2] The brief discussion of noise in Edmund Burke's seminal *Essay on the Sublime and the Beautiful* (first published in 1757) epitomised the ambivalent polite response to the soundscape of popular politics:

> Excessive loudness alone is sufficient to over-power the soul, to suspend its action and to fill it with terror. The noise of vast cataracts, raging storms, thunder, or artillery, awakes a great and awful sensation in the mind, though we can observe no nicety or artifice in those sorts of music.

> The shouting of multitudes has a similar effect; and by the sole strength of the sound, so amazes and confounds the imagination, that in this staggering, and hurry of the mind, the best-established tempers can scarcely forebear being borne down, and joining in the common cry, and common resolution of the crowd.[3]

This is 'nuisance' scaled up to 'imperialistic' proportions: unlike the 'excessive' noise of the natural sublime and European warfare which 'over-powers' normal perception, the 'shouting of multitudes' can actually sway the polite 'ear-witness' (another of Shafer's coinages) into surrendering their better judgement and joining the 'common resolution of the crowd' – in effect, a sensory *coup d'état.*

Burke's encoding of a wider cultural anxiety about the *vox populi* may well have been a response to topical events. In addition to regular food riots and the assertion of crowd power which was an accepted tactic of the 'moral economy' of the urban lower classes, Britain at this time was entering a tumultuous phase of popular political protest centred around the figure of the renegade parliamentarian John Wilkes.[4] What Burke had heard, literally or metaphorically, was the sound of the radical sublime, the swelling crescendo of popular protest and agitation which would reverberate all the way to Peterloo and beyond into the Chartist era (ear): a sound of sufficient volume that it could be heard in Italy by the exiled Percy Shelley ('There came a voice from over the Sea');[5] a sound that the British government periodically attempted to 'gag', muzzle, extinguish and contain; a sound that vibrated through the echo-chamber of radical institutions and radical print culture, meaning that 'live' sound (at meetings and rallies) was immediately converted into 'recorded' sound in print reportage; a sound composed of (and by) orators, journalists, men and women activists, writers, poets and satirists, musicians and bands, and vast numbers of the uncredited; a sound that was both real and ideal, audible and symbolic, agitational and aspirational. To its enemies and detractors, this was the sound of Pandemonium, chaos, anarchy and misrule; to its supporters, it was the voice of the many, not the few, the 'unvanquishable number' of a 'sacred' melody of irresistible reform: 'Eloquent, oracular; / A volcano heard afar'.[6]

When, in 1790, the dissenting minister Richard Price listened to the French revolution, he heard 'THIRTY MILLIONS of people, indignant and resolute, spurning at slavery, and demanding liberty with an irresistible voice'. Burke heard something more sinister: 'The horrid yells, and shrilling screams, and frantic dances, and infamous contumelies, and all the unutterable abominations of the furies of hell, in the abused shape of the vilest of women.'[7] In Manchester on 16 August 1819, the tone-deaf authorities would not allow the 'unutterable' to be uttered; and as their sabres slashed like demented batons, these vilest of violators conducted their own unhallowed symphony of the bad sublime ('And many more Destructions played / In this ghastly masquerade').[8] Far from 'stopping the throats' of reform,[9] this 'infamous' intervention immortalised a routine political event and gave Peterloo a unique 'eloquence'. As this chapter will show, shifting from the eye- to the ear-witness can be productive and illuminating. Listening to the sounds of Peterloo enables us to newly appreciate and re-evaluate its political and cultural impact.[10]

Recording Peterloo

The most obvious place to begin re-tuning our ears to Peterloo's soundscape is with diegetic or represented sound, the noises that ear-witnesses actually heard on 16 August. Contrary to the smears of the loyalist press, monster meetings were co-ordinated rituals with their own narrative logic and attendant sounds: assemblage in local areas, formation marching and chanting (often accompanied with bands), arrival at the venue and the allocation of space, communal singing of both patriotic and radical songs, platform oratory (often preceded by presentation of gifts and addresses), crowd response such as huzzas and cheers, and orderly dispersal. It is hard to state definitively which was the loudest moment in this procedure as the whole event would be noisy, but two points of crowd power stand out: the arrival of the main speaker (the hero), and the thunderous applause a skilled orator could elicit (a third component, the riot, was never part of the plan, though it became the dominant impression in polite culture). At Peterloo, the authorities were determined to prevent the second of these crescendos and – as they had done at Smithfield just weeks earlier – arrested Henry Hunt before he could get into his verbal stride, but not before his sublime acoustic presence was established by the assembled crowd's deafening cheers – according to Samuel Bamford, Hunt 'was hailed by one universal shout from probably eighty thousand persons' – and their singing 'See the Conquering Hero Comes' to musical accompaniment.[11] Intriguingly, it is possible that the local ruling class also specifically targeted female radical discourse, as the formal proceedings were about to commence with the presentation of an address by the Female Reformers of Manchester.[12] Women had been active members of reform movements for many years, but the newly formed women's political associations in the north of England were a new phenomenon, comprising many working-class women and engaging in high-profile public events alongside the men.[13] Only the previous month, a successful shared platform had taken place in Blackburn: widely reported in the radical press (but mocked by the mainstream media), the women asserted their authority by linking economic deprivation to political intransigence:

> Our beds, that once afforded us cleanliness, health and sweet repose, are now torn away from us by the relentless hand of the unfeeling tax-gatherer, to satisfy the greatest monsters of cruelty, the borough-mongering tyrants, who are reposing on beds of down . . . come forward and join the general union, that by a determined and constitutional resistance to our oppressors, the people may obtain Annual Parliaments, Universal Suffrage, and Election by Ballot, which alone can save us from lingering misery and premature death.[14]

Even though their words were recited by the male chairman, and despite their reliance on melodramatic and sentimental flourishes to expose their families' suffering, this politicisation of the domestic sphere was a direct challenge to the stereotype of compliant, quietist femininity. George Cruikshank's caricature *The Belle Alliance, or the Female Reformers of Blackburn!!!* (1819) threw the anti-Jacobin book at the problem, depicting the women as a reincarnation of Burke's 'vilest of women', a gaggle of boisterous and indecent lower-class haridans merely parroting the political obscenities of their male counterparts.[15] Yet the print is testimony, albeit negatively, to the arrival of a new type of political women with a new sound that blended feminine and masculine discourses: poignancy and declamation, sensibility and analysis, victimisation and retaliation. None of this is evident in the well-known visual prints of Peterloo which foreground trampled and terrified women in order to create an instant myth of the slaughter of the innocents. As much as Henry Hunt's absent harangue, the Female Reformer's Address is one of the lost, haunting aural presences at Peterloo.[16]

The acoustic strophe of Peterloo – the moment when Peterloo came into being as an inversion of the original planned event – was of course when the authorities fulfilled their own prophecy and turned a 'peaceable' crowd into the bad sublime: 'For a moment the crowd held back as in a pause; then there was a rush, heavy and resistless as a headlong sea; and a sound like thunder, with screams, prayers and imprecations from the crowd-moiled, and sabre-doomed, who could not escape.'[17] This description by Samuel Bamford is, rightly, often cited for its vivid evocation of the violence of Peterloo, though its sonic drama has been neglected. In fact, Bamford amplified the soundscape of Peterloo in interesting and significant ways. In another gripping episode, he puts his status as an ear-witness at the centre of the drama:

> The meeting was all in a tumult; there were dreadful cries; the soldiers kept riding amongst the people, and striking with their swords. I became faint, and turning from the door, I went unobserved down some steps into a cellared passage; and hoping to escape from the horrid noise, and to be concealed, I crept into a vault, and sat down, faint and terrified, on some fire wood. The cries of the multitude outside, still continued, and the people of the house, up stairs, kept bewailing most pitifully. They could see all the dreadful work through the window, and their exclamations were so distressing, that I put my fingers in my ears to prevent my hearing more; and on removing them, I understood that a young man had just been brought past, wounded. The front door of the passage before mentioned, soon after opened, and a number of men entered, carrying the body of a decent, middle aged woman, who had been killed. I thought they were going to put her beside me, and was about to scream, but they took her forward, and deposited her in some premises at the back of the house. (1:222–3)

The rich cluster of explicit and submerged Burkean tropes in this account speaks volumes. Ironically, the chaos transforms Bamford into one of Burke's 'best tempered' individuals who is terrorised by the shouting multitude; like a Gothic nightmare, the 'horrid noise' even pursues him into a 'vault' where, sitting on incendiary firewood, he is taunted and tortured by a new sound, the 'bewailings' and 'exclamations' of the domestic spectators of the massacre. This reminds us that Peterloo is still a visual horror, but the writing is remarkable for showing the autonomy of sound, its reverberation and transmission through three aural 'passages': victim, spectator and ear-witness. Bamford skilfully gives the episode a final visual-acoustic twist: having stopped his ears to muffle the aural violence, he is suddenly confronted with the central symbolic casualty of the tragedy in radical propaganda, a fatally wounded 'decent' woman. Had the body not been removed, he would have screamed, and this sound would have completed the echoing and internalisation of the exterior violence, the traumatic recording of the 'horrid noise' on his psyche.

The Peterloo Soundtrack

Like all the other ear-witnesses, Bamford was as much haunted by the sounds as the sights of Peterloo; unable to mute or 'deposit' these sounds at the 'back' of his mind, writing at least offered him the opportunity to build aural defences, mount noisy counter-attacks, and undermine the 'imperialistic' noise of the ruling classes that another, anonymous poet captured so graphically:

> Who is it that flies from the tumult so fast
> When the yeomanry's bugles are mingling their blast?
> The mother who folds her dear child to her breast,
> And screams, as around her expire the oppress'd.[18]

In the poetry he wrote from prison, Bamford deployed a variety of aesthetic strategies to achieve these ends, several of which move away from deigetic to the extra-diegetic or imagined sonic realm, the equivalent of a 'soundtrack' or added acoustic dimension which does not represent actual events. One of the most intriguing poems, 'The Arrest', shows a high degree of self-consciousness about the ideological implications of the formal sounds of poetry.[19] The poem recreates his detention as a metrical assault:

> They came at night, and did surround
> My humble dwelling whilst I slept –
> And I awoke, and heard a sound

Of feet, as if they softly crept;
And then, a firmer foot there stept:
And then, I heard a number more,
As if a marching pace they kept –
I guessed there might be a score,
And then they knocked at my door.[20]

Recalling Hazlitt's infamous denunciation of 'right royal' poetry,[21] the poem imagines state power as a hegemonic cultural force. The noise of the invasive 'feet' swells from 'soft' to 'firm' to militaristic 'marching' until the poet realises there is a 'score' – the latter word brilliantly encapsulating a double pun on metre (the 'number' twenty) and music.[22] Like his more famous peer Percy Shelley, who also 'slept' until awoken by 'a sound Of feet', the 'humble' Bamford responds by composing his own, sardonic Peterloo score:

And so the fools have sent me here,
'Tis for my benefit no doubt. . . .
And feeling grateful, as I ought,
How can I less than sing a lay,
The memorable deeds about—
Of Hulton and of Parson Hay,
And that famed corps of yeomanry. (81)

Bamford lived up to this promise of mock-epic contempt with several full-throated re-enactments of the massacre. The aptly named 'Song of Slaughter' aimed to tell 'another story / For the page of history' (84) by emphasising the violence. Indeed, the poem reads like a verbal commentary on Cruikshank's famous caricature prints:

Ah, behold their sabres gleaming,
Never, never known to spare;
See the flood of slaughter streaming
Hear the cries that rend the air.

Youth and valour naught availed,
Naught availed beauty's prayer,
Even the lisping infant failed
To arrest the ruin there. (83)[23]

Each stanza ends with a conspicuous, heartbreaking human cry that recalls anti-slavery poetry of the 1780s and 1790s. In the 'lisping' infant we also hear a distant echo of the grand master of satire Alexander Pope, who famously 'lisped in numbers'. If there is a literary allusion here, it implies that numbers do indeed count, both poetically and politically. Heard in isolation, the lone voice of the 'humble' poet may be unable to 'arrest the ruin' of oppressive power (indeed, this was one of the central problematics of literary Romanticism, as Coleridge recognised when he abandoned his 'squeaking baby trumpet of sedition' for the aeolian harp), but in the echo-chamber of the radical press and the imagined community of reformers it represented, the single 'lay' could amplify (or imagine it was amplifying) its volume to sublime levels. As Thomas Brown declaimed in *The Field of Peterloo* (1819):

> Think you we will our wrongs sustain,
> In silent dread, and *not* complain?
> Or, through our only means, the PRESS
> We will not seek – *enforce* redress?[24]

In the immediate aftermath of the tragedy, what E. P. Thompson called the 'heroic' role of the radical press came to the rescue,[25] though quite how it could '*enforce*' justice remained another question. As the Six Acts loomed, it was perhaps sufficient that radical print culture remained a 'nuisance noise', as this would sustain and even boost morale. One way to 'arrest' the sanguine flow of brutality was to turn the aural tables, either by vaunting the radical sublime, or by imagining retribution for the perpetrators. One of Bamford's first Peterloo poems, 'Lines Written During Confinement in the Castle of Lancaster, Sept. 1819', takes the latter approach:

> The Patriot on his cell-bed,
> Can sleep an undisturbed sleep:
> The Pander on his hell-bed
> May curse, and groan, and madly weep. (25)

This is a neat re-inversion of 'The Arrest' that reduces the guilty to the same abject acoustic condition as the Peterloo victims. Bamford rejects this disempowerment and revives the English custom of skimmington or public cursing and verbal abuse. In 'Ode to a Plotting

Parson' his target is Parson Hay, one of the Manchester magistrates who received a promotion for taking a tough line with the protestors:

> And when the gloomy famine doth stalk through the land,
> No comfort the poor shall receive at thy hand;
> And the widow shall curse thee whilst life doth remain,
> And the orphan shall lisp back her curses again. (48)

Unlike the helpless infant in 'The Song of Slaughter', lisping is now empowered. Moreover, sublime nature adds its own blasts to the chorus of damnation:

> And the night-wind shall sound as a scream in thy ear,
> And the tempest shall shake thee with terrible fear; (48)

Even the picturesque joins in the radical heckling:

> And the zephyr that fans thee shall bring thee no cure,
> It will whisper a tale which thou canst not endure. (48)

Bamford's decision to give the final harrowing word to the normally consolatory and comforting pastoral 'zephyr' is a stroke of considerable poetic skill. There is also a poignant contrast with another poem, 'Lines: Relating to a Beautiful Rural Cottage in Hopwood' in which the conventional pastoral tones evoke a quest for inner peace and security:

> Cooling seat, where breezes sing,
> To the harp's melodious string;
> Sounds combining which might be,
> Murmur of heavenly minstrelsy. (99)

This Arcadian, Keatsian murmur is one possible ending to the Peterloo soundtrack, a respite from the raucous din of the radical sublime. But the more urgent task was to continue on the dual (sound)track of rallying the troops and damning the enemy. In the words of a tribute poem:

> The God of Justice grant it may
> Be thine to see, to sing that day,
> Magnificent and grand.

And thine to write the funeral song
Of the base tyranny which long
Hath cursed our native land. (86)

The radical consumer of the poetry could also join in this community singing. The anonymous author of *The Free-Born Englishman Deprived of his Seven Senses* (1819),[26] a pamphlet which included a pull-out caricature of John Bull with a padlocked mouth (an ironic image of the so-called 'freeborn Englishman' first used in the 1790s and revived after the reintroduction of the Two Acts in 1817),[27] struck an upbeat note:

Thy power, oh reader! may be small,
Yet many a little makes a great,
The voice which echoes 'one and all,'
May turn the scale of adverse fate.

This recovery of the *vox populi* took numerous literary forms. In reportage, it could include the personalised address of a leader, the prose equivalent of a poetic ode or lyric. This was a powerful but high-risk genre as the speaker was dangerously exposed. Sir Francis Burdett's incensed 'Address to the Gentlemen of England', which was reported widely in the radical press, earned him a jail sentence. His defiant statements required dramatic typographical enhancement in order to imitate the declamatory style of platform oratory: 'the GENTLEMAN OF ENGLAND . . . [must] . . . JOIN THE GENERAL VOICE, loudly demanding justice and redress'.[28] If capitalisation was one way to turn up the volume, another was to invoke the benevolently sublime power of the crowd that had been stifled at Peterloo. Henry Hunt's spectacular entry into London in early September 1819 was presented in the radical press as the Other Peterloo, the 'magnificent and grand' event that never happened:

> The shouts which rent the air on [Hunt's] approach might, we safely assert, have been heard a mile on either side . . . The waving of hats and handkerchiefs, the clapping of hands, the shouts of applause mingled with the sounds of musical instruments, and the voices of some thousands who accompanied them in the national air of 'Rule Britannia,' presented to the eye and to the ear such a combination of scene and sound, as we believe has seldom, if ever, been equalled in London.[29]

Striking the perfect balance between visual and aural stimulation, this scene could be regarded as another closure of the dismal Peterloo narrative, but as Wooler noted, this was only the 'second act' in a three-act drama. The third act 'will close with due poetical justice executed upon the offending parties' (ibid.). The term 'Peterloo' refers to much more than the 16 August 1819; it encompasses a whole new phase of struggle including resistance to the Six Acts and the Queen Caroline Affair. The acoustic stakes were not new: gagging versus free speech; censorship versus a free press; tyranny versus liberty. The new element was the emergence of a powerful new tool of propaganda which was invented by the radical print culture but soon taken up by loyalists: the illustrated, satirical pamphlet.

Satirical Blasts

The new genre was the brainchild of the radical publisher William Hone and his artistic collaborator George Cruikshank, the leading caricaturist of the day. By the time of Peterloo, the pair had been a formidable partnership for some years, having excelled in the Cádiz Mortar ('Regent's Bomb') controversy in 1816, the huge amount of publicity surrounding Hone's three trials in 1817, and the Bank Restriction Note furore earlier in 1819. Independently of Hone, Cruikshank had already given Peterloo its definitive visual identity with two devastating prints, *Massacre at St Peters, or "Britons Strike Home"!!!* and *Manchester Heroes*, both of which used sound in innovative ways (see Figures 2.1 and 2.2). Cruikshank's intervention is not at all surprising, as Peterloo was a gift to the caricaturist. After decades of maligning the reform movement as violent and anarchic, the state had finally shown its hand and destroyed its credibility with each stroke of the flashing sabres. Of all artistic forms, caricature was the best-suited to making an immediate and incisive graphic response to the tragedy: the technology and infrastructure for producing images within days of the 'trigger' event was well established, giving caricature the function of visual reportage in the pre-photography era. It was also the ideal medium for conveying the Peterloo 'soundtrack' and giving the visual a verbal dimension. Unlike all other visual genres except the outdated emblem books, caricature routinely incorporated textual matter. Speech bubbles and

Figure 2.1 *Britons Strike Home!* by George Cruikshank (Anne S. K. Brown Military Collection, Brown University Library)

Figure 2.2 *Manchester Heroes* by George Cruikshank (Anne S. K. Brown Military Collection, Brown University Library)

other types of paratextual devices (printed matter, subtitles, signs, names and quotations) litter the often rowdy and spectacular confrontations staged within the caricature scene. Unlike painting, characters actually speak and shout (to say nothing of indulging in other unseemly and noisy bodily activities). Cruikshank's Peterloo prints are memorable for the way they both capture and mock the military brutality of the massacre, juxtaposing (ludicrous) chubby-faced, axe-wielding mounted cavalry with trampled protestors. Viewed in conjunction with press reports, it is not hard to imagine the 'horrid noise' of the slaughter. Crucially, Cruikshank adds speech bubbles to exaggerate the 'imperialistic' aural dominance of the authorities, with the cavalry egging each other on and the Prince Regent appearing from a cloud to promise everlasting fame for their bravery. The acoustic masterstroke, however, is entirely extra-diegetic, as both prints allude ironically to significant popular songs. 'Britons Strike Home', originally written for Purcell's opera *Bonduca* in 1695, soon became so popular that it has been called a second national anthem.[30] Its patriotic words and accompanying tune would have been known by most viewers of the print:

> Britons, strike home!
> Revenge, revenge your Country's wrong.
> Fight! Fight and record. Fight!
> Fight and record yourselves in Druid's Song.
> Fight! Fight and record. Fight!
> Fight and record yourselves in Druid's Song.[31]

There are two ironies at work here. First, if one imagines the cavalry singing (or performing to) this tune, the self-satirising mockery conveys both their malice and ideological conditioning: in their eyes (and ears) they were indeed defending the nation against an internal enemy that had replaced Napoleon as the greatest threat to the country's well-being (and it is worth adding that 'Britons Strike Home' was revived during the invasion scares and featured in several anti-French caricatures).[32] Second, the song can be heard emerging from the saturnalian, carnivalesque subculture of the radical 'free and easy' in which patriotic songs and tunes were 'remastered' or 'sampled' (in today's musical parlance) as part of the radical songbook – that repertoire of satirical musical forms which included songs, toasts, sentiments and curses.[33] Most radical meetings actually featured an element of this travestying musical culture in their rituals, as it was quite normal to sing patriotic songs such as 'Rule Britannia' alongside alternative versions of the national anthem; and as already noted, Henry Hunt entered St Peter's Field to the tune of 'See the Conquering Hero Comes', a famous chorus from Handel's *Judas Maccabaeus* (1746), an opera which was originally composed to celebrate the Duke of Cumberland's brutal victory at Culloden. Listened to in this way, the agency of resistance is transferred from the military to the people through a remastered soundtrack which inverts the 'record' of Peterloo. The same point can be made about the second key allusion, the Prince Regent's promise in *Manchester Heroes* that his troops will figure in a 'new Chevy Chase'. This story of a futile border war between the Earls of Percy and Douglas was one of the most popular of all English ballads and would have been known in some form to most viewers of the print; its tune had also been widely adopted by other songs, including radical broadsides.[34] The effect is again to strike a note of extreme dissonance that reinforces the print's satirical force.[35]

Not content with having made this innovative contribution to the Peterloo soundscape, Cruikshank teamed up with Hone to invent a new form of caricature that combined the agitational potency and utility of the pamphlet with the visual power of graphic satire. The new format was enabled by switching from metal to wood engraving. This allowed letterpress and image to be printed on the same page, thus reducing costs considerably. Typically, a Hone-Cruikshank pamphlet such as the trendsetting *The Political House that Jack Built*, published in December 1819, would give the purchaser between a dozen and twenty pages and images for their shilling, the same price they would pay for just one single-print caricature, and this must have been a factor in the incredible popularity of the new genre amongst the middle classes (by March 1820 *The Political House that Jack Built* had gone through fifty-two editions). This reconfiguration of the relationship between text and image also bridged the gap between caricature and the unillustrated radical press: most satirical pamphlets, both radical and loyal, were forms of mock-reportage narrating the ongoing story of the struggle for freedom of expression. In terms of sound, the importance of these pamphlets is that they replayed the central aural drama of Peterloo, the right of the grievances of the people to be heard and the determination of the state to muzzle dissent. The rest of this chapter will take an acoustic tour through the Peterloo pamphlet wars, visiting sites where the *vox populi* is represented and contested.

The Voice of The People

There is no better place to begin than *The Political House that Jack Built*, the sensationally successful text that launched the new genre. The satire comprehensively lampoons the structure of the British state which is founded on the interlocking institutions of monarchy, government, church and military. Peterloo (though never named) appears about half-way through the mock-nursery rhyme: 'These are THE PEOPLE all tatter'd and torn, / Who curse the day wherein they were born'.[36] The illustration shows a small group of ragged individuals, possibly a family (two men who could be brothers, a child, and a woman, presumably the wife of one of the men, with a baby) in the foreground; in the background there is a depiction of the massacre that could be a portion of one of Cruikshank's graphic prints. The acoustic make-up of the whole Peterloo page (text, epigraph and illustration) is actually quite complex (Figure 2.3). At first sight, it looks like the plebeian group have escaped from the violence, but on closer scrutiny it is clear that the scene works like a satirical diptych where the emphasis is on the extreme contrast between the two visual

Figure 2.3 'These are the People' from William Hone and George Cruikshank, *The Political House that Jack Built* (Working Class Movement Library, Salford)

units. The upturned stool and the straw on which the woman is sitting (which is much clearer in the de luxe coloured version) indicate that this is in fact a cutaway of a domestic scene. So, the point is that the people are indeed both 'tattered and torn' (or, in Shelley's alliterative modulation, 'starved and stabbed'):[37] it is socio-economic misery rather than political injustice that has driven them 'peaceably' to 'ask for Reform' (41), only to be 'torn' apart by the sabres of the cavalry. The two mini-scenes condense Peterloo into stark vignettes of social and political deprivation, both of which are curable by the talismanic 'watchword' of reform, as a later episode declares (51). The illustration's caption, an excerpt from William Cowper's *The Task*, appeals to the reader's sensibility and humanity: 'What man seeing this, / And having human feelings, does not blush, / And hang his head, to think himself a man?' The poet's response is exemplary: 'I cannot rest / A silent witness of the headlong rage, / Or heedless folly, by which thousands die' (40). The poet's own 'rage' converts the visualised 'folly' of poverty and warfare depicted in the vignettes into virtuous verbal action. This is a worthy aural outcome that complements the main text's campaign, but there is also an intriguing acoustic dimension to the images themselves. Far from cursing the day they were born, the working-class family are precisely a 'silent witness' of the deafening carnage in the background, and it is this acoustic contrast that adds such a poignancy to the scene (notice that the next illustration shows Castlereagh speaking to Sidmouth, a 'driv'ller', and Canning, 'the spouter of froth' (48–9)). Indeed, the pose of man on the left is particularly striking, as he is deep in thought, ignoring the tugs of his pleading child: his silent, solemn and profound meditation creates a pocket of contemplation in the midst of a tempest, and converts him into a symbol of working-class intelligence and intellectual enquiry. His ruminative stance is poised on the boundary between surrender and revolutionary retaliation, despair and defiance: he represents the power of silence, the poetics and politics of the ineffable, the radical dialectics of 'unheard melodies' and 'thoughts that lie too deep for tears'.

Introspection is not, of course, the same as gagging. In their next pamphlet Hone and Cruikshank went straight for the jugular of the Six Acts, the repressive legislation which became law in December 1819, only a few months after Peterloo. *The Man in the Moon* (January 1820) is a parody of the Prince Regent's parliamentary speech which authorised the new measures. In the satirical version, it is a 'Speech from the Throne, to the Senate of Lunaria In the Moon', in other words an act (in more senses than one) of lunacy. To the liberal-radical reader, the self-satirising sound of the king's voice would undoubtedly have been a source of entertainment and empowerment, but there were many more acoustic pleasures and nervous thrills to come. In order to justify the suppression of free speech, the Prince rants that 'CONSPIRACY and TREASON are abroad'. His evidence is aural: 'Reform, Reform, the swinish rabble cry — / Meaning, of course, rebellion, blood, and riot' (90). The cure for these 'grumbling habits' (90) is 'STEEL LOZENGES', or oral bayoneting. Lozenges were pills taken to (allegedly) cure headaches and other ailments: in the hands of Hone and Cruikshank this nostrum became a peculiarly violent and horrific metaphor of censorship.[38] To get this point across, Cruikshank made some gory adjustments to his Peterloo template: instead of cavalry using axes, there are infantrymen sticking their bayonets into the mouths of kneeling men (Figure 2.4). Shocking as the scene is, it was not in fact so far from the historical truth: although the tragedy is remembered as a grotesque travesty of a cavalry charge, the 88th Foot, who were deployed to cut off all routes of escape, committed many atrocities, including the bayoneting of women.[39] As Michael Scrivener has argued, the imagery also evokes oral rape,[40] and 'Steel Lozenges' could be criticised for being gratuitously violent and disempowering, but Cruikshank was reacting to the double degradation and desperation of Peterloo and the Six Acts. The conventions of caricature allowed him to embellish and exaggerate, and to wield his own steel (the engraver's burin) with the same brutality and swagger as the original offence. He pushed the image of the mouth-padlocked John Bull to new levels of grotesquery and gave Peterloo its most disturbing visual image of the loss of free speech. Compared to this episode, the pandemonium which closes the text is a more palatable satirical denouement that surveys the riven soundscape of England in 1819:

> His Highness ceased –
> The dissonance of Babel
> Rose from the motley
> Moonitarian rabble:

STEEL LOZENGES

will stop their pain,
And set the Constitution
right again.
My L—ds and G—tl—n,
The foreign powers
Write me word frequently
that they are ours,
Most truly and sincerely,
in compliance
With our most

Figure 2.4 'Steel Lozenges' from William Hone and George Cruikshank, *The Man in the Moon* (Working Class Movement Library, Salford)

> The yell of loyalty –
> The dungeon groan –
> The shriek of woe –
> The starving infant's moan –
> The brazen trumpet's note –
> The din of war –
> The shouts of freemen
> Rising from afar –
> Darted in horrid discord
> Through my brain . . . (98)

Bamford's 'horrid noise' has now become a national 'dissonance', a 'horrid discord' of imperialistic 'din', groaning victims and the distant (though emergent) 'shouts of freemen'.

This dystopian score expressed the dark mood of early 1820, though the tone was soon to change in an unexpected way. In the meantime, Hone and Cruikshank's satirical pamphlets were proving so popular that loyalists began to issue their own counterblasts. These were parodies of the originals, usually with modified titles, the exact same format of illustrated satirical text, and the same price. The aim was to restore the bad sublime and reimpose anti-Jacobin conventions of representation in which the 'People' are always a rowdy, rebellious rabble. In *The Loyal Man in the Moon* (1820), the story of a monster meeting is retold from a loyalist perspective. As the unsavoury mob of men and women march to the venue, 'What yells, and groans, and hootings rent the air!' (119). At the meeting, 'they rent the very air and skies, / With every species of infernal noise, / That either men or demons could devise' (127). The accompanying cuts recycle the stereotypes of baying, disreputable crowds and barking agitators that had been a mainstay of caricature from Gillray's *Copenhagen House* (1795) onwards. The final applause, which occurs after Cobbett (depicted as the Hampshire hog) delivers his harangue, explicitly evokes Milton's depiction of Pandemonium in *Paradise Lost*, a scene in which the fallen angels erect a parliament of their own to the accompaniment of martial music:

> Imagine, reader, twice ten thousand devils,
> Holding in Pandemonium their revels;
> Call every frightful picture to thy view,
> That Dante or great Milton ever drew . . .

And altogether were not half so bad,
As that which my perturb'd imagination
Depicted of the strange association,
Of every sort of uproar, yell and screech,
That followed this Reformer's daring speech. (131)

Faced with this 'dire tremendous storm' (ibid.), the Six Acts seem like a sensible and necessary measure.

Other reactionary pamphlets sang the same tune. *The Radical Letter Bag* (1820)[41] also rewrites Peterloo, this time from the point of view of a demagogic, Hunt-like figure, who is determined to provoke a riot:

To this riotous, round-headed, Radical town
Of Manchester. Here are plenty of boys,
Full of mischief, and notions of something, and noise:
Just the things we want . . . (9)

He is the epitome of 'nuisance noise', a stirrer up of dangerous enthusiasm:

Then up with the Radicals – they are the boys
For rowing, and mowing, and making a noise;
'Tis the very best thing in the nation –
Exhilaration! (36)

The soundscape of the massacre is replayed from the loyalist song-book:

A legion of soldiers march'd up the street smack;
The people cry'd 'Shame on't' and all in a crack
Began to throw brickbats, and potsherds, and stones,
And tiles from the houses, and rubbish, and bones,
At the soldiering tribe . . .
. . . We shouted, and rallied, and shouted again;
And call'd these fine lobsters a thousand fine names;
But this work was chiefly perform'd by the dames;
Fine spirited lasses who mounted a cart,
And play'd mighty well their exemplary part,
In bawling, and bouncing, and shoulder-knot tearing,
And screaming out 'Cowards!' and stamping, and swearing. (40)

The most confident and strident of these loyal satirical assaults was published after the Cato Street Conspiracy of May 1820. The arrest and execution of a group of conspirators who were plotting to murder the Cabinet was an embarrassment to the radical movement, and pro-government propagandists were quick to exploit the situation. One pamphlet called *The Radicals Unmasked and Outwitted; Or the Thistle Uprooted in Cato-Field*[42] blasted out its smug message:

> Who will now the RADICALS applaud and defend!
> Who will now believe they meet only to mend!
> Let CATO STREET speak, as in thunder, their meaning. (5)

Cato Street was the proof that Peterloo was a justified disarming of a terrorist movement. The bad sublime was back with a vengeance. Most of the text of *Radicals Unmasked* comprises an ekphrasis of the cover image which shows the agitator 'Thistle' (Thistlewood) haranguing the shouting multitude:

> 'Revenge! Revenge!' the thistle cries,
> 'Revenge! Revenge!' his mob replies:
> 'Royalty's name and power defy,
> 'This night let all the COUNCIL die.' (8)

But this clamour soon gives way to the 'curse' of penitence:

> The Radicals outwitted, lodg'd safe in a jail,
> Curse their folly and madness, and their last hour bewail;
> And lessons of industry, contentment and quiet,
> Preach to lunatic Radicals, inclining to riot. (12)

Where Bamford had imagined the tortured last hours of the Peterloo perpetrators, this text goes one step further and offers salvation: seeing the errors of their ways, the condemned men abandon rabble-rousing speech and willingly 'preach' the 'quiet' loyal gospel of social and political conformity. If all radicals would follow suit, the pamphlet argues, the country could finally achieve a state of peace:

> Then a CHORUS should rise from the dwellers on mountains
> Which sweetly should echo o'er woods, rocks and fountains,
> And the thick-crowded cities should catch the sweet strain,

And the grand, charming song re-echo again,
Which, uniting in chorus with the swains on the plain,
Should a harmony swell which all England should hear;
And SCOTLAND, and IRELAND, and the ISLES far and near
Should resound the grand anthem to BRITTANIA dear. (14–15)

This sublime reimagining of the national anthem is the loyalist antidote to Peterloo's radical soundtrack. The new 'harmony' is a fantasy of national unity in which country and city sing the same 'charming song', though ironically there is little in this tribute that could not be re-appropriated for a radical songbook.

As the pamphlet war grew more raucous, no one could have foreseen the next twist in the extended Peterloo narrative. At the end of January George III finally died, and one of the consequences of the succession was a completely new scandal that took the nation by storm. The new King George IV, formerly the Prince Regent, suddenly found himself embroiled in colossal domestic tiff in the shape of his estranged wife Caroline. Having lived separately for most of their married life, she was now insisting on claiming her nuptial rights and being installed as the new queen, a thought that filled the king with horror. He flatly refused to countenance her demand and put her on trial for adultery. Usually referred to as the Queen Caroline Affair (even though she never acquired the title), the controversy was a gift to the radical movement as it offered the opportunity to rally behind Caroline in order to embarrass and harass the king. Moreover, it provided a new platform for radical satirists to continue the Peterloo narrative of a tyrannical and bigoted government blatantly ignoring the rights of its people, in this case personified by the most elevated female victim of all, the queen. In a bizarre twist, the radical and imperialistic soundtracks merged into a sublime, patriotic anthem of national reconciliation, justice and liberty. A typical example comes from a pamphlet called *A Non-Coronation* (1820),[43] whose cover shows a plebeian man kneeling and touching the hand of Caroline to the applause of a watching crowd:

And ev'ry voice be with her praises swell'd,
Till her Fame's trump resound thro' ev'ry nation
A louder blast than that at a Coronation. (8)

This chorus echoes the original purpose of Peterloo, the election of a legislatorial attorney or people's representative: Caroline represents the general will of the people who, through the sheer loudness of their unvanquishable numbers, will force the king to submit. In Bakhtinian terms, this is a people's coronation. In the appositely entitled *A Groan from the Throne* (1820),[44] Caroline's appearance, 'welcom'd by unnumber'd millions' cheers' (20) strikes such terror into the court and cabinet that the king flees. The next scene is pure popular theatre:

> When lo! as coming from the
> EMPTY THRONE
> Proceeds a death-like, dreadful, horrid
> GROAN!!!
> And then the panic-struck astonish'd P—rs
> All heard a VOICE that thus assail'd their ears. (26)

As the cover design shows, this is a blast from the royal past: the ghost of the deceased King George III appears to warn his son to 'DESIST'.

The warning, of course, went unheeded, but the Caroline controversy was the acoustic climax of an emboldened radical print culture that refused to be silenced by repressive legislation. As Wordsworth noted, somewhat nervously, in his poem 'On the Power of Sound' (1828):

> When civic renovation
> Dawns on a kingdom, and for needful haste
> Best eloquence avails not, Inspiration
> Mounts with a tune, that travels like a blast . . .
> That voice of Freedom, in its power
> Of promises, shrill, wild, and sweet![45]

Who blasts loudest, blasts last? Perhaps. In his anti-Six Acts caricature, *Loyal Addresses & Radical Petitions* (4 December 1819), George Cruikshank shows the Prince Regent emitting an enormous fart over his opponents: the blast has sufficient force to knock some of them over, while others are overwhelmed with the stink.[46] The scatalogical representation of 'Fame's trump'[47] was one way for radical popular culture to deflect Peterloo's 'horrid noise' back onto its perpetrators. Another was to imagine the gagging of the imperial mouth. In *The Political Showman – at Home!* (1821), Hone and Cruikshank invented the 'Legitimate Vampire', a monster with a giant 'ravening maw' that consumes its worshippers. Thankfully, there was a way to slay this monster: force-feed it with doses of the illustrated radical press, the revolutionary equivalent of Peterloo's steel lozenges:

> These PAPERS are to be *forced down his throat* DAILY, *morning and evening*, and on the *seventh* day a *double* dose should be administered. The operation is accelerated by the powerful *exhibition* of the WOOD DRAUGHTS.[48]

As the creature expires, 'all mankind, relieved from the deadened atmosphere under which they had been *gasping*, will make the first use of their *recovered breath*, to raise an universal shout of joy' (296). Ye are many, they are few.

Notes

1. F. Murray Shafer, *The Soundscape: Our Sonic Environment and the Tuning of the World* (London: Destiny Books, 1994).
2. Ellis describes newspaper accounts of a slave rebellion in Jamaica in 1760 as 'a kind of nightmare bad sublime for this period' (*The Politics of Sensibility: Race, Gender and Commerce in the Sentimental Novel* (Cambridge: Cambridge University Press, 1996), p. 67).
3. Edmund Burke, *A Philosophical Enquiry into the Origin of our Ideas of the Sublime and Beautiful* [1757], 4th edn (London: R. and J. Dodsley, 1764), pp. 159–60.
4. See E. P. Thompson, 'The Moral Economy of the English Crowd in the Eighteenth Century', *Past and Present* 50 (February 1971), pp. 76–136; George F. E. Rudé, *Wilkes and Liberty: A Social Study of 1763–1774* (Oxford: Oxford University Press, 1965).
5. P. B. Shelley, *The Mask of Anarchy* [1819], l. 2; in *Shelley: Poetical Works*, ed. Thomas Hutchinson (Oxford: Oxford University Press, 1991), p. 338.
6. Shelley, *The Mask of Anarchy*, ll. 369, 362–3; *Poetical Works*, p. 344.
7. Richard Price, *A Discourse on the Love of Our Country* [1790], in *Political Writings*, ed. D. O. Thomas (Cambridge: Cambridge University Press, 1991), p. 195; Edmund Burke, *Reflections on the Revolution in France* [1790] (Oxford: Oxford University Press, 1989), p. 122.

8. Shelley, *The Mask of Anarchy*, ll. 26–7; *Poetical Works*, p. 338.
9. The phrase 'stopping the throats' is adapted from the words spoken by Prime Minister William Pitt in a caricature by Isaac Cruikshank, *The Royal Extinguisher or Gulliver Putting out the Patriots of Lilliput!!!* [1795]; British Museum Satires 8701.
10. For an overview of the neglected place of the 'soundscape' in the study of Romanticism and radical print culture, see my article 'Pandemonium: Radical Soundscapes and Satirical Prints in the Romantic Period', *Republics of Letters* 5:2 (November 2017), pp. 1–26.
11. Samuel Bamford, *Passages in the Life of a Radical*, 2 vols (London: Simkin, Marshall, 1844), vol. 1, p. 205.
12. Michael Bush states that 'the authorities at Peterloo felt threatened by a double revolution: one which would place the propertyless in charge; a second which would end male rule' (*The Casualties of Peterloo* [Lancaster: Carnegie Publishing, 2005], p. 2).
13. Helen Rogers, *Women and the People: Authority, Authorship and the Radical Tradition in Nineteenth-Century England* (Aldershot: Ashgate, 2000), pp. 18–23.
14. See William Cobbett's *Political Register*, 23 October 1819.
15. British Museum Satires 13257.
16. Percy Shelley could have read reports of this meeting in *The Black Dwarf* in July 1819, and this may have influenced his decision to make Earth, the principal speaker in *The Mask of Anarchy*, implicitly female. See Ian Haywood, 'Shelley's *Mask of Anarchy* and the iconography of female distress', in *Romanticism and Popular Culture*, ed. Philip Connell and Nigel Leask (Cambridge: Cambridge University Press, 2009), pp. 148–74.
17. Bamford, *Passages*, vol. 1, p. 207.
18. 'The Sword King', *The Black Dwarf*, 22 September 1819, p. 628.
19. For a much fuller exploration of the dual sound of Romantic poetry (representation and enunciation), see the Romantic Praxis volume, *Soundings of Things Done: The Poetry and Poetics of Sound in the Romantic Era and Ear*, ed. Susan J. Wolfson (April 2008) <http://www.rc.umd.edu/praxis/soundings/index.html> (last accessed 10 May 2018).
20. Samuel Bamford, *Miscellaneous Poetry* (London: Thomas Dolby, 1821), p. 76. Further page references are placed after the quotation.
21. William Hazlitt, 'Coriolanus', *Examiner*, 15 December 1816.
22. That 'score' carried this meaning at the time is documented by the *Oxford English Dictionary*, s.v. score, def. 6a. *OED Online* (Oxford: Oxford University Press, March 2018) <http://www.oed.com/view/Entry/173033> (last accessed 16 May 2018).

23. According to John Gardner, this poem garnered a fair degree of publicity. It was first published by Henry Hunt in his *Letter to Radical Reformers* (July 1820), along with the reminder, 'This song is the exclusive property of Samuel Bamford, for whose benefit it is published separately, price One Penny'. See John Gardner, 'The Suppression of Samuel Bamford's Peterloo Poems', *Romanticism* 13:2 (2007), pp. 145–55, 152.
24. Thomas Brown, *The Field of Peterloo: A Poem. Written in Commemoration of the Manchester Massacre* (London: J. Fairburn, 1819), p. 27.
25. E. P. Thompson, *The Making of the English Working Class* [1963] (London: Penguin, 1977), p. 660.
26. Anon. *The Free-Born Englishman Deprived of his Seven Senses* (London: J. Fairburn, 1819).
27. See British Museum Satires 8711 and 13287.
28. *The Black Dwarf*, 25 August 1819.
29. *The Black Dwarf*, 15 September 1819.
30. Martha Vandrei, '"Britons Strike Home": Politics, Patriotism and Popular Song in British Culture, c. 1695–1900', *Historical Research* 87:278 (2014), pp. 679–702.
31. Available at <https://www.youtube.com/watch?v=CwSBEWY1sEs> (last accessed 22 July 2017).
32. See, for example, Charles Williams, *After the Invasion, the Levee en Masse, or Britons Strike Home* [1803].
33. Iain McCalman, *Radical Underworld: Prophets, Revolutionaries and Pornographers in London, 1790–1845* (Oxford: Clarendon Press, 1993).
34. See Ruth Perry, 'War and the Media in Border Minstrelsy: The Ballad of Chevy Chase', in *Ballads and Broadsides in Britain, 1500–1800*, ed. Patricia Fumerton and Anita Guerrini (Aldershot: Ashgate 2010), pp. 251–70.
35. See also Hone and Cruikshank's *A Political Christmas Carol* [1820] which even provided the music for the first stanza, a skit on a well-known English carol:

    God rest ye merry gentlemen, let nothing you dismay
    Remember we were left alive upon last Christmas day,
    With both our lips at liberty to praise Lord C—h,
    For his practical comfort and joy, And joy,
    For his practical comfort and joy.

36. *Radical Squibs and Loyal Ripostes: Satirical Pamphlets of the Regency Period, 1819–1821*, ed. Edgell Rickword (Bath: Adams and Dart, 1971), p. 40. Further page references in parentheses.

37. P. B. Shelley, ‘Sonnet: England in 1819’ [1819], l. 7; *Poetical Works*, p. 575.
38. Compare Cobbett’s pastiche of the loyalist case for suppressing free speech: ‘it is not a *reform* but a *subversion* that we want; and that, therefore, the only answer for us ought to come from the mouth of a musket’ (*Political Register*, 4 December 1819).
39. Bush, *Casualties*, pp. 50–5.
40. Michael Henry Scrivener, *Radical Shelley: The Philosophical Anarchism and Utopian Thought of Percy Bysshe Shelley* (Princeton: Princeton University Press, 1982), pp. 201–2.
41. *The Radical Letter Bag* (London: J. Wright, 1820).
42. *The Radicals Unmasked and Outwitted; Or the Thistle Uprooted in Cato-Field* (London: G. Greenland, 1820).
43. *A Non-Coronation* (London: J. Fairburn, 1820).
44. *A Groan from the Throne* (London: J. Fairburn, 1820).
45. *The Poetical Works of William Wordsworth* (Boston: Phillips, Sampson and Company, 1850), p. 439.
46. British Museum Satires 13280.
47. The *Oxford English Dictionary*, s.v. trump, shows uses of the verb to mean ‘the act of breaking wind audibly’ dating back to 1552 and occurring in 1719 and 1798. *OED Online* (Oxford: Oxford University Press, March 2018) <http://www.oed.com/view/Entry/206929> (last accessed 16 May 2018).
48. Rickword, *Radical Squibs*, pp. 296–7.

Chapter 3

Henry Hunt's White Hat: The Long Tradition of Mute Sedition

Murray Pittock

Henry Hunt (1773–1835), nicknamed 'Orator' Hunt, was the star turn at St Peter's Field on 16 August 1819, being welcomed to the platform with the airs of 'See the Conquering Hero Comes', 'God Save the King' and 'Rule Britannia'. 'God save the King' was played with a particular reference beyond that of loyalty, for Hunt had refused to 'stand and uncover' for the anthem in Manchester's Theatre Royal that January. As in more visible features of the giant meeting that day, the music alluded to the radical purpose of the assembly while lying beyond the reach of prosecution under British treason and sedition legislation, which depended on language, whether printed or spoken. The subject of this essay is the mute – but similarly unprosecutable – sedition of colour in clothing to express radical views, and in one article of clothing in particular: Hunt's white hat.[1]

Henry Hunt, an agitator who was radical candidate for Westminster in 1818, was already notorious for his capacity to draw large crowds to hear him speak. On this occasion, his white hat, for which he was already known, was central to the wide range of symbolic allegiance to the radical cause on show: as James Epstein suggests, 'it would be difficult to exaggerate the importance of the emblems and banners carried into Manchester on 16 August 1819', which included 'numerous caps of liberty on poles ringing the hustings, as if imparting apotropaic protection to the meeting'. In the midst of this tableau, Hunt's removal of his white hat was the signal for his speech to begin. As Samuel Bamford recalls, 'Mr Hunt, stepping towards the front of the stage, took off his white hat, and addressed the people'.[2]

Hunt's speech was interrupted by the charge of the yeomanry that precipitated the outrage of Peterloo, and his white hat 'was staved in by a sword and became the symbol of reform' (although indeed, as we shall see, the colour and the hat were both in use in radical and oppositional contexts before Hunt was born).[3] However, Peterloo undoubtedly helped to make Hunt's choice of headgear notorious: cartoons of Hunt before Peterloo do not show the white hat, even when it is reported by onlookers. Afterwards, matters changed. 'White hats' began to distinguish Hunt's followers, and 'the wearing of white hats to divine services and Sunday schools in Lancashire opened a new theatre of resistance'. Within a few weeks of that fateful day in August 1819 the white hat of liberty was sufficiently widespread in the Manchester area to become the subject of an anxious broadside by Anglican Sunday Schools. By October, Thomas Teulon took it as the title of his periodical, 'THE WHITE HAT, worn by so many steady and dedicated patriots', and thereafter white hats and green ribbons (to which I shall return later) were for some time worn on the anniversary of Peterloo. Within weeks then, not only Peterloo but Hunt's white hat had become notorious: the 'condensed symbolic nomenclature' of Hunt's hat offering a narrow and deep point of reference for the importance of reform and the folly of repression. The hat was a badge of good manners and gentility, a reassurance that the radicalism represented by Hunt resided comfortably within the bounds of civil discourse. Its colour was important to this implicit claim in more ways than one.[4]

On the day of Peterloo itself, both Hunt's white hat and the act of taking it off were significant. The colour white was worn by radical sympathisers on a number of occasions: it symbolised purity of intention as opposed to corruption, much as when ex-BBC reporter Martin Bell (b. 1938) wore a white suit as the victorious independent candidate in Tatton at the General Election of 1997 (and indeed for many years afterwards). Hunt had refined the use of the colour white by attaching it to a single specific object – his hat – which became his badge and brand, and the piece of materiality by which he was both recognised and remembered. Hunt wore this white top hat, possibly for the first time, speaking at Spa Fields at the monster rally there on 15 November 1816, the first in a series of meetings which – it has been claimed – 'inaugurated the mass platform' into British public life. This may be too strong a claim: the London

Corresponding Society (LCS) meetings at Copenhagen Fields on 26 October and 12 November 1795 were attended by a 'vast crowd'.[5] Whoever is granted priority in their organisation, such mass gatherings went on to be a model for Daniel O'Connell's repeal movement, itself developed from O'Connell's engagement in the latter stages of reform agitation. These gatherings were themselves part of 'the era of large monuments . . . a "performing century" – and the century of monster meetings, large assemblies, festivals, and street illuminations', the cultural semiotics of public memory. In this sense Hunt's rallies anticipated not only future reform gatherings but covert Tory attempts to turn rallies to more traditional uses, such as was evident in some of the planning for the Burns Festival in Ayr in 1844. In the first age of mass industrial urbanisation early modern outdoor socialisation practices continued in the context of the poor availability of artificial light, but they could now be on a new scale, not just by virtue of population concentration but by the means of the velocity of circulation made possible by an expanding media. Both state and revolutionary actors took full advantage, beginning with the *fêtes révolutionnaires* of the 1790s, out of which the LCS and Hunt's gatherings grew.[6]

The first appearance of the white hat may have been deliberately linked to the cap of Liberty banner displayed at Spa Fields, where Hunt had made what seems to have been his first appearance in the hat in front of a cap of Liberty banner and tricolour (a red (England), white (Scotland) and green (Ireland) British flag rather than the French version) in November 1816. The 'British' tricolour was commissioned by Arthur Thistlewood (1774–1820), later executed for his part in the Cato Street Conspiracy, and made by his wife, Susan. Its British as opposed to French colouring was meant to symbolise native rather than imported radicalism, but radical meetings used political symbols from both traditions in a manner which government found discomfiting. Although Hunt emphasised the roots of the cap of Liberty in Roman manumission, pointing out its 'representation . . . on the front of the town hall at York', the 'red cap' that preceded him to the earlier 4 January 1819 meeting at St Peter's Field was a *bonnet rouge* version of the Phrygian cap clearly referencing the French Revolution. The display of the cap of Liberty, not only here, but at Rochdale, Blackburn and Leigh, London and Huddersfield in the weeks leading up to Peterloo 'was clearly a calculated gesture, making claims on the control of public space'. The cap was an overt challenge to the magistracy when it was exhibited, being seen as 'that bloody ensign of *French Rebellion*!' Hunt, who had used it at the Bristol by-election of 1812, was very aware of what it meant, and when the 'red cap of liberty' appeared at the Spa Fields meeting on 15 November 1816, his white hat complemented it and both amplified and confused its message, as well as identifying Hunt with a native tradition of liberty personified in himself.[7]

In the developing organisation of the monster rally at St Peter's Field in August, Hunt's efforts to avoid 'any breach of the public peace' have been viewed by his biographer as 'truly remarkable and extremely successful'. This determined avoidance of breaching the peace had earlier been evident in the Blanketeers' march of spring 1817, when 'the Manchester radicals decided to petition in groups of twenty, in strict conformity with Stuart legislation against tumultuous petitioning' (see below). Rather interestingly for the argument that follows, the Blanketeers also 'chose to follow Charles Edward's route through Leek and Ashbourne to Derby, rather than the easier route through Staffordshire' on their way to London, echoing mutely – and beyond the reach of prosecution – an earlier challenge to the Hanoverian state.[8]

The House of Commons' Secret Committee's distaste and suspicion concerning the 'symbols of the French Revolution' was in part because of the manner in which they lay beyond the reach of prosecution, even though – as George Canning protested – 'banners, ribbons, and other such devices, might be as clear an indicator of purpose as words'. In the Jacobite era, tartan had irritated the authorities just as much because of its semantics of opposition. Tartan cloth signified – in both Scots and English garb – support for the Stuart dynasty and opposition to the Hanoverian British state, and indeed a distinctively Jacobite tartan sett seems to have been produced in Edinburgh from 1713. In the 1760s, tartan – seen as the badge of Stuart absolutism – was associated with support for Bute against Wilkes and opposition to reform. The cloth's prohibition and then reintroduction under the limited terms of British military identity, sentimental ethnicity and vaudeville have only in recent years been challenged, while Jacobite flags were ritually burnt. Likewise at Peterloo, the cavalry cried 'Have at their flags' (such as one bearing the legend 'LIBERTAS' on a cap of crimson velvet with laurel, symbolising the victory of radicalism) precisely because such symbols provoked while being difficult to reduce to the language and intention of sedition. The crowd for their part struggled forcefully for their symbols just as a regiment might over its colours, for 'the mounted caps marked some of the few points where unarmed working people offered resistance' on 16 August. Hunt's hat was also a target.[9]

A post-Peterloo broadside, *The White Hat*, glorified Hunt's symbolic garb in terms redolent of earlier political struggles. Hunt was compared to Cromwell, but that was not all, as the broadside threatened to 'lay the Throne and the Altar flat, / With a whisk of Harry the Ninth's White Hat!'.[10] 'Harry the Ninth' had been a nickname for Henry Dundas (1742–1811), a representative of old corruption and the reputed Scottish taste for absolutism, close associate of Pitt, and Secretary for War from 1794–1801, impeached for misappropriation of public funds and acquitted in 1805. It was also the title of 'King' Henry IX, the Stuart heir and brother of Charles Edward Stuart, who 'reigned' from 1788 to 1807. Hunt was the ironic antithesis of the representatives of absolutism; he was also, as we shall see, the heir of their era. Just as 'old Jacks' was a term used for Jacobins, it had been a term used for Jacobites: and the symbolism and public presentation of these two kinds of oppositional politics was markedly similar in ways which are not yet fully appreciated.[11]

Hunt's white hat was a moniker for the orator, who would be barely visible from the back of huge crowds, such as the 10,000–153,000 variously estimated at St Peter's Field; later Daniel O'Connell's far more complex floats and pageants would serve the same purpose, framing a single speaker and his significance to monster meetings which could not hear his words. The inaudibility of star speakers was a major problem: 'at the prodigious meeting on Peep Green in May 1839 . . . the *Northern Star* admitted that perhaps not even 10 per cent of the vast crowd were able to hear'. When Hunt took off his hat to address the crowd at Peterloo, they were aware that he was now beginning to speak, even though they could not necessarily hear him. Then, as now, hat etiquette for gentlemen demanded that the hat be kept on outdoors (except when temporarily removed as a gesture of respect) but removed indoors. Thus Hunt's action was both symbolic of his respect for the popular cause of reform and the thousands who had gathered to hear him speak in its support, and it was a gesture signifying entering private space, of conversation *sub rosa*, a symbolic claim to be offering intimate and confidential discourse, which most of the crowd could not hear, but which was symbolised by the hat. When on, it was a silently respectful affirmation of the principles voiced explicitly when it was off. But of course, Hunt spoke in public: the removal of the hat was thus also a challenge, a making of the private public, the hidden open, and the conspiratorial, political. And yet it was also – given the wide recognition of what constituted appropriate hat wearing and doffing – an act of gentlemanly intimacy extended to a mass audience, a signal of a speech especially for them, even though its message was intended to be broadcast far and wide. The people gathered at St Peter's Field might not be able to hear the speech, but the hat and Hunt's gestures with it reassured them both that it was for them and the nature – if not the detail – of its contents. Hunt's white hat was thus a quintessentially 'treacherous object': a sign of political challenge arising from an everyday item and utilising its semantic position in society. Removing it was a sign of the onset of the prosecutable language of sedition in what the authorities were to term a seditious assembly. Indeed, Hunt was initially pursued for treason.[12]

John Barrell's *Imagining the King's Death* (2000) was the first major study to outline the continuing importance of the treason legislation of 25 Edward III with its stress on 'compasser ou ymaginer' (to compass or imagine [the king's death]) in the radical era. As I argued in *Material Culture and Sedition* (2013),[13] the moves made against the dissemination of radical opinion in the 1790s were themselves in close alignment with those made against the Jacobites in a previous era, and in both cases writing and speech were the key signifiers of what might constitute treasonable activity. In addition, medieval English legislation on '*scandalum magnatum*' (speaking ill of the great) mutated in the environment of the Reformation and the religious wars of the seventeenth century into an extension of treason law into 'seditious words and rumours' as provided for explicitly in 1 and 2 Philip and Mary c.3 (1554–5) and implicitly present in extensions of 25 Edward III to include reflection on the monarch's religious beliefs (as in 26 Henry VIII c.13 and 13 Elizabeth c.1). Seditious language began to morph into being regarded as potentially treasonous in the seventeenth century. In 1606, legislation regarding seditious libel was introduced, while the 1661 Sedition Act (13 Car 2 st1 c1) included 'tumultuous petitioning' among a list of new seditious categories which could be in effect treasonable. By 1681, Chief Justice Francis Pemberton noted that what was simply 'uttered and spoken' was increasingly regarded as treasonous, and indeed 'the conjoining of "seditious libel" and "treasonable words" charges in the context of the Rye House Plot of 1683–4 showed how porous these categories were becoming'. While the prosecution of seditious words and the penalties attending conviction waned in the eighteenth century as the state began to feel itself more secure, language was always a flashpoint for prosecution at times of crisis, and just as the concept of an attack on the Crown had been extended into religion so it mutated into more general forms of ideology. Supporters of King James and later radicals both responded to this in the same way: by the use of material culture, gestures and codes to exhibit political sympathies beyond the reach of action under the terms of 'compasser ou ymaginer' in all their forms.[14]

Such activities could hardly be grouped under the fashionable rubric of the public sphere, as the 'differentiation of civil society from the state' which they manifested was not an alternative political sphere, but an oppositional one: in echoes of both the Restoration and Jacobite eras, the Seditious Meetings Act of 1817 not only 'restricted the right to hold mass public meetings and censored the radical press', but also gave 'magistrates . . . powers to monitor all lecture rooms, coffee houses and inns' for seditious material.[15] Thus, rather than utilising the infrastructure of newspapers and coffee houses, oppositional groups manifested the unity of their subcultures in 'a material form', expressing through the inexpressive the moral force they believed their case to possess, beyond the reach of the monopoly of physical force in the hands of the state.[16] Thus the trial of Henry Sacheverell (1674–1724) in 1710 was accompanied by the production of pictures of him for dining rooms and door signage and his profile in letter seals, tobacco stoppers and coat buttons: an 'urban icon . . . within a culture of political celebrity that could redefine the most quotidian practices and performances . . . unbuttoning a coat, smoking a pipe or having a drink'.[17] In the years that followed, even 'printsellers who published gallows portraits' of those convicted of Jacobitism were prosecuted. It was this era, with its strong distribution networks of everything from medals (7,000 in one 1699 smuggling run to Kent alone) to pincushions sold 'through provincial merchants, markets, fairs and pedlars', which defined the possible uses of oppositional materiality for generations to come. So strongly entrenched was Jacobite material culture as a political statement that the government propaganda against it had stressed the 'superior relationship to reality' enjoyed by the Whig administration compared to the 'symbolic practices' of the Jacobites that were in their turn to shape the definition of the materiality of sedition in the Radical era, where coat buttons and blue ribbons both were used to denote loyalty to the Crown, just as white was used by the radicals.[18]

Party colours gained a major popular presence for perhaps the first time in the conflicts of the Stuart and Jacobite eras, and they persisted in public political demonstrations. They had first appeared extensively in the Exclusion Crisis, with green ribbons signifying support for Exclusion, red for the Crown and blue for supporters of Monmouth. After William of Orange came to the throne, orange replaced green as the colour of the Whigs (although green as a radical colour was to reappear), while white and yellow (sun and sunflowers for legitimacy and renewal) for the Stuart Crown were used, and black for Hanover. White was the Bourbon colour, and the white rose was certainly associated with the Stuarts from the attempt to exclude the Duke of York from the succession at the beginning of the 1680s (the White Rose of course had been the badge of the House of York in the Wars of the Roses). White was also associated with the origins of the Stuart dynasty, as Scotland was 'Alba', the white land 'by virtue of a Latin pun which appeared in Caroline masques'. King James 'VIII''s badge later bore the legend 'Alba maxima'; likewise, James Duke of York was Duke of Albany in Scotland. White was found as a Stuart colour in England in Bath as late as 1749, and was adopted – probably in this sense – by the first major Irish agricultural protest movement, the Whiteboys/*Buachaillí Báin* in the 1760s. One of James' codenames was the 'Little white-headed cow'. 'True Blue' Tories on the other hand were initially Protestant Jacobites, and later the colour was used by Lord George Gordon's supporters in the anti-Catholic riots of 1780. The colour characterises the Conservative and Unionist Party to this day. In 1776, blue cockades and blue ribbons were worn in the Ballymena election, and Orange cockades appeared among loyalists in 1789, while the United Irishmen adopted green. Green became Ireland's colour in British radical display also, and at the same time made its return as a more general radical colour, though often one tinged with reference to Ireland: when James Fleming opened the welcoming speeches in Paisley to celebrate Hunt's release from prison in 1822, for example, Ireland was his primary subject amid concern that 'Scotland might soon be in a similar situation'. The nature and colour of dress and accessories thus both had a long history of association with political expression.[19]

It was thus no surprise that colours were and are evident in unprosecutable displays of political radicalism and disaffection. In the Jacobite period, 'white gloves, signifying innocence, were prominent' in public gatherings. The same use of the colour was made by the White Rose anti-Nazis in Hitler's Germany and by the anti-Bolshevik forces in 1918–20. White ribbons are still used in a more contemporary frame to express opposition in today's Russia.[20] In the immediate aftermath of the French Revolution, white was used by the French Royalists as a sign of loyalty to the Bourbons, before being adopted in England as a sign of purity, just as the Stuart oak was often used as the basis for the Tree of Liberty. In the Rockite disturbances in Ireland, a scarlet band worn round the neck was a sign of 'such as were deputed officers and serjeants under Captain Rock'.[21]

As Nicholas Roe has observed and has already been evident in Hunt's use of the tricolour, the radical era used a good deal of the panoply and symbolism of the revolutionary *fêtes*. On Hunt's march into London on 13 September 1819, white wands were carried with red cockades and laurel leaves; a green Liberty banner was carried by six Irishmen, and a white flag announced in its black border and inscription respectful mourning for those who had died at Peterloo, together with a red flag inscribed 'Universal Suffrage' and the red, white and green tricolour for England, Scotland and Ireland: the embedded reference to Scotland as the 'White Land' is worth noting. Hunt supplemented his usual white hat with white trousers on this occasion. The inscriptions on the banners articulated more direct political discourse than usually found in treacherous objects. As Roe points out:

> Most striking, perhaps, is the frequency with which the colour white appears in flags, on the wands, in Henry Hunt's dress: as in revolutionary France, white was an expression of the reformers' untainted ideals and motives which (like the laurel) invoked the precedent of the classical world.

Roe does, however, also refer in a footnote to the Jacobite use of such symbols. Laurel symbolised future triumph, and had been used to signify this by supporters of the Stuarts.[22]

Both the nature of materiality and its colour had specific contextual uses. Ribbons were used at elections as both relatively cheap and 'instantly recognizable to the illiterate or to mass crowds'. Green ribbons symbolised radicalism and later Irish or Irish tinged radicalism: more broadly still, they became associated with general political dissent. The wearing of white hats with green ribbons on the anniversary of Peterloo may have referenced not only Hunt, but also the support for annual parliaments (and hence elections) which was central to the views of many Radicals. Blue 'sashes and cockades' had reappeared to 'demonstrate . . . loyalism at the burning of effigies of Paine' in 1792–3, while orange – never entirely out of fashion – made a major reappearance as a statement of Protestant identity with the development of the Orange Order in Ireland from 1795 onwards. By the 1820s, yellow had begun to be used by liberal reformers, and was later adopted by the Liberal Party. Black denoted collectivity in identity and purpose as well as sobriety of manners.[23]

There was also the register of dress by which the 'body politic' distinguished itself. 'Sunday best' clothing was often worn by radicals to dissociate their reformist aims from the 'covert and seditious world of underground clubs and mob violence', which the political cartoon – whether or not realistically – associated with scruffiness of person and attire. At the opposite end of the spectrum was the use of disguise to mask illegal activities aimed at the damage of people or property. Cross-dressing was a favoured disguise: in the Rebecca Riots of 1839 and again in 1842–3, men appeared in women's clothes with blackened faces, echoing the 'wearing of women's dress' with 'blackening of the face' used by the Rockites in Ireland. Another Irish radical agricultural group, the Strawboys, used yellow paint or head coverings of straw to disguise themselves.[24]

Henry Hunt was a gentleman – his *Memoirs* suggest an ancestry going back to an officer of William the Conqueror's – and his white hat as a hat signified gentlemanly intent and status. It was also carelessly visible and was associated in one dimension of its colour with feminine purity, such as the white ribbons worn by ladies to greet George III in 1789 or the plain muslin gowns – often white – which became fashionable from the turn of the nineteenth century.

In Hunt's hands the symbol became so widely known that it was hooted at by crowds as a sign that the wearer's politics had been identified and were disapproved of; Francis Burdett is depicted carrying it on his lap in *The Real or Constitutional House that Jack Built* (1819).[25] Subsequently it became associated with the Chartist movement: James Taylor, a Methodist Unitarian manufacturer in Rochdale, 'as a special line, made white hats for Chartists'. Taylor stood in the first reform election of 1832. Two other Methodist Unitarians stood locally in that year in Todmorden and Bury: the latter, Edmund Grundy (1781–1857), had gone bail for Hunt when he had been arrested. In August 1840, 'on his liberation from Chester Castle, Peter McDouall was presented with a "splendid white beaver hat" by the men of Andershaw'.[26]

The white hat, though, had a longer history of public display, which took two main forms, one general and one specific. The cap of Liberty, although by origin Roman, had arguably been seen as a 'Dutch symbol', symbolising the struggle to free the Netherlands from the 'absolutist' monarchy of Catholic Spain: as such, it entered English political discourse after the Revolution of 1688. It was a patriotic symbol, with overtones of support for the Protestant succession: it could not easily become white until the close of the Jacobite era, for white was a core Jacobite colour, as is discussed further below. John Wilkes (1726–97) appears to have been initially identified with the 'red Phrygian cap' of Liberty in the 1760s, but soon his depiction changed. William Hogarth's famous 1763 caricature of Wilkes with the cap of Liberty on a pole (BMC 4050) appears to show the cap as white, as indeed it more clearly is in the pro-Wilkes print of 1768, *The Many Headed Monster of Sumatra* (BMC 4231): this is interesting, as 'the red cap of liberty' was to be its definitive colour in the French Revolutionary era.[27] A white liberty cap on a pole can also be seen in prints such as *Association, or Public Virtue* (BMC 5638), *Your Petitioner Sheweth* (BMC 5665) and *The R-y-l Hunt or the Petitioners Answer'd* (BMC 5675), all from 1780, while in 1793, Thomas Rowlandson's *The Contrast* depicts a white cap of Liberty on the end of Britannia's trident. Hunt's white hat was thus a visible expression of a definitive political commitment which could trace its symbolism back beyond the French Revolution's red caps to the radical Whigs of the 1760s and the Revolution of 1688. But it appears not only to have been related to radical symbolism divided from it by time and/or space, but to have deliberately reiterated one particular aspect of that symbolism – the hat – because of its association with the cap of Liberty.[28]

But the white hat had a still earlier and equally pertinent presence in symbolic politics. When James, Duke of York, returned to London from Edinburgh at the close of the Exclusion Crisis in 1682, his 'triumph was celebrated . . . by the performance of Thomas Otway's *Venice Preserv'd* at the Duke of York's playhouse in Dorset Garden', where Antonio, the villain in chief, is a thinly disguised version of the Earl of Shaftesbury and Pierre – though he too is politically compromised – is seen as the vehicle for an attack on Whig values. Subsequently, *Venice Preserv'd* became both a popular and a Jacobite play, being performed eighty-nine times in London between 1729 and 1745 alone. Otway's commentary on the politics of the Exclusion Crisis was accompanied by a 'curious stage tradition'. Both John Mills and James Quin, 'who had the role of Pierre at Drury Lane from 1707 until 1748' consistently 'wore a white hat when performing the part', identified by Aline Mackenzie as a sign of support – on the head of the conspiratorial Pierre – for the Stuart dynasty. White was the Stuart colour and the colour of James as Duke of York and Albany. The white hat thus had almost half a century of public tradition at one of London's major theatres as a sign of public display of conspiratorial and anti-Hanoverian sympathies long before Hunt was born. Drury Lane was also the only theatre operational in London during the Stuart Restoration.[29]

Productions of *Venice Preserv'd* continued at Drury Lane until at least the 1780s, and it was at Drury Lane that James Hadfield attempted to assassinate George III on 15 May 1800 while the national anthem was being played before the staging of a Cibber play. *Venice Preserv'd* had nearly caused a riot when it was staged following a previous assassination attempt on the king, and when it was produced again in 1802 Pierre's part was censored. The play continued to be politically referenced: John Wilkes Booth (whose favourite roles included Brutus and Wallace) said in 1865 on hearing of the surrender of Robert E. Lee that 'he was done with the stage, and the only play he wanted to present now was *Venice Preserved*', an indication that he was now determined to assassinate rather than (as he had previously planned) kidnap Lincoln. The associations of Pierre's white hat could thus suggest a much more radically violent attack on corrupt government than that symbolised by the white cap of Liberty.[30]

In more recent times, 'White hats' have become a slang description for the good guys in Westerns following the use of white hats to identify the heroes in the black and white era, and today the term is used of computer hackers who test rather than compromise the security of the systems they hack as well as a certain subgroup of American college student who is morally conservative, dresses up unnecessarily and maintains contact with home and high-school friends. Most of the varied uses of the term 'White hat' involve ascriptions of virtue, integrity or moral conservatism in various contexts, and take us back all the way to both Hunt and Pierre. Hunt's white hat is thus not only an accidental detail of the carnage at Peterloo, but a denominator of the deep meaning of materiality and culture in political protest, one often powerfully and specifically referenced, while resting beyond the reach of prosecution – if not, as on that fateful 16th August, assault.

Notes

1. James A. Epstein, *Radical Expression: Political Language, Ritual, and Symbol in England, 1790–1850* (New York and Oxford: Oxford University Press, 1994), p. 82; see Murray Pittock, *Material Culture and Sedition, 1688–1760: Treacherous Objects, Secret Places* (Basingstoke: Macmillan, 2013) for a full discussion of the semantics of the expression of treason and sedition beyond language.
2. Epstein, *Radical Expression*, p. 82; Samuel Bamford, *Passages in the Life of a Radical* [1841], Preface by T. M. Hilton (Oxford: Oxford University Press, 1984), p. 151.
3. See <https://www.britannica.com/biography/Henry-Hunt> (last accessed 31 January 2017).
4. See for example BMC 12819 which does not show it at the November 1816 Spa Fields meeting; *At a Special Meeting of Members of the Committee of the Sunday Schools in Manchester and Salford Belonging to the Established Church*, 24 September 1819; Paul A. Pickering, 'Class Without Words: Symbolic Communication in the Chartist Movement', *Past and Present* 112 (1986), pp. 144–62 (155); Epstein, *Radical Expression*, pp. 94–5.
5. John Belchem, *'Orator' Hunt: Henry Hunt and English Working-Class Radicalism* (Oxford: Clarendon Press, 1985), pp. 58–9, 64; H. T.

Dickinson, *Caricatures and the Constitution* (Cambridge: Chadwyck-Healey, 1986), pp. 166–7.

6. Joep Leerssen and Ann Rigney, 'Introduction', in *Commemorating Writers in Nineteenth-Century Europe: Nation Building and Centenary Fever*, ed. Leerseen and Rigney (Basingstoke: Macmillan, 2014), pp. 1–23 (6); Murray Pittock and Christopher Whatley, 'Poems and Festivals, Art and Artefact and the Commemoration of Robert Burns, c.1844–c.1896', *Scottish Historical Review* 93:1 (2014), pp. 56–79.
7. Epstein, *Radical Expression*, pp. 72–4, 77, 80–1.
8. Belchem, *'Orator' Hunt*, pp. 74, 81, 91, 106; Paul Monod, *Jacobitism and the English People, 1688–1788* [1989] (Cambridge: Cambridge University Press, 1993), p. 341; *Memoirs of Henry Hunt Esquire*, 3 vols (London: Dolby, 1820).
9. Katrina Navickas, '"That sash will hang you": Political Clothing and Adornment in England, 1780–1840', *Journal of British* Studies 49:3 (2010), pp. 540–65 (552); Murray Pittock, 'Plaiding the Invention of Scotland', in *From Tartan to Tartanry: Scottish Culture, History and Myth*, ed. Ian Brown (Edinburgh: Edinburgh University Press, 2010), pp. 32–47; see Dickinson, *Caricatures*, pp. 47, 99, for the association of tartan with Bute; Epstein, *Radical Expression*, pp. 81, 82, 85.
10. <http://chethamslibrary.blogspot.co.uk/2012/09/putting-on-my-white-hat.html> 21 September 2012 reproduced this broadside.
11. E. P. Thompson, *The Making of the English Working Class* [1963], rev. ed. (Harmondsworth: Penguin, 1968), p. 544.
12. See Murray Pittock, 'Treacherous Objects: Towards a Theory of Jacobite Material Culture', *Journal for Eighteenth-Century Studies* 34:1 (2011), pp. 39–63; Pickering, 'Class Without Words', p. 153.
13. John Barrell, *Imagining the King's Death: Figurative Treason, Fantasies of Regicide, 1793–96* (Oxford: Oxford University Press, 2000); Pittock, *Material Culture*.
14. David Cressy, *Dangerous Talk* (Oxford: Oxford University Press, 2010), pp. 29, 40, 42, 49, 57, 63, 208, 235; Pittock, *Material Culture*, pp. 6–7.
15. Jürgen Habermas, *The Structural Transformation of the Public Sphere* [1962], trans. Thomas Buger with the assistance of Frederick Lawrence (Cambridge: Polity, 1992); Penny Young, *Two Cocks on the Dunghill: William Cobbett and Henry Hunt: Their Friendships, Feuds and Fights* [2009] (South Lopham: Twopenny Press, 2010), p. 123.
16. Jeremy Tanner, 'Introduction: Sociology and Art History: A Reader', in *The Sociology of Art: A Reader*, ed. Tanner (London and New York: Routledge, 2003), pp. 1–26 (3). See also Emile Durkheim, 'Symbolic Objects, Communicative Interaction and Social Creativity', in Tanner,

pp. 63–8 (67), and Jürgen Habermas, 'Art Criticism and the Institutions of the Public Sphere', in Tanner, p. 157.

17. Mark Hallett, *The Spectacle of Difference: Graphic Satire in the Age of Hogarth* (New Haven and London: Yale University Press, 1999), p. 30.
18. Neil Guthrie, *The Material Culture of the Jacobites* (Cambridge: Cambridge University Press, 2013), pp. 18, 20, 124; Thompson, *Making*, p. 544; Corrinne Harol, 'Whig Ballads and the Past Passive Jacobite', *Journal for Eighteenth-Century Studies* 35:4 (2012), pp. 581–95 (589–90); Katrina Navickas, 'The "Spirit of Loyalty": Material Culture, Space and the Construction of an English Loyalist Memory 1790–1840', in *Loyalism and the Formation of the British World, 1775–1914*, ed. Alan Blackstock and Frank O'Gorman (Woodbridge: Boydell and Brewer, 2014), pp. 43–59 (59).
19. Petri Mirala, *Freemasonry in Ulster 1733–1813* (Dublin: Four Courts, 2007), pp. 151, 173; Pittock, *Material Culture*, pp. 26, 56, 75–6, 96, 98, 107, 157, 160, 163, 164; Pickering, 'Class Without Words', p. 154; *Report of the Meeting, Held at Paisley, In the Saracen's Head, on the 31st October 1822 in Celebration of Mr Hunt's Release from Ilchester Bastile* (Paisley: Neilson, 1822), p. 7.
20. Paul Monod, 'Pierre's White Hat: Theatre, Jacobitism and Popular Protest in London, 1689–1760', in *By Force or By Default? The Revolution of 1688–1689*, ed. Eveline Cruickshanks (Edinburgh: John Donald, 1989), pp. 159–89 (174); Pittock, *Material Culture*, p. 153.
21. James Donnelly, Jr, *Captain Rock: The Irish Agrarian Rebellion of 1821–1824* (Cork: Collins Press/University of Wisconsin Press, 2009), p. 51; Pittock, *Material Culture*, pp. 154–6.
22. Nicholas Roe, *John Keats and the Culture of Dissent* (Oxford: Oxford University Press, 1998), pp. 71–3; Pittock, *Material Culture*, p. 164; Pickering, 'Class Without Words', p. 154.
23. Navickas, '"That sash"', pp. 541, 544, 547, 550, 552, 557.
24. George Rudé, *The Crowd in History 1730–1848*, 2nd edn (London: Lawrence and Wishart, 1981 [1964]), pp. 157, 159; Donnelly, *Captain Rock*, p. 110; Navickas, '"That sash"', p. 559.
25. Navickas, '"That sash"', pp. 544, 556; Christina Parolin, *Radical Spaces: Venues of Popular Politics in London, 1790–c.1845* (Canberra, ACT: Australian National University E Press, 2010), p. 140; 'Communism Amongst Us', *The Spectator*, 30 January 1849, p. 15.
26. Herbert MacLachlan, *Essays and Addresses* (Manchester: Manchester University Press, 1950), p. 214; Pickering, 'Class Without Words', p. 155.

27. Epstein, *Radical Expression*, pp. 77–8; Navickas, '"That sash"', p. 542; Pickering, 'Class Without Words', p. 154; Dickinson, *Caricatures*, pp. 54, 68.
28. Epstein, *Radical Expression*, p. 79; Dickinson, *Caricatures*, pp. 94, 100, 102.
29. Monod, 'Pierre's White Hat', pp. 162, 164, 170, 176; Aline Mackenzie, 'A Note on Pierre's White Hat', *Notes and Queries* cxcii (1947), pp. 90–3.
30. Michael W. Kauffman, *American Brutus: John Wilkes Booth and the Lincoln Conspiracies* (New York: Random House, 2004), p. 207.

Chapter 4

Staging Protest and Repression: Guy Fawkes in Post-Peterloo Performance

Frederick Burwick

In the aftermath of Peterloo many plays were performed that featured violent military repression directed against a gathering of the downtrodden. Censorship prevented playwrights from directly identifying the stage representation with the events at Manchester on 16 August 1819.[1] Fearing that the unarmed citizens, gathered to urge reform, were instead planning riot or rebellion, the cavalry, directed to disperse the crowd, charged with drawn sabres, killing eighteen and wounding over 700. News of the massacre was reported in newspapers and periodicals throughout Britain and was the subject of many literary works. In drama, however, the representation of Peterloo was possible only under the guise of heterotopia. In order to gain the approval of the Examiner of Plays, the playwright must claim a setting in some other place or time. A convenient disguise was Guy Fawkes, who had been transformed from a villainous conspirator into a hero of the oppressed. The historical transformation was strikingly evident in the rowdy festivities of Guy Fawkes Night (5 November).

What was originally intended as a celebration of the salvation of James I had become a celebration of Guy Fawkes as the rebel against tyranny. In Lewes, Guildford and other towns the street bonfires turned into violent assaults by the lower classes on the homes and shops of wealthy merchants. Because Guy Fawkes Night had legal sanction as an official holiday, performances could still be performed with the sanction of the Examiner of Plays. The most popular post-Peterloo version was George MacFarren's *Guy Fawkes; or, The Gunpowder Treason* (Coburg, September 1822),[2] one of many being performed throughout the provinces. The crucial scene in MacFarren's play is the interrogation of Guy Fawkes. All depends on how the actor plays the role. As a play written to slip through censorship, in the interrogation scene Guy Fawkes might be played as an arrogant anarchist defying a well-ordered monarchy – or as a sympathetic advocate of the people opposing a brutal reign of tyranny.

Another version was Edward Stirling's *Guido Fawkes; or, The Prophetess of Ordsall Cave*, which introduces the protesters as meeting secretly in Manchester.[3] After his arrest, Guy Fawkes proudly declares that he and his friends may have been stopped, but the doom of tyranny is still underway. This melodrama was originally written for performance in Manchester. Samuel Hibbert, a Manchester historian, declared that Ordsall Cave, Fawkes' hiding place, was a site where 'sacrifices, divination and compacts appertaining to worship of the hero of the Edda were regularly practiced'.[4] Fighting abroad for ten years for the Catholic cause in Europe during the Eighty Years' War, Fawkes adopted the Italian name Guido. Using the assumed Christian name that was also Catholic, Stirling's Guido also acquires an Old English pedigree.

In the streets as well as on stage the *coup de théâtre* was the capture of the enemy to be burned in effigy. But who was the enemy? In early years it was a dummy costumed as the Pope, often giving rise to conflict between local Anglican and Catholic contingents. By the beginning of the nineteenth century, however, the effigy was a nobleman dressed in coat and waistcoat decorated with gold braid, shiny buttons, and fine lace at the neck and sleeves. Torching the effigy was sometimes accompanied by property damage and *violent* scuffling between the propertied and labouring classes. As performed in the post-Peterloo era, Guy Fawkes had become a sympathetic character struggling against persecution. On stage his character was akin other defiers of authority: Robin Hood, or Jack Sheppard the Highwayman, or William Tell, or Karl Moor of *The Robbers*.

Guy Fawkes as the heroic rebel, rather than as the villainous traitor, was a character revision that evolved slowly with the temperament of revolution in the 1790s,[5] but gained impetus during the years of riot and economic depression following the Napoleonic Wars. The massacre at St Peter's Field, Manchester, gave impetus to the idea of resisting violent oppression. William Hazlitt and Charles Lamb were among the critics who sought to refurbish the reputation of Guy Fawkes as a champion of the downtrodden and martyr to a just cause. Not only did Hazlitt and Lamb cite each other, each would prompt the other to a bolder defence of Guy Fawkes. During 1811, rampaging Luddites destroyed 1,000 of the power looms that left them underpaid or unemployed.[6] The violence prompted Lamb's speculation, 'On the Probable Effects of the Gunpowder Treason in this Country if the Conspirators had accomplished their Object' (1811). Hazlitt would subsequently argue that the notorious attempt of 5 November 1605 had been an act of desperation by the persecuted Catholics.

In 1808 Leigh Hunt and his brother John had launched a liberal weekly newspaper, *The Examiner*, which advocated abolition of the slave trade, Catholic emancipation, reform of Parliament and the criminal law. For their satirical treatment of the unpopular Prince Regent, the Hunt brothers were imprisoned in 1813. Hunt presented the Prince Regent as a corrupt ruler whose habits would infect the nation at large. He printed a series of sharp satires, including Charles Lamb's 'The Triumph of the Whale'. The article responsible for sending Hunt to jail was entitled 'The Prince on St Patrick's Day', published on 22 March 1812 with two epigrams written by Lamb. The Prince Regent was described as

> a violator of his word, a libertine over head and ears in debt and disgrace, a despiser of domestic ties, the companion of gamblers, and demireps, a man who has just closed half a century without one single claim on the gratitude of his country or the respect of posterity![7]

As a result, Hunt and his brother John (*The Examiner*'s printer) were prosecuted for libel on 9 December 1812. On 3 February 1813 they were sentenced to imprisonment, fined £500 and required to pay a further £250 as a guarantee for their good behaviour. Hunt was imprisoned at Horsemonger Lane Gaol, where he was joined by his wife and young son. He carefully decorated his cells, transforming them into a 'bower' with blue sky on the ceiling. Here he continued as editor of *The Examiner*. He was released on 3 February 1815.[8] In 1821 John Hunt was again imprisoned for libel; to avoid persecution Leigh Hunt left for Italy in November 1821. The Hunt brothers left the publication in the hands of their nephew, Henry Leigh Hunt, and to help maintain circulation Hazlitt contributed his three-part essay on 'Guy Faux' to the issues of *The Examiner* for 11, 18 and 25 November 1821.[9]

Hazlitt developed three ideas: (1) that Fawkes was truly committed to the idea of restoring the civil and religious rights of Catholics; (2) that in the intervening two centuries religious tolerance ought to have advanced sufficiently to raise the stature of Fawkes in British history; (3) that in spite of the extreme violence of the Gunpowder Plot, Fawkes' intentions were in accord with the practical moral standard of revolutionary consequentialism. As Hazlitt knew, the argument that 'ends justify the means' could be adopted by either of the opposing parties: by the persecuted Catholics or by the Parliament that upheld the supremacy of the Church of England; by the disenfranchised populace gathered at St Peter's Field or by the military authorities who sent the cavalry charging into the unarmed crowd with sabres drawn.

> We burn Guy Fawkes in effigy, and the hooting and buffeting and maltreating of that poor tattered figure of rags and straw makes a festival in every village in England once a year . . . Guy Faux is made into the figure of a scare-crow, a fifth of November bug-bear, in our history. Now that Mr Hogg's *Jacobite Relics* have dissipated the remains of an undue horror at Popery, it may seem the time to undertake the defence of so illustrious a character, who has hitherto been the victim of party-prejudice and national spite.[10]

As a reassertion of national pride Scottish poet and novelist James Hogg, 'the Ettrick Shepard', assembled *Jacobite Relics of Scotland: Being the songs, airs, and legends, of the adherents to the house of Stuart* (2 volumes, 1819–21). The songs, a number of them composed by Hogg himself and others written or adapted by Robert Burns, celebrated the return of James II as Catholic monarch of England, or of Bonnie Prince Charlie as rightful heir to the throne.

In spite of his failure, Hazlitt wrote, Fawkes attained notoriety 'for his unsuccessful attempt to set fire to the House of Lords, and blow up the English Monarchy, the Protestant Religion, and himself, at one stroke'.[11] Because he failed, he 'has had the honour to be annually paraded through the streets, and burnt in effigy in every town and village in England from that time to this'.[12] The failure was not absolute. Compassion for the disenfranchised Catholics increased during the intervening two centuries, just as public opinion was swayed on behalf of the multitude of martyrs at Peterloo. Hazlitt set up a number of binaries that place 'the hero of the Gun-Powder plot' on the positive side of the equation:

> a fanatic, but he was no hypocrite . . .
> a fool, a madman, an assassin; – still he was neither knave nor coward . . .
> he did not murder in sport; it was serious work that he had taken in hand . . .
> a picture of the strange infatuation of the human understanding, but not of the depravity of the human will.[13]

If they could visualise Fawkes in the act preparing for the explosion, Hazlitt declared, readers would recognise him as a dedicated martyr to the cause.

> To see this arch-bigot, this heart-whole traitor, this pale miner in the infernal regions, skulking in his retreat with his cloak and dark lanthorn, moving cautiously about among his barrels of gunpowder, loaded with death, but not yet ripe for destruction, regardless of the lives of others, and more than indifferent to his own.[14]

Fawkes may not have been alone in the plot, but he was the only one of the conspirators prepared to ignite the gunpowder train.

> There were thousands of pious Papists privy to and ready to applaud the deed when done: – there was no one but our old fifth-of-November friend, who still flutters in rags and straw on the occasion, that had the courage to attempt it.[15]

Hazlitt emphasised the religious zeal that propelled Fawkes' commitment. 'He was armed with the Holy Spirit and with fire: he was the Church's chosen servant and her blessed martyr.'[16] Identifying Fawkes as 'a true son of the Catholic Church, a martyr and a confessor', Hazlitt argued that Fawkes was driven by 'a high principle of enthusiasm, and a disinterested zeal for truth'.[17] Hazlitt is thus prepared to declare Fawkes Christ-like in his martyrdom. Hazlitt echoes the gospel of John: 'Greater love than this has no one, that he shall give up his life for the truth' (John 15:13 'Greater love hath no man than this, that a man lay down his life for his friends').

Most probably thinking of the plight of Leigh Hunt and his brother John during that November of 1821, Hazlitt regretted that 'we have no Guy Fauxes now'; wrongs need to be righted, but there is only 'a little unmeaning splutter' of protest.[18] None of us, Hazlitt observed, is ready 'to fling ourselves into the gap, and blow up the system and our own bodies to atoms at once, upon an abstract principle of right'. Hazlitt modifies his praise for Fawkes' Christ-like 'spirit of martyrdom' by acknowledging the unchristian opposition among Anglicans, Puritans, Presbyterians and Catholics that intensified under James I; the beginning of the seventeenth century was 'an age that had virtue enough in it to produce the mischievous fanaticism'.[19]

The defence of Fawkes as a martyr to the reform of religious persecution entailed a shift in moral perspective. That shift was well-practised by the audiences of Edward Moore's *The Gamester: a Tragedy* (Drury Lane, 1753) and Susanna Centlivre's *The Gamester; a Comedy* (Drury Lane, 1767), and by those who cheered the villain in *Richard Turpin, the Highwayman* (Royal Amphitheatre, November 1819) and John Baldwin Buckstone's *Jack Sheppard* (Adelphi, 28 October 1839).[20] 'Gamesters and highwaymen', Hazlitt wrote, 'are so far heroes that it is neck or nothing with them: they set consequences at defiance' while their motives are selfish, uninformed by a rational goal: 'Before a man can fight for an idea, he must have an idea in his head to fight for.'[21] They are not to be compared to true martyrs like Fawkes, for 'their actions are disinterested – but their motives are not so'. The Gunpowder Plot and Peterloo were key moments in the suffrage movement. Guy Fawkes' secret conspiracy and Henry Hunt's mass demonstration both sought change in suffrage. 'To have an object always in view dearer to one than one's-self, to cling to a principle in contempt of danger, of interest, of the opinion of the world, – this is the true ideal, the high and heroic state of man.'[22]

Charles Lamb offers a far more playful but no less serious defence in his essay, 'Guy Faux' for the *London Magazine* in 1823.[23] Ten years earlier Lamb had written a defence, 'On the Probable Effects of the Gunpowder Treason in this Country if the Conspirators had accomplished their Object' (1811). He returned to this topic in a long essay incorporating most of his earlier essay and referring to Hazlitt's three papers for *The Examiner* as the work of 'an ex-Jesuit, not unknown at Douay', who had endeavoured to prove that the Gunpowder Plot conspirators were heroic Christian martyrs.[24] Lamb then quotes several paragraphs of Hazlitt's prose before concluding: 'It is impossible, upon Catholic principles, not to admit the force of this reasoning.'[25] Rather than a refutation of Hazlitt, Lamb adds the 'Protestant' perspective of Jeremy Taylor. Lamb's irony lies in the fact Taylor was appointed to preach at St Mary's on the thirty-seventh anniversary of the Gunpowder Plot (5 November 1642). Taylor was eager to dispel suspicions that, after serving as chaplain to King Charles, he still clung to the Catholic faith. For some, Taylor's denunciation of Catholic barbarity was a case of 'protesting too much'. The ceremony that now takes place on Bonfire Night involves 'burning Guy Faux, or the Pope, as he is indifferently called'.[26] Lamb refers to the ritual as 'a sort of Treason Travestie', because it seems to matter little or not at all whether one celebrates Fawkes' execution or his attempt to explode Parliament.[27]

The possibility of annihilating the existing government prompts Lamb to revert to the speculations in his 1811 essay. What 'consequences . . . would have flowed from this plot if it had had a successful issue'.[28] The first consequence, says the whimsical anarchist, would be 'the material change which it must have produced in the course of the nobility'.[29] Having extinguished 'the ancient peerage', the vacancies must be filled with a 'new race of peers'.[30] And what if this grand act of overthrow and restoration were to occur *now* rather than then.

> Why, you or I, reader, might have been Duke of —, or Earl of —. I particularise no titles, to avoid the least suspicion of intention to usurp the dignities of the two noblemen whom I have in my eye; but a feeling more dignified than envy sometimes excites a sigh, when I think how the posterity of Guido's Legion of Honour (among whom you or I might have been) might have rolled down . . . What new orders of merit think you this English Napoleon would have chosen? Knights of the Barrel, or Lords of the Tub, Grand Almoners of the Cellar, or Ministers of Explosion?[31]

Whimsical or not, Lamb constructs an entirely new Parliament upon the ruins. Plebeians like himself now have titles to sit in the House of

Lords. Further, if there is to be an explosion in our own times, Lamb cautioned, 'then we better know what a House of Commons is in our days'.[32] Lamb's proposal for the new House of Commons was on the same trajectory of reform that could be traced from Henry Hunt's platform in St Peter's Field to the Representation of the People Act (Great Reform Act, 1832): extending suffrage, abolishing 'rotten' boroughs. Presenting serious reform under the guise of wild fantasy, Lamb defines the necessity of extending the right to vote, and he also inserts a flight of fancy to promote freedom of the press.

Lamb asks his readers to imagine themselves seated as MPs at the very moment of explosion:

> Faux just ready with his train and matches below, – in his hand a 'reed tipp'd with fire.' He applies the fatal engine. To assist our notions still further, let us suppose some lucky dog of a reporter, who had escaped by miracle upon some plank of St. Stephen's benches, and came plump upon the roof of the adjacent Abbey; from whence descending, at some neighbouring coffee-house, first wiping his clothes and calling for a glass of lemonade, he sits down and reports what he had heard and seen (*quorum pars magna fuit*) for the *Morning Post* or the *Courier*.[33]

For this explosion Lamb imagines for his reporter a happier experience than encountered by the *Courier* reporter at Peterloo, whose frustrations led to his anonymous publication of his *Suppressed Narrative* (1819).[34] He imagines, too, a thorough cleansing of government corruption, an 'absolute purification of the house'.[35] Major Thomas Trafford led the sabre-wielding Yeomanry Cavalry to purge St Peter's Field of Dissidents and Dissenters.[36] Sir Thomas Pride, parliamentarian commander in the Civil War, conducted 'Pride's Purge' to rid the House of Commons of Presbyterians and Royalists so that, instead of negotiating a settlement with King Charles I, the business of the House could turn directly to regicide. Lamb imagined a kindred purge, 'a renovation' in defence of Dissenters and disenfranchised Commoners:

> Let the most determined foe to corruption, the most thorough-paced redresser of abuses, try to conceive a more absolute purification of the House than this was calculated to produce. Why, Pride's Purge was nothing to it. The whole borough-mongering system would have been got rid of, fairly exploded; with it the senseless distinctions of Party must have disappeared, faction must have vanished, corruption have expired in air.[37]

Putting aside his imagined re-enactment of the destruction of Parliament, Lamb concludes with straightforward advice on how, in 1823, to bring about needed reform:

> It is the duty of every honest Englishman to endeavour, by means more wholesome than Guido's, to ameliorate, without extinguishing, parliaments; to hold the lantern to the dark places of corruption; to apply the match to the rotten parts of the system only; and to wrap himself up, not in the muffling mantle of conspiracy, but in the warm, honest cloak of integrity and patriotic intention.[38]

'On the Pleasure of Hating' (1826) is the essay in which Hazlitt argues that 'the hooting and buffeting and maltreating that poor tattered figure of rags and straw' functions as a purgation of hostility, similar to the catharsis of pity and fear in Aristotle's account of tragedy. Now that 'Protestants and Papists' no longer 'burn one another at the stake', they must seek emotional release in venues safely buffered from the extremes of violence, such as reading Fox's *Book of Martyrs* or Scotch novels that,

> carry us back to the feuds, the heart-burnings, the havoc, the dismay, the wrongs and the revenue of a barbarous age and people – to the rooted prejudices and deadly animosities of sects and parties in politics and religion and of contending chiefs and clans in war and intrigue.[39]

Because hatred is an impulsive passion readily satisfied vicariously, one may find release in indulging the histories and fictions of enmity without adopting the convictions of either Fawkes or the Monarchical/Anglican authority. 'We feel the full force of the spirit of hatred with all of them in turn.'[40] In the essay, 'Of Persons One Would Wish to Have Seen' (1826), Hazlitt recollects attending the table-talk of the Charles Lamb circle in 1808.[41] Lamb suggested the subject of 'Wish to Have Seen', and when called upon named Guy Fawkes and offered his rationale and defence of the notorious treason. Lamb distinguished 'that poor, fluttering annual scare-crow of straw and rags' from the actual Fawkes whom he considered 'an ill used gentleman', reduced to desperation as a victim of anti-Catholic prosecution.[42] 'I would give something', Lamb declared, 'to see him sitting pale and emaciated, surrounded by his matches and his barrels of gunpowder, and expecting the moment that was to transport him to Paradise for his heroic self-devotion'.[43]

Anti-Catholicism was the stuff of Gothic novels and melodrama, where the villains were perverted and depraved priests, as in Matthew Gregory Lewis' *The Monk* (1796).[44] Anti-Catholicism among the English arose from the fear of subjugation to a foreign power and exploitation by Rome and the Catholic allegiance of France, Spain and Italy. After James II was deposed in the Glorious Revolution of 1689, William III, a Dutch Protestant, was brought to the throne. The Act of Settlement of 1701 stipulated that no Catholic could ever become an heir to the throne. The provisions of the Popery Act were matched by the restrictions imposed on non-conformists. The acts granting educational and property rights sparked the anti-Catholic Gordon Riots (1780). The Roman Catholic Relief Act (1791) allowed Catholics to enter the legal profession, excused them from the Oath of Supremacy, and permitted schools.[45] Protestant dissenters who took the oaths of supremacy and allegiance, and made the declaration against transubstantiation, were allowed freedom to worship in public provided their meeting places had been registered. Ministers, in addition, had to subscribe to thirty-six of the Thirty-Nine Articles of the Church of England. They were excused from those directly concerned with the governance of the Anglican Church. Those who qualified themselves under the act were given liberty from some penal laws, but not the exclusionary Corporation and Test Acts. The only other major political gain made by dissenters in the eighteenth century was the 1779 Dissenters' Relief Act, which freed ministers from the need to subscribe to the Thirty-Nine Articles of the Church of England as required by the Toleration Act and permitted tutors and schoolmasters to teach without needing to be licensed. The crowds at St Peter's Field may have included Catholic immigrants from Ireland and Scotland, but their numbers were more largely from the religiously and politically disenfranchised. 'At the time of Peterloo', wrote Donald Read of the religious constituency, 'nonconformists of all sorts in Manchester probably outnumbered Anglicans by about two to one', while those in positions of authority upheld the conviction that 'dissent from the Established Church implied dissent also from loyalty to the established constitution'.[46]

The industrialists, who were cutting wages without offering relief, blamed market forces generated by the aftershocks of the Napoleonic

Wars.[47] The plight of the poor was made worse by the Corn Laws of 1815, which supported the reliance on English grain, and kept prices artificially high, by imposing a tariff on foreign grain. Those most adversely affected by conditions of poverty had no political voice. The need for political reform – to vote, to hold office – was inseparable from the economic blight. Repeal of the Test and Corporation Acts was finally achieved in 1828, though in practice most dissenters had to wait until 1835. The repeal of the Penal Laws culminated in the Roman Catholic Relief Act in 1829. The 1832 Reform Act extended the parliamentary franchise to a wider constituency.

The discontent was sufficiently strong to attract an enthusiastic audience to any performance featuring a character determined to kill virtually all members of the government – the king, the House of Lords, the members of the House of Commons. Such plays were extremely popular.[48] Highly portable, thoroughly adaptable and appropriately explosive were the popular dramatisations of Guy Fawkes, especially George MacFarren's *Guy Fawkes; or, The Gunpowder Treason* (Coburg, 22 September 1822; BL Playbills 174).[49] MacFarren's final scene of the co-conspirators dying in the explosion did not necessarily impress the audience with retributive closure, but rather revealed additional barrels of gunpowder and the *karma* of a continuing causality.

At its premiere performance, *Guy Fawkes, or, The Gunpowder Plot* (Coburg, 7 October 1822; BL Playbills 174) was performed together with another of MacFarren's plays, *Edward, the Black Prince*, which had opened a couple of months earlier (Coburg, 19 August 1822; BL Playbills 174). The two plays continued to be performed together for the ensuing two weeks. The playbill cites the passage in David Hume's *The History of England*[50] describing that moment when a Catholic soldier named Guy Fawkes has been caught in the basement of Parliament, with a couple tons of gunpowder, prepared to kill virtually all members of the government – King James I, members of the House of Lords, members of the House of Commons, and King James' heir Henry – in an explosion when James addresses the opening session of Parliament.

> The subject of this piece is founded (as Hume expresses it) 'on a Fact as certain as it appears incredible. Being one of the most memorable that History has conveyed to posterity, and containing, at once, a singular

> proof both of the strength and the weakness of the human mind; its widest departure from morals, and most steady Attachment to erroneous prejudices.' – An attempt has been made to build an interesting Story upon the principal Facts and incidents developed on the Trial of the Conspirators, and the various Memoirs published on the occasion, avoiding, with becoming delicacy, the religious Fanaticism which gave rise to the Plot, and endeavouring to inculcate the most Patriotic and Loyal Principles, by exhibiting the Terrors of Conscience, the obduracy of Human Wickedness, and the Retribution of Providence, in the Punishment of the Traitors by their own diabolical means, forming the completest Dramatic Moral that Ancient or Modern History has ever furnished. (Coburg, 7 October 1822; BL 174)

Act I opens in the gardens of the Percy mansion near the House of Lords, where Robert Catesby and Thomas Percy discuss the plot and solicit the complicity of Guy Fawkes, a soldier who fought for the Spaniards in Holland. Following a scene in the courtyard of Montegle's house as he receives the mysterious warning to stay away from the Parliament, the first act closes in Tresham's lodging in Dean's Gate. Act II commences in King James' study, depicting a paternal monarch concerned with the welfare of all of his people and disturbed by an unruly faction among the Catholics. In the next scene the king prepares to address the combined assembly of Lords and Commons in the Old Parliament House, followed by a scene in the vaults where Guy Fawkes is interrupted by Montegle at the moment of firing a train to explode thirty-six barrels of gunpowder to destroy the king, the royal family and members of both houses of Parliament. The crucial scene in the play takes place in the council room at Westminster in Act III. During the interrogation of Guy Fawkes, what is revealed is not a Catholic zealot, nor a revolutionary. Fawkes emerges, rather, as a 'Saturnine Character' who appraises the richness of his experiences in terms of the audacity of his crimes. Following the scene in which Guy Fawkes is led to his execution is the final scene with the conspirators still at large gathered in Digby's House. The 'Retributive Annihilation of the Conspirators' takes place with the accidental blowing up of a remaining barrel of gunpowder.

Guy Fawkes had been celebrated since the eighteenth century more vigorously in Shrewsbury than elsewhere, and apparently without the violent conflict between propertied and labouring classes or between Anglicans and Catholics,[51] as occurred in such towns such as Lewes[52] and Guildford.[53] A crucial factor that distinguished Shrewsbury from other weaving centres in Britain was the presence of tradesmen guilds established in the fourteenth century that provided collective strength to the drapers, the fellmongers, the spinners, weavers and dyers of Shrewsbury.[54] Especially relevant were the performances at Shrewsbury of MacFarren's *Guy Fawkes; or, the Gunpowder Plot* (6 November 1829; BL Playbills 282) in the aftermath of the Catholic Emancipation, when dialogue denouncing the pretence of the Catholic plot was added to the play's examination of Guy Fawkes in the Council Room at Westminster (III, ii). Similarly, when *Guy Fawkes* was again performed in Shrewsbury (5 November 1834; BL Playbills 282) after the founding of the Grand National Consolidated Trade Unions, the theatre manager, J. Bennett, expanded the scene depicting the procession to the Palace of Whitehall (I, ii) so that the leaders of the local guilds could don their vestments and join in the march across the stage.

MacFarren's *Guy Fawkes; or, the Gunpowder Plot* was frequently staged throughout the provinces for the annual commemoration on 5 November, but performances were by no means restricted to the anniversary. It was played in Nottingham, along with *Jane Shore* (5 October 1825), and years later billed as the explosive complement to the terrifying melodrama of the man who discovers that his wife had murdered all of her previous husbands, *Pedlar's Acre; or, The Wife of Seven Husbands* (19 November 1832; BL Playbills 297). It was offered off calendar at Worcester (17 July 1826; BL Playbills 289) but performed for the Guy Fawkes Night celebrations in Shrewsbury (6 November 1829 and 5 November 1834; BL Playbills 282).

In the aftermath of passing the Great Reform Bill, the Shrewsbury performance of *Guy Fawkes, or, The Gunpowder Plot* on 5 November 1834 had even further significance. As theatre manager, J. Bennett, reminded his audience, the cellar that Fawkes tried to blow up was destroyed in a fire, reducing to ash and rubble the former Houses of Parliament. Three weeks earlier, on 16 October 1834, citizens of London witnessed the most intense inferno since the Great Fire of 1666. Small wooden tally sticks, convenient aids for the bookkeepers of the Exchequer in past centuries, were being disposed of in the two furnaces under the House of Lords. The furnaces were overloaded and the sticks burnt hotter and faster than anticipated, setting a chimney fire in the flues that ran beneath the floorboards of the Lords' chamber, up through the walls to the rooftop. The event was reported, not as a vindication or validation, but nevertheless as a belated fulfilment of Fawkes' plot.

When *Guy Fawkes* was offered at Halifax (27 February 1833; BL Playbills 279), theatre manager Manly promised 'a Tremendous Explosion'. In Stockton, *Guy Fawkes* was paired once more with *Jane Shore* (10 October 1835; BL Playbills 284). At the theatre in St Albans, which had the regular patronage of the local lodges of both the Odd Fellows and the Ancient Order of Druids, theatre manager John Saville Faucit offered double explosions for Guy Fawkes Night by billing *Guido Fawkes; or, The Powder Plot of 1605* alongside Pocock's *The Miller and his Men* (5 November 1835; BL Playbills 280). In spite of the altered title the play adhered closely to MacFarren's script, which Faucit included in his company repertory at the several theatres under his management: Deal, Greenwich, Margate, Ramsgate, St Albans and Sandwich.[55]

Edward Stirling, in *Guido Fawkes; or, The Prophetess of Ordsall Cave* (Queen's, Manchester, June 1840), offered a very different approach to the Gunpowder Plot. Stirling was acting manager of the Adelphi in 1838, and stage director in 1839, and went on to serve successively as manager of Covent Garden, Surrey, Olympic, Lyceum (English Opera House) and Drury Lane. Originally intended for a Manchester audience, *Guido Fawkes; or, The Prophetess of Ordsall Cave* appropriated the local history that the Gunpowder Plot had actually been conceived when Fawkes met Catesby in Ordsall Hall,[56] and, further, that Guy Fawkes was supposed to have escaped capture by the king's soldiers by way of an underground tunnel from Ordsall Hall to an inn at the cathedral end of Hanging Bridge. In Stirling's melodrama, this underground passage was connected to the cave known as Woden's Den at the ford across the River Irwell. The cave was the site for pagan ritual and for worship held by persecuted Catholics. Stirling's version adds to the traditional lore of Woden in the Edda a dimension of supernaturalism and a prophecy that anticipates the inevitable explosion. Stirling's Guido Fawkes proceeds with the conviction that he cannot fail. Even after he is apprehended, he knows the doom will take place as foretold.

Lamb's defence of Guy Fawkes relied on light humour and a comic exposition of consequences to defang the conspirators' intended slaughter. Perhaps the cleverest of the satirical versions was *Guy Fawkes A Gingerbread Tragedy* (Lyceum, 3 and 4 January 1821). 'Gingerbread' in the title refers to the spicy bakery ware shaped like a man, but it also means 'lavishly decorated, highly ornamented'; both meanings applied to the straw-dummy effigy carted through the streets before being set ablaze. Samuel James Arnold, owner and manager of the Lyceum, produced this piece in defiance of the order from the office of the Lord Chamberlain. Since 1809 Arnold had permission to stage opera and other musical dramas, but the licence had been granted with the condition that the Lyceum, like the Haymarket, would open only for four months in the summer. When Drury Lane burned down (24 February 1808), Arnold offered the Lyceum for performances by the Drury Lane company.

After the rebuilt Drury Lane reopened (10 October 1812), Arnold assumed that he had gained sanction to perform throughout the regular season. The London Magistrates thought otherwise. Arnold, however, contrived a series of special engagements that allowed him to open on occasions throughout the year. The conflict persisted in the season of 1820–1, when Arnold was denied the permission to open during the lucrative holidays. Thus, on the playbill for the new year, Arnold announced his conformance to the mandate:

> *Soirées Amusantes*. 'The Law allows it.' – Shakespeare. The Publick are respectfully informed that on Wednesday and Thursday, Jan. 3rd & 4th 1821, and every Evening till further notice, Their Magistrates' Servants, (not being allowed at this festive Season to '*act, represent or perform, any Interlude, Tragedy, Comedy, Opera, Play, Farce, or other Entertainments of the Stage*',) will mis-represent, as a short Christmas Revel, an *extra-Dramatick Comico Musico Burlesque Olio,* comprising a variety of fantastical Entertainments, made up of *new Fancies and old Pastimes.* (Lyceum, 3–4 January 1821; BL Playbills 360–2)

Because terms of the closing specifically stipulated that actors must not appear on the stage to '*represent or perform*', Arnold decided that his 'Company of the first-rate Talent' would 'mis-represent', appearing in boxes as talking heads or behind screens as shadows:

> The Proprietor has collected a Company of the first-rate Talent, consisting of a considerable number of *Heads* of the Profession (that have *cut* their Bodies to come within the Licence) – A Troop of Spirits, who have

> been expressly called from '*the vasty deep*' for this occasion, will '*come like shadows so depart*' – and a variety of breathing Puppets not '*as large as life*.' (Lyceum, 3–4 January 1821; BL Playbills 360–2)

To bring England's arch-anarchist onto the stage in defiance of legal closure was a bold stroke, but Arnold was confident that the holiday playfulness would win sufficient audience approval to enable him to escape prosecution. The 'breathing Puppets not "*as large as life*"' were the children who pulled the cart with the effigy across the stage. Arnold's playbill further announced that this *Gingerbread Tragedy* was 'supposed to have been performed in the time of Shakespeare', a subtle reminder that the first performance of Macbeth's regicide must have taken place at approximately the same time as the trial and execution of those involved in the Gunpowder Plot. The villain of the piece is Sir Everard Digby, 'a Gentleman Pensioner', who counts on his wealth to seduce Joan Tothill, 'a wise child, in love with Guy'. Sir Godfrey Tothill, 'Knight and Gingerbread Baker', would much rather see his daughter debauched by Sir Everard than have her elope with Guy Fawkes, the 'mysterious Hero' with incendiary inclinations. Sir Godfrey's harsh response to his daughter's defiance prompts her ironic twist of Ophelia's line, 'They say the owl was a baker's daughter. Lord, we know what we are, but know not what we may be' (*Hamlet* IV, v, 35–7).

Performed frequently in the theatres of the provinces as well as in the theatres of London, the plays on Guy Fawkes had far more numerous performances in domestic theatre, uncontrolled by the office of the Lord Chamberlain and the Examiner of Plays. Webb, Hodgson and Skelts – three of the major publishers of toy theatres – were circulating hundreds of printings of the plays and the cut-out characters.[57] How these plays were performed varied, no doubt, with household politics, but the fate of Guy Fawkes was no doubt subjected to a course and conclusion more varied than had been allowed by history, tradition and the 'legitimate' theatre. Children of the 1820s had access to a schooling in protest and rebellion that had not belonged to previous generations.

Destroying the king and both houses of Parliament was a plot that seemed less extreme and perhaps more appropriate after the senseless massacre at Peterloo. Certainly it seemed both rational and just to the conspirators arrested at Cato Street six months later (23 February1820), in the midst of their scheme to murder all the British cabinet ministers and Prime Minister Lord Liverpool. Of the thirteen arrested, five conspirators were executed and five others were transported to Australia.[58] The Cato Street Conspiracy may not have attracted many supporters, but more than a few would not have found the idea repugnant. There were high hopes during the 1820s that reforms sought at St Peter's Field were in fact being negotiated. When the House of Lords repeatedly voted against reform, hostilities broke out once more. In Exeter on 5 November 1831 the citizens set fire to an effigy, not of Guy Fawkes, but of the new Bishop of Exeter, Henry Phillpotts, a High Church Anglican and High Tory who opposed parliamentary reform. Attempts by the authorities to suppress the celebrations resulted in violent protests.[59] The violent attack of the Yeomanry Calvary could scatter the demonstration in 1819. Government spies could betray the schemes of Cato Street in 1820. With the second effort to pass the Reform Bill in 1831, the protestors gained an advantage over the authorities. In Derby, local citizens raided the city jail to free falsely charged prisoners. In Nottingham, rioters set fire to the castle of the Duke of Newcastle. In Bristol, rioters kept the city in tumult for three days. When it seemed that the Reform Bill would be defeated a third time in the House of Lords, public violence again ensued. Barrels of gunpowder might well have been brought to Parliament, had not a negative vote been forestalled by efforts from King William IV and Prime Minister Charles Grey. The Bill passed and received the Royal Assent on 7 June 1832.

Notes

1. David Worrall, *Theatric Revolution: Drama, Censorship and Romantic Period Subcultures, 1773–1832* (Oxford: Oxford University Press, 2006), pp. 136–40; L. W. Conolly, *The Censorship of English Drama 1737–1824* (San Marino: Henry E. Huntington, 1976), pp. 127–8; Malcolm Chase, '"Love, bitter, wrong, sad pity, and lust of power"', in *Politics, Performance and Popular Culture: Theatre and Society in Nineteenth-Century Britain*, ed. Peter Yeandle, Katherine Newey and Jeffrey Richards (Manchester: Manchester University Press, 2016), pp. 199–215, 211.

2. George MacFarren, *Guy Fawkes: or, The Gunpowder Treason: an historical melo-drama in three acts, performed at the Royal Coburg Theatre* (London: Jackson and MacFarren, 1822).
3. Edward Stirling, *Guido Fawkes; or, The Prophetess of Ordsall Cave* (London: J. Duncombe, 1840).
4. Samuel Hibbert, *History of the Foundations in Manchester of Christ's College, Chetham's Hospital, and the Free Grammar School*, 4 vols (Manchester: T. Agnew and J. Zanetti, 1828–48), vol. 2, pp. 11–12.
5. *Guy Fawkes; or The Fifth of November a Prelude in One Act* (Haymarket, 5 November 1793). Review: *The Times of London* (6 November 1793), p. 2, col. C.
6. Frederick Burwick, *British Drama of the Industrial Revolution* (Cambridge: Cambridge University Press, 2015), pp. 249–58.
7. *The Examiner*, 22 March 1812, p. 179.
8. Nicolas Roe, *Fiery Heart: The First Life of Leigh Hunt* (London: Pimlico, 2005).
9. William Hazlitt, 'Guy Faux', *The Examiner*, 11, 18 and 25 November 1821. *The Collected Works of William Hazlitt*, ed. A. R. Waller and Arnold Glover (London: J. M. Dent and Sons, 1904), vol. 11, pp. 317–22.
10. William Hazlitt, 'On the Pleasure of Hating', *The Collected Works of William Hazlitt*, ed. A. R. Waller and Arnold Glover (London: J. M. Dent and Sons, 1903), vol. 7, p. 128.
11. Hazlitt, 'Guy Faux', p. 317.
12. Ibid. pp. 317–18.
13. Ibid. pp. 318–19.
14. Ibid. p. 319.
15. Ibid.
16. Ibid. p. 318.
17. Ibid. p. 320.
18. Ibid.
19. Ibid.
20. Edward Moore, *The Gamester: A Tragedy*, As it is acted at the Theatre-Royal in Drury-Lane [1753], 5th edn (London: Printed for T. Davies, in Russel-Street, Covent Garden, 1771); Susanna Centlivre. *The Gamester; a comedy: as it is acted at the Theatre-Royal* (London: Printed for T. Lowndes, W. Bathoe and R. Horsfield, 1767); *Richard Turpin, the Highwayman* (Royal Amphitheatre, 8 November 1819); John Baldwin Buckstone, *Jack Sheppard* (Adelphi, 28 October 1839).
21. Hazlitt, 'Guy Faux', p. 326.
22. Ibid. p. 320.

23. Charles Lamb, 'Guy Faux', *London Magazine* [1823], in *The Complete Works and Letters of Charles Lamb* (New York: The Modern Library, 1935), pp. 340–5.
24. Ibid. p. 345.
25. Ibid. p. 346.
26. Ibid. p. 348.
27. Ibid.
28. Ibid. p. 349.
29. Ibid.
30. Ibid.
31. Ibid.
32. Ibid.
33. Ibid. p. 350.
34. *The Suppressed narrative of the Courier reporter: who, through the faithful and affecting manner in which he described the tragical events of the 16th of August, lost the confidence of his employers* (London: Printed for Limbird, 1819).
35. Lamb, 'Guy Faux', p. 350.
36. John Wade, *Manchester massacre!! An authentic narrative of the magisterial and yeomanry massacre at Manchester: with remarks on the illegal conduct of the magistrates in suppressing the meeting, and their proceedings towards Mr. Hunt: also anecdotes of the yeomanry cavalry and police* (London: J. Fairburn, 1820).
37. Lamb, 'Guy Faux', p. 350.
38. Ibid.
39. Hazlitt, 'On the Pleasure of Hating', p. 129.
40. Ibid.
41. William Hazlitt, 'Of Persons One Would Wish to Have Seen', *New Monthly Magazine* [January 1826], in *Hazlitt: Selected Essays*, ed. George Sampson (Cambridge: Cambridge University Press, 1958), pp. 46–59.
42. Ibid. p. 59.
43. Ibid.
44. Diane Long Hoeveler, *The Gothic Ideology: Religious Hysteria and Anti-Catholicism in British Popular Fiction, 1780–1880* (Cardiff: University of Wales Press, 2014).
45. J. R. H. Moorman, *A History of the Church in England* (London: A. & C. Black, 1973), pp. 312–13.
46. Donald Read, *Peterloo: The 'Massacre' and its Background* (Manchester: Manchester University Press, 1958), pp. 25–6.
47. Ian Hernon, *Riot! Civil Insurrection from Peterloo to the Present Day* (London: Pluto Press, 2006), p. 22.

48. See the chapter titled 'Explosions, Conflagrations, and Other Happy Endings' in Frederick Burwick, *British Drama of the Industrial Revolution* (Cambridge: Cambridge University Press, 2015), pp. 230–54.
49. British Library Mic. C 13137. All subsequent references to the volumes of Playbills in the British Library will be cited parenthetically with the theatre, performance dated, volume number.
50. David Hume, *The History of England, with a continuation from revolution in 1688 to the death of George II, by Tobias Smollet*, 2 vols (London: J. S. Virtue, 1800), vol. 1, pp. 263–5.
51. Bernard Ward, *The Sequel to the Catholic Emancipation*, 2 vols (London: Longmans, Green and Co., 1915), vol. 2, pp. 130–45.
52. David Cressy, 'The Fifth of November Remembered', in *Myths of the English*, ed. Roy Porter (Cambridge: Polity Press, 1992), pp. 70–86; J. A. Sharpe, *Remember, Remember: A Cultural History of Guy Fawkes Day* (Cambridge, MA: Harvard University Press, 2005), pp. 77–100, 110–15.
53. George Charles Williamson, *Guildford in The Olden Time, side-lights on the history of a quaint old town* (London: G. Bell; Guildford: Woodbridge Press, 1904).
54. W. G. Rimmer, 'Castle Foregate Flax Mill, Shrewsbury', *Transactions of Shropshire Archaeological Society*, 56 (1957–60), pp. 49–62.
55. Allardyce Nicoll, *History of English Drama 1660–1900*, vol. 4, 2nd edn (Cambridge: Cambridge University Press, 1960), pp. 239–44.
56. William Harrison Ainsworth, *Guy Fawkes* [1840], 3 vols (London: Richard Bentley, 1841).
57. [Toy theatre:] *Guy Fawkes; or, The Gunpowder Treason. A Drama, In three Acts* (London: Hodgson's Juvenile Drama, 1822); *Guy Fawkes, Hodgson's Theatrical Characters* (London: Hodgson, 1822–4); *Guy Fawkes, or, The gunpowder plot: an historical drama in three acts, based on original by McFarren, George, written expressly for, and adapted only to Webb's characters and scenes in the same* (London: Printed and published by W. Webb, 1822); Skelt, M., *Harlequin and Guy Fawkes; Or, The 5th of November: a comic pantomime, written expressly for, and adapted only to Skelt's characters and scenes in the same* (London: Printed and published by M. and M. Skelt, 1830).
58. John Stanhope, *The Cato Street Conspiracy* (London: J. Cape, 1962). See also John Gardner, *Poetry and Popular Protest: Peterloo, Cato Street and the Queen Caroline Controversy* (Hampshire: Palgrave Macmillan, 2011).
59. Sharpe, *Remember, Remember*, pp. 157–9.

Chapter 5

Responses to Peterloo in Scotland, 1819–1822

Gerard Carruthers

No doubt replicated elsewhere in the British Isles, the response to 'Peterloo' in Scotland could be a contrasting one. In Paisley in the West of Scotland, an estimated 14,000–18,000 people attended a well-planned protest meeting under a month later, gathering on Saturday, 11 September.[1] They had been 'summoned by a placard with a mourning border' and arrived to a band from the nearby district of Neilston playing Robert Burns' 'Scots Wha Hae'.[2] Burns' composition, ostensibly about the medieval wars of independence with England, was in reality a slight allegory on the contemporary 'tyranny' that had actually concerned its author when composing it in 1793, and increasingly as the nineteenth century went on the song became anthemic for reform-minded groups including the Chartists.[3] Contingents gathered in Paisley from Dalry, Glasgow, Kilbarchan, Kilmarnock and elsewhere in the west, marching into town behind banners and flags, coming especially from those places where weavers and other mechanics made up a large part of the populace. During the course of 11 September, resolutions were formed condemning the Manchester magistrates along with the biased reporting of the events of 16 August in the *Glasgow Chronicle*, and praising the radical leaders who had been in attendance at St Peter's Field. A collection was taken up 'for the relief of the relatives of the Manchester sufferers', and it was announced that a Mr Laing was offering to produce a 'Radical reform newspaper . . . in the cause of universal suffrage'.[4] In the course of the rest of the day, scuffles broke out between a sizeable Glasgow contingent of protestors and special constables in the High Street of Paisley. Soon after ten o'clock in the evening, the Riot Act was read, the cavalry called in and, with their efforts, the main streets were eventually cleared by three o'clock in the morning. However, Paisley experienced another six days of tense agitation and for many months after 11 September the authorities in the large Renfrewshire town, in Glasgow and elsewhere were extremely nervous.[5]

Exactly one week earlier, in a letter of 4 September 1819, Walter Scott (1771–1832) wrote to his eldest son, Walter, serving as a lieutenant in Ireland with the 18th Hussars:

> The Manchester Yeomen behaved very well upsetting the most immense croud ever was seen and notwithstanding the lies in the papers without any unnecessary violence. Mr Hunt pretends to have had several blows on his head with sabres but has no wound to show for it. I am disposed to wish he had got such a one as once on a day I could have treated him to. I am apt to think his politic pate would have broached no more sedition.[6]

Eight days later Scott's supposed identification of fake news shifted uncomfortably as he upbraided his friend and publisher James Ballantyne (1772–1833) for having the temerity to criticise the disorganised actions of the Manchester magistrates at Peterloo and the unleashing of an overzealous yeomanry. Ballantyne's comments had appeared in the paper he edited, *The Edinburgh Weekly Journal* of 24 August, and on eventually turning his mind to these, Scott wrote to Ballantyne that for an editor:

> it may be often highly adviseable that he should supress an opinion formd even on good grounds because the publishing it may lead to evil consequences. It is an obvious thing that 50,000 men are not a deliberative body – they cannot be assembled for any proper or useful purpose and they are in the case in hand avowedly assembled for the overthrow of the constitution.[7]

In the same letter, a huffy Scott talked of withdrawing his own interest (he owned shares) in *The Edinburgh Weekly Journal* since as a Crown-sworn magistrate himself, 'I should have acted and will in the same circumstances act upon the peril of life & fortune & fame precisely like those in Manchester'.[8] Instead, however, he published three letters in the paper, anonymously, across December 1819 and January 1820, castigating the evils of radical unrest. Towards the end of 1819, Scott also offered to the government his raising of a corps of volunteers 'to be calld the Loyal Foresters to act any where South of [the] Forth'.[9]

As James Chandler has pointed out, there is a step-change in Scott's historical fiction in *Ivanhoe* (1819) as it is his 'first novel not to take Scottish history for its subject matter', and this, it can be suggested, was because Scott's mind had been recently and disturbingly fixed south of the border, specifically on Peterloo.[10] Stephen Basdeo, an expert on Robin Hood has eloquently argued in his blog that Scott's depiction of the famous outlaw in the novel as a commoner or yeoman was because the yeomanry at Peterloo had received such bad press and that the Scottish novelist was looking to redress the balance.[11] Without suggesting that Peterloo is the sole *raison d'être* for the novel, it can be advanced that Scott's tale of 'merry England' in *Ivanhoe* has at the core of its mythic fabric a valorisation of the yeomen of England, loyal to the true king (the deposed Richard the Lionheart) as it draws on the 'good yeomen' of Agincourt in Shakespeare's *King Henry V* (a play more than once referenced in the novel[12]), and – in one chapter-epigraph (allegedly from an 'old play', often code for Scott making up his own inter-texts) – we find this declaratory verse:

> Trust me each state must have its policies:
> Kingdoms have edicts, cities have their charters;
> Even the wild outlaw, in his forest-walk,
> Keeps yet some touch of civil discipline.[13]

Something recently for Scott – Peterloo and the radical agitation following it in places like Paisley – was beyond the 'wild outlaw' (the 'Loyal Foresters', in the case of Robin Hood and his men). Out of the ethnic strife and confusion in *Ivanhoe*, the contest of Saxon and Norman, a strong England was in time formed, but the strain of radicalism in the nineteenth century clearly was not seen by Scott as in any way moving through its disruptive nature towards a better Britain. And it is implicitly clear in *Ivanhoe* that it is the new class-consciousness among the reform-minded that he does not like. This becomes particularly apparent in Scott's 1830 introduction to

Ivanhoe (1830 seeing the death of George IV and the prospect of the Reform Act of 1832 opening up), where he heaps up further references to good-natured stories of king and commoner, alongside his version of Robin Hood, including King Edward and the Shepherd, and the medieval Scottish metrical romance, *Rauf Coilzear*; Scott writes in the introduction to the 1830 iteration of the novel, 'In merry England there is no end of popular ballads on this theme . . . the King and the Tanner of Tamworth, the King and the Miller of Mansfield, and others on the same topic.'[14] King and commoner (especially king and mechanic), then, are historically united in society, united in the one nation rather than riven by class division. This harking back to a somehow more organic (though actually no less violent) past, with supposed national unity slowly but surely emerging in Scott's novel, as Graham McMaster has argued, shows its author in 1819 experiencing, actually, a crisis in his thinking about the British people that had been precipitated by Peterloo.[15]

We might return once more to Paisley on 11 September 1819 and note amidst the heightening violence as the day progressed that William Motherwell (1797–1835) was knocked unconscious.[16] Motherwell was sheriff clerk depute in the town and a Tory, who was to become an outspoken opponent of all attempts at constitutional reform, including Catholic Emancipation. He was also an accomplished literary scholar who would go on to produce an edition of Burns and he had already begun a project that would occupy him throughout the rest of his life, the active encouragement of the Burns 'movement' (which had started with his Secretary-ship of Paisley Burns Club in 1817). Later, in the 1830s, as a logical extension of his cultural and political interest, Motherwell would go on to promote the growth of the Orange Order in Scotland, and so we might note his long-concerted conservative attempt to control the hoi polloi. In both his Burns movement and Orange endeavours, Motherwell was intent on harnessing the efforts of the working man away from radicalism and towards loyalism: in the arena of Burns, emphasising much more the rural, safely patriotic aspects of the Bard's works and not so much the poet's approbatory views on the French Revolution. We might also attend to a related aspect of Motherwell's cultural work that was part of a tradition going back to the 1790s, where the Scots language, couthy, signalling social stability and common sense, was appropriated at least as much by the politically reactionary as by the reform-minded. In 1832, Motherwell produced his *Memoirs of a Paisley Bailie*, a fictional autobiography after the style of John Galt with a Scots-speaking narrator. Bailie Pirnie finds himself at a reform meeting in Kilsyth, one of the districts replete with weavers that, like Paisley, was rightly seen as a hotbed of potential insurrection in 1819–20. Pirnie becomes the object of some rough handling, and this follows on from the reformers tediously, egotistically jockeying among themselves for personal advancement:

> Weel, the meeting was nae like to skail, and me being anxious to get out to the cauler air, was making my way to the door, when the cry got up — 'He's a Tory — he's a bourough-mongering spy', and I felt my coat tails pookit, and a gude wheen of the lovers of freedom dunching me with their elbucks in the ribs sae devilitsch hard that my corruption began to rise; but ye may guess what kind of a tirravee I was in, when a lump of a chield came ahint me, and with ae dunkle on the crown of my split-new thirty-shilling hat, drave it clean ower my face, and shaved the skin aff my unoffending nose at the same time. Seeing my dilemma and confloption, and that the bloody rabeatours were set upon insulting and abusing me, up springs my young friend on the table, kicking ower ane of the twa penny candles, which brought its lowe richt into the peery e'ed secretary, and burned half a thin whisker that the creature had on its chafts, and then putting himsell in a grand attitude like a play-actor, to my utter astonishment roared out: 'Mr President and gentlemen, I am grieved and mortified at the conduct of my countrymen this evening'.[17]

Pirnie is defended from the bullying reformers by a young man he has met by chance, but the would-be assailants are stayed only briefly as they proceed to put our Tory protagonist in a chair and parade him home (whether genuinely to make amends or to further the mockery it is not clear). Out in the open, however, the procession is charged by a herd of stots (castrated male cattle). Pirnie records the response of one of his 'bodyguard', who urges, 'stand fast in the cause of freedom, they're no bills, only stots'.[18] However, the panic continues as the cattle continue their attack, roaring all the while, so that, as Pirnie recounts, 'my body bearers flung me, chair, barrow and all down, and magnanimously, like reasoning animals, betook themsells to flight', while one beast goes on to demolish the reformers' flag.[19] The heavy irony, including the wordplay on 'bulls' / [reform] 'bills', and the herding, bovine nature of the Kilsyth men reduced to panicked flight by real cattle requires little unpacking. However, it might be suggested that we see here Motherwell, long-traumatised by his own experience following the Paisley Peterloo meeting, practising a kind of revenge on his real-life attackers. Like others of his persuasion, the Mob was the mob and it deserved little sympathy following Peterloo and Paisley.

Motherwell was, unsurprisingly, sympathetic to the broadly Tory politics of the 1817-founded *Edinburgh Monthly Magazine*, later *Blackwood's Edinburgh Magazine* and colloquially in time known more simply as the 'Maga'. In 1828 he even founded a publication modelled in political interest on the 'Maga', the *Paisley Magazine*, so that the radical print bounty promised on 11 September for Paisley (Mr Laing's putative newspaper) was, some years later, precisely reversed with a periodical more reactionary than any other in Scotland. Writers more directly associated with the Tory-minded *Blackwood's* and the publisher William Blackwood, more generally, such as John Galt (1779–1839), usually deployed greater nuance than Motherwell about the radical activity of the early nineteenth century and of earlier periods.[20] Galt's fiction *The Gathering of the West* appeared in *Blackwood's Magazine* for September 1822. It was received by fellow Blackwoodians such as John Gibson Lockhart as a set of largely pleasant character and place sketches and its most recent editor – Bradford Allen Booth – in 1939 – sees it as a site of 'tranquility',

> offer[ing] quiet charm and a haven for jaded emotions . . . Here is a society that is simple in its habits, persistent in its ideals, warm-hearted in its loyalties; yet with all the frailties and petty foibles which mankind is heir to.[21]

Such judgements, contemporary and over a century later, remarkably miss the point that Galt's is a text that registers deeply the trauma of the events of 1819–20, especially those which were somewhat shaped in the light of Peterloo: the Scottish 'Radical War' of 1820, the Cato Street Conspiracy and the Queen Caroline Affair. *The Gathering of the West* centres on the visit of King George IV to Edinburgh in 1822, the event Walter Scott stage-managed. In the most infamous sublimation of insurrection or rebellion inherent in the Edinburgh visit, Walter Scott was instrumental in the king being garbed in Royal Stuart tartan, or as a kind of Jacobite monarch, and this precise historic Scottish context was complemented by a more contemporary *raison d'être*, a public royal charm offensive designed to play a part in quelling recent reformist sensibilities.[22]

Unlike Scott's 'pageantry' of the royal visit, the human ceremony essayed by Galt in *The Gathering of the West* is more chaotic, has more to do with the ordinary folk clamouring to be at Edinburgh for the event, and is explicitly satirical. Galt knowingly collaborates with the sublimation or displacement of insurrection, reference to which is never far from the surface, including in the title of his text, the western counties of Scotland recently having been the epicentre of so much post-Peterloo agitation. Sincere Presbyterian too, born and growing up in the West of Scotland (in Irvine and Greenock), Galt was as acute historically as Walter Scott, and the title of his fiction also recognises Scotland's covenanting heritage, centred particularly in Ayrshire and Renfrewshire with its disruptive, revolutionary potential in matters of both state and church. In *The Gathering of the West*, we see the Greenock folk preparing for their jaunt to the Scottish capital (in Greenock on 8 April 1820, the Port Glasgow volunteers had killed eight people and injured another ten, at least, who were protesting about the incarceration of five radical prisoners in the town gaol). Likewise, we also see the weavers of Paisley and the burghers of Glasgow, among others, and so the text is studded with the sites of recent political unrest that had led to the pressure for the Scottish royal visit as a means of displaying executive accessibility and responsibility. Galt slyly but suitably intrudes the theme of governing the urban spaces in a discussion of Greenock's inadequate roads and pavements, where a 'learned clerk' exhorts the Bailies of the town to remember:

> The Roman Consuls and Athenian Archons, and to recall to mind how Tarquinuius Priscus constructed the cloacae of the Eternal City, how Provost Pericles built the Parthenon, and with what dignity Epaminondas performed his duty as a bailie, even with respect to the common sewers and dunghills of Thebes.[23]

Lucius Tarquinius Priscus, or Tarquin the Elder, was the fifth king of Rome from 616 to 579 BCE. He reigned amid times, directly before and after him especially, when hereditary monarchy was not practised, and he massively expanded the Roman Senate bringing in senators from beyond the elite families. He also constructed an effective sewerage system for Rome ('the cloacae') and was adept as a military general in leading his men in street-fighting combat. 'Provost Pericles' bestows a nicely jarring epithet on the great orator and general, who was too, however, a practical statesman. Epaminondas led the successful Theban fight for freedom against their Spartan overlords. Galt's clerk, then, exhorts the great men of the present to be mindful of basic, material civic duties including their duties to the ordinary people. At the same time, the overly busy frame of reference to these classical figures references ideas of unstable kingship, oratory and urban insurrection among the anxieties of the present. Galt's clerk's rather chaotic heap of classical detail mirrors the whirling energy of the people gathering to see the king, which also reflects the urban chaos recently surrounding reform. There is much happening between the king and the gutter and it is far from clear if anyone is managing this particularly well: this would seem to be Galt's point. We might also note Galt's usage of history, which is so different from Scott's in *Ivanhoe*, so that similarity with the past (of the classical but nonetheless eventful, often unsettled ancient stories of Greece and Rome) rather than radical break with it is brought to the fore.

In the course of *The Gathering of the West*, Galt turns explicitly to the radicalism of 1819–20 and to an incident in Paisley in particular:

> Among other extraordinary effects of the radical distemper which lately raged in the West, was a solemn resolution, on the part of a patriotic band of weavers' wives, to abjure tea and all other exciseable articles; in conformity to which, and actuated by the fine frenzy of the time, they seized their teapots, and marching with them in procession to the bridge, sacrificed them to the Goddess of Reform, by dashing them, with uplifted arms and an intrepid energy, over into the river,— and afterwards they ratified their solemn vows with copious libations of smuggled whisky.[24]

Galt's narrator adduces this story as evidence of 'what Cobbett calls a thinking people', and the irony is left somewhat indecisive.[25] Are we to laugh at the slightly ludicrous smashing of teapots (with its echo of the seismic American Revolution) and the demotic alcohol imbibing, or are we to see in these crude events, indeed, quotidian philosophy (the Goddess of Reform, incidentally, no more laughable than the idealised Gods of Greece and Rome)? Galt leaves these questions decidedly open for the readers of the 'Maga'.

Throughout *The Gathering of the West* there is the collision of political philosophy and the common, provincial realities of the people. The Paisley weavers discuss the king's visit to Edinburgh and how it might open up other possibilities. Could the monarch even on his journey to Scotland 'think o' coming to Paisley, it would be a glorious job for trade', opines one practically-minded weaver.[26] This in response to another's remarks about the metropolitan conceit hampering the monarch, which he is taken to be aware of so that it,

> looks as he had himself some thought o' flitting; and I dinna wonder at it, for the Lononers hae been made sae het and fou by the lang residing o' the Court amang them that they hae forgotten themselves, and acted as if the Crown was na a moveable'.[27]

Again, Galt has set up something nicely poised: the possibility of compact between king and discontented people, if the sovereign informs and educates himself about the condition of the country and also the idea of blasé Londoners for whom (rather than the weavers) the Crown has lost its mystique. As sovereignty is over Scotland as well as England (and since it was only 1603 when the Scottish Stuarts went south), there is no reason why the court should not relocate to the northern nation. As ever with Galt, there is a splendid mixture of the seeming ludicrous with the historically accurate, and here in the mouths of the common folk, who are, indeed, a 'thinking people'. Another of the weaver-debaters concludes, however, that with Paisley's recent radicalism the king would be too scared to come near; and yet another, Peter Gauze, is under-awed by the monarch, seeing a trip to Edinburgh for his visit as justifiable even though (as Gordon Millar has summed up Gauze's view) 'the King is only a magistrate and deserves respect because of the position he holds in the community of which they are all members'.[28] *The Gathering of the West* has a thoroughly unsettled texture, seen in the passages just cited and throughout. The political condition of Britain is uncertain, unstable and the thoughts of reformers and radicals are as alive as the reactionary powers that have recently checked their political agitation. In Edinburgh itself, in contrast to the cogent if not entirely convincing Walter Scott theatre of the king's visit, Galt's text sees events misfire. The king is to attend worship at St Giles Cathedral and one Mrs Goroghan, desperate for proximity to her sovereign, manages with the help of Mr Snodgrass the minister to have herself located by the church door with the collectors of offerings. However, immediately prior to the king's entrance, overzealous security has the area cleared so that,

> not only was the lady cruelly prevented from seeing his Majesty, and his Majesty disappointed of placing with his own hands in the plate his mite to the poor, according to the simple and affecting usage of the Presbyterian church; but our friends Wilkie and Allan were frustrated of their design to paint the King humbly depositing his offering.[29]

The artists, David Wilkie and David Allan, great painters of the Romantic historical age of Scotland, are not deployed. Instead we have Scott's garishly-garbed king as the presiding record of the royal visit of 1822. The next evening Mrs Goroghan feels happily sure her monarch has looked at her at a ball, and the day following again she like most of the West Country folk departs contentedly (for the moment) for home. The text ends with the idea that the Edinburgh people have been sometimes rather mocking of the visit, but:

> notwithstanding all the jokes and jeers of the modern Athenians, the Provost and Magnates of that Royal City continue in as happy a state of good-humour with themselves, as all gentlemen of loyal principles, social manners and liberal minds, ever deserved to be.
>
> GOD SAVE THE KING![30]

Galt, our author of conservative bent, is far from blind that dissatisfaction and unsolved problems lurk not far below the surface of British society. The metropolis, whether Edinburgh or London, ought rightly to be more aware of the potential for disruption coming from the provinces. The 'tranquillity' of Galt's text, identified by Bradford Allen Booth, is – most decidedly – an illusion.

Between Peterloo and the king's visit to the Scottish capital in August of 1822, several other establishment-upsetting events occurred: the thwarted Cato Street Conspiracy, the misfiring 'Radical War' in the West of Scotland, and the return of Queen Caroline of Brunswick to

England for her husband's coronation and the subsequent legal attempts by King George IV and his advisors to discredit her. The Cato Street conspirators, intent on murdering the Prime Minister, Lord Liverpool, and the rest of the Cabinet undoubtedly had within their portfolio of grievances, Peterloo, and especially the 'Six Acts' banning reform meetings, which were passed as a consequence of events in Manchester. Walter Scott, as he put it in a letter of 21 April 1820, 'heard the last day of that bloody dog Thistlewood's trial', though later, elsewhere and in private he annotated a rather one-sided book on the conspiracy, which claimed that Cato Street leader Arthur Thistlewood's 'countenance [bore] an additional degree of malignancy', with the comment, 'I do not think he was ill-looked: He was worried and care-worn [with the] look of a decayed gentleman.'[31] As extremely dramatic as the Cato Street episode in Scotland, and equally misfiring, was the series of uprisings in April 1820 in Glasgow, led by Andrew Hardie (d. 1820), in Condorrat, marshalled by weaver John Baird (1790–1820), and in Strathaven, commanded by yet another weaver James Wilson (1760–1820). Indeed, as Gordon Pentland has written, 'There is a compelling case for seeing the radical activity in Scotland during this period in the context of the failed Cato Street conspiracy of February 1820 and of violent activity in parts of northern England.'[32] Pentland suggests that 'Scottish radicals were certainly in correspondence with their counterparts in Lancashire and elsewhere, though such evidence falls short of proving the existence of a co-ordinated plan of insurrection'.[33] On 1 April a 'provisional government' had been declared by radicals at Glasgow, and a few days later at the 'Battle of Bonnymuir', near Bonnybridge, a group led by Baird and Hardie were intercepted by the cavalry as they sought to seize armaments from the Carron Iron Works near Falkirk. Refusing to surrender, a skirmish ensued with the arrest of some eighteen radicals. Action on the same day by Wilson's contingent petered out and his band dispersed, though the leader was arrested shortly afterwards in his home and joined Baird and Hardie in being sentenced to death. A final episode in April, already alluded to above, involved the death of people coming to the aid of arrested radicals in Greenock at the hands of the Port Glasgow Volunteers. The three leaders, Baird, Hardie and Wilson, never led a total force of more than 150 men, and did little, particularly, to frighten the authorities; writing cheerfully to his son in Ireland again on 12 June 1820, magistrate Walter Scott says:

> Every thing here is quiet. The radicals are no [more] heard of than if they never existed. But next week the Commission of Oyer and Terminer as it is calld a temporary court erected for the trial of the crime of High Treasons begins its sittings. They are to commence with the trial of the Bonnymuir warriors at Stirling some two or three will assuredly swing & the rest be sent off to Botany Bay. They are terribly frightened.[34]

In radical memory the 1820 'Radical War' led by Baird et al. was far from forgotten, with a series of publically subscribed monuments at Strathaven (erected 1846), Sighthill, the '1820 Martyrs' Monument' in Glasgow (1847), Paisley (1867), and Bonnybridge itself (2007). In recent years, a particularly (Scottish) nationalist and republican interpretation has been placed on the rising of 1820, which Gordon Pentland sees as a marked phenomenon 'only after 1945' and related largely to the rise of modern Scottish nationalism.[35] It is interesting to note that an excellent play on 'Peterloo', *Thistlewood* was authored by the Scottish playwright, Stewart Conn (b. 1936), performed in Edinburgh, at the Traverse Theatre in February 1975, and broadcast in revised form on the radio from the Manchester studios of the BBC in 1976. Conn's play assumes a common British history emanating from Manchester and London and has no particular Scottish slant.[36] Shortly afterwards, in 1978, the contemporary political novelist James Kelman (b. 1946) wrote his equally fine play, *Hardie and Baird* (1978) for BBC Radio Scotland so as to present in his own words, 'an episode of suppressed radical history in Scotland' dealing with the Radical War of 1820.[37] This was also produced at the Traverse in Edinburgh, although not until 1990. Kelman's play does a compelling job of disinterring the sacrifice of Hardie and Baird, through imagining their last excruciating days in gaol. It is related to – but does not necessarily or at least entirely accord with – the more recent, 'after 1945' nationalist/republican iteration of the radicals' uprisings of 1820. There is an implicit or even explicit claim in Scottish republican nationalist historiography that the Radical War of 1820 is inconveniently *nationalist*, and this is why it has been partially forgotten or, indeed, never really remembered in Anglo-centric accounts of the 'period of Peterloo'. However, as Catriona Macdonald has noted, the cause of Queen Caroline in Scotland 1820, 'attracted far greater support than the fabled Radical War of 1820 and encompassed a far wider geographical area than the depressed west-central belt'.[38] As

Macdonald shows, reformers in Scotland as in England opened a new constitutional front and indeed made some effective moral capital from the ostracised and poorly-treated queen, whose behaviour (presented in forbearing light) could be seen to counterpoint the long-standing immorality of George IV. Walter Scott, indeed, was more worried by the Caroline affair than by the radical war; he writes in July 1820: 'The Queen is making an awful bustle . . . [S]he has the whole mob for her partisans'.[39]

The Queen Caroline Affair, the Radical War and Cato Street were certainly related to one another and to Peterloo in Scotland. However, the main story so far as Scottish reformers in the period were concerned was Peterloo itself. We see compelling proof for this perspective in a remarkable, published document that records a public meeting in Paisley, *Report of the meeting, held at Paisley in the Saracen's Head on 31st October 1822, in celebration of Mr Hunt's release from Ilchester Bastile* [*sic*].[40] The preamble to the pamphlet tells us that 'a respectable, and harmonious meeting' on this evening took place to celebrate Henry Hunt's release that month from his Somerset prison. More than 200 attended, and such was the lack of room that 'many well-wishers had to retire'.[41] From the start, then, Hunt's supporters are intent on emphasising and publicising their orderly behaviour, aware of the government's principal moral tool against them, censuring the mob. Indeed unlike the early hours events in Paisley of 11 September 1820, the Saracen's Head meeting ended at two o'clock in the morning, with 'each congratulating one another, that so much true patriotism had been manifested'.[42] Speeches began the evening with James Fleming in the chair, remarking that 'Mr Hunt, like the ancients of old . . . had come through great tribulation, and had suffered much in the good cause of the reformers'.[43] Fleming elaborates that 'a system' had attempted to quash Hunt, one which,

> had introduced a fallacious species of paper money, subject to every kind of fluctuation, and which had often occasioned the deepest distress to the people . . . [a] system by which wars had been carried on, the most bloody and ruinous, destructive of every social tie, and virtuous feeling of the human heart.[44]

'Boroughmongers' are blamed as 'chief supporters of the war', since they profiteer from it as they do from dealing in parliamentary power.[45]

The system with these people at the heart of it, Fleming opines, has brought a 'decaying' situation to British farmers and 'uproar and confusion, hunger and turbulence' to Ireland, with the possibility that Scotland might soon end up in the same condition.[46] What was required was 'a speedy and effectual reform of the Common's House of Parliament' and, on the bright side claimed the chairman, 'the reformers might be persecuted, imprisoned and calumniated, but they would ultimately triumph'.[47] In similarly upbeat mood, he said that Hunt had been

> zealously employed in promoting the sacred cause of universal liberty. And such was the benign influence of truth, attended with experience and reflection, that the name of Mr Hunt was now very generally classed with all that was brave, with all that was liberal, and with all that was enlightened'.[48]

Fleming's command of an economic, political and moral vocabulary is eloquent enough, even as it is fairly standard reformist rhetoric of the period. What is a little more remarkable, perhaps, is Fleming's idea that the intellectual tide was turning, even if things might yet become worse. Related to this was Hunt's pivotal position here, his reputation 'still rising in the estimation of his countrymen, as their sufferings were increasing'.[49] And, most probably related to his apprehension of changing attitudes, Fleming also shows awareness that the memory of Peterloo increasingly was taking root (although as it had perhaps also functioned almost from the start), 'the horrible transactions . . . would never be forgotten by the British public', given the 'unoffending women and children, who were unexpectedly and inhumanly thrown down, bruised or sabred'.[50]

The major ideas established from Fleming's speech, the company moved through a series of eight major toasts and around forty performances, of songs and 'glees'. The first toast was to 'the people, the only true source of legitimate power', followed suitably enough by a rendition of Robert Burns' 'A Man's a Man for a' that', then another song, 'a parody of the same' (the 'parodic' nature probably similar sentiments to the same tune), followed by a 'glee': 'None are happy but the free.'[51] Here authorship is unclear, but there was no shortage of radical Paisley versifiers who could produce such material to order. The second toast was to 'Henry Hunt Esq. Being restored to his fellow citizens, may he live to see and enjoy the fruits of his exertions in the cause of liberty and humanity.'[52] A suite of 'original' songs followed the salutation to Hunt, including 'Ye who revere the Patriot's Name', 'Rejoice, brave Albion's Sons' and 'The Tyrants smiled in their lordly hall' (the British or 'Albion' 'patriotism', then, of the widest national kind). The band then played Burns' 'Scots Wha Hae wi Wallace Bled', William Wallace having been incorporated into a general iconography of British liberty-fighters since the 1790s, rather than as a figure expressing any kind of contemporary desire for Scottish independence. A third toast was to a canon of British reformers: Major Cartwright (1740–1824), Nottinghamshire campaigner for parliamentary reform; Sir Charles Wolsey (1769–1846), who like Hunt had been imprisoned for sedition following his involvement in a mass pro-reform meeting in Birmingham in 1820; Sir Francis Burdett (1770–1844), friend of John Horne Tooke and Thomas Paine, who had been particularly outspoken against the actions of the authorities at Peterloo; and 'messrs [Thomas] Wooller [?1786–1853] and [William] Cobbett [1763–1835]', reformist journalists both of whom had faced the legislative wrath of the state, with the two being linked together as successive editors of 'The Statesman', a newspaper that practised close scrutiny of the British parliament.[53] A fourth toast was to 'The Friends of Freedom' followed by a number of performances including a glee, 'Freedom to the Slave'.

A fifth toast to Scotland was followed by yet another rendition of Burns' 'Scots Wha Hae' ('the last verse sung by the whole company, accompanied by the band') and another song, 'The Deluge of Carnage' (another local composition).[54] In this section of the evening there was a tone of general Scottish (but not separatist) patriotism, with further performances of a song about William Wallace and 'The Flowers o' the Forest' (a folk song lamenting the defeat of the Scots at the Battle of Flodden in 1513). A sixth toast was to 'Lord Cochrane . . . and the speedy establishment of liberty in South America' – Admiral Thomas Cochrane (1775–1860), a highly successful Royal Navy commander against Napoleon, who had gone on to command the rebel Chilean navy in their quest for independence from Spain from 1818.[55] This was followed by a another suitably cosmopolitan song, 'Columbia's sons their burst shackles display', celebrating American liberty and independence, and the Jacobite song, 'Johnny Cope' (a popular Scottish song most likely performed for its general, upbeat martial tone rather than associating Scottish Jacobitism with radical politics). The seventh toast was especially centred on 'Greece, the cradle of liberty, and the nurse of heroes', and enjoined, 'may they continue their exertions till every remnant of tyranny and superstition be banished and consumed in Europe'.[56] Among other performances following was the band playing the 'Tyrolese Hymn of Liberty', a song by Thomas Moore, and ironically enough particularly popularised in the vicinity of Paisley by William Motherwell who had published it in his *Harp of Renfrewshire* (1820). Toast eight was to 'The Liberty of the Press', followed by nine other performances before the closing of proceedings. The last song of the evening was 'The Muckin' o' Geordie's Byre', which had a long history as a Jacobite attack on sovereigns named George and was retooled particularly by Alexander Rodger (1784–1846), the Glasgow weaver-poet, his version most likely being employed on the night.

Not all of the songs of 31 October 1822, as indicated, can easily be disinterred and identified but some lyrics are published in *Report of the meeting, held at Paisley in the Saracen's Head*. These include one of the renditions following the toast to Hunt, 'Ye who revere the patriot's name', which was set to the tune of the most popular song of the evening, 'Scots Wha Hae'. The scansion of the song is robust if not over-compelling compared to the original, as stanza one calls on the attention of 'Ye who revere the patriot's name / whose bosom glows with freedom's flame', and ends with the line 'For brave Hunt and liberty'.[57] In stanza five, we find the hymning of Queen Caroline:

> Shall we forget fair Caroline,
> Whose virtues shall for ever shine,
> The worthiest of the Brunswick line,
>   Forsaken by our hierarchy[58]

Stanza eight recalls Peterloo, painfully etched on the Scottish, on the British, consciousness:

> By Manchester's bloody plain,
> By our friends for freedom slain,
> We shall yet our rights regain
>   And triumph o'er all knavery[59]

The Saracen's Inn occasion at Paisley shows us how enduringly heartfelt was the response to Peterloo and to Henry Hunt in the West of Scotland. Certainly, with a strong Scottish (frequently Burnsian) accent, the approbatory commemorations of the reform efforts at Manchester alongside the reactionary responses to 16 August 1819 show a Scotland largely in kilter with sentiments elsewhere in the British Isles. This in itself is worth knowing about Peterloo as it provides a window onto the powerful public opinion formation that had resulted from that bitterly sad day at St Peter's Field.

Notes

1. W. M. Metcalfe, *A History of Paisley, 600–1908* (Paisley: Alexander Gardner, 1909), p. 374.
2. Ibid. p. 373.
3. For Burns' setting of his text in a contemporary political context, see *The Letters of Robert Burns*, vol. II: 1790–1796, ed. G. Ross Roy (Oxford: Clarendon Press, 1985), p. 236; for the performing of the song at Chartist dinners, see, for instance, James Epstein, *Radical Expression: Political Language, Ritual and Symbol in England, 1790–1850* (Oxford: Oxford University Press, 1994), p. 193.
4. Metcalfe, *History*, p. 374.
5. Ibid. pp. 375–7.
6. *The Letters of Sir Walter Scott 1817–19*, ed. H. J. C. Grierson (London: Constable, 1933), p. 483.
7. Ibid. pp. 485–6.
8. Ibid. p. 487.
9. *The Letters of Sir Walter Scott 1819–21*, ed. H. J. C. Grierson (London: Constable, 1934), p. 54.
10. James Chandler, *England in 1819: The Politics of Literary Culture and the Case of Romantic Historicism* (Chicago: University of Chicago Press, 1998), p. 11.
11. See <https://gesteofrobinhood.com/2016/11/02/the-peterloo-massacre-walter-scotts-ivanhoe-1819/>. For Scott's own experience in the 'yeomen-cavalry' during the late 1790s, see also Eileen Dunlop, *Sir Walter Scott: A Life in Story* (Edinburgh: NMS Enterprises, 2016), pp. 77–82.
12. See for instance the epigraph to chapter xxxi: Walter Scott, *Ivanhoe*, ed. A. N. Wilson (London: Penguin, 1984), p. 331.
13. Scott, *Ivanhoe*, p. 347.
14. Ibid. p. 539.

15. Graham McMaster, *Scott and Society* (Cambridge: Cambridge University Press, 1981), p. 90.
16. Metcalfe, *History*, p. 375.
17. Printed as an appendix to Mary Ellen Brown, *William Motherwell's Cultural Politics* (Lexington: University Press of Kentucky, 2001), pp. 221–2.
18. Ibid. p. 222.
19. Ibid. pp. 222–3.
20. In *Annals of the Parish* (1821), for instance, Galt bases an episode in Ayrshire of a magistrate crassly condemning two Christian weavers in a pastiche of the brutal rhetoric of Lord Braxfield against Thomas Muir and his fellow reformers of 1793, whom the judged sentenced to transportation to Botany Bay; see *Four Galt Novels*, ed. Ian Campbell (Edinburgh: Kennedy & Boyd, 2015), p. 73.
21. John Galt, *The Gathering of the West*, ed. Bradford Allen Booth (Baltimore: The Johns Hopkins University Press, 1939), see Booth's introduction, p. 38.
22. For details, see the still highly-useful, Robert Withington, 'Scott's Contribution to Pageantic Development: A Note on the Visit of George IV to Edinburgh in 1822', *Studies in Philology* 17:2 (1920), pp. 121–5.
23. Galt, *The Gathering of the West*, p. 42.
24. Ibid. p. 49.
25. Ibid.
26. Ibid. p. 51.
27. Ibid.
28. Gordon Millar, 'Pioneering the Political Novel in English', in *The International Companion to John Galt*, ed. Gerard Carruthers and Colin Kidd (Glasgow: Association for Scottish Literary Studies, 2017), p. 109.
29. Galt, *The Gathering of the West*, p. 101.
30. Ibid. p. 103.
31. *The Letters of Sir Walter Scott 1819–21*, p. 178; see Scott's annotation in his copy of George Theodore Wilkinson, *An Authentic History of the Cato-Street Conspiracy* (London: Thomas Kelly, 1820), p. 20. I am grateful to the Faculty of Advocates (and especially Ms Andrea Longson, Senior Librarian at the Advocates Library) and to the Honorary Librarian at Abbotsford House, Professor Alison Lumsden, for permission to quote from Scott's book.
32. Gordon Pentland, '"Betrayed by Infamous Spies"? The Commemoration of Scotland's "Radical War" of 1820', *Past and Present* 201 (November 2008), pp. 141–73 (146).
33. Ibid.

34. *The Letters of Sir Walter Scott 1819–21*, p. 209.
35. Pentland, "'Betrayed"', p. 169; see Pentland's article for a superb tracing of the cultural and political significance, indeed the usability, of the rising from 1820 to the twenty-first century. Claims made for a distinctively nationalist tincture to 1820 are made in the much more partisan works of P. Berresford Ellis and Seumas Mac a'Ghobhainn, *The Scottish Insurrection of 1820* (London: Victor Gollancz, 1970) and in James D. Young, *The Very Bastards of Creation* (no publisher, no date, but appearing in 1996), pp. 54–63. Prior to such works, 1820 was largely seen on the Scottish left as a phenomenon which was part of a common British working-class experience; see, for instance, Thomas Johnston, *The History of the Working Classes in Scotland* (Glasgow: Forward Publishing, 1920), pp. 236–48. The most nuanced political and historiographical context to 1820 in Scotland, however, is provided by Gordon Pentland, *Radicalism, Reform and National Identity in Scotland, 1820–1833* (Woodbridge, Suffolk: Boydell, 2008). See also the excellent article by John Gardner, 'Preventing Revolution: Cato Street, Bonnymuir, and Cathkin', *Studies in Scottish Literature* 39:1 (2013), pp. 162–82.
36. Stewart Conn, *Thistlewood* (Todmorden, UK: Woodhouse, 1979).
37. James Kelman, *Hardie and Baird & Other Plays* (London: Secker and Warburg, 1991).
38. Catriona M. M. Macdonald, 'Abandoned and Beastly?: The Queen Caroline Affair in Scotland', in *Twisted Sister: Women, Crime and Deviance in Scotland since 1400*, ed. Yvonne Galloway and Rona Ferguson (East Linton: Tuckwell Press, 2002), p. 103. See Macdonald's essay (pp. 101–13) for a very full narrative of the engagement in Queen Caroline's cause by Scottish reformers.
39. *The Letters of Sir Walter Scott 1819–21*, p. 235.
40. *Report of the meeting, held at Paisley in the Saracen's Head on 31st October 1822, in celebration of Mr Hunt's release from Ilchester Bastile* (Paisley: J. Neilson for R. Smith, 1822). I am grateful to Professor Murray Pittock for pointing me towards this pamphlet. Clearly Hunt's well-wishers at Paisley had been reading his pamphlet, *A Peep into a Prison; or, the inside of Ilchester Bastile* [*sic*] (London: Thomas Dolby, 1821).
41. *Report of the meeting, held at Paisley in the Saracen's Head on 31st October 1822*, p. iii.
42. Ibid. p. iv.
43. Ibid. p. 5.
44. Ibid. pp. 5–6.
45. Ibid. pp. 6–7.

46. Ibid. p. 8.
47. Ibid. p. 9.
48. Ibid. p. 12.
49. Ibid.
50. Ibid.
51. Ibid. p. 15.
52. Ibid.
53. Ibid.
54. Ibid. p. 16; this is the one text from the occasion that is anthologised in Tom Leonard's excellent collection, *Radical Renfrew: Poetry from the French Revolution to the First World War* (Edinburgh: Polygon, 1990), pp. 90–1; this is an anthology which, for all its many good things, is fairly scant on Peterloo.
55. Ibid. p. 17.
56. Ibid.
57. Ibid. p. 24.
58. Ibid. p. 25.
59. Ibid.

Chapter 6

'The Most Portentous Event in Modern History': Ireland Before and After the Peterloo Massacre

James Kelly

Daniel O'Connell, the Irish barrister who emerged in the late 1810s as a leading agitator for Catholic Emancipation, described the Peterloo massacre as 'the most portentous event in modern history'.[1] Writing in 1821, while the memory of the massacre was still fresh, O'Connell saw it as a potential first step either to 'a military despotism established in England' or a 'fall into the horrors of revolution'.[2] The massacre in Manchester struck many observers as repeating violent repressive measures that had been enacted in Ireland previously. T. J. Wooler's radical magazine *The Black Dwarf* warned in September 1819 that 'the system that disgraced Ireland during the reign of Castlereagh and his colleagues will be introduced into England, if the temper of the times will bear it'.[3] The kind of political repression that was enacted in Manchester in August of that year was more common in Ireland, and reformers made common cause with Irish Catholics, many of whom were beginning to migrate to the industrial towns of Northern England. Ireland gave English reformers a cautionary example of tyrannical government, while Irish writers and politicians saw in Peterloo an illustration of the English establishment's true coercive colours. Peterloo may have portended military despotism or anarchic revolution, but for many observers in the early nineteenth century these were often seen as the contradictory but simultaneous conditions of Irish society.

In a speech in Liverpool in 1838, by which point Peterloo had become a defining moment in radical histories of the early nineteenth century, the reformer H. T. Atkinson spoke on the need for the disestablishment of the Church of Ireland, invoking the Manchester massacre as an example of Tory coercion that was all too familiar in Ireland:

> Let them not forget that even the very freedom of discussion which they now enjoyed was but the creation of yesterday. Within the memory of those whom he then addressed, a drunken and infuriated yeomanry, hounded on by a Tory magistracy, had trampled under their horses' hoofs, men, women, and children, on the plains of the ever memorable and infamous Peterloo. – But, during the many ages that Ireland had groaned under the infliction of Tory domination, these scenes of blood and terror had been as familiar as household words.[4]

Indeed, Atkinson's point about the familiarity of such events to Irish audiences was borne out a few years previously. O'Connell had invoked the memory of Peterloo to draw attention to the Tithe War in Ireland, when there were a series of disturbances and violent reprisals against the payment of taxes by Catholics towards the maintenance of the Protestant Church. Tithes were bitterly resented by the Catholic population, and the early 1830s saw the escalation of protests against their payment. Visiting Manchester in September 1835, O'Connell invoked Peterloo to draw attention to the killing of a dozen protesters in Rathcormac, County Cork, on 18 December 1834. 'Did Sir R. Peel never hear of Peterloo, of what has been called the Manchester massacre?', asked O'Connell before invoking the Irish situation:

> Did he never hear of Rathcormac, and Rathangan, red with the blood of the grand-daughter of a blind and aged man? Did he never hear of Wallscourt? Was it the democratic principle that for 4s. 6d. slaughtered nine men in Rathangan? Did he never hear of the widow Ryan, who breakfasted in the morning with her two sons, fine youths, one eighteen and the other twenty-two, neither of them married, nor even thinking of it till their sister should be provided for, and their mother taken care of. One of her sons left her in the morning. A demand for 4s 6d. was made upon her for tithes. The military fired. She ran out wild – 'Where are my sons?' She found a dead body. She took it up to see the face. It was not her son; and she laughed – the poor woman laughed aloud, forgetting there was another woman to weep for that boy. She took up a second

> body. She laughed again – a frantic laugh: it was not her son. She went to the third. It was her boy: the boy who had left her a few hours before, blood-bolten, stiff, and dead. As she said to herself, 'I did not cry; I never shed a tear; but my eyeballs are coals in my head, and I shall never have them quenched on this side the grave. Did Sir Robert Peel never hear of Mooncoyne? . . . There were two parsons at Rathcormac; and I believe you had some clergymen at your massacre here. ['Ay, we had.'][5]

O'Connell here was invoking a pathetic story in a long tradition of centring the plight of suffering femininity against the forces of the state. As Ian Haywood has pointed out, Peterloo itself was quickly constructed as 'a gendered confrontation between the brutal, unprovoked, unpatriotic State violence and defenceless, feminized victims'.[6] Certainly, O'Connell would have been aware of the resonance of such imagery on his Manchester audience, as well as aware of the long tradition of Irish representations of 'patriot mothers' cradling their dead sons in their arms.

The news of Peterloo provoked uneasy responses in Irish observers. The Belfast radical and former United Irishman William Drennan was an old man when he surveyed the post-Peterloo political situation and felt that 'all was uncertain'. His comment about Major John Cartwright in a letter of late 1819 to his sister may have been partially self-reflective: 'He has grown too old – most patriots and heroes live too long.'[7] Drennan had lived through the 1798 United Irishmen Rebellion and witnessed the repressive measures that followed, and he recognised in the Six Acts that followed the massacre at St Peter's Field legislation that had been familiar to Ireland. The 1790s had been marked, for United Irish radicals, by a 'reign of terror and coercion'.[8] The violent dispersion of reformers by the Manchester Yeomanry had revealed a contempt for the lower classes that Drennan felt would be the ruin of the gentry and spoke to a panic in officialdom about political demonstrations. He wrote to his sister about the difference in a post-Peterloo world between reform as espoused by private political clubs such as Cartwright had initially been involved in and that by public assembly and protest: 'The ministry would overlook anything that passed in a room but what happens on a heath, or common, or in a square, this they dread, and how can millions of people assemble but under the canopy of kites and crows?'[9]

Drennan was aware that post-war radicalism was, as E. P. Thompson put it, 'less a movement of an organised minority than the response of the whole community'.[10] Public assembly was central to post-Napoleonic political agitation and would become central to Irish political movements in the 1820s and 1830s. The violent massacre of radical reformers at Manchester in 1819 occurred at a moment when Irish writers and reformers were considering the nature and extent of how public assembly and public speech were linked to political agency. Indeed, for a brief period in 1817 to 1819 Ireland went from being the scene of violent disorder that it was characterised as for much of the nineteenth century, to being invoked by politicians across the political spectrum as a calm, tranquil polity in contrast to an England that was in turmoil.

This was not to last, though. As James Chandler notes, the fervour of radical politics from 1815 to 1819 would dissipate to such an extent that George Canning in an 1820 speech could declare that 'November 1819 and March 1820 effectively belonged to different "epochs" in the nation's history'.[11] Such a rapid progression did not happen in Ireland, where late 1819 saw the development of agrarian disturbances in the southern counties of Ireland; disturbances that would reinforce a view of Irish history as a nightmarish cycle of violence rather than a Whiggish narrative of progression. When seeking to locate Irish dimensions of Peterloo, it is less a task of identifying overt references to the 'Manchester massacre' in speeches and writings by Irish authors and orators as identifying both practical links and overarching structures of feeling. Peterloo and the radical politics surrounding it were on the one hand closely observed by Irish politicians, and on the other fed into larger issues surrounding representation, violence and political speech. Reading Peterloo against Irish literature and politics in the period brings to light unusual and unexpected aspects of Ireland as discussed in both British and Irish literary culture. 'Ireland! What a fearful word! What a copious and never-failing source of injury, insult, and weakness to the empire!', wrote one observer in 1831,[12] but reducing Ireland to the eternal signifier of disturbance and fearful violence diminishes the complexity of how observers spoke about the Irish situation in the immediately post-Napoleonic context of Peterloo.

Coercion and Tranquillity in the Age of Peterloo

When the radical agitator and poet Samuel Bamford was arrested and transported from Salford to London in 1817 he advised his 'conductor' as they approached Chadderton Hall near Oldham that it would be best to return to Manchester:

> I pointed to Chadderton Heights, and the neighbouring country, over which scores of people were running like hunters, as if to meet the coach near Royton: all the country was up, I said, and every one whom he might want, would be apprised of his coming. He growled a deep oath, saying he had never seen anything like that before: the officer commanding the dragoons, who rode by the coach door, observed that he had seen something like it in Ireland, but never any where else.[13]

It is unsurprising that a soldier looking for a similar situation to the radicalised and restless northern counties of England should think of the 'sister isle' of the United Kingdom. Ireland was a model of a country 'all up' throughout most of the nineteenth century. The Act of Union between Great Britain and Ireland that came into law on 1 January 1801 had been a response in part to the bloody carnage of the 1790s which saw the United Irishmen Rebellion of 1798 bring sectarian conflict to numerous regions across the island. In the space of three months some 30,000 people were killed, the majority by government and loyalist forces, even if the atrocities committed by Catholic rebels quickly entered the public consciousness. What had been a rebellion inspired by Enlightenment ideals of liberty, democracy and religious toleration came to be seen as more a return to an atavistic religious conflict and brutal state oppression. '[A] potent source of spectacular violence', as Ian Haywood points out,[14] the Rebellion was a foundational event in the subsequent entrenchment of sectarian politics. Robert Emmett's subsequent abortive rebellion of 1803 in Dublin provided British and Irish radicals with a romantic image of the doomed idealistic youth, even as it introduced a suspension of habeas corpus that would usher in a century of coercion in Ireland. Unsurprisingly both 1798 and 1803 entered into Irish imaginative writing: the former as a traumatic violent shock and Gothic backdrop for a number of poets and novelists; the latter as the locus of a sentimental nationalism informing some of Thomas Moore's most famous Irish Melodies. Moore himself in *Memoirs of Captain Rock* (1824) gave a savage indictment of coercion policies in Ireland, tracing the history of the titular Captain's family of insurrectionists:

> It has been said, that 'you may trace Ireland through the Statue-book of England, as a wounded man in a crowd is tracked by his blood', and the footsteps of the Captain are traceable, in the like manner, through the laws that have prevailed during the last four-and-twenty years. For instance:
> The Insurrection Act, in force from 1800 to 1802
> Martial Law, in force from 1803 to 1805
> The Insurrection Act, in force from 1807 to 1810
> Ditto, from 1814 to 1818
> Ditto, from 1822 to 1824.[15]

Given the reputation of Ireland for discontent and violence then, it is surprising to note that when Lord Castlereagh introduced the first reading of the Seditious Meetings Bill in February 1817 he proposed not applying it to Ireland. The Bill was a response to the previous riots of November and December 1816 in Spa Fields, London. Growing dissatisfaction with the effects of the 1815 Corn Laws, the demobilisation of some 200,000 soldiers into a crowded and depressed labour market, and the developing movement for reform led to a febrile atmosphere in Britain. The riots in London, provoked arguably more by government *agent provocateurs* than the speeches of the radical leader Henry 'Orator' Hunt, provoked repressive measures by a government darkly prognosticating a revolution at home. Castlereagh's speech on the Seditious Meetings Bill contrasted an agitated England where 'a wicked conspiracy existed in the country for the subversion of the constitution and the state'[16] with a peaceful Ireland, a nation that 'was at present tranquil to that degree, that he hoped the people of that country had at length drawn a useful lesson from their experience; and were determined to set a noble example to the rest of the united kingdom'.[17] Yet just a few months later the same government argued for the renewal of the Irish Insurrection Bill, a coercive measure that as Moore pointed out would be renewed in 1822 and would continue to be renewed throughout the century. When Castlereagh committed suicide in 1822 the liberal *Examiner* printed a castigating obituary in which the minister's earlier brutality in Ireland was painted as the model for dealing with radical protests in England: 'The various suspensions of the Habeas

Corpus were the work of that mind, which knew no other mode of checking Reform in England than what had succeeded in suppressing (for a time) rebellion in Ireland, – namely, *force*.'[18]

The rhetoric of tranquillity was present on the other end of the political spectrum in Ireland, though, with Daniel O'Connell and others contrasting the state of Ireland with turmoil in England. In an article published in *The Dublin Evening Post* on 28 October 1819 O'Connell wrote of how the 'enemies of every Liberty, Civil as well as Religious, say that the English people are seeking a revolution' and noted that 'the People of Ireland show not the least assumption of revolutionary tendency'. An England that 'has been agitated to her centre' was held by O'Connell in contrast to an Ireland 'perfectly tranquil'.[19] O'Connell went on to advise that Irish Catholics, even if temperamentally inclined to support the twin claims of universal suffrage and annual parliaments, should retain focus on the cause of Catholic Emancipation:

> In theory I admit the right to Universal Suffrage, and I admit that curtailing the duration of Parliament would be likely to add to its honesty. Nay, I am ready to go the fullest possible practical length to obtain Parliamentary Reform. But we have a previous duty to perform – a favourable opportunity now presents itself to add to the general stock of liberty, by obtaining our Emancipation – and the man would, in my judgement, be a false Patriot, who, for the chance of an uncertain Reform, would fling away the present most propitious moment to realise a most important and almost certain advantage.[20]

Now was not the time for O'Connell to advise Irish Catholics 'to throw the sword and the pike into the scale of Reform'.[21] O'Connell had given similar speeches in the years prior to Peterloo. A vast open-air meeting at Harold's Cross on 13 January 1816 in support of reform had seen a similar focus on Emancipation prior to Universal Suffrage.

The 1819 article appeared alongside a much more rhetorically fiery piece by Valentine Lawless, Lord Cloncurry. Cloncurry had been involved with the United Irishmen and continued to take a strongly national interest in Catholic Emancipation and then repeal of the Union. In his letter in the *Post* he raised the spectre of 1798 as a moment in which misgovernment and coercion provoked the populace into sanguine rebellion:

> It is above twenty years since the People of Ireland, peaceably demanding this Right [of representation], were, by every species of injustice and cruelty, goaded into Rebellion by an Administration and a Magistracy who escaped legal punishment in an Act of Indemnity granted by the same Parliament who soon after sold their Country, and by the Union, which destroyed Ireland, rendered the Legislation of England more corrupt than it was.[22]

For Lawless Peterloo stood as a parallel to 1798, with a similar sense that the magistracy was going to escape any consequences of the massacre. Irish Catholics ought to 'join in such measures as will save the Country from absolute Despotism, and the people from that Eastern extravagance and that Military Execution, with which they are threatened'.[23]

Cloncurry's warnings about 'despotism' were often echoed in discussions about coercion and state violence in the period. Debates about the suspension of habeas corpus or the limiting of political freedoms in times of emergency often returned to Ireland as a test case for whether coercion worked, whether it could be applied locally rather than nationally, and how British ideals of liberty were tested and undermined when conditions in Ireland were considered. Government responses to Spa Fields and later Peterloo would raise the spectre of Irish coercion to British radicals. The harsh repressive measures of the Six Acts which followed Peterloo coincided with an increase in disturbances in the southern counties of Ireland. Indeed, the Irish tranquillity invoked by politicians was increasingly hard to reconcile with conditions on the ground. There were sufficient concerns about agrarian violence in the southern counties of Ireland in particular to mark a renewed concern about the state of Ireland in the early 1820s. The previous talk of calm was replaced by a renewed rhetoric of violence when describing the Irish situation.

While English radicals had, admittedly with some resistance in their own constituency, aligned their cause with that of Catholic Emancipation, there were other unique factors in Ireland that exacerbated tensions between landowners and tenants. John Ramsay McCulloch,[24] reviewing a series of books on the present state of Ireland for the liberal *Edinburgh Review*, singled out tithes as one of the most pressing causes of agrarian disturbance, and the 1820s can be seen as a moment in which the disturbances of the 1830s that

O'Connell would align with Peterloo were formed. A Catholic population forced to sustain a bloated Church of Ireland represented for liberal British opinion an appalling injustice, and McCulloch's attack on the tithe system concluded by noting that coercion alone could not bring about a tranquil nation:

> No severity of punishment will ever be sufficient to induce men quietly to submit to such unparalleled extortion. We may send hundreds of thousands of troops into Ireland – we may erect a gibbet in every village, and fence every cottage with bayonets; but until this monstrous and complicated system of abuse and oppression be put down, the flames of civil war, and the inhuman attacks of the midnight murderer, will never cease to spread terror and desolation throughout the country.[25]

By the 1820s Ireland had returned to being the land of intractable violence by both discontented agitators and oppressive state forces.

The Irish at Peterloo

Among the many broadsides published in the immediate aftermath of Peterloo was the reactionary 'The Answer to Peter-loo' which saluted the yeomen and soldiers:

> Success attend those warlike-men, our Yeomen Volunteers,
> And all their Gallant Officers who knows [*sic*] no dread or fears,
> Likewise the Irish Trumpeter, that loud his trumpet blew,
> And took a cap of liberty from them at Peter-loo.[26]

The 'Irish Trumpeter' is a reference to Edward Meagher, who by common account was one of the first of the Manchester Yeomanry to rush into the crowd. Meagher was held to be responsible for some of the worst injuries inflicted,[27] and his house was subsequently surrounded by an angry mob on 5 September, with Meagher firing into the crowd to disperse it. He was one of the defendants in a trial held in 1822 but, like the others, was acquitted with costs met by the government.

It is not clear if Meagher was first or second generation Irish, but the identification of his nationality aligns him with the rapidly growing Irish population of Manchester in the early decades of the nineteenth century. If an Irishman may be responsible for starting Peterloo, there is some evidence that the Irish community suffered the consequences of the violent repression of the radical meeting. In his report to Parliament, the Reverend William Hay, one of the Manchester magistrates responsible for the reading of the Riot Act, reported that disturbances after the dispersal of the meeting continued:

> During the afternoon, and part of the evening, parts of the town have been in a very disturbed state, and numerous applications made for military. These have been supplied, but in some cases have, in the Irish part of the town, been obliged to fire, I trust without any bad effect as to life, in any instance.[28]

Irish emigration to the northern centres of industry would increase throughout the century. A steep population rise aligned with a relative lack of industrialisation and repeated subsistence crises fed into the movement of formerly rural workers to the cotton industry of Lancashire. The year before Peterloo had seen the introduction of regular steamboat services between Ireland and Britain, increasing the connectivity of the two islands.[29] Manchester had already seen some radical connections with Ireland going back to 1798. The city had seen up to 900 men take the United Englishman oath, a kindred organisation to the United Irishmen, in 1797,[30] even if the energy of that movement fizzled out after the arrest of Colonel Despard in 1802.

When remembering the processions towards St Peter's Fields Samuel Bamford gave an account of a natural enthusiasm and sympathy among Irish emigrants and political reformers, even if couched in a rather patronising language:

> At Newtown we were welcomed with open arms by the poor Irish weavers, who came out in their best drapery, and uttered blessings and words of endearment, many of which were not understood by our rural patriots. Some of them danced, and others stood with clasped hands and tearful eyes, adoring almost, that banner whose colour was their national one, and the emblem of their green island home. We thanked them by the band striking up, 'St Patrick's day in the morning;' they were electrified; and we passed on, leaving those warm-hearted suburbans capering and whooping like mad.[31]

While Irish weavers may have had some enthusiasm for the radical cause, they were absent from the participants at Peterloo. The *Dublin Weekly Register* included a special sub-article on its reporting of the massacre on the conduct of the Irish in Manchester. It assured its readers that the Irish had been peaceable and 'completely aloof' from all participation in the plans of the Reformers: 'Their conduct has been marked by the utmost prudence and circumspection, and this we learn, is in a great degree attributable to the influence and advice of two most respectable Roman Catholic Clergymen in Manchester.'[32]

If there was not a coherent Irish cohort among the participants among Peterloo, however, it was not because of a distance between radical and Catholic political projects. British radicals had been keen to include references to Ireland in their writings and proposals, often in the face of local opposition to include Catholic Emancipation as an aim alongside Universal Suffrage and annual parliaments. This made practical as well as ideological sense given the increasing population of Irish emigrants as well as the increased possibilities of political representation from Ireland in Parliament. There may also have been an element of self-interest at work too. As Donald MacRaild argues, English radicals thought that improved conditions in Ireland 'might result in the voluntary repatriations of thousands of migrant labourers – 'temporary sojourners' in Britain – to the enormous benefit of the native working class'.[33]

Major Cartwright had written to O'Connell on 24 December 1816 urging him to exert himself in persuading the Catholic population to join in with petitions from England and Scotland for reform:

> May the Petitions of Ireland, therefore, be, if it were possible, as numerous as her wrongs! This, after all, is the artillery with which the fortress of corruption must be battered down. Compelled to write in great haste, I can only offer it as an opinion that we are likely to be in a condition to carry annual election and suffrage to the extent of all householders, whether taxed directly or indirectly; but, should Ireland pour in her hundreds of petitions – and why shall she not? – I should reckon on the thing as certain.[34]

Henry Hunt also promoted the inclusion of Ireland in the project of reform, visiting Dublin and including Catholic Emancipation in the programme of radical politics in the run up to the Manchester meeting. Hunt allowed his name to be attached to an *Address of the People of Great Britain to the People of Ireland*, with 4,000 copies sent to Dublin and Cork promoting a union of those interested in civil and religious liberty.[35] Attempts to join with O'Connell though were always hampered by the latter's focus on Emancipation and hedged, lukewarm support of the twin planks of Universal Suffrage and annual parliaments.

O'Connell would later in life move to a much more openly hostile position in relation to Chartism, which had by the 1830s and 1840s appropriated Peterloo as a foundational moment in the development of a mass working-class political movement. Chartist demonstrations in the 1830s and 1840s would often combine representations of Peterloo alongside memorials of Robert Emmett, and the latter's doomed rebellion became part of a pantheon of republican moments for later radicals. An 1834 speech by the Tyneside Chartist Robert Lowery invoked both Peterloo and Ireland in the long tradition of British republicanism:

> They knew what tyrants could effect by law; it was by law that Sydney perished at the block; it was by law that Emmet died upon the scaffold; and it was by law that the field of Peterloo was strewn with unoffending men and women – law it might be called, but never justice.[36]

Emmet's speech from the dock at his trial became one of the foundational texts of nineteenth-century Irish nationalism, as well as inspiring a generation of British radicals and republicans. The speech, widely reproduced in the immediate aftermath of his abortive rebellion of 1803, can be seen as setting the tone for Irish political rhetoric, and it spoke to the power and force of oratory in the new century.

Eloquence, Politics and Popular Protest

The infamous 'hanging judge' John Toler, 1st Earl of Norbury, addressed the assizes in Mullingar on 9 August 1819 and celebrated the peace and tranquillity of both the county of Westmeath and the wider country at large: '[All] is quiet; no tumult, no confusion, no meetings; a prospect of a fine harvest; a likelihood of a plenteous crop; every thing composed from Derry to Dingle; fine corn fields, and a not a single *orator.*'[37]

Norbury regretted that this was not the case in England, and the readers of *Saunder's News-Letter* on 18 August would be reading this speech in light of the events in Manchester. '[The Irish] are an imitative people' argued Norbury: '[the] historian observes there never was a convulsion in England that was not followed by one in Ireland'.[38] Norbury went on to praise the Irish but note that '[their] sensibilities make them liable to be easily worked on, and they are too readily worked on by every itinerant orator; any preacher of nonsense and sedition will be listened to'.[39] The role of public speaking, the control of potentially subversive speech, and the challenge of radical politics to traditional standards of rhetoric and oratory were all areas that were affected by the increased prominence of Irish voices in favour of Catholic Emancipation and English radical voices in favour of reform. Norbury's suspicion of orators and radical 'preachers' was part of a much wider debate about the role and nature of public speech in the post-Napoleonic years. Leading Irish orators such as Richard Lalor Shiel, Daniel O'Connell and Charles Phillips were seen as importing a dangerously irrational, illegitimate form of orality into Britain, and concerns about Irish eloquence prefigured and ran alongside official condemnation of Henry 'Orator' Hunt and other radical public speakers. Alongside the rise of such dangerous oratory, the period 1816–20 saw the deaths of Richard Brinsley Sheridan, John Philpott Curran and Henry Grattan, which prompted eulogising meditations on what the main characteristics of 'Irish eloquence' might be. We can see in the reactions to both Irish speech and Peterloo a growing concern at establishing proper codes of public speaking, while the legacy of Peterloo sees an impassioned rhetoric of blood and violence familiar to Irish readers and auditors brought into English radical discourse.

The Irish had a long-standing association with oratory prior to this period and Irish public speakers were often charged with bringing a florid, unruly language into public life in the years after the Union. A letter to the *Morning Chronicle* in 1811, for instance, defended the 'intemperate' language of the growing movement for Catholic Emancipation by reference to the Irish national character:

> We must not judge of the Irish in this respect by ourselves. The national character, habits, feelings, eloquence, all are different. They are a quick, sprightly animated people. Their tone is always impassioned. The Athenians themselves delighted not more in speeches. With the Irish oratory is not only a natural endowment; it is absolutely a passion; which therefore cannot be extinguished, and must be indulged; humour it, and it will not be perverted: freeze not its genial current – let it flow on; but if you will, divert its course. But seek not to dam it up: the rash attempt will not succeed, and it will cost you dear; it will burst your flood-gates – overflow – and in a torrent impetuous and irresistible, carry with it desolation.[40]

Three years earlier Francis Jeffrey had reviewed a collection of speeches by the lawyer John Philpott Curran, and characterised Irish eloquence as 'more vehement, and figured and poetical than any that is now attempted in this country' with the aim of 'dazzling the imagination, or enflaming the passions, as much at enlightening the understanding'.[41] For Jeffrey, as for many commentators, this style could be traced to the example of Edmund Burke, although since that great orator's example it '[had] been defiled . . . by base imitations and disgusting parodies' as well as '[being] naturalised and transfused into the recent literature of our country'.[42]

Whether Irish eloquence was aimed at 'enflaming' or 'enlightening' an audience became central to debates about its nature and efficacy in the post-Napoleonic period. 1819 saw the publication of the first major anthology of Irish oratory, Charles Phillips' *Specimens of Irish Eloquence*, a book partly inspired by a drawn-out quarrel between Phillips, a Protestant lawyer and advocate of Catholic Emancipation, and Henry Brougham, the liberal MP and contributor to the *Edinburgh Review*. Phillips and Brougham clashed on the nature of Irish eloquence and the manner in which oratory ought to be judged. Central to the quarrel was precisely the extent to which oratory ought to operate on a crowd's passions or reason. Phillips had come to the attention of British literary culture in 1815 with the publication of his speech in an adultery case in Dublin which ran to multiple editions. His elegy *A Garland for the Grave of Richard Brinsley Sheridan* followed in 1816. For many reviewers, Phillips' forensic oratory was typical of what John Wilson Croker called 'that inflated and jargonish style which has of late prevailed among a certain class of authors and orators in the sister kingdom'.[43]

Sentimental, florid and figured, it collapsed the difference between registers and genres, and could be compared elsewhere to the excessive and emotional style of low literary genres like the sentimental or Gothic novel. Indeed, when in 1816 another Irish author, Charles Robert Maturin, saw his wild tragedy *Bertram* performed at Drury Lane, reviewers noticed a similarity across genres:

> [*Bertram's*] characteristics appear to be – language copious to verbosity – imagination luxuriant to rankness – a style resembling the celebrated productions of the Minerva Press . . . but even going beyond them, – and strewed over with a profusion of the 'daisies and dandelions' of Irish eloquence and Della Cruscan poetry . . . [Maturin's] *own* manner is at once grovelling, monotonous, and hyperbolical; and reminds us a good deal of the poetico-prosaic raptures of [Charles] Phillips. Indeed, if we were to compare this tragedy to any thing which *we* have read, it would be to the performance of the orator to whom we have alluded.[44]

Central to the debate between Phillips and Brougham was the question of whether oratory could be measured by success in achieving its aims. An 1817 edition of Phillips' speeches contained a preface by the Irish barrister John Finlay which considered the extent to which imagination, passion and reason ought to be employed by the orator:

> With judges it is to be hoped that the passions will be weak: with public assemblies it is to be hoped that reasoning will be strong; but although the imagination may, in the first case, be unemployed, in the second it cannot be dispensed with; for if the advocate of virtue avoids to address the feelings of a mixed assembly, whether it be a jury or a political meeting, he has no security that their feelings, and their bad feelings, may not be brought into action against him: he surrenders to his enemy the strongest of his weapons, and by a species of irrational generosity contrives to ensure his own defeat in the conflict.[45]

Finlay's acknowledgement of the role of passion and feeling in public assemblies was objected to strongly by Brougham, and the former's contention that oratory ought to be judged by 'the fitness of its means to the attainment of its end'[46] was particularly rejected. For Brougham, the idea that 'success with a jury or a mob . . . is the criterion of good oratory' was reprehensible 'for everyone who knows anything of those audiences, but especially in Ireland, is aware that they are liable to be led away by the glare of the worst style of speaking'.[47] The role of passion and imagination in oratory would not have seemed so objectionable in the eighteenth century, when a 'New Rhetoric' associated with Scottish rhetoricians like Hugh Blair and George Campbell emphasised the connection between eloquence and emotion. But in the changed and charged context of radical culture in the early nineteenth century, public speech was now connected to vulgar politics. Assemblies quickly become mobs in Brougham's review. The example of the Spa Fields riots the year previously and the growing popularity of Henry 'Orator' Hunt fed into a new paranoia about public speech, a paranoia which often found expression in the manner in which British reviewers characterised Irish oratory as containing far too much 'glare'.

In his 1825 biography of Richard Brinsley Sheridan, Thomas Moore was more hesitant to identify a particularly Irish variety of oratory, and less inclined to see the union of imagination and the practical as a distinctively Irish creation:

> It is also, I think, a mistake, however flattering to my country, to call the School of Oratory, to which [Edmund] Burke belongs, *Irish*. That Irishmen are naturally more gifted with those stores of fancy, from which the illumination of this high order of art must be supplied, the names of Burke, Grattan, Sheridan, Curran, Canning, and Plunkett, abundantly testify . . . [Francis] Bacon, by making Fancy the handmaid of Philosophy, had long since set an example of that union of the imaginative and the solid, which, both in writing and speaking, forms the characteristic distinction of this school.[48]

Moore's biography of Sheridan had been in gestation since 1818, although its progress was interrupted when Moore fled Britain due to bankruptcy in 1819, and it was while travelling through Italy that Moore makes one of his few references to Peterloo. Moore was part of a group of Irish visitors to Florence that autumn that included the novelist Lady Morgan and her husband, and the Irish peer Henry Dillon. According to Moore's journal, on 19 October the Italian tragedian Giovanni Battista Niccolini 'said that the massacre of Manchester was a lucky event for English liberty & exclaimed "Would to God that the Arch-Duke would this night order 400 Tuscans to be sabred!"'[49]

Moore did not record his response, but when speaking to Sir Robert Adair, the British Ambassador to Constantinople, ten days later on 29 October they agreed 'that England is a desolated country & hastening fast to its ruin'.[50] Moore was the pre-eminent Whig satirist of post-Napoleonic Britain, and so it was unsurprising that his pseudonym was co-opted by the anonymous author of *The Field of Peterloo* (1819). Moore himself remained relatively silent on the matter, his modern biographer speculating that his own precarious financial position and desire for a smooth return to England may have made him reluctant to enter the contentious public debate about the massacre.[51] Lady Morgan was less reticent, railing against those who 'On Peterloo's blood-letting fondly gloat' in her 1822 satire on the administration of Lord Liverpool, *The Mohawks*.[52] As the 1820s progressed though, the sectarian conflicts engendered by the evangelical Protestant 'Second Reformation', the increasingly mass-organised movement for Catholic Emancipation, and continued agrarian disturbances drew the attention of Irish writers. When Moore came to write *Memoirs of Captain Rock*, for instance, after an 1823 tour of the disturbed southern counties of Ireland, Peterloo had been eclipsed by the larger history of British coercion in Ireland.

Conclusion

In Maria Edgeworth's novel *Patronage* the noble Lord Oldborough berates a servant who has cursed a mob of poor people who assaulted him:

> 'Do not curse them, my good Rodney,' said Lord Oldborough, smiling. 'Poor people, they are not ungrateful, only mistaken. Those who mislead them are to blame. The English are a fine people. Even an English mob, you see, is generous, and just, as far as it knows.'[53]

Appeals to the generosity of the English mob grew scarcer in the years following the publication of Edgeworth's novel. Peterloo was a foundational moment in the nineteenth-century development of public assemblies as political moments. Edgeworth's Lord Oldborough blames those who mislead crowds, rather than the people themselves. Whether such magnanimity would be possible later in the century is open to question, as only a few short years later a far stronger suspicion of popular orators was being expressed. In Ireland there was a longer history of fearing the violent crowd, whether they were a crowd of pike-bearing 1798 rebels or a detachment of soldiers enforcing the payment of tithes. The type of repressive measures enacted by the state after Peterloo was the rule rather than the exception in Ireland for much of the nineteenth century. While there may be a paucity of direct references to the Manchester massacre by Irish imaginative writers, who perhaps had enough home-grown atrocities to draw on for imagery of political violence, there are wider suggestive connections between the events in Manchester and the post-Union, post-Napoleonic cultural moment in Ireland. Sharing a language of civil disruption, state coercion, and the nature of public speech and action, Peterloo and Ireland were both troubling signifiers for subsequent writers and thinkers in the violent nineteenth century.

Notes

1. *The Life and Speeches of Daniel O'Connell, M.P.*, ed. John O'Connell, 2 vols (London, 1846), vol. 2, p. 311.
2. Ibid.
3. 'Hints to the Reformers of the British Empire, as to the real authors of the Manchester Massacre!', *The Black Dwarf* 36:111 (8 September 1819), p. 581.
4. Reported in 'Justice to Ireland', *Freeman's Journal*, 15 November 1838, p. 3.
5. 'Mr O'Connell in Manchester', *Reading Mercury*, 21 September 1835, p. 4.
6. Ian Haywood, 'Shelley's *Mask of Anarchy* and the visual iconography of female distress', *Romanticism and Popular Culture in Britain and Ireland*, ed. Philip Connell and Nigel Leask (Cambridge: Cambridge University Press, 2009), pp. 148–73 (149).
7. *The Drennan-McTier Letters, 1802–1819*, ed. Jean Agnew and Maria Luddy (Dublin: Irish Manuscripts Commission, 1999), p. 709.
8. Richard Robert Madden, *The United Irishmen: Their Lives and Times*, second series, 2 vols (London, 1843), vol. 2, p. 322.
9. *Drennan-McTier Letters*, p. 709.
10. E. P. Thompson, *The Making of the English Working Class* [1963], rev. ed. (London: Pelican, 1968), p. 663.
11. James Chandler, *England in 1819: The Politics of Literary Culture and the Case of Romantic Historicism* (Chicago: University of Chicago Press, 1998), p. 22.

12. 'Ireland!', *The Age*, 12 June 1831, p. 188.
13. Samuel Bamford, *Passages in the Life of a Radical*, 2 vols (London, 1843), vol. 1, pp. 83–4.
14. *Ian Haywood, Bloody Romanticism: Spectacular Violence and the Politics of Representation, 1776–1832* (London: Palgrave, 2006), p. 104.
15. Thomas Moore, *The Memoirs of Captain Rock* [1824], ed. Emer Nolan (Dublin: Field Day, 2008), p. 183.
16. 'Seditious Meetings Bill', Hansard, HC Debate, 24 February 1817, vol. 35 cc590-639, col. 594.
17. Ibid. col. 597.
18. 'Death of the Marquis of Londonderry', *The Examiner* 763 (18 August 1822), p. 515.
19. Daniel O'Connell, 'To the Catholics of Ireland', *The Dublin Evening Post*, 28 October 1819, p. 4.
20. Ibid.
21. Ibid.
22. Lawless, Valentine, Lord Cloncurry, 'Reformers', *The Dublin Evening Post*, 28 October 1819, p. 3.
23. Ibid.
24. The *Wellesley Index to Victorian Periodicals* lists the Irish MP Henry Parnell as a possible alternative author for this article.
25. John Ramsay McCulloch, 'Reflections on the State of Ireland in the Nineteenth Century', 37:73 *Edinburgh Review* (June 1822), pp. 60–109 (78).
26. Anon., *The Answer to Peterloo*, Online Image, Manchester Archives, GB127.Broadsides/F1819.2.E <https://www.flickr.com/photos/manchesterarchiveplus/6048991522/in/photolist-j95wKR-adwErh-ecFfzf-ouK4CW-yJsUTY> (last accessed 28 June 2017).
27. Robert William Reid, *The Peterloo Massacre* (London: Heinemann, 1989), p. 176
28. 'Papers Relative to the Internal State of the Country', Hansard, HC Debate, 24 November 1819, vol. 41, col. 262.
29. Lynn Hollen Lees, *Exiles of Erin: Irish Migrants in Victorian London* (Manchester: Manchester University Press, 1979), p. 33.
30. Michael Hebert, *The Wearing of the Green: A Political History of the Irish in Manchester* (London: Irish in Britain Representation Group, 2001), p. 29.
31. Bamford, *Passages*, vol. 1, pp. 202–3.
32. 'Conduct of the Irish at Manchester', *Dublin Weekly Register*, 21 August 1819, p. 2.
33. Donald MacRaild, *The Irish Diaspora in Britain, 1750–1939*, 2nd edn (London: Palgrave, 2011), p. 117.

34. *The Correspondence of Daniel O'Connell Volume 2: 1815–1823*, ed. Maurice O'Connell (Dublin: Irish University Press, 1972), p. 128.
35. John Belchem,*'Orator' Hunt: Henry Hunt and English Working-Class Radicalism* (Oxford: Clarendon Press, 1985), p. 104.
36. Quoted in Dorothy Thompson, 'Ireland and the Irish in English Radicalism before 1850', in *The Chartist Experience: Studies in Working-Class Radicalism and Culture, 1830–1860*, ed. James Epstein and Dorothy Thompson (London: Macmillan, 1982), pp. 120–51 (137).
37. Reported in 'Mullingar Assizes', *Saunder's News-Letter*, 18 August 1819, pp. 2–3 (2, emphasis in the original).
38. Ibid. p. 2.
39. Ibid. p. 3.
40. 'Ireland', *The Morning Chronicle*, 11 November 1811, p. 2.
41. Francis Jeffrey, 'Speeches of the Right Honourable John Philpot Curran', 13:25 *Edinburgh Review* (October 1808), pp. 136–48 (136).
42. Ibid. p. 137.
43. Quoted in James Kelly, 'Earnestness and Reality: Oratory and Speech in the Fiction of John and Michael Banim', *European Romantic Review* 26:6 (2015), pp. 743–56 (747).
44. Review of 'Bertram: or, The Castle of St Aldobrand', *The Augustan Review* 3:16 (August 1816), pp. 178–85 (179).
45. John Finlay, 'Preface' to *The Speeches of Charles Phillips, Esq Delivered at the Bar and on Various Public Occasions* (New York, 1817), p. xi.
46. Ibid.
47. Lord Henry Brougham, 'Speeches of Mr Phillips', 29:57 *Edinburgh Review* (November 1817), pp. 52–70 (56).
48 Thomas Moore, *Memoirs of the Life of the Right Honourable Richard Brinsley Sheridan*, 2 vols (London, 1825), vol. 1, p. 525.
49. *The Journal of Thomas Moore: Volume 1*, ed. William S. Dowden (Newark: University of Delaware Press, 1983), p. 235.
50. Ibid. p. 243.
51. Ronan Kelly, *Bard of Erin: The Life of Thomas Moore* (Dublin: Penguin, 2008), p. 346.
52. Lady Morgan, *The Mohawks: A Satirical Poem* (London, 1822), p. 103.
53. Maria Edgeworth, *Patronage* [1814], in *Tales and Novels*, 18 vols (London, 1833), vol. 16, p. 41.

Chapter 7

Political Suicide: Castlereagh, Rebellion and Self-Directed Violence

Michelle Faubert

> '[S]hall we mourn for Castlereagh whose vices had reached such a climax as to render life insupportable? No, we will rejoice.'[1]

Attention to the violence of the Peterloo massacre of 1819 usually focuses on that of the soldiers who attacked the peaceful protesters gathered to demand equal representation and workers' rights. However, this chapter will demonstrate that the event and its aftermath brought into sharp focus the intense concern with, and conflicting attitudes towards, self-directed violence and its ultimate expression, suicide, in Romantic-era Britain. P. B. Shelley framed the murders of the peaceful protesters in St Peter's Field in Manchester as the victims' martyrdom – as their self-sacrificing political agitation – in not one but two poems: *The Mask of Anarchy: Written on the Occasion of the Massacre at Manchester* and 'England in 1819'. In doing so, the poet built upon an attitude towards suicide that was familiar in classical times, but that had only begun a resurrection, so to speak, in eighteenth-century literature, in which self-directed violence was sometimes presented sympathetically as a courageous political act that asserted individual autonomy in the face of implacable tyranny. This theme was threatened, however, when Viscount Castlereagh – Conservative defender in the House of Commons of the government's attack at Peterloo, and the very figure of despotism in the period – slit his own throat with a pen knife in 1822. Awkwardly for some Romantic writers and other radicals, Castlereagh's death put him in the camp of those he had tormented: rebels, slaves, the disenfranchised. Thus, when Byron mocked his suicide and called Castlereagh the 'Werther of Politics' in *Don Juan*, the poet seems to struggle with the accepted literary signification of suicide as sympathetic, the last courageous act of protest in the struggle for equality.

Suicide Across Britain

Officially, suicide was considered to be a crime in religious, legal and popular realms during the Romantic period, but individuals increasingly queried whether a more lenient, humanitarian attitude towards suicide was appropriate. Donna Andrew comments that, in eighteenth-century Britain, suicide was 'debated and discussed at least twenty-one times through the last three decades of the century at nine of London's commercial debating societies', in response to what they judged to be 'a late alarming number of Suicides'.[2] Britons believed that they had a propensity to self-directed violence, and the rest of Europe agreed: France and Germany defined their own suicidal tendencies as minimal relative to that of Britain. Changing and sometimes contradictory laws and attitudes towards suicide in Britain reflected the intense soul-searching created by the perceived scale of the problem.

Two of the most common claims about suicide in Romantic-era Britain are that laws were becoming increasingly lenient and secular with the growing medicalisation of suicide, and that popular attitudes towards suicide were more humanitarian than legal. However, R. A. Houston stipulates clearly that jurors did not adopt 'the medical interpretation of suicide' after the 1750s, and that doctors 'almost never supported juries' automatic link between suicide and insanity'.[3] In fact, doctors sought to distance themselves from the assumption that they were experts on suicide and were almost never called upon to make such an assertion as part of their coroners' reports.[4] Notably, though, there were differences in the legal treatment of suicide between the various countries in the United Kingdom.[5] The treatment of suicide in Scottish courts was more centralised, private and medicalised than in English courts, as doctors were frequently called in to study the cadaver and open the head of the corpse to ascertain whether the suicide was a victim or not, rather than to comment on the suicide's mental state.[6] Nor is there evidence of the increasing medicalisation of suicide in Irish courts, and particularly not of an increasingly secular attitude towards it.[7] What appears to be unique to Ireland is belief: both that the Irish killed themselves less often than did the English and Scottish, and that this difference was the effect of the greater religiosity of the Irish and the Catholic injunction against suicide.[8] However, there is no proof that the Irish committed suicide less often than did their other British counterparts.

Another common historical claim about suicide in Romantic-era Britain is that the establishment – the law, the government – sought to instil a horror of committing suicide in the living by inflicting punishments on the suicide's corpse and family, but the historical record is more complex than that view implies. All countries in the United Kingdom present evidence of punishments to the suicide's corpse during the Romantic period, such as burial at a crossroads and the denial of burial in a churchyard.[9] Equally common was that the 'goods and chattels', or the so-called 'movables', of a suicide (as opposed to land or real estate) were forfeit to the Crown. However, James Kelly claims that, at least in late sixteenth- and early seventeenth-century Ireland, 'forfeited goods were acquired, not by or on behalf of the Crown, but by family members or local landowners', suggesting either that the treatment of suicide became more aggressive over time or that Ireland was more lenient in its response to the act than were other areas of the United Kingdom.[10] Also of note in this case is that the Crown did not benefit from the forfeited goods, which undermines the notion that such a punishment was always an expression of state power. The historical response to suicide is surprisingly complex and cannot be held up as evidence of the brutality of the law in every case.

There were also various approaches to punishing the suicide's body across Britain and over time. Houston comments that 'Staking was unusual in the north of England and unknown in Scotland, but there were similarities between these regions in the way some corpses were shamed prior to burial that seemingly have no parallel in most of the rest of England.'[11] The brutality of driving a stake through the suicide's heart is undeniable, but early punishments for the suicide's body were much worse in some areas of the United Kingdom:

> the branks or scold's bridle . . . [, an iron gag worn around the head as punishment for disorderly women, was] found in Scotland and in the towns of the north of England, [but it] does not seem to have been used in Wales and Ireland (outside Ulster), though other shaming punishments were. Staking was found in Wales and in Ireland.[12]

Notably, though, ameliorations of the punishments for suicide could materialise in court, where it was increasingly recognised over the course of the eighteenth century that the insane could not be held responsible for their actions, mitigating the criminality of the suicide's final act:

> juries in England and Scotland in the late seventeenth century . . . [often] return[ed] verdicts of *non compos mentis* [of unsound mind] rather than *felo de se* [felon of one's self] on the grounds that it was 'impossible that a man in his senses should' kill himself because it was 'so contrary to nature, and all sense and reason'.[13]

Houston also provides an important caveat: 'profane burial [was] a legal but not statutorily sanctioned punishment – until 1823', which shows that not every level of governance agreed on the appropriateness of the official responses to suicide.[14] Along the same lines, by 1700 'punishments that had been judicial or para-judicial . . . became primarily extra-judicial or "popular" . . . Suicide was a felony, but forfeiture was a civil liability and corporal punishments were primarily associated with criminal justice.'[15] In other words, different levels of British society – legal, religious, popular – had different responses to suicide.

It is difficult to draw a single conclusion regarding the social power dynamics signified by one type of response to suicide, such as corporal punishments, since these responses were not always meted out by legal or governmental entities. Houston notes that corporal punishment was 'primarily associated with criminal justice', but he also claims that: 'Burying a suicide in unconsecrated ground with a stake through the heart had not authority at law, but was a "customary" or local usage sanctioned by warrant of an English coroner.'[16] Houston's use of the phrase 'criminal justice' does not mean an official legal reaction to suicide, but, more broadly, a judicial response required by a community, which is composed of the populace, professionals in the legal system, and elected officials. Evidently, then, historical punishment for suicide was not invariably proof of Foucauldian or Agambean 'biopower' in Britain, wherein the individuals in a society are controlled bodily by political power structures. In fact, as Kelly comments, 'the public at large was not neutral in its response to suicide. The public countenanced, indeed enforced sanctions (albeit in a minority of cases) through the eighteenth and into the nineteenth century that were palpably more severe than those provided for by the Church of Ireland', for instance.[17] Moreover, as tempting as it is to think that the post-Enlightenment spirit of scientific knowledge and democracy created increasingly lenient responses to suicides, other evidence suggests that these changes were the result of rather less informed and humanitarian concerns: 'Rather than the onset of civility or humanity, changes in the law towards greater certainty and consistency cause the decline of officially sanctioned corporal punishments', Houston reveals.[18] In several ways, the response to suicide in the Romantic era challenges our easy assumptions regarding the Whiggish march of history towards greater beneficence in society. The cruel response to Castlereagh's suicide late in the Romantic period – especially from those whom we would expect to be most sympathetic – is just one additional example of the complexity of historical attitudes towards suicide in Britain.

Sympathetic Suicide in Literature

Sympathetic suicidal characters abound in the sentimental literature of the period: suicide appears often as the pitiable last act of the insane or amorously desperate. Outside of Gothic fiction, one would be hard-pressed to provide an example of a suicidal character in Romantic-era literature who is not pitiable or even heroic. The list of sympathy-inspiring suicides is long and includes: Mary Wollstonecraft's Maria in *The Wrongs of Woman* (1798); Mary Shelley's protagonist in *Mathilda* (1959); William Wordsworth's speaker in 'The Complaint of a Forsaken Indian Woman' (1798); Felicia Heman's suicidal female speakers; and Thomas Chatterton and Werther in many other adoring and sentimental poems, such as by Mary Robinson. Arguably, this beneficent attitude to suicide was an extension of the judicial treatment of suicide as blameless when committed by an insane person, a judgment increasingly returned by juries throughout the period. Yet, because insanity exculpates the suicide from moral responsibility by denying intention, it also negates the possibility that it was an act of courage, such as a political statement, another iteration of sympathetic suicide in Romantic-era literature. It is therefore necessary to distinguish between these different portrayals of sympathetic suicide.

Particularly prominent in establishing the theme of sympathetic suicide are Jean-Jacques Rousseau's *Julie, ou La Nouvelle Héloïse* (1761) and the novel it influenced, Johann Wolfgang von Goethe's *The Sorrows of Young Werther* (1774). As the foundational texts of the literature of sensibility – a mode that gave rise to many of the most recognisable features of high Romanticism, such as excessive emotion and the celebration of personal response – these novels are usually studied for their representation of the love relationships within them. The novels' protagonists, St Preux and Werther respectively, are both suicidal on account of their unsatisfied romantic attachments, and the latter character accomplishes the act in the novel's final pages. But what is less often recognised is that both protagonists are also class rebels of sorts: their failed romantic relationships and resultant suicidality follow from this political stance. St Preux's class is below that of Julie, rendering his desire for her an attempt at class levelling. Werther also refuses to act the part of his class, often waxing poetic about his love of the lower classes when he is not pining for Lotte, his beloved. Because they are of the same class, Werther should be as industrious and dependable as Albert, the fiancé of Lotte, but Werther remains idle for most of the novel and quits his good position working for the Envoy late in the novel. Significantly, Lotte and Albert finally get married while Werther is actively failing at his role as a member of the bourgeoisie; since Albert is the ultimate figure of staid reliability and he 'gets the girl', the message appears to be that Werther's refusal to embrace his class responsibilities is tied to his romantic disappointment, for which he kills himself. Audience reaction to these suicidal characters was almost uniformly sympathetic, and often fanatically so, in keeping with what would come to be recognised as the usual reaction of the audience to the lovelorn characters in novels of sentiment.

Byron's 'mental drama' *Manfred* (1817) is, perhaps, the most significant Romantic-era text on suicide for the present discussion because Byron's comments on Castlereagh's suicide are so famous. Manfred's Wertherian identity is well established: Manfred is a classic Byronic hero and all Byronic heroes are loosely modelled on Werther in their intense emotionalism and outsider statuses. True to form, Manfred's suicidality follows from the death of his beloved, Astarte, and he is careless about his aristocratic lineage, much to the amazement of the Chamois Hunter. Not to be outdone by the suicidal rebels before him, Manfred wishes for death throughout Byron's 'mental drama', but he refuses to accept death from a divine tyrant. In the opening scene, Manfred is asked by a Spirit what he requests from the great powers of the universe, whom he has gathered to serve him. He names his desire for 'Oblivion, self-oblivion' and continues to do so in various ways throughout the play.[19] Despite Manfred's many requests for death, though, it eludes him until the last moments of the drama because he refuses to gain it at the cost of his existential freedom when it is offered to him in exchange for obeisance to a greater power.[20] Manfred is a Werther whose rebellion exceeds earthly bounds. Even though Byron mocked Werther at times, such as in a letter he wrote to his publisher John Murray, his adoption of the Werther figure for his non-satirical works shows that he also used it as shorthand for the themes it conveyed, particularly suicide and rebellion in *Manfred*.[21]

Suicide and Martyrdom

Literary figures like Werther were not the only means through which suicide and rebellion became linked conceptually in the Romantic period, and, indeed, such artistic representations were themselves a reflection of other instances of rebellious suicide. Richard Bell has delineated the phenomenon of slave suicide in the long eighteenth century, noting the popularity of texts describing slaves 'choosing liberty through death' during the American Revolutionary era (1765–83), when slave suicide was often framed as 'principled resistance to tyranny'.[22] By contrast, after the Romantic era, abolitionist texts 'offered instead a remarkably consistent vision of subaltern suicide as the inexorable product of a culture of oppression'.[23] Perhaps contributing to the Romantic-era interpretation of slave suicide as rebellion was the influence of another national revolution: the French. Initially, 'animated by anticlerical zeal, the Jacobins repealed the law prohibiting suicide', clearly in defiance of the religious injunction to avoid suicide.[24] However, they soon reimposed this law, and with a vengeance: 'French institutions of power rigorously legislated against suicide . . . with particular severity during the Reign of Terror' because it 'perceived suicide as a threat to its power [, which] is suggested by the regular guillotining of political prisoners even after their suicides', notes Kelly McGuire.[25]

Such strictures only emphasised the revolutionary notion of suicide as a noble act of autonomy in the face of implacable oppression. When political figures killed themselves in heroic Roman style during the French Revolution, suicide acquired the firm significance of courageous rebellion and the opposition to tyranny at the greatest personal cost.[26] Inspired by the French Revolutionaries, rebels against the British government followed suit.

Thus, when Wolfe Tone, hero of the United Irishmen, asserted that he willingly laid down his life for a 'sacred' cause in his final speech at his court martial before the British government in 1798, his audience would have understood the revolutionary subtext of his words: 'I entered into the service of the French Republic [which aided the Irish rebels against the English] . . . After all I have done for a sacred cause, death is no sacrifice.'[27] Tone subsequently committed suicide while in captivity to avoid execution at the hands of his oppressors, the British government, the public face of which was none other than Castlereagh: as Chief Secretary of Ireland at the time of the 1798 United Irishmen Rebellion, Castlereagh ordered the suppression of the rebels. Tone's clear delineation of his death as a martyrdom for his political cause – freedom from the tyranny of the British government – outlived him and became part of the accepted narrative of political suicide, while Castlereagh became inscribed as the figure of oppression that necessitates such martyrdom.

By framing his death as martyrdom, Tone brought into the Romantic-era suicide debate another consideration: that putting oneself in the way of danger and being killed as a result – such as by protesting or otherwise rebelling against a hostile government and being executed for treason – is a kind of suicide. His political descendent, Robert Emmet – a latter-day United Irishman who was executed for treason upon attempting to reinvigorate the Irish Rebellion in 1803 – was duly dubbed 'the Irish martyr'. Notably, though, the close link between suicide and virtuous martyrdom was not introduced by the Irish rebels. The Christian tradition lauded the voluntary self-sacrifice of the saints and early Christians as a replication of Jesus' death, emblematic of the charity itself, but Edward Gibbon 'viewed the deaths of early Christians who provoked the Roman authorities to kill them as suicides'.[28] Part of the Romantic-era suicide debate therefore involved whether martyrdom – or even military service and duelling – might be considered forms of suicide, since the person in question willingly puts his or her own life in danger, with frequently fatal consequences. For instance, William Godwin discusses martyrdom as 'a species of suicide' in *Enquiry Concerning Political Justice* (1798).[29] The conceptual link between suicide, martyrdom and political rebellion in the period reveals why the 'Scottish martyrs' have acquired this title, despite surviving their brutal punishment for their efforts to effect parliamentary and constitutional reform in Scotland. Their French Revolutionary sympathies and willingness to risk their lives in a penal colony out of devotion to their cause are evidence of their political suicidality.

Long before Martin Luther King Jr. and Mahatma Ghandi counselled their followers to submit to the violence of their oppressors in their fight for human rights, the disregard for one's own life was honed as an effective tool of political agitation. P. B. Shelley's implication that the Peterloo protesters were martyred, rather than simply killed, by the British government fits into this cultural conversation about choosing death. In *The Mask of Anarchy* (written in 1819; published 1832), 'indignant Earth' urges the 'Men of England, heirs of Glory' to submit to the violence of the British government to achieve political change, reframing the deaths of peaceful protestors during the Peterloo massacre as efficacious and powerful.[30] The poem continues:

> And if then the tyrants dare,
> Let them ride among you there,
> Slash, and stab, and maim, and hew –
> What they like, that let them do.
>
> With folded arms and steady eyes,
> And little fear, and less surprise,
> Look upon them as they slay,
> Till their rage has died away.[31]

Some might take offence at Shelley's suggestion that the victims of the Peterloo massacre were martyrs, since it seems to shift some of the blame for the victims' deaths away from the government and onto the protesters, as though they chose to die. This very notion of the victims' agency is precisely Shelley's point, though: considered in this light, their deaths gain political value and their victimhood is transformed into courage. A similar sentiment appears in Shelley's 'England in 1819', which was inspired in part by Peterloo: it was written on 23 November 1819, only months after the event, and – like *The Mask of Anarchy* – it provides further reasoning for Shelley's identification of the protesters' deaths as martyrdom, a species of suicide. Shelley writes of the victims of Peterloo: 'A people starved and stabbed in th' untilled field; / . . . / Are graves, from which a glorious Phantom may / Burst, to illumine our tempestuous day'.[32] The deaths of the protesters, in other words, are politically useful, for they may shine a light on the social problems of 1819 and create necessary change. The description 'a glorious Phantom may / Burst, to illumine' is a clear reference to the legend of the phoenix, the mythical bird that immolates itself every 500 years, only to be born anew and more perfect; therefore, also clear is the implicit comparison of the protesters to Christ, who is often associated with the Phoenix myth. In this way, Shelley again frames the victims of Peterloo as martyrs – and their deaths as socially useful.

Traitorous Self-Killing and Castlereagh's Long History of Self-Violence

What is considerably more opaque in Shelley's 'England in 1819' is the implication about self-destruction that follows these famous lines set in the 'untilled field' of St Peter's: the poet writes of 'An army, which liberticide and prey / Makes as a two-edg'd sword to all who wield'.[33] Murky as they are, these lines demonstrate an essential Romantic-era understanding of the significance of the event. Shelley reasons that the victims of Peterloo are threefold: the protesters (the 'prey'), liberty (the event was 'liberticide'), and the soldiers (as representative of the government) themselves, for they wield a 'two-edg'd sword' that cuts themselves as surely as it cuts their targets. Shelley's identification of the soldiers and government as victims seems mysterious until one considers that they, too, are part of British society, the liberty of which has been destroyed by their actions. In this way, the soldiers of Peterloo destroy themselves – a kind of suicide – by killing the protesters. Nor is this view of the matter arcane: after all, the massacre at St Peter's Field by former soldiers of the Battle of Waterloo (and the local yeomanry) is most commonly known as 'Peterloo', a nickname that signifies self-directed violence. The 'loo' in 'Peterloo' recognises that the hussars – former heroes of the famous Battle of Waterloo, soldiers whose violence was celebrated for defending British interests against hostile foreigners – turned on their fellow Britons while wearing their medals from Waterloo. That the massacre is almost always referred to as 'Peterloo', an epithet that appeared directly after the event in the *Manchester Observer*, shows how significant was the hussars' identity as decorated soldiers of Waterloo to the contemporary understanding of the event.[34] The coinage 'Peterloo' denotes the ironic turnaround of violence that becomes self-directed fatal violence.

The name 'Peterloo' therefore manifests a different aspect of the Romantic-era concern with self-directed violence as the ultimate betrayal of one's community. This conceptualisation of suicide was not new to the events of Peterloo, but the massacre may be said to have inscribed this meaning of suicide indelibly into the British psyche. The notion of suicide as social betrayal was cited often by anti-suicide campaigners in the eighteenth century, such as the minister Charles James, who argues in *Suicide Rejected* (1797) that 'society has a claim on your life' before launching into the familiar litany of positive benefits that suicidal people may offer to society through continued life.[35] This notion was repeated in legal texts, such as in Sir Matthew Hale's *Historia Placitorum Coronæ: The History of the Pleas of the Crown* (1778), which contains the injunction: 'No man hath the absolute interest of himself, but I. God almighty hath an interest and propriety in him, and therefore self-murder is a sin against God. 2. The king hath an interest in him, and therefore the inquisition in case of self-murder is' to determine feloniousness.[36] The king is the representative and leader of British society; to offend against the king is to offend against Britain. Radical writers also considered the social impact of suicide as a cogent argument against the act. In *Political Justice*, Godwin reasons that 'the usefulness I may exert in twenty or thirty years of additional life' could well outweigh the desire for 'a voluntary death'.[37] Meanwhile, in Rousseau's *Julie*, Bomston scolds the suicidal St Preux, 'How about society to which you owe your preservation, your talents, your lights; the fatherland to which you belong[?] . . . Where is that virtuous patriot [in you?].'[38] Peterloo consolidated, rather than created, a growing conceptualisation of self-directed violence as a betrayal of community. That Castlereagh soon became identified as the government face of Peterloo only compounded this association.

Since at least 1798, Castlereagh emblematised the violent betrayal of one's community, a kind of self-murder. Tone's suicide was not the only political self-violence associated with the United Irishmen Rebellion: one of the lasting reproaches against Castlereagh – what made him so virulently hated long before his involvement with Peterloo – was his vicious suppression of the 1798 United Irishmen Rebellion of which Tone was the leader, a violence that was viewed as all the more despicable because Castlereagh was himself Irish. Thus, when he ordered the torture of his countrymen at the Derry Down Triangle – the wooden frames upon which the Irish rebels were tied – his identity as a vicious traitor to his community was complete.[39] Even before Peterloo, then, and long before his suicide, Castlereagh had contributed to the understanding of self-directed violence as the betrayal of community, challenging what was for many Romantic-era writers its chief signification: a courageous assertion of the individual's political power in the face of social oppression.

In the twenty years spanning the Irish Rebellion to Peterloo, Castlereagh was, as Clara Tuite has observed, strongly associated with violence.[40] However, I contend that he was linked to a particular iteration of violence on one hand – autocratic, authoritarian oppression of the less powerful – and, on the other, violence against one's own community, a self-directed violence that overlaps confusingly with suicide. Indeed, Castlereagh epitomised the kind of cruel tyranny that inspired suicidal rebellion, such as through his opposition to the abolition of slavery. He was also loosely associated with the sort of despotism against which the French Revolutionaries heroically killed themselves, since the United Irishmen of the 1798 Rebellion were supported by the army of the French Republic. Castlereagh spearheaded the Six Acts of 1819, as well, to shut down protest and free speech, and supported the unjust settlement at the Congress of Vienna after Waterloo. For such reasons and many others, Castlereagh was one of the most caricatured politicians in the Tory government, often appearing as a cackling villain, or, even more pointedly (excuse the pun), as having the body of a dagger.[41] He was an emblem of why suicidal rebellion happens via his part in violently betraying his fellow Irishmen in 1798 and the British government's betrayal of Britons at Peterloo, but he also obscured a favourite understanding of suicide for Romantic writers when he killed himself in 1822. These writers responded in a way that seems, to their readers today, out of step with their usual sympathetic approach to suicide, but Castlereagh had prepared the way for such a reaction more than two decades before his death.

Because the usual portrayal of suicide in the Romantic era is as pitiful, inspiring the audience's sympathy for the afflicted figures, it comes as something of a shock to read of the Romantics' jeering response to Castlereagh's suicide, as hated a political foe as he was. Notably, though, such vitriol about Castlereagh was not inaugurated by his death: second generation Romantic writers had written critically about Castlereagh before his suicide. Shelley's *The Mask of Anarchy* provides the most striking image of the politician: the speaker claims to have

> met Murder on the way –
> He had a mask like Castlereagh –
> Very smooth he looked, yet grim;
> Seven blood-hounds followed him.
>
> All were fat; and well they might
> Be in admirable plight,
> For one by one, and two by two,
> He tossed them human hearts to chew.[42]

Castlereagh's cruelty is partially covered – masked – by his 'smooth' face, a description of the politician that appears repeatedly in critical commentaries about him, as though his youthful good looks were an added insult to his victims. Such descriptions recognise the duplicity and hypocrisy of Castlereagh, who repeatedly did what his critics viewed as *à rebours*, against nature, the unexpected: he first turned on his fellow Irishmen and then he defended the British government's decision to kill Britons. Such a disavowal of natural loyalty is figured as monstrous, and the country itself becomes unrecognisable under the rule of such leaders: Mary Shelley writes from Italy to her friend Marianne Hunt that her homeland was 'no longer England, but Castlereagh land or New Land Castlereagh, – heaven defend me from being a Castlereaghish woman'.[43] It is as though Castlereagh's cruel disloyalty has not only killed his own identity as Irish or British (as well as that of the hussars) in a kind of political suicide, but he has also thereby destroyed the national identity of others, who no longer recognise a Britain ruled by an enemy government. In the 'Dedication' to *Don Juan* in 1818, Byron presents Castlereagh as the representative of tyranny itself and, like P. B. Shelley, he invests the politician's youthful looks with great significance: Castlereagh's handsome features mask his evil nature, covering his inner ugliness with beauty, like Oscar Wilde's Dorian Gray. Calling him 'intellectual eunuch Castlereagh', Byron describes him as a 'Cold-blooded, smooth-faced, placid miscreant! / Dabbling its sleek young hands in Erin's [Ireland's] gore, / . . . / The vulgarest tool that tyranny could want'.[44] Indeed, even before Peterloo, Castlereagh had gained a reputation as a hypocritical criminal – a 'smooth-faced . . . miscreant', 'placid[ly]' murdering his own countrymen. In this context, Byron's harsh response to Castlereagh's suicide is not surprising.

'We will rejoice': Byron's Preface on Castlereagh's Suicide

In a long footnote to the Preface to Cantos VI to VIII of *Don Juan*, Byron jeers at Castlereagh's suicide and seems, in fact, to revel in it. He does so while essentially summarising and mostly criticising the many factors that could attenuate the traditionally harsh reaction to suicide at the time, rendering this passage a kind of guidebook to the Romantic-era treatment of suicide. Byron begins, 'Of the manner of his death little need be said, except that if a poor radical . . . had cut his throat, he would have been buried in a cross-road, with the usual appurtenances of the stake and mallet', a clear reference to the punishment of the suicide's body – as well as to the uneven application of this penalty.[45] Byron implies that in death, as in life, Castlereagh is rewarded by the conservative regime to which he contributed, a system that rewards the powerful and resists the change for greater equality that radicals sought to establish. The truth of the poet's complaint is recognised by historians of suicide today. McLynn comments that, to avoid the traditional punishments visited upon the suicide's body and family, not to mention the 'social stigma' attached to suicide,

> relatives of the deceased had . . . [strong] motives for concealing suicide and passing it off as natural or accidental death . . . Suicides therefore, tended to be concealed and underreported . . . To a large extent this was a class phenomenon, since the wealthy could more easily cover the

> tracks of a suicide; after all they could bring all kinds of social pressure to bear on coroners and in any case constituted a large proportion of coroners' juries.[46]

In other words, laws and customs regarding the treatment of suicide were easily evaded; such demands were only followed closely when the dead had no champions powerful enough to intercede for him or her. Driving this point home, Byron recognises in several of the following mocking comments that the medical assessment of a suicide tended to moderate harsh reactions to it, suggesting that doctors were puppets of the wealthy. He writes of Castlereagh, 'he merely cut the "carotid artery" (blessings on their learning!)', implying that the published coroner's report containing these words was designed to evoke the reader's mercy for perpetrator, as 'merely cut[ting]' the vein sounds much more acceptable than slashing one's throat.[47] When Byron sarcastically exclaims his admiration for the coroner's medical education ('blessings on their learning!'), which provided such technical vocabulary as '"carotid artery"', then he also suggests that medical jargon was used to distance the public from Castlereagh's suicide. Such jargon conveys that the average person is not knowledgeable enough to come to his or her own conclusions about the meaning of the suicide.

Byron moreover suggests why Castlereagh's death earned such an outpouring of affection: 'the Minister was an elegant Lunatic – a sentimental Suicide', the poet comments sardonically.[48] Again, Castlereagh's wealth and social status – his 'elegan[ce]' – overshadows his humble posthumous status as *non compos mentis*, designating him as 'a sentimental Suicide' and therefore deserving of an outpouring of love, pity and sympathetic tears. Byron's judgement is not without basis. Castlereagh's physician, Dr Bankhead, 'convened an inquest that found Castlereagh had suicided as a result of overwork'.[49] In other words, Castlereagh's supporters claimed that he had driven himself insane as a result of his devotion to his job, rendering his suicide a noble one. Castlereagh's enemies were quick to oppose this finding, though. In *The Republican* (1822), Richard Carlile reasons, 'It has been discovered that Castlereagh purchased the knife on the Friday . . . in the street, with which [knife] he destroyed himself on the following Monday. This is a proof that the act was deliberate and premeditated.'[50] Byron's closing invitation – 'let Ireland remove the Ashes . . . from the Sanctuary of Westminster', a place of honour – also demonstrates that the politician wore the stain of betraying his native community beyond the end of his life.[51] In his suicide, Castlereagh's self-directed, anti-Irish violence had hit its truest mark.

Byron thus contextualises his cruel remarks about Castlereagh's death in terms of the cultural conversation about suicide in the Romantic period. Before identifying Castlereagh as the 'Werther of Politics', Byron prepares his reader to understand his epithet as a reference not just to Goethe's novel, but to the entire tradition of literary sensibility heralded by it. Byron's mocking comment about the funeral of Castlereagh as a histrionic display of grief frames it as a replication of Wertherians' excessive reactions to the suicidal character, responses so extreme that Europe was said to be infected with 'Werther-mania'. Byron describes Castlereagh's funeral: 'and lo! the Pageant, and the [Westminster] Abbey! and "the Syllables of Dolour yelled forth" by the Newspapers – and the harangue of the Coroner in a eulogy over the bleeding body of the deceased'.[52] This sarcastic portrayal accords with those of the many eighteenth-century Wertherians who cried loudly over the protagonist's tragic end, replicating Werther's passionate emotionalism and 'maudlin indulgences'.[53] Notably, though, by dubbing his target the 'Werther of Politics', Byron modulates the position for which he himself was well known, having published *Manfred* only five years previous to Castlereagh's death. *Manfred* was one of the best-known treatments of suicide in the period, and Byron presents the act not only as sympathetic in it, but even as heroic, making Werther one of the key sources for the Byronic hero. Tuite argues that Byron's Preface registers the poet's 'outrage at Castlereagh's appropriation of the hero's mode of suicide', which gains added significance in consideration of Byron's poetic creations.[54] Manfred and the self-destructive Byronic hero convey the poet's investment in Wertherian, sentimental suicide, regardless of Manfred's distinct machismo. Castlereagh's death undermined the conceptualisation of suicide upon which Byron had built a poetic identity and forced him to disavow it in the Preface to *Don Juan*.

How does Byron's Preface on Castlereagh relate to the popular Romantic understanding of the social meanings of suicide? As a politician, Castlereagh's suicide might be considered political, but a tyrant's suicide cannot be understood in the same light as that of a subaltern raging against despots and championing the cause of the oppressed. Just as Shelley presents the protesters' deaths at Peterloo as suicidal rebellion, Byron mockingly figures Castlereagh as serving his country through his suicide: 'It may at least serve as some consolation to the Nations, that their Oppressors are not happy, and in some instances judge so justly of their own actions as to anticipate the sentence of mankind.'[55] Byron suggests that, by killing himself, Castlereagh saves Britain the trouble of a trial and execution for his crimes, thereby doing his countrymen a patriotic favour. The poet offers the same perspective in a few acerbic epigrams on Castlereagh, which first appeared in *The Liberal* 1822: 'So Castlereagh has cut his throat! – The worst / Of this is, – that his own was not the first'.[56] Another offers a more detailed view of Castlereagh's suicide:

> Oh, Castlereagh! thou art a patriot now;
> Cato died for his country, so didst thou:
> He perish'd rather than see Rome enslaved,
> Thou cutt'st thy throat that Britain may be saved![57]

With dark humour, Byron implies that Castlereagh has committed self-sacrificing suicide to defend his country – from himself.

Byron follows a well-worn philosophical path in considering how suicide might be beneficial to one's country, a topic that David Hume, Godwin and Rousseau all discuss. Hume comments that, in the case of criminals, 'voluntary death is . . . advantageous to society, by ridding it of a pernicious member'.[58] On the same topic, Godwin quotes Lycurgus (fl. ~seventh century BCE), the legendary lawgiver of Sparta, to comment that '"a man ought, if possible, to render his death a source of . . . benefit"' to his society.[59] Finally, in *The Social Contract*, Rousseau asserts that 'Whatever services the citizen can render the state, he owes whenever the sovereign demands them', including his very life in a time of war.[60] In some cases, these philosophers reason, suicide is positively beneficial to society, and far from a crime against it. Byron agrees this was the case when Castlereagh killed himself.

However, Byron is also careful not to invite earnest admiration of Castlereagh's suicidal patriotism, concluding his epigram on the minister with an invitation to the reader to heap shame upon Castlereagh's grave:

> Posterity will ne'er survey
> A nobler grave that this:
> Here lie the bones of Castlereagh:
> Stop, traveller and — [.][61]

By implicity instructing his audience to urinate on Castlereagh's place of interment, Byron implies that the mode of the minster's death – and not just his life – are deserving of the kind of social disapprobation traditionally expressed through the physical desecration of the suicide's body. Here is a vulgar echo of the physical punishments visited upon the suicide's corpse that continued to be required by the community in many places throughout Romantic-era Britain, even if they were not statutorily required, as Houston notes.[62] Many people felt that suicide is a shameful way to die, as well as that people often kill themselves as a response to some ignominy that they wish to escape through death. As such, the 'shaming' of the suicide's corpse, to use Houston's phrasing, manifests the community's insistence that the suicide should not escape the moral punishment of humiliation.[63]

Part of the mythological aftermath of Peterloo was the belief that Castlereagh killed himself out of his guilty feelings over his violent policies towards his countrymen. Mary Fairclough suggests that the British people demanded physical violence be visited upon the bodies of those responsible for Peterloo in a retaliatory response to the violence of the massacre:

> The political outrage of Peterloo is generated by the marks of violence on the bodies of the people. On August 25, 1819[,] the *London Alfred* asserts: 'The Manchester Magistrates . . . have fleshed the swords of their young trained bands in the bodies of Britons . . . [They] should have thought of the consequence of spilling one drop of citizen's blood. A soldier's blood is not of the same political value.'[64]

This thinly veiled threat expresses the public desire for bloody justice, which was satiated in part by stories of the perpetrators' suicides. Henry Hunt attested to the suicides of two of the yeomen of Peterloo on 16 August 1819, supposedly in response to the crushing guilt they felt for their murderous actions upon their own people.[65] Castlereagh, many believed, was similarly plagued by remorse over Peterloo. Carlile asserts:

> He acted wisely for himself, in cutting his throat. His continuation of life must have been that of despair and wretchedness, such as attends the corrodings of a guilty conscience; and it is more than probable that the 'working of events' might have caused its extinction upon a public scaffold.[66]

Both Carlile and Byron echo the attitude of their community towards Castlereagh's death: British society reportedly celebrated it and nearly rioted in reaction to his lavish state funeral.[67] Carlile declares, 'All is joy throughout the two islands of Britain and Ireland at his self-destruction', adding, 'It was an expression of a detestation of tyranny, a cheers of gladness, to think that a tyrant was going to his grave prematurely, and had himself been destroyed by the hand that had assisted in so much destruction.'[68] Many Britons apparently revelled in the poetic justice of Castlereagh's suicide.

Conclusion

James Chandler has identified the Peterloo massacre as one of the great defining events of Romantic period politics: Peterloo 'names an event of indeterminate duration that marks a major transformation in the practices of modern literary and political representation, one understood in its moment to have revolutionary potential'.[69] So much is also true with regard to its effect on attitudes towards suicide. The Romantic-era literati's cruel lack of sympathy towards Castlereagh's suicide shocks readers today, but I have shown that such jeering comments as Byron's are a recognisable aspect of the – admittedly various and sometimes contradictory – attitudes towards self-directed violence in the period, which was partially bound up with the Peterloo massacre and Castlereagh's connection to it. Although attitudes towards suicide were becoming increasingly sympathetic throughout the Romantic period, the violence of Peterloo may be judged to have reversed some of these gains, even amongst the most sympathetic of British citizens, the Romantic writers.

Notes

1. Richard Carlile, 'To the Republicans of the Island of Great Britain', *The Republican*, 14:6 (1822), pp. 417–21 (417).
2. Donna T. Andrew, *Aristocratic Vice: The Attack on Duelling, Suicide, Adultery, and Gambling in Eighteenth-Century England* (New Haven: Yale University Press, 2013), p. 96.
3. Robert Houston, 'The Medicalization of Suicide: Medicine and the Law in Scotland and England, circa 1750–1850', in *Histories of Suicide: International Perspectives on Self-destruction in the Modern World*, ed. John C. Weaver and David Wright (Toronto: University of Toronto Press, 2009), p. 91.
4. Ibid. pp. 109, 94.
5. Ibid. p. 94.
6. Ibid.
7. James Kelly, 'Suicide in Eighteenth-Century Ireland', in *Death and Dying in Ireland, Britain, and Europe: Historical Perspectives*, ed. Mary Ann Lyons and James Kelly (Newbridge: Irish Academic Press, 2013), pp. 95–142 (97).
8. David Lederer, 'Suicide Statistics as Moral Statistics: Suicide, Sociology and the State', in *Death and Dying*, ed. Lyons and Kelly, pp. 221–48 (231).
9. Robert Houston, *Punishing the Dead?: Suicide, Lordship, and Community in Britain, 1500–1830* (Oxford: Oxford University Press, 2010), p. 374.
10. Kelly, 'Suicide', pp. 95–6.
11. Houston, *Punishing*, p. 6.
12. Ibid. pp. 6, 370.
13. Kelly, 'Suicide', p. 96.
14. Houston, 'Medicalization', p. 91.
15. Houston, *Punishing*, p. 5.
16. Ibid.
17. Kelly, 'Suicide', p. 97.
18. Houston, *Punishing*, p. 5.
19. George Gordon Lord Byron, *Manfred* [1817] in *The Longman Anthology of British Literature: The Romantics and Their Contemporaries*, vol. 2A, ed. Susan Wolfson and Peter Manning, 4th ed. (New York: Pearson Longman, 2010), pp. 660–95 (I, I, 144).
20. Byron, *Manfred*, II, ii, 166–71.
21. George Gordon Lord Byron, *Byron's Letters and Journals: A New Selection*, ed. Richard Lansdown (Oxford: Oxford University Press, 2015), p. 380.

22. Richard Bell, 'Slave Suicide, Abolition and the Problem of Resistance', *Slavery & Abolition: A Journal of Slave and Post-Slave Studies*, 33:4 (2012), pp. 525–49 (526).
23. Ibid. p. 537.
24. Thomas Szasz, *Fatal Freedom: The Ethics and Politics of Suicide* [2002] (Syracuse: Syracuse University Press, 2009), p. 15.
25. Kelly McGuire, *Dying to be English: Suicide Narratives and National Identity, 1721–1814* (London: Pickering & Chatto, 2012), p. 177.
26. Jeffrey Merrick, 'Suicide and Politics in Pre-Revolutionary France', *Eighteenth-Century Life* 30:2 (2006), pp. 32–47 (43).
27. Eugene Regnauld, *The Criminal History of the English Government: From the First Massacre of the Irish, to the Poisoning of the Chinese* (New York: J. S. Redfield, 1843), p. 44.
28. Elizabeth G. Dickenson and James M. Boyden, 'Ambivalence toward Suicide in Golden Age Spain', in *From Sin to Insanity: Suicide in Early Modern Europe*, ed. Jeffrey R. Watt (Ithaca: Cornell University Press, 2004), pp. 100–15 (107); Szasz, *Fatal Freedom*, p. 12.
29. William Godwin, *Enquiry Concerning Political Justice: and Its Influence on Morals and Happiness* [1793], 3rd edn (London: G. G. and J. Robinson, 1798), pp. xliii; 139–40.
30. P. B. Shelley, *The Mask of Anarchy* [1832], *Romanticism: An Anthology*, ed. Duncan Wu [1994] (Oxford: Blackwell Publishers, 1996), pp. 943–53 (ll. 139; 147).
31. Shelley, 'Mask', ll. 340–7.
32. P. B. Shelley, 'England in 1819' [1839], in *Romanticism: An Anthology*, ed. Wu, p. 876 (ll. 7; 13–14).
33. Shelley, 'England', ll. 8–9.
34. John Gardner, *Poetry and Popular Protest: Peterloo, Cato Street and the Queen Caroline Controversy* (Basingstoke: Palgrave Macmillan, 2011), p. 17.
35. Charles James, *Suicide Rejected, An Elegy, Founded upon Principles of Christian Confidence against Worldly Despondency* (London: Hookham and Carpenter, 1797), p. 12.
36. Sir Matthew Hale, *Historia Placitorum Coronæ: The History of the Pleas of the Crown* (London: T. Payne, 1778), p. 412.
37. Godwin, *Enquiry*, p. 87.
38. Jean-Jacques Rousseau, *Julie, Or, The New Heloise: Letters of Two Lovers who Live in a Small Town* [1761], trans. and ed. Philip Stewart and Jean Vaché (Lebanon: University Press of New England, 1997), p. 321.
39. Clara Tuite, *Lord Byron and Scandalous Celebrity* (Cambridge: Cambridge University Press, 2015), p. 97.

40. Ibid. p. 100.
41. Ibid.
42. Shelley, 'Mask', ll. 5–12.
43. Jane Blumberg, *Mary Shelley's Early Novels: 'This Child of Imagination and Misery'* [1993] (Basingstoke: Macmillan, 2016), p. 78.
44. George Gordon Lord Byron, Dedication to *Don Juan* [1819], in *Romanticism: An Anthology*, ed. Wu, pp. 769–74 (l. 88; 89–90; 93).
45. George Gordon Lord Byron, Preface to *Don Juan* VI–VIII [1823], in *The Major Works*, ed. Jerome McGann [1985] (Oxford: Oxford University Press, 2008), pp. 589–90 (589).
46. Frank McLynn, *Crime and Punishment in Eighteenth-Century England* (London: Routledge, 1989), p. 53.
47. Byron, Preface, p. 589.
48. Ibid.
49. Tuite, *Lord Byron*, p. 122.
50. Carlile, 'To the Republicans', p. 418.
51. Byron, Preface, p. 590.
52. Ibid. p. 589.
53. Michael Hulse, 'Introduction', in Johann Wolfgang von Goethe, *The Sorrows of Young Werther*, ed. Michael Hulse (London: Penguin, 1989), pp. 5–19 (12).
54. Tuite, *Lord Byron*, p. 109.
55. Byron, Preface, p. 590.
56. George Gordon Lord Byron, 'Epigrams' [1822], in *The Complete Poetical Works of Lord Byron*, ed. Paul Elmer More (Boston: Houghton Mifflin, 1905), p. 238 (ll. 1–2).
57. Byron, 'Epigrams', ll. 1–4.
58. David Hume, *Essays on Suicide, and the Immortality of the Soul* (London: Printed for M. Smith, 1783), p. 20.
59. Godwin, *Enquiry*, p. 92.
60. Jean-Jacques Rousseau, *The Social Contract* [1762], trans. Maurice Cranston (London: Penguin Books, 2004), pp. 32, 33.
61. George Gordon Lord Byron, 'Epigrams on Castlereagh', in *Lord Byron*, ed. Paul Muldoon (New York: Faber & Faber, 2010), p. 101 (ll. 11–14).
62. Houston, 'Medicalization', p. 91.
63. Houston, *Punishing*, p. 6.
64. Mary Fairclough, 'Radical Sympathy: Periodical Circulation and the Peterloo Massacre', *Romanticism and Victorianism on the Net* 57–58 (2010): 19 paragraphs (8).
65. Robert Walmsley, *Peterloo: The Case Re-opened* (Manchester: Manchester University Press, 1969), p. 512.

66. Carlile, 'To the Republicans', p. 418.
67. John Bew, *Castlereagh: A Life* (Oxford: Oxford University Press, 2012), p. 549.
68. Carlile, 'To the Republicans', p. 417.
69. James Chandler, *England in 1819: The Politics of Literary Culture and the Case of Romantic Historicism* (Chicago: University of Chicago Press, 1998), p. 18.

Chapter 8

William Cobbett, 'Resurrection Man': The Peterloo Massacre and the Bones of Tom Paine

Katey Castellano

No radical leader loomed so large and yet was so noticeably absent from the mass gathering at St Peter's Field on 16 August 1819 as the journalist William Cobbett. Most scholars agree that Cobbett's *Political Register* and Henry Hunt's oratory were the most persuasive radical influences encouraging the people to demand reform before Peterloo.[1] Yet Cobbett was living in America during the Peterloo massacre. He had fled to America in order to continue publishing his *Political Register* unimpeded by threats of imprisonment due to the suspension of habeas corpus in 1817. Even though Cobbett was physically absent from England when Peterloo occurred, conservative and pro-government broadsides and pamphlets published after the event blamed Cobbett's *Political Register* for the working-class discontent that culminated in the mass gathering at St Peter's Field. Cobbett provoked and shaped working-class discontent first and foremost through his widely disseminated address, 'To the Journeymen and Labourers of England, Wales, Scotland and Ireland'. Working-class readers bought and distributed 200,000 copies of the open letter, which appeared in Cobbett's unstamped two-penny *Political Register* on 2 November 1816.

'To the Journeymen and Labourers' insists, 'the real strength and all the resources of a country, ever have sprung and ever must spring, from the *labour* of its people'.[2] Cobbett's focus on labouring bodies' rightful place in the body politic counters the idea of the working class as an animalised surplus population. The radical Samuel Bamford documented the influence of Cobbett's cheap *Register* on the working class: 'Cobbett's books were printed in cheap form; the labourers read them, and thenceforward became literate and systematic in their proceedings'.[3] Cobbett's 'Two-Penny Trash', as his detractors called it, was considered so dangerous that two short-lived journals, the *Anti-Cobbett* and *The Detector*, were published in 1817 exclusively to counteract its message. Thus, even though Cobbett was not living in England at the time of the Peterloo massacre, conservatives and radicals alike understood that his argument for working-class inclusion in the body politic circulated amongst the people as they gathered for the mass political protest on St Peter's Field.[4]

Due to the time delay in news reaching America, Cobbett did not find out about the Peterloo massacre until he read the Irish newspapers on 26 September 1819.[5] Cobbett was outraged by what he called the 'Manchester Murders', and the government's indiscriminate injury and slaughter of the men, women and children protesting at St Peter's Field confirmed Cobbett's suspicion that the linguistic animalisation of the working class was accelerating into institutionally sanctioned violence. Cobbett alleged that the representation of the poor as animals by those in power – such as in Burke's reference to the working class as the 'swinish multitude' in his *Reflections on the Revolution in France* (1790) and Malthus' depiction of the poor as a population whose fertility should be managed similarly to farm animals – was designed to disenfranchise them of their political and common rights. Cobbett's political enemies, moreover, called him the 'Hampshire Hog' throughout his life; thus he had intimate experience with the strategy of animalising the working class to undermine their political status.[6] Cobbett's concern about the animalisation of the working class, I argue, reflects his prescient understanding of Giorgio Agamben's observations about the biopolitical animalisation of humans in modernity: the 'anthropological machine of the moderns' is a representational and political force that functions 'by animalizing the human, by isolating the nonhuman within the human' and thus strategically denies animalised humans full political rights and protections.[7]

Cobbett's response to the Peterloo massacre was based on his attunement to the ways in which the working class were animalised by contemporary discourse. On 29 September, three days after reading about the Peterloo massacre, Cobbett writes that he had personally disinterred the body of Tom Paine as his first step in a plan to return Paine's bones to England in order to create a memorial to the 'Noble of Nature'.[8] Paine died in obscurity after publishing *The Age of Reason* (1792), in which he denied the sacredness of the Bible. After his death, the Quakers refused to bury his body in a churchyard, so he was buried unceremoniously in a field at his farm in New Rochelle, New York.[9] Although Cobbett had considered a memorial to Paine previously, it was the event of Peterloo – the slaughter of working-class people like animals – that spurred him finally to disinter Paine's body.[10] While both his enemies and allies were baffled by Cobbett's response to Peterloo, Cobbett enthusiastically believed that establishing a memorial in England for the remains of an influential, working-class, political writer would validate radicalism as an important intergenerational movement that could not be snuffed out by the murder and prosecution of present-day radicals. Even his allies, however, distanced themselves from the project, and Cobbett's enemies emphasised the material ghastliness of Paine's disinterment with delighted derision. At least ten caricatures were published in pamphlets or broadsides (1819–20) that depict a deranged Cobbett carrying or interacting with Paine's skeleton or coffin.

Isaac Robert Cruikshank's caricature, *The political champion turned resurrection man!* (December 1819), for example, depicts Cobbett riding a flying demon-like monster across the Atlantic. Suspended between America and England, Cobbett holds a quill in his right hand, a symbol of his writing in the *Political Register*, and in the other hand he grasps the skeleton of Tom Paine (Figure 8.1). Paine's skull is capped with the bonnet rouge, while Cobbett says, 'How to delude the populace – An advantageous distribution of the words Liberty, Tyranny, Slavery & c'. Behind Cobbett follow four smaller flying monsters in the shape of scourge-carrying insects: they carry Cobbett's *Political Register*, Paine's *Age of Reason*, plague, revolution and corruption, with other monsters following in the distance. The flying monsters that trail behind Cobbett and Paine's skeleton suggest that the mass publication of working-class political ideas might amount to a dangerous, uncontrollable contagion. On the coast of America, people are celebrating that Cobbett has left the country; however, on the coast of England, post-Peterloo radicals welcome him waving their red caps of liberty and carrying banners.

Figure 8.1 *The political champion turned resurrection man!* by Isaac Robert Cruikshank (The British Museum, London, © The Trustees of the British Museum. All rights reserved.)

By calling Cobbett a 'resurrection man', Cruikshank was unfairly associating Cobbett's disinterment of Paine's body with the widely reviled men who robbed graves in order to sell the dead for anatomical dissection. However, Cruikshank's caricature nonetheless is uncannily perceptive about Cobbett's political influence on the working class in the years just before and after Peterloo. This essay analyses, first, Cobbett's 'advantageous distribution of words' in 'To the Journeymen and Labourers', which contributed to the mass meeting in St Peter's Field and, second, Cobbett's reaction to the violence of Peterloo, disinterring Paine's bones and shipping them back to England in order to create a memorial. Cobbett's 'resurrection-man' style of politics has been criticised as politically ineffectual nostalgia. E. P. Thompson contends that Cobbett 'nourished the culture of a class, whose wrongs he felt, but whose remedies he could not understand'.[11] Yet I argue that Cobbett's radically-conservative, 'resurrection-man' style of politics arose from his prescient understanding that violence against the working class stemmed from the rise of biopolitical discourse that animalised the poor. The animalisation of the poor sought to silence them, and both Cobbett's *Register* before Peterloo and his resurrection of Paine's bones after Peterloo were meant to engender forms of relational discourse that would interpellate the working classes into a conversation that would weave their collective voices into demands for inclusion in the body politic.

Countering the Animalisation of Labour in 'To the Journeymen and Labourers'

In 'To the Journeymen and Labourers', Cobbett uses rhetorical strategies to shift the affect of his working-class readers from those who are downtrodden and begging for help to those who are in a position of power to claim assistance and representation. First, by addressing his audience in a conversational style as equals, he interpellates the working class into the political realm. Second, Cobbett creates class solidarity by addressing his prose to all the striations of the working class: journeymen, labourers, women and children. Third, Cobbett asserts that workers' bodies are the producers of England's intergenerational wealth, not a drain on it.[12] Representing working-class bodies as the producers of wealth serves as a counter-discourse to the animalisation of the poor in Malthusian discourse.

By explicitly addressing the working class in epistolary form, Cobbett interpellates readers into a relationship with him. Cobbett wrote letters in the informal vernacular, and, moreover, he was continually talking with his readers and including accounts of those conversations in his letters. As Thompson argues, 'Cobbett's thought was not a system but a relationship', and it contained an element of reciprocity within the discourse.[13] In his journalistic style of the open letter, Cobbett thus modelled a central element of the early modern moral economy, reciprocity between those in power and those without it. 'To the Journeymen and Labourers' emphasises the structural violence and exclusion experienced by skilled and unskilled labour due to their common animalisation by those in power. He argues, they 'call you the *mob*, the *rabble*, the *scum*, the *swinish multitude*, and say, that your voice is nothing; that you have no business at public meetings; and that *you* are, and ought to be, considered as nothing in the body politic!'[14] By addressing this particular letter to both journeymen, who were highly-skilled labourers with access to guilds and social protections, and labourers, who were often unskilled and completely subject to the vicissitudes of wage labour, Cobbett sought to create relational discourse between those classes.[15]

The style of the open letter, in which Cobbett gave an account of his personal life alongside his political ideas, brought the English masses into a relationship not only with him but also with other workers, and engagement with readers was an important precursor to Peterloo because it created community while situating the working class within a world of political discourse. As James Grande argues, 'Within early nineteenth-century literary culture, letters carried particular strong associations with reading aloud within the domestic sphere, a practice that Cobbett was keen to encourage'.[16] Perhaps even more radically, Cobbett's *Register* was intentionally designed to conflate the public/private distinction by politicising working-class domestic life. Describing the benefit of his cheap publication, he argues,

> And besides, the expense of the thing itself thus becomes less than the expense of going to the public-house to hear it read. Then there is the time for reflection, and the opportunity of reading over again, and of referring to interesting facts. The *children* also have an opportunity of reading. The expence of other books will be saved by those who have this resource. The wife can sometimes read, if the husband cannot. The women will understand the causes of their starvation and raggedness as well as the men, and will lend their aid in endeavoring to effect the proper remedy. Many a father will thus, I hope, be induced to spend his evenings at home in instructing his children in the history of their misery, and in warming them into acts of patriotism.[17]

Cobbett seeks to move radical meetings out of the taverns frequented by men and into the home occupied by men, women and children. Addressing women and children greatly expands Cobbett's audience and also those who might be involved in agitation for radical change. Women are admonished to understand politics 'as well as the men' and even serve as leaders and teachers of the family. As Cobbett would later outline in more detail in his *Cottage Economy* (1822), he viewed domestic space as a place of political activism where even mundane domestic decisions, such as baking bread instead of buying it or drinking beer instead of tea, were legible signs of political engagement.[18]

By publishing 'To the Journeymen and Labourers' and other two-penny *Registers*, Cobbett seeks to politicise the home and make reading the *Register* and political conversation a daily habit. As Altick argues, Cobbett's *Register* was a 'revolutionary development in the history of the reading public'.[19] Habitually reading and discussing political issues prepares the working class to enter politics, even if they had not yet won the franchise. Ian Dyck notes that the two-penny *Register* was designed for 'the pedlar's pack, from where it was vended at hiring-fairs, market-places and public houses, together with other cultural productions such as chapbooks, almanacs, broadside songs'.[20] Cobbett's cheap *Register* may have been sold along with other cheap pamphlets and tracts, yet at the same time the *Register* countered the messages of the widely distributed 'moral tracts' intended for the poor. Directly after his 'Address' was published and just before leaving for America, Cobbett warned about the debilitating effect of moral stories written for the poor:

> Simple, insipid dialogues and stories, calculated for the minds of children seven or eight years old, or for those of savages just beginning to be civilised. These conceited persons have no idea that the minds of the working classes ever presume to rise above this infantine level.[21]

The *Political Register*'s open letters invited its readers to rise above being the mere recipient of didactic, moral discourse into being critical and informed participants in an open-ended political dialogue.

After creating such a broad audience and interpellating them into the national conversation about politics, Cobbett further develops a new sense of subjectivity for the labourers. 'To the Journeymen and Labourers' opens with a description of the dignity and necessity of labour: 'the real strength and all the resources of a country, ever have sprung and ever must spring, from the *labour* of its people'.[22] Cobbett then advises workers to see themselves reflected in the affluence around them:

> Elegant dresses, superb furniture, stately buildings, fine roads and canals, fleet horses and carriages, numerous and stout ships, waterhouses teeming with goods; all these, and many other objects that fall under our view, are so many marks of national wealth and resources. But all these spring from *labour*. Without the journeyman and the labourer none of them could exist; without the assistance of their hands, the country would be a wilderness, hardly worth the notice of an invader.[23]

In this revision of biopolitical discourse about the poor, the 'numerous' and 'teeming' bodies of the working class are reflected in 'elegant', 'superb', 'stately' and 'fine' durable objects. Such numerous bodies, instead of being a drain on England's wealth, created the wealth and civilisation of England.

To depict the working classes of England as the creators of intergenerational wealth counters the representation of the working class as animals. Cobbett argues, 'With this correct idea of your own worth in your minds, with what indignation must you hear yourselves called the Populace, the Rabble, the Mob, the Swinish Multitude'.[24] This list of dehumanising epithets alludes to the animalisation of the working class as the 'swinish multitude' in Edmund Burke's *Reflections on the Revolution in France* (1790) and as a 'populace' in Malthus' *Essay on Population* (1798). Cobbett's argument suggests that this discourse has done representational violence to the poor and has limited their understanding of their place in the body politic. Stephen F. Eisenmen reminds us that Burke's term 'swinish multitude' was meant to 'explicitly recall market day mayhem at Smithfield'.[25] Cobbett understood that the conceptual erasure of localised human communities precedes a real erasure through forced emigration or restrictions on marriage and childbearing. He argues, 'these corrupt and insolent men are busied with schemes for *getting rid of you*'.[26] Cobbett, whose opposition to the Malthusian understanding of the poor would only increase in frequency and ferocity in the 1820s, disliked Malthus' writings because of the way they animalised the people. He argues, 'The writings of MALTHUS, who considers men as *mere animals*, may have had influence in producing of this change; and we now frequently hear the working classes called, "the *population*," just as we call animals upon a farm, "the *stock*."'[27] Unlike working-class Romantics such as William Blake and John Clare, who try to draw parallels between the working class and animals as a form of radical solidarity, Cobbett performs his resurrection politics by reinforcing the divide between animal and human life.[28]

Cobbett suspects that the animalisation of the working classes sought to render them submissive, silent animals in all political matters. Cobbett argues that those in power seek to:

> Keep all *quiet*! Do not *rouse*! Keep *still*! Keep *down*! Let those who perish, perish in *silence*! It will, however, be out of the power of those

> Quacks, with all their laudanum, to allay the blood which is now boiling in the veins of the people of this kingdom; who, if they are doomed to perish, are, at any rate, resolved not to perish in *silence*.[29]

The poor are biopolitically controlled and made to be subservient, Cobbett reveals, because there is another kind of quiet violent resentment seething under the veneer of their submissiveness. While often the working class were accused of committing violence, Cobbett warns, presciently, that this linguistic and systemic violence might turn into real violence: 'Such men, would kill you or me or any man who talks of the people's sufferings . . . And I have not the least doubt, those men would see one half of the people's throats cut in order to reduce the rest into silent submission.'[30] This prescient statement all but predicts the violence of the Peterloo massacre, during which working-class people lost their lives over their refusal to remain politically silent.

As 'The Political Champion Turned Resurrection Man' suggests, Cobbett's 'advantageous distribution of words' was thought of as a plague-like contagion that spread among the working class. The radical Samuel Bamford records,

> At this time, the writings of William Cobbett suddenly became of great authority; they were read on nearly every cottager hearth in the manufacturing districts of South Lancashire; in those of Leicester, Derby, and Nottingham; also in many of the Scottish manufacturing towns. Their influence was speedily visible; he directed his readers to the true cause of their sufferings – misgovernment; and to its proper corrective – parliamentary reform.[31]

Bamford describes the way in which reading Cobbett's two-penny *Register* prompted the working classes to assert themselves into the political order. 'To the Journeymen and Labourers' clearly argues that misgovernment, resulting in taxation, paper money and the national debt are leading to the suffering of the poor, but, most importantly, he seeks to expose the rhetoric that is used to blame the poor for their own bodily existence. As Olivia Smith argues, 'Cobbett's prose is essentially an act of healing, of transforming previously domineering and antagonistic images and styles into a resource of self-knowledge and a basis of action'.[32] Cobbett's rhetoric seeks a transformation of the affect of the poor, to give them a 'correct idea of your own worth in your minds', that might counter negative messages internalised from a culture that describes them as an over-large, supplemental population. By attempting to resurrect the intergenerational, historical significance of the working class as a collective political body, Cobbett sought to ground their existence in a history that discursively transcends their individualised, animalised bodies.

'Nothing New': Resurrecting the Bones of Tom Paine after Peterloo

'To the Journeymen and Labourers' challenges the rhetoric of animalisation in discourse about the poor by interpellating all striations of the British working class into a political conversation that represents the working class as stable, intergenerational contributors to British politics and culture. The mass production and distribution of Cobbett's two-penny *Register* undoubtedly inspired much of the radical discontent that culminated in the large crowds gathering in St Peter's Field to agitate for parliamentary reform. The suspension of habeas corpus in 1817, in Cobbett's view, was designed at least in part to intimidate him from continuing to publish his *Register*. Thus, Cobbett fled to America to continue publishing without the threat of imprisonment. Cobbett's hasty departure for America just as he was beginning to persuade the working class to agitate for political reform left other radicals in dismay, yet his choice of self-exile in America is not all that surprising. Although Cobbett is often represented as a local, rural British writer, he always demonstrated, as James Chandler observes, a 'deeply ingrained transatlantic orientation' through his creation of a knowledge commons that promoted the exchange of periodicals and ideas across the Atlantic.[33] In 'To the Journeymen and Labourers', Cobbett suggested that residual British liberty and freedom can be found only in America: 'The Americans, who are a very wise people, and who love liberty with all their hearts, and who take care to enjoy it too, took special care not to part with any of the great principles and laws which they derived from their forefathers'.[34] Because the Americans ostensibly preserved British principles, Cobbett sought to associate the reform movement with the American Revolution rather than the French, which dangerously cut ties with the past.[35] Cobbett sought to invoke discontent among the working classes which might be channelled into a resurrection of ideals from the past, such as the moral economy and common rights.

'To the Journeymen and Labourers' argues for working-class inclusion in the body politic through the resurrection of ideas and values from the past: 'We want *great alteration*, but we want *nothing new*. Alteration, modification to suit the times and circumstances; but the great principles ought to be and must be, the same, or else confusion will follow.'[36] Cobbett refers here to what Leonore Nattrass calls the 'radical ancient constitution', the common right to food, clothing and living space.[37] A pamphlet deriding Cobbett's reaction to the events of Peterloo, *Sketches in the Life of Billy Cobb* (1819), argues that Cobbett's desire for 'nothing new' culminates in the absurdity of disinterring the body of Thomas Paine and travelling back to England with his bones. The pamphlet asserts, 'B STANDS FOR BONES, that "nothing new"', and the page is illustrated with an image of Cobbett stooped over the earth, putting Paine's arm and skull in a coffin, as more human bones are scattered around the coffin in disorder.[38] Digging up and attempting to memorialise the bones of Paine is the most material version of Cobbett as 'resurrection man', and figuratively it is consistent with Cobbett's radically conservative politics that sought to ground political radicalism in past principles and institutions. In the wake of the Peterloo massacre, Cobbett resurrected Paine's body in order to establish a monument to which the working class would make a bodily pilgrimage. By meeting together at a memorial in the landscape, a collective, intergenerational working-class body might emerge and persist.

Starting in the 1810s, Cobbett increasingly acknowledged his debt to Paine's thought, and he was disturbed by Paine's life ending in obscurity without a proper memorial. Yet it was the event of Peterloo that prompted him to take action. Two days after reading about Peterloo while in America, Cobbett writes, 'I have just done here a thing, which I have always, since I came to this country, vowed that I would do: that is, *taken up the remains of our famous countryman*, PAINE, *in order to covey them to England*'.[39] Wanting 'nothing new', Cobbett seeks to establish an influential political ancestor to continue the project he began in 'To the Journeymen and Labourers': symbolically elevating working-class life above animal life by establishing their intergenerational importance and dignity. Seeking 'to do *justice to the memory* of our famous countryman; this child of the "*Lower Orders*"', Cobbett resurrected Paine as a form of working-class nobility whose writing would be forever recorded in the nation's history and whose body would permanently mark the English landscape.[40]

Paine would have been dismayed at becoming one of the 'manuscript authority of the dead' that he railed against during his lifetime,[41] yet Cobbett's radical conservatism always melded Burkean and Painite ideas. As Olivia Smith argues, Cobbett's cheap *Register* 'writes the swinish multitude into a dignified and traditional, particularly Burkean, social fabric'.[42] In his resurrection of Paine, Cobbett attempts to establish Burke's political foe, Paine, as a forefather in the Burkean sense. Given the intensity of the Burke/Paine debate in the 1790s, it is remarkable that almost thirty years later, spurred by the event of Peterloo, Cobbett collapses the theories of the two opposed thinkers. Yet Cobbett's project of intergenerational stability – his 'nothing new' – can be located both in the stately and fine goods created by the working class that were lauded in 'To the Journeymen and Labourers' and in the proposed memorial to Paine. Materially, both durable goods and memorials create 'a partnership not only between those who are living, but those who are living, those who are dead, and those who are to be born'.[43] Tying the working class to durable material objects that last beyond their lifetimes performatively pulls the working class away from being associated with transient animal bodies into an intergenerational political movement.

Cobbett argues that his memorial to Paine will serve an active function among the working class: 'the tomb of this "*Noble of Nature*" will be an object of pilgrimage with the people'.[44] During the Romantic period travelling to the memorials of writers become fashionable. Paul Westover calls this phenomenon 'necromanticism', which demonstrates 'Romanticism's dependence not just on the past, but more precisely on bodies dead and buried'.[45] Most travel to writers' memorials contributed to middle-class canon-formation; somewhat similarly, by creating a memorial for Paine, Cobbett seeks to establish Paine as the forefather of a working-class canon. Paine's *The Rights of Man*, as Haywood argues, initiates the plebeian public sphere, as it was widely published in cheap form and written in accessible language.[46] Mass publication was central to an important affective shift in the working class, as John Klancher describes, such mass-produced radical texts 'confront their readers as collectives and representatives of collectives – "an *inseparable* part" of the social order, undetachable members of an audience contesting its position in social and cultural space'.[47] Paine is indeed a forefather of Cobbett's two-penny *Register* and other radical publications of the same time such as *The Black Dwarf*, *Gorgon* and *Republican*, which all used mass publishing to cultivate a working-class audience.

Cobbett's project for Paine's memorial aspires to more than literary canonisation; by encouraging pilgrimage to Paine's tomb, Cobbett sought to initiate a process of self-formation through the bodily mobility of the working class. Pilgrimage prompts the working class to exercise the 'right of loco-motion': 'The laws of England secure to us the right of loco-motion; that is to say, the right of moving our bodies from one place to another.'[48] The right of locomotion amounts to what Foucault called a 'technology of the self', a 'mode of action that an individual exercises upon himself' in creating political freedom.[49] 'To the Journeymen and Labourers' had also admonished the working class to exercise the 'right of loco-motion': 'Any man can draw up a petition, and any man can carry it up to London, with instructions to deliver it into trusty hands, to be presented whenever the House shall meet.'[50] This particular piece of advice caused a great deal of agitation: a journal that sprung up in response to the popularity of Cobbett's cheap *Register*, the *Anti-Cobbett* (1817), addressed it directly. It warns that if people travel to London with petitions, then large groups of men will starve and die together on the roads, creating nothing more than an embarrassing spectacle. Instead, the people were advised, 'by waiting patiently at your own homes, you will certainly gather the fruit of these exertions made by your best and real friends [the upper classes]'.[51] Cobbett, however, insightfully suggested that exercising a freedom of movement to travel is a technique for self-formation; it transforms the working class from penned-in animals that wait quietly in their homes like animals in a barn to an empowered collective body. Cobbett later performs the political 'right of loco-motion' in his *Rural Rides* in the 1820s.

By creating a memorial for Paine, Cobbett sought to establish a working-class necro-geography in the wake of the senseless deaths of the Peterloo massacre. Thomas Lacqueur argues that in the nineteenth century, people 'engaged with creating, through bodies, specific memorial communities and specific histories'.[52] Cobbett indeed considered the project to be communal; he argued, 'Let this be considered the act of the *reformers of England, Scotland, and Ireland*. In their name we opened the grave, and in their name will the tomb be raised.'[53] In a private letter to J. W. Francis, Cobbett further explained:

> I have done myself the honour to disinter his bones . . . they are now on their way to England. When I myself return, I shall cause them to speak the common sense of the great man; I shall gather together the people of Liverpool and Manchester in one assembly with those of London, and those bones will effect the reformation of England in Church and State.[54]

Cobbett wanted Paine's body to engage in what Lacqueur calls 'the work of the dead' as they 'speak the common sense' of radical politics. The memorial to Paine would thus establish a necrogeographic meeting point for people from different locations to gather together in 'one assembly', a collective working-class body. Whether by memorialising Tom Paine or by inviting the working classes to see themselves in the wealth and built environment of England, Cobbett gestures towards a working-class collectivity to come. Brian Massumi suggests, 'resistance is of the nature of a *gesture*. Resistance cannot be communicated or inculcated. It can only be gestured. The gesture is a call to attunement.'[55] Both the memorial for Paine and the reciprocal nature of Cobbett's writing are gestures towards an attunement, invitations into affective shift in the working class that resists their individualisation and animalisation in order to assert a collective political body.

Cobbett brought Paine's bones back to England during a resurgence of interest in Paine's ideas. In 1818, Richard Carlile published an edition of Paine's *Age of Reason*. He was sent to prison for blasphemous publication for almost ten years, but the sensationalism of the trial and his subsequent imprisonment caused the book to sell in great quantities.[56] Haywood argues that the figure and ideas of Paine reasserted a 'spectropolitical' presence of the 'deferred promise' of revolution after the end of the Napoleonic Wars. Cobbett's 'hagiographical adventure', however, was the most literal resurrection of Paine's ghost.[57] While figures on the right resurrected Paine in caricatures that demonised his legacy, Cobbett sought to establish him as a saint or 'natural Noble' who would legitimise a tradition of working-class politics.

In the *Political Register*, Cobbett documents the dismay of both radical activists and loyalist, pro-government writers at his return with Paine's body. He records,

> To bring *the bones of* PAINE amidst such a state of things was to put public opinion, and especially with regard to myself, to the severest test. By way of preparation, the newspapers (about three hundred in number) had proclaimed me to be coming with a design to carry the bones at the head of a Revolutionary army.[58]

Indeed, due to the fear of another popular uprising, the constables of Manchester prevented Cobbett from entering the city with Paine's bones. At the same time, loyalists published many caricatures, pamphlets and broadsides ridiculing Cobbett's venture.[59] One response to Cobbett's return was to emphasise the instability in his political views by republishing Cobbett's own *The Life of Thomas Paine* (original publication in 1796, republished in 1819) – a vitriolic attack on Paine that Cobbett wrote during his earlier career as the loyalist Peter Porcupine during the 1790s. In the preface, the new editor performs shock and horror by asserting no one could believe that Cobbett 'would actually bring over his [Paine's] mouldering bones from a distant land, and expose them as relics to the veneration of the British public'.[60] The ghastliness of Cobbett's venture is emphasised in the number of British caricatures that depict him literally carrying the coffin and/or bones of Tom Paine on his back. *The Life and Times of Billy Cobb and Tom Paine* describes a custom house scene that accuses Cobbett of mental instability:

> Look! how the officers did stare,
>   Transfixed – like stocks or stones,
> When they beheld BILL COBB was there,
>   And with him TOM PAINE's BONES!
> Prepared they were for taking heed,
>   If fever they should find;
> But quite at fault how to proceed,
>   With *what infects the mind*.[61]

The attack on Cobbett's mental state sought to delegitimise Cobbett's goal of creating Paine's memorial. Similarly, radicals disapproved of the project: 'Former friends, or pretended friends, shrugged up their shoulders; and looked hard in my face, as if in wonder that I was not dismayed.'[62]

Without support for the memorial, Cobbett promptly abandoned the project and stored Paine's bones unceremoniously in his attic. Cobbett's failure at this point mars his legacy. William Hazlitt's sketch of Cobbett records,

> The only time he ever grew romantic was in bringing over the relics of Mr Thomas Paine with him from America to go a progress with them through the disaffected districts. Scarce had he landed in Liverpool when he left the bones of a great man to shift for themselves . . .'.[63]

While his plan to create a memorial for Paine was not successful, it arose out of an impulse to elevate the poor above an animal death into an intergenerational existence in the wake of the Peterloo massacre. Death and burial were a locus for treating the poor as animals, as Lacqueur argues:

> In life the pauper was a drain on the commonwealth; in death she was pure waste, a relic that might only be redeemed if it could somehow find a use in anatomy theaters or, more fantastically, in marling the field. Anonymous mass graves in urban churchyards and in specialised new grounds belonging to poorhouses starting in the early eighteenth century and the mass graves in the nineteenth century cemeteries largely worked to erase the poor from the community of the dead.[64]

Cobbett sought to restore Paine to the community of the dead and thus ensure the dignity and continuity of the working class. To establish a celebrated memorial and funeral for Paine accompanied by the spectacle of 'twenty waggon loads of flowers . . . to strew the road before the hearse' is a territorial gesture on behalf of the working class to confirm their part in the larger political and social body.[65]

Cobbett believed that the violence of Peterloo occurred because of a rhetorical rendering of the poor as animalised 'stock' and 'surplus population' who were excluded from political rights.[66] As mentioned previously, before Peterloo, in 'To the Journeymen and Labourers',

Cobbett warned that those who wrote about the problem of the poor were 'busied with schemes for *getting rid of you*' through emigration, prisons and workhouses, and the prohibition of marriage. Due to the decline of the commons and common right and the simultaneous rise of a capitalist economy, the poor were being turned into what Giorgio Agamben would later call 'bare life', excluded from rights within the established political order.[67] The violence of Peterloo confirmed Cobbett's suspicion that linguistic and conceptual violence against the poor easily morphs into institutionalised physical violence, so he literally resurrects the bones of Tom Paine in order to build the intergenerational value of the working class. Both of these movements may have been conservative, resurrecting something from the past, but they were also attempts at inclusion, at countering the animalisation and marginalisation of the working class by insisting that they are connected to intergenerational monuments and institutions beyond their animal bodies. While Cobbett ultimately failed in his role as 'resurrection man' for Paine's memorial, he continued to refine and rearticulate his theory of working-class inclusion through resurrection of the past and recourse to intergenerational stability in his publications of the 1820s such as *Rural Rides*, *Cottage Economy* and *History of the Protestant 'Reformation'*.

Notes

1. E. P. Thompson argues that in the 'groundswell of Radical propaganda' of that period, the most influential journalistic voice was that of William Cobbett and the most compelling orator was Henry Hunt (*The Making of the English Working Class* [1963] [New York: Vintage, 1966], p. 601). Similarly, Ian Haywood documents, 'The turning point in the development of "cheap" political reading in this period is undoubtedly Cobbett's decision in November 1816 to issue his *Weekly Political Register* in a reduced, two-penny format' (*The Revolution in Popular Literature: Print, Politics, and the People, 1790–1860* [Cambridge: Cambridge University Press, 2004], p. 86).
2. 'To the Journeymen and Labourers of England, Wales, Scotland, and Ireland', *Political Register* 31 (2 November 1816), pp. 545–76 (545).
3. Samuel Bamford, *Passages in the Life of a Radical* (London: J. Heywood, 1841), p. 7.

4. For example, the post-Peterloo caricature, *Fanatical Reformists, Or the Smithfield Assembly of New Legislators* by Charles Williams (1819) depicts Henry Hunt riding an ass that bears the face of Cobbett. The working-class radicals that surround Hunt and Cobbett are depicted as cattle and swine, which bears further testimony to the animalisation of the working class during the time before and after the Peterloo massacre.
5. 'To Henry Hunt, Esq.', *Political Register* 35 (13 November 1819), pp. 375–8 (375).
6. Illustrations of Cobbett with the body of a pig can be found in *The Loyal Man in the Moon* (London: C. Chapple, 1820) and *The Men in the Moon: Or, the 'Devil to Pay'* (London, 1820).
7. Giorgio Agamben, *The Open: Man and Animal*, trans. Kevin Attell (Stanford: Stanford University Press, 2004), p. 37. In the period, the term brutalisation was frequently used to describe the strategy of animalising humans to disempower them. Brutalisation and animalisation are synonyms. However, I choose to use the term animalisation in order to emphasise Cobbett's prescient theoretical understanding of the consequences of biopolitics for the poor. Animalising racial difference was used to justify nineteenth-century colonisation and slavery. Debbie Lee explores the animalisation of Africans as monkeys and apes in chapter 4 of *Slavery and the Romantic Imagination* (Philadelphia: University of Pennsylvania Press, 2002). Although Cobbett was against slavery, he focused almost singularly on the condition of the English working class. The animalisation of the working class in England tended, somewhat differently, to associate the working-class 'crowd' with cattle and swine. As Stephen F. Eisenman points out, the 'unreasoned outbursts of the mob' were considered to be eruptions of animal behaviour ('The Real "Swinish Multitude"', *Critical Inquiry* 42 [Winter 2016]), pp. 339–73 (347–8).
8. *Political Register* 35 (29 September 1819), pp. 382–4 (382).
9. For more information about Paine's obscure burial, see Leo Bressler, 'Peter Porcupine and the Bones of Tom Paine', *Pennsylvania Magazine of History and Biography* 82 (April 1958), pp. 176–85, and Paul Collins, *The Trouble with Tom: The Strange Afterlife and Times of Thomas Paine* (New York: Bloomsbury, 2005).
10. 'A Letter to Lord Folkestone', *Political Register* 35 (18 September 1819), pp. 129–55 (131–2).
11. Thompson, *The Making*, p. 762.
12. In *The Ecology of British Romantic Conservatism, 1790–1837* (Basingstoke: Palgrave Macmillan, 2013), I argue that Romanticism is invested in an 'intergenerational imagination' that seeks to reinvest value in

collective cultural identity through honoring continuities between past and future generations. The grand buildings and stately furniture with which Cobbett seeks to associate working-class bodies aspires to develop an intergenerational imagination on their behalf (pp. 1–14).

13. Thompson, *The Making*, p. 758. Moreover, as James Grande points out, in Newgate (1810–12) Cobbett wrote many prison letters, which influenced the style of the open letters published in his two-penny *Register*: 'Cobbett formulated a radical mode of correspondence, which draws on aspects of manuscript, oral and material culture' (*William Cobbett, the Press and Rural England: Radicalism and the Fourth Estate, 1792–1835* [Basingstoke: Palgrave Macmillan, 2014], p. 60).
14. 'To the Journeymen and Labourers of England, Wales, Scotland, and Ireland', *Political Register* 31 (2 November 1816), pp. 545–76 (562).
15. According to Jon Klancher, Cobbett's *Register* was innovative and influential because his 'vantage point shapes a discourse that brings rural and urban, northern and southern, handcraft and artisan labourers within a broader, national sense of being a public' (*The Making of English Reading Audiences, 1790–1832* [Madison, WI: University of Wisconsin Press, 1987], p. 128).
16. Grande, *William Cobbett*, p. 85.
17. 'To the Readers of the *Register*', *Political Register* 31 (16 November 1816), pp. 609–24 (611–12).
18. For more on Cobbett's politicised domestic economy, see 'Subsistence as Resistance: William Cobbett's Food Politics' in my *Ecology of British Romantic Conservatism*, pp. 113–40.
19. Richard Altick, *The English Common Reader: A Social History of the Mass Reading Public 1800–1900* (Chicago: University of Chicago Press, 1957), p. 325.
20. Ian Dyck, *William Cobbett and Rural Popular Culture* (Cambridge: Cambridge University Press, 1992), p. 82.
21. 'Mr. Cobbett's Taking Leave of His Countrymen', *Political Register* 32 (5 April 1817), pp. 1–32 (7).
22. *Political Register* 31 (2 November 1816), pp. 545–76 (545).
23. Ibid. pp. 545–6.
24. Ibid. p. 546.
25. Eisenman, pp. 339–73 (349).
26. *Political Register* 31 (2 November 1816), pp. 545–76 (564).
27. 'Mr. Cobbett's Taking Leave', p. 6.
28. Cobbett denies the vulnerability that humans share with animals. Ron Broglio points out the representative connections between animal and working-class vulnerability: 'The machinery of biopower at work on the material, biological, and political body of the agricultural labourer

can be read through the figure of animal death.' This shared vulnerability prompted Cobbett to deny vehemently any connection between animals and the working-class. (Ron Broglio, *Beasts of Burden: Biopolitics, Labor, and Animals Life in British Romanticism* [Albany: State University of New York Press, 2017], p. 36).

29. *Political Register* 31 (2 November 1816), pp. 545–76 (573).
30. 'Letter to Mr. Hunt', *Political Register,* 31 (14 December 1816), pp. 737–68 (761).
31. Bamford, *Passages*, p. 7.
32. Olivia Smith, *The Politics of Language: 1791–1819* (Oxford: Clarendon Press, 1984), pp. 230–1.
33. James Chandler, *England in 1819: The Politics of Literary Culture and the Case of Romantic Historicism* (Chicago: University of Chicago Press, 1998), p. 459. As his vision of American agrarian freedom collapses with his medievalism, Cobbett develops an affinity for Tom Paine. David A. Wilson argues that 'American liberty, for Cobbett, was a means to the end of strengthening British reform, and British reform was itself a means to restore Britain's former greatness' (*Paine and Cobbett: The Transatlantic Connection* [Georgetown, ON: McGill-Queen's University Press, 1988], p. 170).
34. *Political Register* 31 (2 November 1816), pp. 545–76 (567).
35. Cobbett warned, 'when you hear a man talking big and hectoring about projects which *go farther than a real and radical reform of Parliament*, be you well assured, that that man would be a second Robespierre if he could . . .' (Ibid. p. 569).
36. Ibid. p. 568.
37. Leonore Nattrass, *William Cobbett: The Politics of Style* (Cambridge: Cambridge University Press, 2007), p. 112.
38. *Sketches of the Life of Billy Cobb, and the Death of Tommy Pain* (London, 1819), p. 15.
39. *Political Register* 35 (29 September 1819), pp. 382–4 (382).
40. Ibid. p. 383.
41. Paine argued: 'I am contending for the rights of the *living*, and against their being willed away, and controlled and contracted for, by the manuscript authority of the dead; and Mr. Burke is contending for the authority of the dead over the rights and freedom of the living' (*The Paine Reader*, ed. Michael Foot and Isaac Kramnick [New York: Penguin, 1987], p. 204).
42. Smith, *Politics*, p. 230.
43. Edmund Burke, *Reflections on the Revolution in France* (New York: Penguin, 2004), pp. 194–5.
44. *Political Register* 35 (29 September 1819), pp. 382–4 (383).

45. Paul Westover, *Necromanticism: Travelling to Meet the Dead, 1750–1860* (Basingstoke: Palgrave Macmillan, 2012), p. 48.
46. Haywood, *Revolution*, pp. 11–25.
47. Klancher, *The Making*, p. 100.
48. 'To Mr. James Paul Cobbett', *Political Register* 35 (4 December 1819), pp. 385–418 (393).
49. Michel Foucault, 'Technologies of the Self', in *Ethics: Subjectivity and Truth*, ed. Paul Rabinow (New York: The New Press, 1994), p. 225.
50. *Political Register* 31 (2 November 1816), pp. 545–76 (576).
51. *Anti-Cobbett, Or, The Weekly Patriotic Register* 5 (1817), pp. 131–2, 146.
52. Thomas Lacqueur, *The Work of the Dead: A Cultural History of Mortal Remains* (Princeton: Princeton University Press, 2015), p. 93. Cobbett can also be considered to be part of the larger movement in the nineteenth century in which, as Esther Schor puts it, 'the living imaginatively bring the dead to life, and by so doing, invent history' (*Bearing the Dead: The British Culture of Mourning from the Enlightenment to Victoria* [Princeton: Princeton University Press, 1994], p. 9).
53. *Political Register* 35 (29 September 1819), pp. 382–4 (383).
54. Quoted in *The Life and Letters of William Cobbett in England & America: Based Upon Hitherto Unpublished Family Papers*, ed. Lewis Melville, vol. 2 (London: J. Lane, 1913), p. 116.
55. Brian Massumi, *Politics of Affect* (Cambridge: Polity, 2015), p. 105.
56. See Altick, *English Common Reader*, p. 327. See also Leo Bressler, 'Peter Porcupine and the Bones of Tom Paine', *Pennsylvania Magazine of History and Biography* 82 (April 1958), p. 183.
57. Ian Haywood, *Romanticism and Caricature* (Cambridge: Cambridge University Press, 2013), pp. 102, 118.
58. 'To Mr. James Paul Cobbett', *Political Register* 35 (27 January 1820), pp. 775–86 (777).
59. For example, see *The Men in the Moon* (London, 1820), *The Loyal Man in the Moon* (London: C. Chapple, 1820), *The Real or Constitutional House That Jack Built* (London: J. Asperne, W. Sams and J. Johnston, 1819), Robert Cruikshank, *The Book of Wonders* (London: H. Stemman, 1821), and *An Excellent New Song, called 'Rascals Ripe!'* (London, 1820).
60. The same publication printed an extract from *The Times* of 27 November 1819 that emphasised the macabre material nature of Cobbett's venture. Describing the custom house: 'When the box was opened, Cobbett observed, –"There, gentlemen, are the mortal remains of *the immortal Thomas Paine*." The skull was shewn, and the coffin-plate accompanied it, but all that could be deciphered was, "—Pain, –180—aged 74 years." Cobbett was extremely attentive to

the box, and looked rather serious during the exhibition' (*The Life of Thomas Paine* [Durham: J. Humble, 1819], p. 25).

61. *Sketches of the Life of Billy Cobb, and the Death of Tommy Pain* (London, 1819), pp. 23–4.
62. 'To Mr. James Paul Cobbett', *Political Register* 35 (27 January 1820), pp. 775–86 (778).
63. *The Character of William Cobbett, M.P.* (London, 1835), p. 14. For more information about the fate of Paine's bones, the whereabouts of which remain unknown, see Collins, *The Trouble with Tom* (cited above in note 9).
64. Lacqueur, *The Work of the Dead*, p. 317.
65. 'To Mr. James Paul Cobbett', *Political Register* 35 (27 January 1820), pp. 775–86 (783).
66. Malthus argues, 'A man who is born into a world already possessed, if he cannot get subsistence from his parents on whom he has a just demand, and if the society do not want his labour, has no claim of right to the smallest portion of food, and, in fact, has no business to be where he is' (*An Essay on the Principle of Population: Or, a View of Its Past and Present Effects on Human Happiness* [London: Joseph Johnson, 1803], p. 249.
67. *Homo Sacer: Sovereign Power and Bare Life*, trans. Daniel Heller-Roazen (Stanford: Stanford University Press, 1998).

Chapter 9

The Church and Peterloo

John Gardner

Attacks on the church became one of the few ways for radicals to confront the government after a series of post-Peterloo crackdowns. With the violence of Peterloo came the end of large public protests to demand reform. The Six Acts of November 1819 brought taxes on knowledge and laws against public meetings. The crushing of the so-called 'rebellions' of 1820, which included the Cato Street Conspiracy, quelled notions of a revolution with eight executions for High Treason in 1820. Finally, the death of Queen Caroline ended hopes that patronage and a royal divorce would bring down the government. Peterloo brought the closeness of the relationship between church and state into the open when the clerical magistrates, Reverend William Hay and Reverend Charles Wicksted Ethelston, instructed the Manchester and Salford Yeomanry and the 15th Hussars to charge through the crowd at St Peter's Field, causing the Peterloo massacre. At around 1.35 p.m. on 16 August 1819, when the crowd had grown to its capacity, Ethelston reputedly read the Riot Act from the window of a Mr Buxton's house, leaning out so far that Hay allegedly held his coat-tails. Many said that it was never read. These magistrates, and with them the Established Church, then became the focus of a range of literary assaults. My argument is that during the suppression of radical and reform activity in the period after Peterloo, attacking the church was one of the few ways that reformers could congregate effectively. Peterloo put a lens on the church and focused on the dominant themes of corruption, hypocrisy, sinecures, representation, spying, taxation and, on the face of it, sexual scandal.

In 1822 a number of writers seized on the homosexual scandal embroiling Percy Jocelyn, the Bishop of Clogher. *The Arse Bishop*

Josling a Soldier, or Do as I Say Not as I Do, illustrated by Robert Cruikshank and published by Fores in July 1822, depicts Jocelyn being apprehended, with his trousers down, alongside a soldier in a similar state of undress. Looking through a window on the event is a young girl, and, at a doorway, three people stare on and make comments, including 'Hang them in chains', 'The Pillory' and 'Send them to China!' A few days before the illustration was published, on 19 July 1822, Jocelyn, the second son of Robert, 1st Earl of Roden, was caught in flagrante with a soldier, John Moverley, in the back room of the White Lion tavern by the landlord's son-in-law James Plant. Plant had seen them through a window and soon gathered the watchman, the landlord and eight pub regulars together to view the scene. Clogher and the soldier were then arrested and charged with carrying out an unnatural act. The soldier was denied bail, but Jocelyn was freed on a £1,000 surety and soon absconded, fleeing first to France and then Scotland where he lived out the rest of his life under an assumed name. Iain McCalman writes that the scandal 'proved a godsend to an increasingly beleaguered radical press . . . the Clogher affair triggered a mass of further exposes of clerical vice and crime'.[1] My argument here is that it was not the Clogher affair that 'triggered' attacks on the church but instead that it was Peterloo. Nonetheless, Clogher gave radicals and reformers much ammunition in a period of intense repression, exemplified by publications such as William Benbow's *The Crimes of the Clergy* and Richard Carlie's *The Republican*, from which the following is representative:

> the right Reverend Father in God, the Lord Bishop of Clogher, (Percy Jocelyn) Commissioner of the Board of national Education; Member of the Society for the Suppression of Vice; Member of the Constitutional Association; Member of the Bible Society, and of the Society for Promoting Christian Knowledge . . . at least every body sees that the Fathers in God are more Vicious, more depraved, more prone to horrible vices, than other men; with all their preaching, and prating, and palavering about religion, they pay no more attention to it than a parrot does.[2]

Here the emphasis is on corruption and hypocrisy rather than homosexual activity. Clogher is associated with societies such as 'the Suppression of Vice', which was then actively prosecuting radical publishers. Carlile asserts the homily that those in power are not subject to the rules they impose on the majority.

Clerical Magistrates

The soldier and the priest were an unpopular combination prior to the Clogher affair, since the roles had come together when Ethelston and Hay orchestrated the massacre at Peterloo. On the third anniversary of Peterloo, Carlile, who had been a scheduled speaker at the meeting, and who was then incarcerated in Dorchester prison for three years for blasphemous and seditious libel, published the following:

> The Bishop and the Soldier certainly represent two very powerful institutions and authorities in this country, but I think we may be allowed upon every principle of morality, to express a wish to put them down as useless, after we have had such a specimen of the purpose for which we are so heavily taxed to support them. To all such institutions and authorities, I am proud to avow myself an enemy, and to say that I do heartily desire to put them down.[3]

Many historians such as E. P. Thompson claim that '1819 was a rehearsal for 1832. In both years a revolution was possible.'[4] This concurs with the view of future Prime Minister George Canning: 'What was the situation of the country in November 1819? Do I exaggerate when I say, that there was not a man of property who did not tremble for his possessions.'[5] The revolution did not happen, of course, and the failure of the Caroline controversy to carry radical demands meant that, as Marilyn Butler states, 'after the noisy demonstration accompanying Queen Caroline's divorce had subsided, a curious period of relative stasis followed'.[6] With other avenues of attack closed down, the established, conservative Church became the soft underbelly for criticism of the state. As Robert Hole writes, the Church had been oppressing reformers in the post-Waterloo years:

> Perhaps the two most notorious were the Reverends W. R. Hay and C. W. Ethelston, who were magistrates involved in the 'Peterloo Massacre' of 1819. But the actions of repressive clerical magistrates in the East Anglian riots of 1816, at Spa Fields in 1816, and later in the Captain Swing riots of 1830–1 also caused much resentment and criticism.[7]

In John Wade's *Manchester Massacre!!* the issue is that '100 000 people were assembled . . . accompanied with nothing but emblems of peace – dressed as for some village holiday – suspecting no harm – anticipating no danger . . . men, women and children – all at once – without notice or alarm of any kind, was attacked, and indiscriminately butchered' on the say of 'ministers of religion'.[8] Wade emphasises that the 'Riot-Act, which was to be the signal for a band of ruffians to plunge their swords in the bowels of an unarmed assemblage of men, women and children, was read by a CLERGYMAN'.[9]

Shortly after Peterloo, two publications appeared within two months of each other with almost the same titles. On 10 October 1819, *The Examiner* led with an article entitled 'Clerical Magistrates', accompanied by a dramatic squib entitled the 'New House that Jack Built'. In early December 1819, William Hone published *The Political House that Jack Built*, which contains within it another shorter poem, 'The Clerical Magistrate'. *The Examiner* and Hone make similar criticisms of the relationship between church and state and both home in on Ethelston and Hay. Published views on clerics reflect what was being said by the class of people affected by Peterloo. William Roach finds that there was a 'general anti-clericalism in 1819–20 displayed at radical meetings'.[10] *The Spirit of the Union* newspaper reports on a meeting in Rutherglen on 23 October 1819 where a banner showed 'a woman with a child in her arms, under the murderous sabre of a Manchester yeoman'. Another said, 'Remember Manchester'.[11] *The Examiner*'s 'Clerical Magistrates' article leads by querying the relationship between the church and the law:

> It has been the avowed opinion of some eminent lawyers that the less Clergymen had to do with being Magistrates the better we think, after the specimens of Clerical Magistracy afforded by the proceedings at Manchester[.] . . . The two most prominent Magistrates at that place, one for his officiousness and the other for his violence, are, as far as we are hitherto acquainted with that strange body of persons, both Clergymen.[12]

The Magistrates were congratulated by the Regent; however, from most quarters they came in for immediate criticism like that in *The Examiner*. Often, churchmen were open in their hostility to reformers in the run-up to Peterloo. In *A Warning Letter to the Prince Regent* the Reverend Lionel Thomas Berguer damns the press as 'the engine of revolutionary principles and the herald of overt REBELLION'.[13] He calls on a middle-class army to arise as: 'Things have reached their climax: but a REVOLUTION will be either prevented, or induced, according as the MIDDLE ranks bestir themselves during the REBELLION.'[14] *The Examiner* states that clergymen are 'belly-gods' destined for corruption due to the nature of their roles:

> the whole nature of the dogmas of faith and of the establishment with which they are connected tends to give them their inclination for power. It is a sensuality not forbidden them by Government, . . . and Clergymen are notorious for indulging in every possible sensuality, which is not in so many words denied them. They are notorious belly-gods and drinkers, smokers, card-players, and gossips; . . . When the same men therefore get power, they use it with double relish of it to themselves, and double scorn of those on who it is exercised.[15]

The Black Dwarf of 10 January 1821 leads in a similar vein with an article entitled 'Character of the Priesthood'. Clergymen are 'slavish dependants' who 'are always either bending before the faces, or clapping the backs of the enemies of the people'. Ethelston, who is singled out in this piece as an enemy of the poor, published several loyalist works including *A Pindaric Ode on the Genius of Great Britain* (1803) and *A Patriotic Appeal to the Good Sense of all Parties in the Sphere of Politics by an Anti-Jacobin* (1817). Ethelston was not known for having sympathy with reformers or the poor. Sentencing two little boys who were found sleeping in brick kilns, he said that they needed 'a good whipping' as sleeping in the kilns was 'the high road to all wickedness'.[16] Ethelston can be found in a range of publications, such as the *Manchester Observer*, *The Black Dwarf*, *The Times* and *The Theological and Political Comet.* He often becomes 'Ethelstone' in these publications, attaching, as Percy Shelley does with Lord Eldon, the image of a stone to a clerical magistrate. In his *The Mask of Anarchy* Shelley writes of Eldon: 'His big tears, for he wept well, turned to mill-stones as they fell.'[17] *The Examiner* of 24 October includes a dramatic squib by Leigh Hunt (signed Harry Brown) entitled, 'Reverend Magistracy'. This has

Ethelston walking to a Court of Justice 'through an avenue of half-starved weavers' saying:

> Yes blackguards; it is ETHELSTONE;
> . . . To death he'll stun
>   All traitors.
> For he's the first of Justices;
> And nothing but mere dust he sees
> In those who eat dry *crusties*
>   And 'tatoes.[18]

The Cap of Liberty of 29 September 1819 would,

> recommend a meeting to be called by the theological or deistical Reformers, to pass a vote of thanks to the Reverend Mr. Ethelstone, for so materially conducing towards bringing the Established Church of England into contempt by his virulent, his biased, his abusive, his any-thing but religious conduct as one of the Magistrates of Manchester . . . Their instigators to the scene of blood were . . . if possible, more guilty, for it was their duty as preservers of the public peace, to restrain (and Mr. Ethelstone particularly as promulgator of the Christian Religion) the Yeomanry from acts of violence.[19]

In 'A New House That Jack Built' published in *The Examiner* there are images and phrases that William Hone would soon use in his best-selling pamphlet:

> A House in Westminster – This is the house that Jack built.
>
> Rotten seats marked with prices – This is the Fault that lay in the House that Jack
>   Built.
> A Reformer – This is the Hand, that met the Fault, that lay in the House that Jack
>   Built.
> Ministers and other Anti-Reformers – This is the Band, that pinned the Hand, that met the
> Fault, that lay in the House that Jack built.
> . . .
> The Manchester Outrage – This is the Row, with the trump and all . . .
> A Reverend Manchester Magistrate – This is the Paid'un all for lawn, that willed the Row

> with the trump and all, . . .
> A poor Englishman – This is the Man, all tattered and torn, that hissed the Paid'un all for
> lawn . . .[20]

Again, Ethelston appears along with government ministers and 'other Anti-Reformers', but most famously he was attacked in William Hone's pamphlet that no doubt owes many debts to *The Examiner* of 10 October where both 'The Clerical Magistrate' and 'The New House That Jack Built' appeared.

Hone and George Cruikshank's *Political House that Jack Built* sold over 100,000 copies. Expanding on the line from *The Examiner*, 'This is the Man all tattered and torn' is an accompanying illustration by Cruikshank that shows a depressed gathering of ragged people, with a child tugging on their pensive father's leg as the yeomanry do their destructive work in the background:

> These are THE PEOPLE all tatter'd and torn,
> Who curse the day wherein they were born,
> On account of Taxation too great to be borne,
> And pray for relief, from night to morn;
> Who, in vain, Petition in every form,
> Who, peaceably Meeting to ask for Reform,
> Were sabred by Yeomanry Cavalry, who,
> Were thank'd by THE MAN, all shaven and shorn,
> All cover'd with Orders – and all forlorn;

Hone, not wanting to credit *The Examiner*, stated that he got his inspiration from one of his children:

> a little girl of four years old, was sitting on my knee, very busy, looking at the pictures of a child's book; 'What have you got there?' said I – "The House that Jack Built" – an idea flashed across my mind; I saw at once the use that might be made of it; I took it from her . . . I sat up all night and wrote 'The House that Jack Built'.[21]

This inspiration seems only partial given how closely the squibs in *The Examiner* correspond to the text and images in Hone and Cruikshank's pamphlet. In 'The Clerical Magistrate' from *The Political House that Jack Built*, George Cruikshank illustrates the doubleness of Ethelston as clergyman and magistrate. Cruikshank's 'Clerical Magistrate', shows Ethelston as a Janus head. Facing right, Ethelston holds a cross and preaches from a pulpit with the Christogram IHS inscribed beneath. Facing left is a rough spiteful Ethelston, holding a gibbet in one hand and a flail in the other. He carries a musket under his arm and has shackles to hand as he 'Commits starving vagrants'. Underneath is written GPR, or George Prince Regent. This woodcut is accompanied by the verse:

> THIS IS A PRIEST, made 'according to Law',
> Who . . .
> Would indict, for Rebellion, those who Petition;
> And, all who look peaceable, try for Sedition;
> If the People were legally Meeting, in quiet,
> Would pronounce it, decidedly – *sec. Stat.* – a Riot,
> And order the Soldiers 'to aid and assist',
> That is – kill the helpless, who cannot resist. . . .
> Breaks the Peace of the Church, to be Justice of Peace . . .
> On God turns his back, when he turns the State's Agent;
> And damns his own Soul, to be friends with the – [Regent].[22]

Hone finds Ethelston a hypocrite because he: 'Breaks the Peace of the Church, to be Justice of Peace'. In Ethelston he sees a state 'Agent' and 'Perjurer' who has renounced God in favour of the Regent, who is here associated with Satan. Ethelston's soul is damned by the alliance. This association is in Shelley's *The Mask of Anarchy* as Anarchy/George bears the mark of the devil: 'On his brow this mark I saw – / I AM GOD, AND KING, AND LAW!' Joseph Brayshaw agrees that magistrates having the law on their side caused the massacre:

> We must not look upon the Manchester massacre as being only the work of the yeomanry and the magistrates; no, they were only the tools of others: the yeomanry would not have ventured to murder the peaceable assembly, had not the magistrates first induced them to believe that they might do it with impunity; neither would the magistrates have dared to order the dreadful work, had they not been assured that the laws would be suspended in their favour.[23]

Thomas Dolby's Hone-like pamphlet, *The Total Eclipse: A Grand Politico-Astronomical Phenomenon, Which Occurred in the Year*

1820 – there was an annular eclipse on 7 September 1820 in Shetland – queries the relationship between the church and reform:

Should Party-Leader dread Reform,
The Church will, orthodox and warm,
Give out a text, with long oration,
Shewing Reform means ruination . . .
'Tis morally impossible,
Tho' Parliament may pass a bill,
One man can serve both GOD and Mammon,–
With the *same* breath, *bless* and *damn* one.
Have we not, this very day,
A Cun[i]gh[a]m, a "Parson H[a]y,"
An Eth[e]ls[to]n "the b__dy poet?"
Instances like these must shew it
Can't be done; our holy pastors
Cannot truly serve *two* masters.[24]

Ethelston is perhaps 'the b[loo]dy poet', having published *The Suicide; with other Poems* in 1803.[25] The *Anti-Jacobin* makes some insightful remarks on 'The Suicide', which, although 'tedious . . . the moral is unexceptionally good and many of the remarks highly excellent'. Of another poem, 'Howard', the paper hits on the perversity of the cleric's character:

> we cannot but view with a suspicious eye that singular species of philanthropy, which selects for its principal objects the votaries of vice; and which seems more anxious to impart comfort to the dungeon of crime, than to speak peace to the cottage of innocence . . . [W]e mean only to suggest, that to give a wrong direction to the best impulses of the human heart, is frequently to convert a source of good into a mine of evil![26]

Ethelston's co-clerical magistrate at Peterloo, William Hay, was a known enemy of reformers. In 'Ogden's Letters to the Treason-Hunting Municipality of Manchester', dated 9 January 1819, there is a poem entitled 'Prelude to Mr. Hay's Letter' which contains the lines:

Justice Hey is in the Chair . . .
When he winks, Heaven blinks,
When he speaks, Hell quakes,

Earth's globe is but his taw.
Cock of the school,
He bears despotic rule.

Hay, like Ethelston, is associated with hell. Ogden's accompanying letter charges,

> As a magistrate, you have taken an active part in committing to prison a great number of not only *innocent* but *worthy* men; . . . those sent to Lord Sidmouth were strictly examined by the Privy Council; and, after nine month's solitary confinement, were liberated and rewarded; so that *they* also must be innocent. Where, then, is your *ability* or *capacity*.

Ogden finishes: 'Reformers, be not dismayed; press on to victory; posterity will bless your name, and children unborn will hail you in their songs.'[27] It is the songs from the labouring classes that will live on and carry the reformer's message through to a future victory that might be generations away.

Robert Walmsley assesses the weaver poet Samuel Bamford's poem, 'Ode to a Plotting Parson',[28] as 'one of the bitterest, most vituperative pieces of writing in all the Peterloo canon, because it was aimed at an individual'.[29]

Come over the hills out of York Parson H__
Thy living is goodly, thy mansion is gay,
Thy flock will be scattered if longer thou stay,
Our Shepherd, our Vicar, the good Parson H__
. . .
Then the joys which thou felt upon Saint Peter's Field,
Each week, or each month some new outrage shall yield;
And thine eye which is failing shall brighten again,
And pitiless gaze on the wounded and slain.

Then thy Prince too shall thank thee, and add to thy wealth,
Thou shalt preach down sedition and pray for his health;
And Sidmouth, and Canning, and sweet Castlereagh,
Shall write pleasant letters to dear cousin ***[30]

Here Hay is an agent of the state, and has profited financially from Peterloo having been given the parish of Rochdale, one of the richest in England with an annual income of £1,730.[31] Raines writes that the 'exasperation of the Reformers towards Mr Hay, as a clerical magistrate, was unbounded when it was found that he had been rewarded with such promotion . . . The ebullition of wrath on the part of political opponents never passed away.'[32] In the poem Hay is an informer to despots, writing letters to the Prince, Sidmouth, Canning and Castlereagh. Raines writes that Hay 'had an unfavourable opinion of the state of the manufacturing districts, both socially and religiously, and did not think that the remedy would be found either in education or an extension of the franchise. He held that Lancashire at any moment was at the mercy of the *mob*.'[33] Hay sent Luddites to trial who were then hanged. Raines writes that Hay 'distinguished himself by his firmness and intrepidity as a magistrate during the political disturbances of 1812 and 1813 owing to the Luddites and their riots, and was thought to be rather too eager to suppress these misguided men, and also their illegal acts'.[34] In 1833 *The Examiner* has not forgotten Hay:

> A Reverend Magistrate, who was promoted for his services on this occasion to one of the best livings in the country, was an eye-witness of the scene, and doubtless took the aristocratic view of it, in which there was no pity for the unwashed; and having in his evidence deposed that he saw a wounded woman sitting by the road-side, he was asked what her condition was, or whether he could recognize her? His reply was that he 'did not take any particular notice, for (laughing as he spoke) she was not very attractive'.[35]

Wrath for Hay can be felt in 'An Epitaphic Satire, Intended to celebrate the Death of — whenever that wish'd for Event shall happen, and will answer for all domineering, cruel-hearted, purse-proud Hypocrites in the Kingdom'. It begins:

> WhilsT on the Earth, with arrogance I trod,
> *Gain* was my CREED, a *Guinea* was my GOD;
> Although for *Character*, on Sunday *Twice*
> I went to CHURCH, and canted about "Vice," . . .
>
> And that my left-hand (though it is forbid
> By scripture) always knew what *t'other* did!

Now, now, alas I departed from the *quick,*
I find the god I worshipp'd was OLD NICK; . . .
And oh! I find, that NOW reduc'd to dust,
All speak of me with – HORROR and DISGUST![36]

A note to this epitaph, signed by 'Veritas', reads 'Your conduct at the Manchester massacre is not forgotten. Your patron Castlereagh used to say, "The system works well." It worked *well* when you got the valuable living you have for your murderous conduct.'[37] Another is 'The One Thing Needful, or Devotion the Road to Preferment':

Says Hull to Hay,
Come tell me pray,
The sure way to promotion;
It can't be Christian piety,
Nor meekness, nor sobriety,
According to my notion.
Quoth Hay to Hull,
You're mighty dull,
Not yet to know the way.
Devotion is the thing I'll prove,
I don't mean to the Lord above,
But to Lord Castlereagh.[38]

Hull was a vicar in Liverpool whose 'outrageous fulminations from the Pulpit' had become briefly famous.[39] Again, Castlereagh is seen as the worst of the government and Hay serves him rather than God. That is how he got his 'promotion'.

The Clerical Spy

The *Manchester Observer* published Bamford's fifteen stanza 'Lines Addressed to H' on 12 August 1820. Bamford, then in jail for his part in arranging the meeting at St Peter's Field, sees Hay and the clergy as a 'host of spies':

O, let them in their darkness sleep,
Whilst hell doth from her ambush creep,
To snatch her mighty prize;

The pimp of power, the venal slave,
The trickster playing fool and knave,
And all her host of spies!

Bamford writes about clergy acting as informers in his memoir *Early Days*. When a small child, around 1792 or 1793, Bamford saw a violent loyalist mob aided by the church:

> This was a real 'Church and King mob', and was too faithful to its employers to suffer the 'Painites' to escape without punishment . . . Such of the Reformers as had the good fortune to escape out of the house, ran for their lives, and sought hiding places wherever they could be found; whilst the parson of the place – whose name was Berry – standing on an elevated situation, pointed them out to the mob, saying – 'There goes one; and there goes one'; 'That's a Jacobin; that's another': and so continued until his services were no longer effectual.[40]

A spy in the employ of Scotland's Lord Advocate wrote in the weeks following Peterloo that radicals 'hold the clergy as the most active tools of the Government in oppressing the people'.[41] In Glasgow, Andrew Scott, the Roman Catholic Priest responsible for building St Andrew's cathedral (1816), and who later became the Titular Bishop of Erythrae in 1828, was sending in reports on his congregation. Amongst these reports, which are to be found in the National Archives at Kew, Scott writes of the 'considerable degree of dissatisfaction in the minds of the Roman Catholics on the west coast of Scotland' who are 'principally Irish of the Lower orders . . . and easily inflamed . . . They are very numerous, very poor, and have nothing to lose in a revolution, and are flattered by the reformists with the hopes of ameliorating their circumstances by a revolution.'[42] Scott asserts that it is an aim of 'the agitators about Glasgow . . . to draw out the military by means of riots in the country' and then to 'seize upon the Barracks in the absence of the military, and to seize on the ammunition contained there'. Scott suggests 'it might be proper to warn the authorities at Glasgow never to leave the barracks without a strong-guard'. However, the priest also has self-preservation in mind, telling Sidmouth that 'my life would be in danger if it came to be known that I had given any information on the subject . . . the Irish Catholics will be exasperated at me, and if any rising or not takes place attempt to make me among the first victims'.[43] In another report of eight pages from 22 September 1820 Scott informs the authorities of a plan to start a rebellion that begins with sabotage: 'Glasgow is lighted with gas. The leading pipes from the Gasometers are to be cut, all at one time, that the town may be thrown into darkness.' Thereafter, ropes are 'to be placed across the narrow streets, a riot to be raised . . . and when the military are called out to quell it, to draw up suddenly these ropes to a certain height to make the soldiers and cavalry stumble'. Scott then details how the rebellion will proceed and warns that 'Some hundreds of the malcontents are already in possession of pistols, a number of pikes . . . I have my information from those who saw the pistols and who saw the pike-heads. The pike-heads were made in the Caltown of Glasgow by a Smith.' Scott goes on to say that he is contacting Sidmouth directly rather than the local authorities in Glasgow as he fears exposure: 'to drag me before an open court of justice would ruin my character, prevent me from ever receiving any information and expose me to be murdered'.[44] Scott wants something back though:

> his Majesty's Government could do something in order to prevent the numerous Irish Catholics in the disturbed districts from being seduced by the Revolutionists. By doing so he would secure the affections and loyalty of at least twenty thousand able bodied men in the Counties alone of Lanark, Renfrew and Ayr. You would do more, you would convert almost every man of them into agents of Government under the influence of their pastors . . . it would be impossible that any conspiracy could be formed without coming to the knowledge of some of them, and if Government was to assist them out of Secret-Service money to pay the debt of their chapels, which in the present distressed times, they are unable to pay themselves, I am certain that I could prevail upon them to give me private information of every thing that was going on.[45]

There are other clergy spies in the archives. A 'Presbyterian clergyman' from Longframlington in Northumbria named Andrew Richardson, writing on 8 October 1819 to Sidmouth, tells of local meetings.[46] Another, John Monteath, a Church of Scotland minister from the manse of the United Parishes of Houston and Killallan in Renfrewshire, wrote to Sidmouth on 6 January 1820 about radicalism in Renfrewshire. Here the minister blames 'Blasphemous Publications . . . they without all doubt have done a world of mischief among mechanics, and weavers, and cotton spinners; yet I think not among the farmers'.[47] Writing again, on 2 March, Monteath refers to Arthur Thistlewood's Cato Street Conspiracy of the week before and the chances of a rebellion if 'Thistlewood's plan, or some other great event having happened in their favour' then this 'was to be the signal for all those desperate men who approved of it, even in the remotest villages, in the counties of Lanark, Renfrew, and Ayr, to rise in a mass, and unite in deeds of violence'.[48] On 31 March, Monteath warns Sidmouth of 'an intended rising tomorrow'. The next night an 'Address to the Inhabitants of Great Britain & Ireland' appeared pasted to walls within a twenty-mile radius around Glasgow, purporting to be from 'the Committee of Organization for forming a Provisional Govern-ment'.[49] Soon after, a sixty-seven-year-old weaver named James Wilson was arrested and later executed for High Treason.[50]

Clerical Corruption

Joseph Brayshaw, in his pamphlet, *Letter to the Lord Advocate*, published in late 1819, also has members of the clergy on the opposite side from their parishioners: 'many of the ministers of religion so far forgot their duty as to insult the distresses of the people; they so far forgot every principle of religion as to take part with the oppressors, and to calumniate and vilify the oppressed'.[51] J. Tela, writing to *The Republican*, links the clergy to financial deceit as 'these are the class of men to whom the people of England and Ireland, are *compelled* to pay a much larger amount in tithes, &c., for their support, than what is paid to all the rest of the Christian bishops and Clergy inhabiting the four quarters of the Globe!!!'[52] John Wade's two volume *Black Book or Corruption Unmasked!* states that 'Church Property is Public Property' and objects 'to the greatness of its possessions, to which it has no just claim, and which possessions are oppressive to the people'.[53] Patronage is attacked and pluralists are named. The system is one where class and blood dominate: 'The patronage not in the Crown is chiefly in the Aristocracy, the Universities, and the Bishops . . . the patronage of the Bishops on their connections and relations to the hundredth degree . . . Probably the total worth of Church Patronage is SIX MILLIONS annually.'[54] There are several dictionary-like publications in the early 1820s that focus on corruption and the people and families who benefit from the unreformed system. *A Peep at the Peers* (1820), which has been variously attributed to W. G. Lewis, William Cobbett and William Benbow,[55] has an 'alphabetical list of all the peers who sit in the House . . . including the Bishops . . . showing the offices, grants, church preferment, and functions, services, and matter and things, belonging or attached to the peers and their families'.[56] Class and a small section of society holding most of the wealth and power in Britain is the issue, along with the church's integral part in perpetuating inequality. Wade's *Political Dictionary* lists corruption from A to Z. The poet laureate, Robert Southey, is listed under 'Apostates'.[57] 'Bible and Crown' is glossed as a 'convenient shelter for every species of vice, servility, and hypocrisy'.[58] Under 'Divinity' is the 'bench of Bishops, in their legislative capacity, uniformly voting against the maxims of the gospel, in support of war, oppression, adultery, and vice'.[59] 'Education' is in 'bondage' to a 'corrupt Government and an exclusive Church'.[60]

The Church against Education

At this political moment, the church fought back by countering labouring-class claims to an education. A post-Peterloo act created a tax on knowledge: 'pamphlets and papers containing any public news, intelligence, or occurrences, or any remarks or observations thereon, or upon any matter in church or state, printed in any part of the United Kingdom' could now not be sold 'for a less sum than sixpence'.[61] The penalty for publishing or selling an unstamped newspaper was £20 per violation. Martin Hewitt notes that the Bill was not fully repealed until 1855 and was thoroughly enforced. Hewitt cites Patricia Hollis' figures that 'between 1830 and 1836 at least 1130 cases of selling unstamped papers were considered by London Magistrates' and over 800 people found themselves in prison for the offence in this period.[62] The conservatism of the church as a blocker of education and reform can be seen throughout the 1820s and 1830s. Mabel Tylecote writes that the new Mechanics' Institutes 'were faced with persistent opposition from the Tory party and the Church of England'.[63] J. W. Hudson concurs that 'Mechanics institutions established in England during the years 1824 to 1835, with few exceptions, received the most direct opposition from that powerful section of the community the clergy of the established church.'[64] In

Aberdeen, the Reverend Dr Forbes told the members of that city's institute that 'Belles lettres, Political Economy, and even History, were dangerous studies'.[65] This sort of criticism led to exclusions in the libraries of these new institutes. The *Mechanics' Magazine* of 19 November 1825 cites Dr Magee, the Archbishop of Dublin, as saying that 'over-educating . . . will make the people uneasy and unmanageable'.[66] By the time of the 1832 Reform Bill, the Established Church was unanimously against reform when twenty-one bishops voted against the Bill with only two in favour and six abstentions.[67]

Some prominent historians identify religion as being one of the reasons why radicalism quietened down in the 1820s. In the aftermath of Peterloo large mass meetings stopped. After the Cato Street, Cathkin and Bonnymuir 'Rising' debacles in 1820, the notion of a possible revolution also dissipated. Iain McCalman writes: 'The execution of the Cato Street conspirators in 1820 and the death of Queen Caroline in 1821 are seen as having marked the end.'[68] E. P. Thompson offers economic and religious explanations for the 1820s being quieter, pointing to 'years of general prosperity, from 1820 to 1825' and draws the conclusion that 'falling prices and fuller employment took the edge off Radical anger'.[69] Thompson also subscribes to Halévy's assertion that revolution in Britain was averted by the growth of Methodism, which reached a peak in the twenties and thirties and encouraged political quietism. This argument has been contested but Thompson insists that his focus had been on 'Methodism's function as a carrier of work-discipline'.[70] In his poem, *Peter Bell the Third*, Percy Shelley makes Methodism a product rather than a cause of despair. Shelley prefigures Marx's claim that religion is an opiate, and associates it with other forms of oblivion: 'Gin – suicide and Methodism'.[71] Ann Hone and Iorwerth Prothero follow Thompson in offering an economic explanation of why radical activity dies down in the 1820s. Hone writes, 'it would be extremely hard to show that the increase in real wages which is measurable after 1820 did not have this effect'.[72] Prothero too represents the Caroline affair as marking the end of a burst of radical activity:

> It had further shaken the prestige of monarchy and government, restored freedom of political agitation, [and] brought trade societies into open political activity . . . The Queen Caroline affair showed, as did the reform crisis later, the reliance of the radicals on a general air of political

> agitation created by those in much more influential situations. Only in that context could large numbers be attracted into political activity. Despite very widespread radical notions among the artisans, the radicals of themselves could not attract large numbers into activity – they needed a context of general political excitement.[73]

It may be true that events such as the Caroline affair would promote radicalism, but it is unlikely that it was sufficient to generate national political excitement. The marital problems of George and Caroline became an 'affair' because they took place within a political atmosphere that was highly charged after Peterloo. Similarly, the Clogher affair was not enough to promote radicalism, instead it was linked with the radical campaign, just like the Caroline controversy.

The Jocelyn scandal allowed radicals and reformers to build on the pressure that had been put on Ethelston and Hay. It highlighted state and church hypocrisy, duplicity and corruption, and also allowed people to have a laugh at the ridiculousness of their enemies – a method that Cruikshank and Hone had used effectively in their pamphlets. In *Passages in the Life of a Radical* Samuel Bamford recounts going to Knightsbridge Barracks with 'Hone's Political Pamphlets, to which we sometimes appealed, and read extracts from. The soldiers were delighted; they burst into fits of laughter; . . .Very soon after this a law was passed, making it death to attempt to seduce a soldier from his duty.'[74] Byron humorously wrote of the Clogher affair on what it might feel like as the recipient of anal sex:

> I have been very unwell . . . with a violent rheumatic and bilious attack – constipation – and the devil knows what – no physician – except a young fellow who however was kind and cautious & that's enough.—Amongst other operations – a Glyster was ordered – and administered in such a manner by the performer – that I have ever since been wondering why the legislature [should] punish Bishop Jocelyn and his Soldado? – since if the Episcopalian instrument at all resembled the damned squirt of the Ligurian apothecary – the crime will [have] carried it's own chastisement along with it.[75]

Byron also pokes at Clogher in his *Don Juan*: 'Then being taken by the tail, a taking / Fatal to bishops as to solders; these'.[76]

The publicity surrounding Clogher brought an old charge back. In 1811 Clogher had been accused of forcing himself on James Byrne, a young coachman. Byrne had made the allegations in a letter and was subsequently prosecuted for malicious libel. Jocelyn was the only witness against Byrne and said the allegation was 'false'. Furthermore, Jocelyn's counsel, C. Kendal Bushe, the Solicitor-General of Ireland, claimed that the charge was impossible, as 'corrupted manners' were unknown in Ireland: 'There is no instance of its existence in the memory of any professional man.'[77] Byrne was sentenced to two years' hard labour in jail. The sentence was preceded with Byrne being tied to a cart and whipped through the streets of Dublin from Newgate to the Royal Exchange and back again. A strong drummer from the barracks was given the job of whipping and reportedly the cat broke under the stress of hitting Byrne. This apparent miscarriage of justice was reawakened by radicals in 1822 and features in a number of publications, including William Benbow's *The Crimes of the Clergy, or the Pillars of Priest-Craft Shaken*. This book sets out to provide a 'completely impartial' account of clerical 'crimes from which human nature shrinks, and of vices, which nought but pampered luxury and idleness could contrive'.[78] Benbow had a variety of publishing interests, producing pirate editions of Shelley and Byron along with a titillating publication called *The Rambler's Magazine*, which combined soft pornography and politics. In *The Crimes of the Clergy* Benbow produces a scandalous spirit of the age. Among the character portraits is the 'Rev. Mr. Ethelston, *a furious Parson*' who 'cleared the garden at Manchester' and would 'make an excellent Mahomedan Priest, to spread the religion of his Prophet by the sword'.[79] Clogher becomes a moniker for sodomy, 'the crime of Clogherism', wherever Benbow finds an instance of it amongst the clergy, such as by John Atherton, executed in 1640.[80] Jocelyn is dismissed with 'bitter contempt' and Benbow hopes that any 'jostling' to get into heaven on the day of judgement doesn't deprive 'the fire of hell of such a deserving faggot'.[81] According to *The Gentleman's Magazine* Clogher died in December 1843 in Edinburgh after living under the name of Thomas Wilson. His coffin-plate is said to read, in Latin, 'Here lie the remains of a great sinner, saved by grace, whose hope rests in the atoning sacrifice of the Lord Jesus Christ.'[82]

Conclusion

My point in re-examining dead church scandals is twofold. It was not the Clogher affair that created attacks on the church, instead it was the outrage of Peterloo that pushed reformers to confront the clergy. Second, these scandals allowed radicals to remain engaged in fighting for reform, when the more conventional routes of protest, rebellion and patronage were blocked after Peterloo. With the rebellions of 1820 and the Queen Caroline Affair coming to nothing, the church was one of the few targets open to radicals who wanted to attack the state. Clogher became, like Peterloo or the Caroline affair, a rallying point for radicals to attack an increasingly defensive government that was avoiding public engagement. This is explicit in many publications including the American dramatist William Bailey's *Records of Patriotism and Love of Country*. Here he makes it clear that criticism of Clogher is not to do with homosexuality, but government corruption:

> 'May the British government in its present form and the world fall together': that identical government in church and state, which bailed and screened away the infamous Bishop of Clogher last year, and this year hanged at Lincoln three defenceless wretches for the self-same crime.[83]

It was not the scandal of the Jocelyn affair that promoted attacks on the church nor a sudden realisation that clergy spied on the poor and taxed them with tithes and increased rents with enclosures. It was Peterloo – and the instrumental way in which members of the church acted at that event – that widened the rift between reformers and religion.

Notes

1. Iain McCalman, *Radical Underworld; Prophets, Revolutionaries and Pornographers in London, 1795–1840* (Cambridge: Cambridge University Press, 1988), p. 206.
2. *The Republican*, 9 August 1822, p. 251.
3. *The Republican*, 16 August 1822, p. 362.

4. E. P Thompson, *The Making of the English Working Class* [1963] (London: Penguin, 1979), p. 737.
5. George Canning, *Speeches of the Right Hon. George Canning Delivered on Public Occasions in Liverpool* (Liverpool: Kaye, 1825), p. 299.
6. Marilyn Butler, *Romantics, Rebels and Reactionaries; English Literature and its Background 1760–1830* (Oxford: Oxford University Press, 1981), p. 173.
7. Robert Hole, *Pulpits, Politics and Public Order, 1760–1832* (Cambridge: Cambridge University Press, 1989), p. 186.
8. John Wade, *Manchester Massacre!! An Authentic Narrative of the Magisterial and Yeomanry Massacre at Manchester* (London: Fairburn, n.d.), p. 6.
9. Ibid. p. 27.
10. William Roach, *Radical Reform Movements in Scotland from 1815 to 1822 with Particular Reference to Events in the West of Scotland* (Glasgow: University of Glasgow, 1970), p. 164.
11. *The Spirit of the Union* 1:1 (Saturday 30 October 1819), p. 5.
12. *The Examiner*, 10 October 1819, p. 641.
13. Lionel Thomas Berguer, *A Warning Letter to His Royal Highness the Prince Regent, Intended Principally as a Call Upon the Middle Ranks, At this Important Crisis* (London: T. and J. Allman, 1819), p. 8.
14. Ibid. p. 36.
15. *The Examiner*, 10 October 1819, p. 642.
16. Ibid.
17. P. B. Shelley, *The Mask of Anarchy* in *The Poems of Shelley*, ed. Jack Donovan, Cian Duffy, Kelvin Everest, Michael Rossington, 4 vols (London: Routledge, 2011), vol. 3, p. 38.
18. *The Examiner*, 24 October 1819, p. 684.
19. *The Cap of Liberty*, 29 September 1819, p. 61.
20. *The Examiner*, 10 October 1819, p. 652.
21. Cited by F. W. Hackwood, *William Hone: His Life and Times* (New York: Kelley, 1970), p. 220.
22. 'The Clerical Magistrate', from *The Political House that Jack Built* (London: William Hone, 1819).
23. Joseph Brayshaw, *Remarks Upon the Character and Conduct of the Men Who Met Under the Name of the British Parliament, at the Latter End of the Year 1819 . . . to which is Added, A Letter to the Lord Advocate of Scotland, on the State of that Country* (Newcastle: Marshall, 1819), p. 21.
24. *The Total Eclipse: A Grand Politico-Astronomical Phenomenon, Which Occurred in the Year 1820* (London: Dolby, 1820).

25. *The Suicide; with other Poems* (London: Cadell and Davies, 1803).
26. *The Anti-Jacobin Review and Magazine . . . from September to December 1803* (London: Hales, 1803), vol. XVI, p. 419.
27. W. Ogden, 'To the Rev. Mr Hay, Chairman of the Manchester Quarter Sessions', in Robert Francis Raines, *The Vicars of Rochdale*, 2 vols (Manchester: Chetham Society, 1883), vol. 2, pp. 288–9.
28. First printed in the *Manchester Observer*, 26 February 1820 and later in *The Black Dwarf* 7 (1821), pp. 670–2.
29. Robert Walmsley, *Peterloo, the Case Reopened* (Manchester: Manchester University Press, 1969), p. 132.
30. Cited in full in Raines, *Vicars*, dated Middleton, 12 January 1820.
31. Robert Reid, *The Peterloo Massacre* (London: Heinemann, 1989), p. 221.
32. Raines, *Vicars*, vol. 2, p. 296.
33. Ibid. p. 318.
34. Ibid.
35. *The Political Examiner*, 10 March 1833, issue 1310, p. 3.
36. Cited in Raines, *Vicars*, vol. 2, pp. 298–9.
37. Ibid. p. 297.
38. Ibid.
39. Ibid.
40. Samuel Bamford, *Early Days* (London: Simpkin Marshall, 1849), pp. 46–7.
41. National Archives, HO 102.30 Lord Advocate to Sidmouth, 19 September 1819, f. 621–2.
42. HO 102.30, f. 526. Letter from Andrew Scott to Lord Sidmouth, 23 August 1819.
43. HO102.30, f. 529.
44. Ibid. f. 649–52.
45. Ibid. f. 652.
46. HO 130/31, f. 13–14.
47. HO 130/32, f. 36.
48. HO 130/32, f. 224.
49. HO 130/32, f. 297.
50. See John Gardner, 'Preventing Revolution: Cato Street, Bonnymuir and Cathkin', *Studies in Scottish Literature* 39:1 (2013), pp. 162–82.
51. Brayshaw, *Letter to the Lord Advocate*, p. 32.
52. *The Republican*, 9 August 1822, p. 340.
53. John Wade, *The Black Book, or, Corruption Unmasked!!* 2 vols (London: Fairburn, 1823), vol. 2, p. 212.
54. Ibid. p. 235.

55. See G. D. H. Cole, *The Life of William Cobbett* [1924] (London: Routledge, 2011), p. 438.
56. *A Peep at the Peers* (London: Benbow, 1820).
57. John Wade, *A political dictionary; or, pocket companion: chiefly designed for the use of members of parliament, whigs, tories, loyalists, magistrates, clergymen, half-pay officers, worshipful aldermen and reviewers; being an illustration and commentary on all words, phrases, and proper names in the vocabulary of corruption* (London: T. Dolby, 1821), p. 3.
58. Ibid. p. 6.
59. Ibid. p. 26.
60. Ibid. p. 28.
61. T. C. Hansard, *The Parliamentary Debates from the Year 1803 to the Present Time, Vol. XLI.* Comprising the Period from the Twenty-Third Day of November 1819 to the Twenty-Eighth Day of February 1820 (London: Hansard, 1820), p. 575.
62. Martin Hewitt, *The Dawn of the Cheap Press in Victorian England* (London: Bloomsbury, 2014), p. 5.
63. Mabel Tylecote, *The Mechanics' Institutes of Lancashire & Yorkshire Before 1851* (Manchester: Manchester University Press, 1957), p. 63.
64. J. W. Hudson, *The History of Adult Education* (London: Longmans, 1851), p. 201.
65. Ibid. p. 59.
66. The *Mechanics' Magazine*, 19 November 1825, p. 76.
67. D. G. Wright, *Popular Radicalism: The Working-Class Experience 1780–1880* (London: Routledge, 2014), p. 96.
68. McCalman, *Radical Underworld*, p. 181.
69. Thompson, *Making*, p. 778.
70. Ibid. p. 918.
71. Shelley, *Peter Bell the Third*, in *The Poems of Shelley*, vol. 3, p. 107.
72. J. Ann Hone, *For the Cause of Truth; Radicalism in London 1796–1821* (Oxford: Clarendon Press, 1982), p. 356.
73. Iorwerth Prothero, *Artisans and Politics in Early Nineteenth-Century London; John Gast and his Times* (Baton Rouge: Louisiana State University Press, 1979), pp. 153–4.
74. Samuel Bamford, *Passages in the Life of a Radical* [1838] (Oxford: Oxford University Press, 1984), p. 24.
75. Byron to Murray, 9 October 1822, Byron's *Letters and Journals, volume X: 'A heart for every fate'*, 1822–3, ed. Leslie A. Marchand (Cambridge, MA: Harvard University Press, 1980), pp. 12–13.
76. Byron, *Don Juan, Cantos VI–VII – and VIII* (London: Hunt and Clark, 1825), Canto VIII, stanza lxxvi.

77. Cited in Matthew Parris, *The Great Unfrocked* (London: Robson, 1998), p. 152.
78. William Benbow, *The Crimes of the Clergy, or the Pillars of Priest-Craft Shaken* (London: Benbow, 1823).
79. Ibid. pp. 23–4.
80. Ibid. p. 25.
81. Ibid. p. 44.
82. *The Gentleman's Magazine: and Historical Review*, March 1844, p. 314.
83. William Bailey, *Records of Patriotism and Love of Country* (Washington, 1826), p. 79.

Chapter 10

'Reform or Convulsion': Jeremy Bentham and the Peterloo Massacre

Victoria Myers

One influential historian of the Peterloo massacre – Donald Read – reports a significant observation concerning the event: local magistrates took alarm, not from the disorder, but rather from the discipline exhibited by the people assembling in St Peter's Field in August 1819.[1] By pre-arrangement unarmed, the hundreds that gathered from the surrounding communities to hear Henry 'Orator' Hunt speak on parliamentary reform marched in practised order with banners waving. There is an uncanny resonance between this account and Bentham's 1776 description in *A Fragment on Government*, in which the magistrate, wielding Blackstone's contract theory of government, attempts to turn back an orderly but determined multitude. Bentham provides a satirical interpretation of the scene, but while the futile gesture of his fictional magistrate renders the blockage of reform efforts absurd, it does not lay to rest the spectre of physical force.[2] Rather, Bentham segues into a key question: when should reform agitation be undertaken – when could it be deemed both legitimate and efficacious enough to risk the counter-force that inevitably would be launched against it? This question indicates two divergent attitudes towards protest that Bentham sought to resolve during his career.

By 1819, Bentham was fully aware that the law courts' entrenched practices, perverting and denying justice, were countenanced by parliamentary inaction and required not only law reform but reform of parliament itself. He had also become fully cognizant that parliament was averse to reforming itself; when he published his *Plan of Parliamentary Reform* in May 1817, therefore, he put the choice as 'reform or convulsion'.[3] Although anticipating the danger of popular uprisings, Bentham understood several other sorts of violence. His earliest (and continuing) target was (1) violence-promoting language, such as references to natural laws, natural rights, social contracts, in short, fictions as well as fallacies, whether by dissidents or by defenders of authority. As he became persuaded of the futility of reform from within institutions, he increasingly targeted (2) 'sinister interest', the self-regarding interest that motivated corrupt practices and subverted the well-being of individuals and society in general; and (3) legalised violence, legally sanctioned punishment directed towards repressing dissident speech and assembly, including quasi-legal practices of intimidation. In combating these sorts of violence, Bentham employed (4) the rhetorical instruments of parody, satire and farce, to induce contempt for corrupters and shame in the corrupted – rhetoric which by 1817 he knew could also be seen as a provocation to legalised violence.

These notions of violence present in Bentham's early writings develop by the time of Peterloo into a strongly articulated position on radical reform, exposing the systemic operation of various sorts of violence in judicial and electoral corruption. Conscious of the danger each sort of violence posed to individual freedom and social harmony, Bentham closely attended to both the psychological operation each sort involved and its systemic expression. Bentham valued security, order and organisation, yet he also valued frankness, inclusiveness, complexity and communication. As he sought means to a permanent resolution of threatened violence, how did he manage – argumentatively and stylistically – these various claims?

Bentham analysed violence-promoting language as early as 1776 in *A Fragment on Government* and its unpublished parent, *A Comment on the Commentaries*. William Blackstone in his *Commentaries on the Laws of England* (1765–9) had argued that the legislature, being sovereign, possessed an absolute 'right' to make laws.[4] Bentham agreed that the legislature should be sovereign, but strenuously opposed Blackstone's rationales: first, that through an original contract, citizens in a polity have implicitly consented to relinquish their independent wills to the will of the legislator; and, second, that natural law is the standard and basis for all valid positive or municipal law. Bentham argued that Blackstone, in his effort to forestall 'contempt' for English law, indeed to gain a quasi-divine source for it, promoted misunderstanding of the nature of legal authority and inadvertently sanctioned revolution. Blackstone's rationales, in Bentham's opinion, left very little room for candid criticism and reform. How to support law reform and constitutional liberties and yet defend against contempt for law constituted a crucial issue for Bentham throughout his long career, during which he frequently recurred to the danger of Blackstonian fallacies and legal fictions.[5]

According to Blackstone's first rationale, an 'original contract' takes human beings out of the 'state of nature' and places them in a governed society, where all submit to one will expressed in the laws. According to Bentham, the original contract, as used by defenders of government, often supposes a promise that not only was never given (that is, it was contrary to historical fact), but also was used to rationalise subservience of people to government, while obscuring responsibility of government to people (that is, it betrayed the mutuality implication in the term 'promise'). But even aside from the question of historical reality, Blackstone's fundamental assumption, concerning the intention of those who remain members of a political society, evidences numerous faults:

> What men intend . . . to do when they are in a state [of governed society], is to act, as if they were but 'one man.' But one man has but one will belonging to him. What they intend therefore, or what they *ought* to intend (a slight difference which our author seems not to be well aware of) is, to act as if they had but one will. To act as if they had but one will . . . is to join [their wills] '*politically*.' [This] . . . is to consent to submit their wills to the will of one. This one will . . . is the will of those persons who are in use to exercise the supreme power [another assumption]; whose wills again, when there happens to be many of them, have, by a process of which our Author has said nothing, been reduced (as we must suppose) into *one* already. (*FG* 478)

Blackstone's logical leaps, as Bentham satirises them here, indicate that the 'original contract' is a 'fiction'.[6] Blackstone replaces an expression of what he thinks people ought to intend and do with an inaccurate expression of what they actually think and do. 'As if' slips into 'is', popular consensus becomes submission to legislative will, while the formation of legislative consensus yet remains unexplained. Bentham does not object to the thesis that the legislature is in some sense supreme, but rather to Blackstone's inattention to the precise conditions in which political will is produced. Bentham's method therefore is 'perpetual commentary', a phrase-by-phrase explication of Blackstone's argument, which Bentham sees as replete with sophistic reasoning that obfuscates the faults in the legal system. By his method, Bentham aims to rescue readers from Blackstone's authority and arm them with the means and inclination for thinking for themselves.[7]

In combatting Blackstone's violence-promoting language, Bentham frequently added ridicule to analysis. To illustrate the absurdity of using the social contract fiction as a logical and efficacious grounding for obedience to any specific law, Bentham invokes a scene from Samuel Foote's popular 1765 comedy *The Commissary*, in which a newly rich nabob, returning from India, attempts to acquire at once all the accomplishments expected of an English gentleman, including the intricate skill of fencing. The nabob unfortunately enlists his landlady to help him show off his skill to his country bumpkin brother – 'unfortunately', for though not an initiate into the mysteries of swordplay, she proves able to parry his stiffly proper moves. As an analogy to the ease with which a commonsensical, self-respecting citizen might refute Blackstone's civil obedience argument, Bentham invites his reader to imagine 'some undisciplined blunderer, like the Commissary's landlady, [who would] thrust in *quart*, when he should have thrust in *tierce*. I doubt much whether he might not get within our Author's *guard*', Bentham says jocularly, adding the citizen's protest:

> I 'intend'? – I 'consent'? – I 'submit' myself? . . . what I know is, that I never 'intended' any such thing: I abominate such men, I tell you, and all they ever did, . . . so far have I been from giving it to their law, that from the first to the last, I have protested against it with all my might. (*FG* 478–9)

This farce is calculated to force Blackstone's readers to cut through the analogies and fictions that legal writers have long favoured and attend to the real people subject to the law. In this hilarious evocation of the common man, Bentham pictures Blackstone stymied, having no plain and honest answer to give him. In short, it is Blackstone who induces contempt, not only via fictions, but also via fallacious reasoning.

The function of a supposed original contract, Bentham contends, can be expressed (and conceived) much more clearly, precisely and consistently by the utility principle: legislative actions ought to be judged by 'the *tendency* they may have *to*, or *divergency* . . . *from* that which may be styled the common *end* of all of them', namely '*Happiness*' (*FG* 415). Bentham's 1789 *Introduction to the Principles of Morals and Legislation* specifies the psychological basis of the utility principle in concrete terms: 'Nature has placed mankind under the governance of two sovereign masters, *pain* and *pleasure*. It is for them alone to point out what we ought to do, as well as to determine what we shall do.'[8] This principle accounts for a person's acceptance (or rejection) of a law. Regarding actions treated by law, 'to point out to a man the *utility* of them or the mischievousness, is the only way to make him see *clearly* that property of them which every man is in search of' (*FG* 415–16). It is, in Bentham's view, this principle of evaluation, not the obligation to keep promises, that fundamentally accounts for inclination towards obedience or towards disobedience of a law (*FG* 439–45).

Bentham's critique reveals no sinister aim in Blackstone's argument, but rather a pervasive tension: Blackstone desires to support the liberties guaranteed by the English constitution but would also shield English law from criticism. In Bentham's view, this tension leads Blackstone to inadvertently promote violence. In his excessive effort to maintain respect for English law, Blackstone avers that only divine and natural laws determine 'true lawfulness'; thus human laws that 'annex a punishment' to a certain act 'do not increase its [an act's] *moral guilt*'; nor do they impose an added obligation (in conscience) to obey the law;[9] the obligation already exists and human law merely declares what the natural law already contains. If this interpretation seems to protect a person's liberties (making them inherent rights), it also, says Bentham, implies that conformity to the law of nature is necessary to legitimate legal decisions, an assumption that potentially undermines the supremacy of legislated law (*Comment* 54). Moreover, recognising that from time to time a judge's decisions are erroneous and to save the common law from the embarrassment of calling such a decision by the name of law, Blackstone justifies the usual recourse to the fiction that a bad law is no law.[10] The mischievous consequence of using this maxim, Bentham points out, is to announce common law's lack of authority: 'if [certain decisions are] no Laws then is the enforcing them an act of violence without authority', therefore 'an act which a man is in the right to resist: now to resist, if the enforcing of them be still persisted in, terminates in rebellion' (*Comment* 55).

Bentham identifies an even more explicit tendency to promote violence in Blackstone's exposition of English law. Blackstone remains true to the lessons of the Civil Wars and the legacy of the Glorious Revolution when he takes the extreme position that the people will sometimes have to disobey a law as a matter of 'duty' if that law contradicts the law of nature or the law of revelation. Although Blackstone hastens to reassert parliamentary supremacy, this admission makes a 'dangerous maxim', says Bentham, not only for the encouragement it gives to religious conflict, but also for the sanction it gives to individual dislike and to individual interpretation (*FG* 482–3). In Bentham's view, law gives rights by imposing duties to do or abstain from doing certain actions and enforces this duty by a punishment.[11] Only positive law should impose punishment, and only in accord with judicial procedure. Blackstone's fiction obscures real law, real authority. Bentham evidently was not eager to approve disorder, but he discerned that legalised violence – punishment – had to proceed from clearly written laws, accessible to common understanding and available for scrutiny. In this principle we may see his continuing effort to avoid the conditions for the non-legalised violence of rebellion.

In the *Fragment*, Bentham's alternative to Blackstone's mode of justifying English law is to maintain that all positive laws are laws, still requiring obedience, and necessarily imposing punishment for disobedience until the law is rescinded. In some respects, he was less liberal than Blackstone: he too sensed the spectre of civil war and sought some solution to the Lockean dilemma of resistance to encroachments on traditional English liberties.[12] But rather than recurring to natural law, Bentham invoked his principle of utility to settle the difficulty of when disobedience is right:[13]

> when, according to the best calculation [a person] is able to make, *the probable mischiefs of resistance* (speaking with respect to the community in general) *appear less to him than the probable mischiefs of submission*. This then . . . is to each man in particular, the *juncture for resistance*. (*FG* 484)

The advantage of Bentham's principle: 'At the worst there is nothing in it to favour the pretensions of fanaticism either political or religious. It places a question difficult to solve in its natural light of difficulty, without deluding men with a false solution' (*Comment* 55). What he recognised as a disadvantage, however, was that his maxim contains the sign for 'each particular person', but not a sign that would automatically unite many, with the result that 'the supreme governor's authority, though not *infinite*, must unavoidably, . . . *unless where limited by express convention*, be allowed to be *indefinite*' (*FG* 484).

If, as Bentham insists, there is no natural limit to a supreme authority's exercise of its power, there must be an explicit contract, not merely an inferred contract or a fictional promise. It seems that, even in 1776 when the Americans were launching their rebellion, Bentham was concerned not only with the question of whether those who wished to instigate reform against a thoroughly recalcitrant government could be warranted in doing so through resistance, but also with the practical question of how individuals so warranted could unite in effective action.[14] Following Locke, Bentham asserts that there must be an express convention, by which 'we are furnished with that common signal . . . A certain act is in the instrument of convention specified, with respect to which the government is therein precluded from issuing a law to a certain effect' (*FG* 489). The government's violation of this constitutional prohibition (which Bentham defines in terms of utility) is the sign that warrants and that unites. The breaking of the explicit convention would be determinable by reference to the principle of utility and could be disputed on the basis of fact, 'that is future fact – the probability of certain future contingencies' (*FG* 491).

Although he may have been sidestepping the issue of non-legalised violence (how can a government ever approve riots and uprisings?), it is very much in keeping with the overall thrust of the *Fragment* that Bentham should dwell on the potentiality for rational debate implied in the utility principle. Bentham clinches his point – that reference to the maxim of utility, made conventional by prior agreement, is the best and only means of securing free obedience – by imagining two opposed scenarios: one of nonsensical wrangling, the other of rational debate. In the latter 'the parties might at length have come to an agreement; or at least to a visible and explicit issue' and might 'solve it' by reference to 'the evidence of such *past* matters of fact as appear to be analogous to those contingent *future* ones' (*FG* 492). Perhaps

Bentham anticipates his later idealising of the American republic or perhaps he only envisions the perfecting of the existing English constitution, when he points to the only way to avoid the violence of uprisings: maintain a free government. He sees a free government as at least 'favourable to resistance' – peaceful resistance – inasmuch as it distributes the power of making laws, allows frequent changes of governors and governed, imposes responsibility on the governors to give reasons for their measures, and (last but not least) allows freedom of the press (*FG* 485). To his imagined scenarios he adds, optimistically, 'Men, let them but once clearly understand one another, will not be long ere they agree' (*FG* 492).

While the violence of the French Revolution temporarily derailed Bentham's development towards democracy, Philip Schofield notes, Bentham continued to work for law reform and in 1808 published *Scotch Reform*, which contains Bentham's 'earliest . . . substantial reference' to the concept of 'sinister interest'.[15] Bentham defines this concept as self-regarding interest, a natural human motive, but dangerous if that interest is pursued by public officials to the detriment of other persons.[16] The Scotch reform proposals before the British House of Lords told Bentham that 'what at first view' had seemed to him 'blindness and imbecility' in individuals administering law was due more to 'sharp-sighted artifice' in the interests of 'profit' to 'the founders, and successive supporters of the system, to give it a direction, opposite at every turn to the ends of justice . . .'.[17] While he addresses the proposal regarding Scotland's judicial system, Bentham also adduces many observations regarding English institutions. One general observation appears throughout Bentham's later institutional criticism as well: corruption is not (always) the opposite of order and organisation, but rather the principle that orders and organises in a certain way.

In sinister interest Bentham discerned a systemic corruption much more threatening than the fallacy-begetting tensions he had identified in Blackstone. Bentham had already seen common law as inconsistent, shapeless and arbitrary, but he now characterised it as intrinsically corrupt. It was 'in the main the work, not of legislators but of judges: manufactured, chiefly in the form – not of real statutory law – but of jurisprudential law'; Bentham called it 'imaginary law, consisting of general inferences deduced from particular decisions', and (he now emphasised) it was law made by judges who have 'power to pay themselves by fees' rather than being paid by fixed salaries (*SR* 5). Possession of power coupled with interest-based motivation, he theorised, produced in judges the will towards corruption. The interest of people in general differed from that of judges and lawyers, the one to avoid 'delay, vexation, and expence', the other to magnify them, especially by means of judicial procedures that multiplied 'the occasions of extracting fees'. This system, moreover, spawned an expert class, 'sole professors of that science, and of the arts belonging to it', and it fostered a '*law partnership*' between judges and lawyers and *mala fide* suitors (*SR* 5). More extensive than Blackstone's substitution of authority for his readers' intellectual capability, this law partnership is linked with the corruption of the people's moral capability.

In early 1809, Bentham composed an essay that gave a much more explicit and detailed picture of the workings of sinister interest in the English judicial system: *Elements of Packing, as Applied to Special Juries, particularly in Cases of Libel Law.*[18] The essay was occasioned by a 20 February 1809 *Times* newspaper article regarding the prosecution for libel of twenty-six persons who had published (or republished parts of) a pamphlet alleged to be a libel. Bentham stated his long-standing opinion that libel law was arbitrary: 'that, in point of *actual law*, a *libel* is any paper in which he, who to the *will* add[ing] the *power* of *punishing* for it, sees anything that he does not *like*'.[19] Aware of the notorious trials for treason and seditious libel in the 1790s and the more recent trials of William Hone and Thomas Wooler,[20] Bentham considered libel law 'incompatible with English liberties', posing a threat as long as libel remained undefined – which (he asserted) only parliament (not the courts) could legitimately remedy (*Packing* 66). For Bentham, libel law was a cogent example of the derailment of legalised violence. Although, he stated hopefully, the resistance of a single juryman in each case can palliate the threat, he had begun to distrust this recourse because a 'publication of the late sheriff, Sir Richard Phillips' provided reasons to question whether jurymen are 'really free to follow their own judgment'; Bentham had thought 'jury packing' characteristic of the Stuart era, but he now discovered it 'had been moulded into a *system*, had become an established practice' among judges and prosecutors and thus had 'acquired the force of *law*' (*Packing* 66). Jury packing, in short, had become an instrument of violence, not legalised but hidden in legal procedures, not employed simply against the person convicted, but against the jury producing the conviction.

In the modern day, says Bentham, the influence exercised over the juryman takes the 'appearance' only of the understanding (of the judge) exercised over the understanding (of the juryman). But as in *Scotch Reform*, Bentham discovers that what has an 'appearance' of justice is really a screen for injustice (*Packing* 67–8).

> In so far as the prescriptions of *duty*, the dictates of *probity*, are taken by the juryman for the rule of his conduct, no *other will* is by *his will* suffered to exercise any influence on it: his *will* takes for its guidance the dictates of *understanding* purely: of *his own* understanding, if it feels itself strong enough: if not, of some *other* understanding, on the relative strength of which . . . its reliance is more assured . . . To the dictates, therefore, of any other *will*, the will of a juryman, as of any other judge[,] cannot so much as listen, but at the expense of probity; such influence would be deemed either *intimidation* or *corruption*. (*Packing* 68)

There are legal protections against intimidation: a juryman cannot be proceeded against separately from his fellows, and the jury may confer 'out of the reach of [the judge's] observation' and of the observation of others. There are protections against corruption as well: namely, '*continual change*: no person being continued in the exercise of that function for any length of time' (*Packing* 69). In *Packing*, Bentham shows, these protections are sidestepped. The jury's independence of the judge had long been seen as a check on 'arbitrary power' (*Packing* 83), but in reality, Bentham says, the judge can indirectly influence the jury's verdict to obtain 'a verdict conformable to his wishes'. In 'pursuance of a *sinister interest*', he tries to 'obtain a jury' he can depend on to follow his will without specific or overt direction, that is, with little or no 'disturbance to his *ease*' (*Packing* 68). In previous eras, packing a jury with favourable members was a matter of 'finding out persons' already well-disposed and putting them on the jury; nowadays, a method of refined packing was available – '[g]oing to work with . . . persons already stationed' by influencing their 'interest or welfare' and 'using them when needed' (*Packing* 71). This will soon appear to be an obscure kind of bribery, more akin to what Bentham calls 'terror' (*Packing* 113).

The moral-psychological dynamic of refined packing, which Bentham outlines in terms of the understanding and the will, requires 'among public men' no special training. The practice being merely a habit of following what other professionals do, it is for the most part performed without conscious or deliberate thought about moral motives or consequences. Judges occupy a 'situation' of power, a position attended with functions that allow them to manipulate 'the matter of wealth or other objects of desire'. Having certain desires (for power, renown, ease) that operate as motives, judges use the means readily available to them, however ambiguous their legality (*Packing* 72). Thus, they have the capacity to entice jurymen to desire (namely) continuance on juries where they receive emoluments and gratefully exhibit 'obsequiousness' to what is expected of them. In characterising the operation of sinister interest according to this psychology, Bentham still implies that the persons involved are prompted simply by natural motives in relation to their 'situation' within the system.

Yet, he shows, the system itself evidences design and intent (*Packing* 71–2). Because overtly continuing a juror's service from one trial to another would be perceived as contrary to a fundamental judicial principle, says Bentham, a disguise or screen is necessary, namely a system in which the judge has virtual power over nomination, in which emolument for jurors is sufficient to corrupt, in which the juror can be removed from his lucrative situation, in which the overall design is imperceptible, and finally in which the plan can be confined to only those instances in which it is needed (*Packing* 72–3). These desiderata Bentham goes on to trace in the multi-layered system of supplying jury members. The official in charge of the jury lists, whom Bentham calls the 'master packer', is wholly a 'dependent of the judge' (*Packing* 77). The master first maintains a traditional list, which is an aggregate of common and special jury candidates nominated by the constable on the basis of legally fixed 'pecuniary and other qualifications'. From this list, the 'qualified special jury' list is selected by the sheriff in accord with parliamentary 'acts relative to *special juries*'. From this list, however, the 'master packer', who is 'well acquainted' with the '*characters*' of the persons on that list, chooses a still shorter 'select qualified jury' list, from which the actually serving jurors will then be chosen in court in the usual manner (*Packing* 78).[21]

As in *Fragment*, Bentham uses ridicule to dramatically illustrate authority's influence of will upon will. Here, however, he exposes the covert violence of sinister interest, operating through hope and fear in the psychology of the juror. Paid a guinea per trial, the jurors on the shorter list, commonly called 'guinea-men', follow a career of pitiable uncertainty. '[C]ontinually-employment-seeking and everlastingly-dependent', the guinea-man deals only with the master packer and Crown solicitor, not with the hidden sources of the corruption.

> In these unknown occupants of the region situated behind the curtain, the trembling guinea-man will behold so many phantoms, to the *will* of every one of which, so far as it can be guessed at, . . . it will be necessary for him to shape his part in the verdict. . . . Meantime, neither with any of the phantoms behind the curtain, nor with either of the two masses of human flesh subsisting, is it possible for the *guinea-man* ever to come to any sort of explanation. . . . His sin, the joining in a wrong verdict, is committed openly in the jury-box: his punishment – removal out of the *select qualified list* – will be inflicted in secret: yea, and so secret, as not to be at any determinate time made known even to the sinner himself. (*Packing* 80)

Although the psychological state of the corrupted juror is deplorable, Bentham renders it satirically in a mock-Gothic style. On the one hand, the juror is a clueless victim, on the other he is a contemptible co-conspirator – on the whole, he represents the despicable moral condition of all those – jurors, packing masters, *mala fide* suitors, advocates and judges – who co-operate in the packing system.

Bentham acknowledges that statutes have been passed to eliminate the 'permanence' of jurymen in an effort to eliminate corruption. But, he says, the parliamentary lawyers who originated the reforming statutes failed to change the mode by which jurors were appointed or to take the nomination of the jurors out of 'the hands of the dependent subordinate of the judge'. Moreover, they in fact made the practice available to other courts (*Packing* 83–4). Despite this reticulating 'impurity' in the system, Bentham reminds the reader ironically, it is legitimised by its longevity and continuity. '[A] judicial practice may be legalized' by common law or by statute law – the former is 'made by the judges' practice and pronouncements', the latter 'through the means of their partners in trade in both houses' (*Packing* 93). Observing this partnership between the judiciary and the legislature, Bentham explains, saps one's confidence in parliament's ability and even willingness to counteract self-interested judicial incursions into law-making (*Packing* 94n). By the time Bentham composes *Scotch Reform* and *Packing*, he has seen sufficient evidence to infer a judicial violence different from the legalised violence of punishment.

In his *Plan of Parliamentary Reform*, the question arises whether Bentham will actually advocate resistance or even revolution against this systemic violence. The core component in this work, called the *Catechism*, was first written in late 1809 but publication was refused, and it remained unpublished 'until the cup of calamity, mixed up by misrule, has been drunk to the very dregs' (*Plan* 435). In 1817, in the wake of 'Gagging Bills and repeated suspension of the Habeas Corpus act', Bentham perceived that 'the country . . . is already at the brink: reform or convulsion, such is the alternative' (*Plan* 435). Believing he possessed the single effectual remedy, he now prepared a lengthy Introduction for the *Catechism* and published them together.[22] Between the two components there is a marked difference in style – the *Catechism* largely expository, the Introduction's first four sections freely declamatory and even alarming, while the last fourteen sections concentrate on rational demonstration. In the works discussed above Bentham had already come close to advocating resistance, though deploring alarmist language and preferring some institutional or ordered remedy for corruption. Why then is he now willing to use violence-promoting language that could validate the fears of the governing class?

Inducements to alarm increase in Introduction Section II, where Bentham deplores the British garrisoning of post-Waterloo France, 'the grave – not only of French, but of English liberties', pointing out that post-war France, under the Bourbons, (pre)figures England, which exhibits the same quelling of 'any information that has not for its object deception . . . [and purveying of] information in which . . . truth is suppressed, and by which pernicious error is circulated and inculcated' (*Plan* 436). In other passages Bentham uses ridicule as he had earlier, to diminish the threat of violence from the people and expose the violence in the government. He describes the argument that supports the garrisoning of France as a fallacy:[23] 'government says we must garrison France since it is a certain fact that "There *have been* Septembrians and anarchists; – *ergo*, no sooner does France cease to be garrisoned by us, than the reign of those miscreants will recommence' (*Plan* 436). But the real purpose of the English garrison, Bentham says, is not 'for the keeping out *bad* government', but 'for keeping out *good* government'. The 'real object of terror to all the newly re-christianized crowned heads' of Europe is a prosperous democracy in France on the American model (*Plan* 436–7). Bentham exhibits their terror in a farcical dramatisation of governing class paranoia:

> There they are – but happily with the Atlantic between us and them – the never-sufficiently accursed United States. There they are – living, and (oh horror!) flourishing . . . flourishing under a government so essentially *illegitimate*! Oh what a reproach to legitimacy! Oh what a reproach, a never-to-be-expunged reproach, to our own Matchless Constitution. . . . But now – suppose the same, or a similar accursed government, with the accursed prosperity, transplanted from that blessed distance – planted under our very noses: planted with no more than one-and-twenty miles of sea to dilute the stench of it. (*Plan* 437)

Far from validating these fears, Bentham's exaggeration exposes them as a melodramatic pretence, a gambit to avoid fundamental reform. To the multitude he directly addresses, such passages diminish the authority of government arguments; to the governing class listening in they may cause a sudden consciousness of shame.

This explanation makes sense of Bentham's revelation of the second real purpose of the garrison, which adopts a less jocular tone. The garrison's purpose is 'to return to all plans of reform, to all petitions for reform – to all groans – to all complaints – to all cries for mercy – the proper, and properly, and already proposed answer, the bayonet' (*Plan* 437). Bentham goes so far as to offer his audience the use of a counter-threat: reminding their governors that the soldiers, being of the 'class . . . of the swinish multitude' themselves, might actually turn their bayonets against the persecutors of that class (*Plan* 437). This sudden and sly break from the farcical style, capturing the surprise the soldiers' about-face would spring upon the governors, is not casual. The number of troops levied for anticipated French duty, Bentham points out, is well in excess of the number needed: 'They are raised and kept at home in *readiness* to be employed in foreign service: and till they are thus employed, they are not distinguishable from those destined to no other than home service' (*Plan* 444n). This, Bentham concludes, indicates that England is 'governed' 'by a standing army' (*Plan* 444), and this fact indicates what sort of constitution England has: not a matchless 'mixed constitution', but 'a military government' (*Plan* 445). In this passage, Bentham reinstates the fears of the governing class, but now he seems to say that these fears are more accurately seen as a product of their own actions.

Bentham's analysis supports this surmise. He describes the cause of the crisis in a way similar to his treatment of the jury-packing practice, but this time the targeted system is not simply the judiciary, but the entire constitution. Like the judges in *Packing*, who have the care of morals but (motivated by self-regarding interests) avail themselves of a system designed for corruption, the governing class claim to be the 'trustees of the people', but assume that 'the substance of the people was a fund, out of which . . . *fortunes* . . . might be . . . made' (*Plan* 438). Comparable to the jury-packing collusion, Bentham perceives that 'the two domineering interests [in the constitution] – the monarchical and the aristocratical' – achieved co-operation with each other without premeditation or plan, but simply in compliance with their natural motives and situation in the system as it is, and together inculcated an ideology of submission into the whole society (*Plan* 438). In this 'system', the superior has control of '[p]ower, money, factitious dignity . . . elements of the *matter of good*',[24] but through this control, items that Bentham considers intrinsically good become transformed into '*matter of corruptive influence*' to induce members of Parliament to serve their 'sinister interest' (*Plan* 438).

Bentham goes on to analyse the rationale behind this unconscious working of the system, in terms redolent of design and intent heightened by satire, as he had done in *Packing*. The exploiters, seeing themselves as guardians and trustees for the country, claim a 'right' to be 'rewarded' for their public service. Their assumption is that the reward should match not the quality of their service but the degree of their desire – which is 'infinite'. However, they discern that 'money in infinite quantity cannot be demanded all at once: [the people] would become desperate; they would rise; better (they would say to themselves) better be shot or hanged at once, than starved' (*Plan* 439). Bentham explains the system as a contrivance of the exploiters' resourcefulness: operating much like the screens in *Packing*, '*drains* must therefore be established and set to work: drains, by and through which, by degrees . . . money may be drawn out of the pockets of the blinded, deluded, unsuspicious, uninquisitive, and ever too patient people' (*Plan* 439). Bentham lists seven of these drains, but they all come down to supporting 'war' and the 'splendours of the crown', which also often involve war. The wasteful contradictions of war are the clearest – because most violent – manifestations of the misery caused by this system (*Plan* 439–40). By analogy with the broken convention in *Fragment*, this waste may function as the sign of constitution violated.

Although his Introduction is alarming, Bentham initiates several moves to palliate the threat and make the remedy attractive. In Britain's supposed 'mixed constitution' of monarchy, aristocracy and democracy, it is the first two that dominate the government. Bentham proposes 'democratic ascendancy', in which 'the *power of the purse* should be actually and effectively in the hands of the real representatives, the freely chosen deputies of the body of the people' (*Plan* 446). He explicitly eschews threats of 'punishment' and class 'extinction' (*Plan* 441). Despite his admiration for the United States' government, Bentham settles for democratic ascendancy rather than demanding 'pure [but representative] democracy', taking the former as the least amount of innovation that can save the country and reasoning that, if total (representative) democracy in the United States has proved not dangerous, *a fortiori* 'partial democracy, with monarchy and aristocracy by the side, and at the head of it, for its support . . . and for keeping it in order, a standing army . . . all around it' would not prove dangerous (*Plan* 447).

He not only accepts the continuation of such institutions, he also advocates a gradual, rather than immediate, shifting of the ascendancy and announces certain 'principles' for conducting the process. He would 'leav[e] the executive part of the government where it is, with the king and his ministers', trusting them to prevent 'waste and corruption' (*Plan* 447–8). To obviate the fears of the aristocracy, '[a]s to what regards money', he would follow 'the *uti possidetis* principle': they would keep what they have and only lose the power of increasing it, especially through corruption (*Plan* 448). As to fears of popular power, he admits that at present the multitude might not be capable of 'making a tolerably apt choice' of 'the persons by whom [the business of government] shall thus be carried on' (*Plan* 448). But he points out that men are willing to follow the advice of experts in private matters and may do so in public as well (*Plan* 448), and he suggests the ability to read be prerequisite to suffrage. At the same time, Bentham also challenges government to cease blocking education and a free press (*Plan* 465–7). Realistically, Bentham concedes the new system may still admit knaves into government, but not as many as under the present system; the new system's securities for maintaining the moral and intellectual aptitude of representatives would diminish opportunities for corruption (*Plan* 454).

These securities are what Bentham means by parliamentary reform. In the rest of the Introduction, Bentham goes on to detail each element in his proposed *Plan* and to explain how they would discourage corruption: (virtually) universal suffrage, annual parliaments, equal representation, and secret ballot. He would also include limitations on the numbers of placemen and their ability to vote in parliament, along with mandatory attendance for members. To discuss each of these items would take this essay too far afield from the topic of violence, but Bentham's treatment of one item in particular will illustrate how he expected reform to eliminate the systemic violence that characterised the corruption of electors.

Distinction between the influence of 'understanding on understanding' and the influence of 'will upon will', as we have seen, is fundamental to Bentham's conception of (a system of) violence. But he also shows that the exertion of will upon will is not always explicitly violent; there is an operation of understanding upon understanding that also manifests itself (as with the *Packing* jurors) as a kind of terrorism, which Bentham again analyses through his notion of pleasure and pain motives.[25] 'As to the sort of motive, through which seductive influence operates, it may be either of the nature of hope, or of the nature of fear.' The first operates through pleasure and is '*alluring*', the second through pain and is '*coercive*' (*Plan* 476). Though the first may include direct bribery in some districts, Bentham finds more effective the favours electors may receive such as 'custom for goods or labor', leniency for tenants, help in payment of debts, transportation to polling places, and so on (*Plan* 479). He considers the second – 'the *painful* – the *terrific*' – to be 'by much the more powerful in its operation' and in the case of electoral influence productive of 'by far the greatest part of the mischief' since favours often constitute an important source of livelihood and solvency (*Plan* 476, 479).[26] Bentham argues that the crucial element in electoral reform is the secret ballot because it would eliminate any confidence corrupters could have in the effectiveness of their influence: 'By terror may a man be driven to the place of election, – true: – but, under the shield of secresy, it is not by terror that, when he is there, the *direction* given to his *vote* can be determined' (*Plan* 487).[27] The remedy, this example suggests, would subvert the dominant class's violence (the influence of will upon will) and make popular violence unnecessary.

By the time of Peterloo, Bentham believed he had constructed a plan that would promote probity and intellectual aptitude in both electors and elected, while protecting their independence of thought and action. But did he, in final desperation, condone a violent revolution to put the plan in place? He often used the word 'contempt', which libel trials consistently used to indict such fundamental criticism as Bentham's, and he certainly employed ridicule in a way that would arouse contempt. Yet he also seriously presented an argument calculated to palliate that feeling or replace it with more constructive feelings. Although his style, in which rational argument is shadowed by satire, could be said to resemble the strategic ambiguity of field orators or the newspaper parody of such popular radicals as Thomas Wooler,[28] Bentham's satire mainly dramatises a complex psychology of unconscious action and its workings through political structures. Bentham clearly meant to accomplish constitutional change, but he did not see this intention as treason.

Finally, by means of his style of persuasion, Bentham developed a complex notion of violence. He recognised that violence was an illegitimate exercise of will upon will, negating persuasion by understanding upon understanding – unless where it supplemented understanding through legalised punishment. But Bentham also showed that, within the existing legal and parliamentary system, will operated upon will to serve sinister interests by taking the opportunities afforded by natural motives and the situations created by the system. He thereby brought systemic violence to a level of comparability with physical force, showing that fallacious and fiction-dependent argument was a screen for electoral and parliamentary corruption and that non-legal (but hidden) violence was the real *modus operandi* of the governing class.

Notes

1. Donald Read, *Peterloo: The 'Massacre' and Its Background* (Manchester: Manchester University Press, 1958), chapters 7–8. For an alternative view, see Robert Walmsley, *Peterloo: The Case Reopened* (Manchester: Manchester University Press, 1969), chapters 3–4, 6–7.
2. Jeremy Bentham, *A Comment on the Commentaries and A Fragment on Government* [1776], ed. J. H. Burns and H. L. A. Hart, and gen. ed. Philip Schofield. (Oxford: Oxford University Press, 1977), p. 481; *Fragment* hereafter cited parenthetically as *FG*.
3. Jeremy Bentham, *Plan of Parliamentary Reform, in the Form of a Catechism, with Reasons for Each Article: with an Introduction, Showing the Necessity of Radical, and the Inadequacy of Moderate, Reform* [1817], in *The Works of Jeremy Bentham*, ed. John Bowring, vol. 3 [1838–43] (New York: Russell and Russell, 1962), p. 435; hereafter cited parenthetically as *Plan*.
4. For Bentham's difference from Blackstone on the term 'right', see Bentham, *Fragment*, pp. 457, 472, 477. Note that legislature includes king with parliament.
5. Both Blackstone and Bentham were aware of the legal use of the word 'contempt' for (verbal) behaviour inciting disaffection for officials and institutions. In *Fragment*, Bentham turns that term against Blackstone.
6. For an evaluation of Bentham's criticism of Blackstone's defence of various fictions, see Ross Harrison, *Bentham* (London: Routledge and Kegan Paul, 1983; pbk 1985), chapter 2.
7. See William Blackstone, *Commentaries on the Laws of England*, facsimile of the First Edition of 1765–1769, intro. Stanley N. Katz, vol. 1 (Chicago: University of Chicago Press, 1979), pp. 6–8; his intended audience was gentlemen, preparing for their functions as magistrates and possibly members of parliament. But see David Lieberman, *The Province of Legislation Determined: Legal Theory in Eighteenth-century Britain* (Cambridge: Cambridge University Press, 1989; rpt 2002), pp. 34–8, on Blackstone's reaching a broader audience.
8. For cogent explications of this and other passages relevant to Bentham's development of a psycho-morality, see Philip Schofield, *Utility and Democracy: The Political Thought of Jeremy Bentham* (Oxford: Oxford University Press, 2006; pbk 2009), chapter 2.
9. Jeremy Bentham, *A Comment on the Commentaries and A Fragment on Government* [1776], ed. J. H. Burns and H. L. A. Hart, and gen. ed. Philip Schofield (Oxford: Oxford University Press, 1977), p. 30; hereafter cited parenthetically as *Comment*.

10. On Bentham's applying the term 'fiction', especially to natural law and the assumption that true law did not change, see Lieberman, *Province*, pp. 43–7.
11. See Harrison, *Bentham*, pp. 90–8.
12. See John Locke, *Two Treatises of Government*, ed. Peter Laslett (Cambridge: Cambridge University Press, 1960; rpt 1988), book II, chapter 19.
13. See Harrison, *Bentham*, chapter 7 for critical comparison of the two principles.
14. Harrison, *Bentham*, chapter 8, discusses the problem of uniting various interests in producing reform – a problem of persuasion.
15. Schofield, *Utility and Democracy*, pp. 117–18.
16. Jeremy Bentham, *Deontology: Together with a Table of The Springs of Action and Article on Utilitarianism*, ed. Amnon Goldworth (Oxford: Clarendon Press, 1983; rpt 2002), pp. 110–11; hereafter cited as *Springs*.
17. Jeremy Bentham, *Scotch Reform; Considered with Reference to the Plan Proposed in the Late Parliament, for the Regulation of the Courts and the Administration of Justice in Scotland* [2nd edn; 1st edn 1808], in *The Works of Jeremy Bentham*, ed. John Bowring, vol. 5 (1838–43; New York: Russell and Russell, 1962); hereafter cited parenthetically as *SR*.
18. See Schofield, *Utility and Democracy*, p. 131, for composition and publication details. Though *Packing* was not published until 1821, Bentham lent a manuscript copy to Thomas Wooler in 1817. See James Epstein, *Radical Expression: Political Language, Ritual, and Symbol in England, 1790–1850* (Oxford University Press, 1994), p. 57.
19. Jeremy Bentham, *Elements of Packing, as Applied to Special Juries, particularly in Cases of Libel Law* [1821], in *The Works of Jeremy Bentham*, ed. John Bowring, vol. 5 ([1838–43] New York: Russell and Russell, 1962), p. 65; hereafter cited parenthetically as *Packing*.
20. See Olivia Smith, *The Politics of Language 1791–1819* (Oxford: Clarendon Press, 1984; pbk 1986), chapter 5; Epstein, *Radical Expression*, pp. 39–56; Marcus Wood, *Radical Satire and Print Culture 1790–1822* (Oxford: Clarendon Press, 1994; rpt 2002), chapter 3.
21. Bentham refers to John Horne Tooke's 1777 trial at King's Bench for libel, where Tooke recounted to the court the manner in which the jury was selected (*Packing* 102–104n).
22. See Schofield, *Utility and Democracy*, pp. 163–4, for composition and publication history.
23. Jeremy Bentham, *The Book of Fallacies*, ed. Philip Schofield (Oxford: Clarendon Press, 2015), pp. 83–91, calls it the 'hobgoblin-crier's argument'.

24. The ultimate superior, the 'Corrupter General', was the king, who could dispense sinecures, seats in parliament, elevation to peerage, and the like. See Bentham, *Plan*, pp. 511–12.
25. In *Plan*, pp. 459, 465, 476n, Bentham refers to his *Springs* for explanations regarding the pleasure-pain foundation of his psychology of motivation. See *Springs*, pp. 98, 105.
26. See Frank O'Gorman, *Voters, Patrons, and Parties: The Unreformed Electoral System of Hanoverian England 1734–1832* (Oxford: Clarendon Press, 1989; rpt 2005), pp. 27–58, 141–71, for a complex assessment of electoral influence.
27. Bentham's argument that reform would greatly reduce corruption of parliamentary candidates is comparable: besides the reformed electoral system, annual parliaments would confine to a shorter length of time the corrupter's hold over the corrupted member because of the greater expense of more frequent elections (*Plan* 511–12).
28. Kevin Gilmartin, *Print Politics: The Press and Radical Opposition in Early Nineteenth-Century England* (Cambridge: Cambridge University Press, 1996), p. 94, comments on Wooler's 'abrupt swerves from the serious to the comic'. Also see p. 15 on the radical strategy of characterising corruption as a 'system' and the adoption of 'a rhetoric of despair'.

Chapter 11

Wordsworth after Peterloo: The Persistence of War in *The River Duddon . . . and other Poems*

Philip Shaw

Silent Ground

On 30 May 1820 Mary Wordsworth records how she and her husband, pausing in Manchester to change coaches on their journey to Banbury, prior to their departure to Belgium in the second week of July, 'took a walk, and inspected Peterloo; the particulars of the Stations of the Performers, the ground upon which certain feats were wrought, etc., we learned from a Person upon the spot, who had witnessed the whole scene'.[1] At once indefinite and exacting, Mary concludes her account by noting that 'William was not inclined to see anything further'.[2] A few weeks later, the field of Waterloo seemed, at first, to present a similarly uninspiring prospect. Yet, as Dorothy Wordsworth observes in her journal entry for 17 July, while there 'was little to be seen' there was 'much to be felt, – sorrow and sadness, and even something like horror breathed out of the ground as we stood upon it!'[3] Responding to Dorothy's impressions, Wordsworth writes in his sonnet 'After Visiting the Field of Waterloo' that even as the field appeared 'joyless, blank, and cold' (l. 6) and 'Meanings . . . could not there be found' (l. 10), yet still 'we felt as Men *should* feel, / With such vast hoards of hidden carnage near, / And horror breathing from the silent ground!' (ll. 12–14).[4] That Wordsworth found significance in the 'great exploits' of Waterloo (l. 12) but felt disinclined to retrieve meaning from the 'certain feats' at Peterloo is unsurprising. Writing to Viscount Lowther the previous autumn Wordsworth had made clear his opposition to 'the revolutionary projects' of those 'active Reformers' who sought to arouse 'public disapprobation of the conduct of the Manchester Magistrates',[5] and as late as December 1820 felt moved to remark critically on the conduct of a Leicestershire bookseller, 'a notorious Jacobin and Incendiary, and Usher of a school', who had appointed a teacher of radical principles 'who had given the "Manchester Massacres" as a Theme for his Boys'.[6]

Civilian pilgrimages to European battlefields were, by 1820, a common enough occurrence, but what the Wordsworths' visit to Peterloo unintentionally reveals is the striking congruity between sites of national and international conflict. That both sites could be regarded as notable additions to the tourist's itinerary compounds the sense in which Peterloo was broadly conceived, in the autumn of 1819, as the ironic counterpart of Waterloo.[7] That the massacre was, at least in part, perpetrated by soldiers who had served at Waterloo, and that at least one of the victims, John Lees, had also fought in that battle, underscored the relationship still further.[8] On the journey to Manchester, Wordsworth, afflicted by the eye disease that would dog him for the remainder of his life, and that was most likely transmitted by soldiers returning from the fight against Napoleon in Egypt, remained 'silent and looked ill'.[9] According to Mary, the poet's spirits were roused only by the sight of the race ground at Manchester, populated by an 'immense concourse of persons – 10,000, as we were afterwards told. The race was just over, and the stream of life that was flowing down from the mass which still seemed stationary, was a sublime sight'.[10] Pre-echoes of this vision were heard the previous summer when, for instance, the radical reformer and journalist Archibald Prentice observed the stream of gaily clad people moving 'slowly and orderly' down Mosley Street on their way to the hustings.[11] Yet, with its emphasis on fluidity and stasis, an optical illusion reminiscent of Wordsworth's encounter with the 'stationary blasts' of the Gondo gorge,[12] Mary's account may also be read as a proleptic response to Samuel Bamford's memorable description of the breaking of the dense, compacted crowd at St Peter's Field:

> For a moment the crowd held back as in a pause; then was a rush, heavy and resistless as a headlong sea; and a sound like low thunder, with screams, prayers, and imprecations from the crowd-moiled, and sabre-doomed, who could not escape.[13]

Here, two versions of the sublime may be compared and contrasted. While Bamford draws on Homeric tropes of catastrophic terror, engulfing the crowd in a tsunami-like wave of destruction, Mary's emphasis on the poised 'stream of life' recalls the observations of the River Duddon that had preoccupied Wordsworth the previous year. By informing her vision with a related affirmation of unity amidst change, Mary endeavours to reverse the current, recasting an 'immense concourse of persons' as a flowing yet stationary mass, in sight of an end that is forever delayed. Those 'certain feats' of which the Wordsworths learn but are reluctant to envision are here effectively consigned to temporal oblivion, annulled by an intelligence in thrall to the recovery of a pre-political society. Witnessed only in glimpses and notably only when on holiday, the Wordsworthian social ideal is characterised nevertheless by a sense of historical indeterminacy, a state in which the distinctions between peace and war become difficult to discern let alone sustain.

Drawing on such observations, this essay argues that while Wordsworth's direct references to Peterloo may be few and predictably conservative, his indirect referential engagements with 'treasons, tumults' and 'wars' in poems published in the aftermath of Peterloo reveal a thoughtful and unpredictable engagement with the place of conflict in civil society.[14] The essay's focus is on a single collection, *The River Duddon, A Series of Sonnets: Vaudracour and Julia and other Poems. To which is Annexed, A Topographical Description of the Country of the Lakes, in the North of England*. Published in April 1820, just prior to the Wordsworths' visit to Manchester, the title page and dedication to Christopher Wordsworth is followed by an advertisement informing the reader that 'This publication, together with "The Thanksgiving Ode," Jan. 18. 1816, "The Tale of Peter Bell," and "The Waggoner," completes the third and last volume of the Author's Miscellaneous Poems'.[15] Purchasers wishing to add the collection to the 1815 two-volume *Poems*, and the aforementioned works, are provided with an alternative title page, 'Poems By William Wordsworth: Including The River Duddon; Vaudracour and Julia; Peter Bell; The Waggoner; A Thanksgiving Ode and Miscellaneous Pieces. Vol. III' and a tipped-in spine label: 'Wordsworth's / Poems / Including The / River Duddon / Vol. III'.[16] Bringing together within one binding poems and prose writings composed during the period of the revolutionary and Napoleonic Wars

(*Peter Bell*, *Vaudracour and Julia*, the guide to the Lakes), verses written in the wake of Waterloo (the 'Thanksgiving Ode' and related poems), the post-Peterloo sonnets and other 'Miscellaneous Pieces' concerned with governance, morality and war, the rare third volume of Wordsworth's *Poems* offers a sustained commentary on the historical origins of political violence while seeking, through meditation on the natural histories of rivers, mountains and lakes, the grounds for a peaceable, albeit reactionary, alternative.[17]

Towards a Poetics of Stasis

Commentary on Romantic poetry and the Peterloo massacre owes much to Jerome McGann, whose 1979 article 'Keats and the Historical Method in Literary Criticism' proclaimed, to the consternation of critics as varied in approach as Paul Fry, Nicholas Roe and Vincent Newey, that 'To Autumn' 'is an historically specified fiction dialectically called into being by John Keats as an active response to, and alteration of, the events which marked the late summer and early fall of a particular year in a particular place'.[18] Sharing common ground with Marjorie Levinson's Marxian critique of Wordsworth's 'repression' of material contradictions in the landscape of 'Tintern Abbey',[19] McGann's reading of 'To Autumn' was widely interpreted as a wholescale denunciation of the high Romantic lyric and its purported evasion of history. Yet what is striking about the criticism written in response to McGann's provocation is the corresponding narrowness of its attention, which with the exception of some notable discussions of Shelley's *Masque of Anarchy* and associated poems, remained almost solely focused on providing subtle defences of Keats' politics and poetics. In the articles, essays and books that emerged in this period and that attempted to engage with Peterloo there are hardly any mentions of poetry by Wordsworth, a surprising omission given that Wordsworth wrote two poems in the autumn of 1819 that may be read, along McGannian lines, as 'an active response to, and alteration of, the events' at St Peter's Field.[20] For reasons that will become clear, the poems in question, 'September, 1819' and 'Upon the Same Occasion', included in *The River Duddon* volume, deserve closer attention.

While hymning the sober pleasures of later life and of the overcoming of 'the anxieties of human love' (l. 23) through submission to the divine, 'September, 1819' presents an image of post-war instability that, in the wake of the more widely read 'To Autumn', appears all too familiar:

> The sylvan slopes with corn-clad fields
> Are hung, as if with golden shields,
> Bright trophies of the sun!
> Like a fair sister of the sky,
> Unruffled doth the blue Lake lie,
> The Mountains looking on. (ll. 1–5)[21]

The mood of peace and plenty is challenged, however, by the inclusion of those 'golden shields' (l. 2). In light of the recent events in Manchester, these spoils of war, assembled under the name of Apollo, god of the sun, of healing and of poetry presents a strikingly troubling image. The impression of internal dissonance is compounded when one recalls Nicholas Roe's discussion of the allusion to the goddess Ceres in Keats' ode. Noting the resemblance between Keats' personification of the season and the female deity of justice, liberty and autumnal abundance depicted on the Peterloo banner, Roe argues persuasively that the ode participates in a radical rereading of classical mythology, drawing on Ceres' associations with husbandry, cultivation and 'common' law to mount a quiet denunciation of the pernicious effects of the Corn Laws in solidarity with the protestors in Manchester.[22] Composed like Keats' poem in a time of economic deprivation and state oppression, 'September, 1819' is, by contrast, ruthlessly combative, marshalling images of armoured fruition to quell political unrest. Where Keats' poem acknowledges the vibrant delights of spring, in order to celebrate the mellow, attenuated pleasures of autumn, Wordsworth offers stark criticism, asserting that the autumnal tone is 'more profoundly dear / Than music of Spring' (ll. 11–12):

> For *that* from turbulence and heat
> Proceeds, from some uneasy
> Seat in Nature's struggling frame,
> Some region of impatient life;
> And jealousy, and quivering strife,
> Therein a portion claim. (ll. 13–18)

In opposition to the constitutional unrest of spring, an echo of the Hobbesian *bellum inter omnia* advanced in the 'Topographical Description of the Country of the Lakes',[23] the poem thus establishes autumn as a season of 'soft harmony' (l. 26) unchecked by internal conflict. Yet, because such seasonal concord is predicated on the suppression of 'impatient life' it becomes increasingly difficult to sustain a distinction between the institution of the peaceable state and the primal antagonism from which it is said to emerge. The peace of autumn, that is, is founded on, or facilitated by, civil war.

In the pendant poem 'Upon the Same Subject' a related attempt is made to shift the focus of attention towards 'undiscordant themes' (l. 20). In concert with the poet's Waterloo poetry, the verse is as much about Wordsworth's aspiration to be acknowledged as a national bard, overcoming faction and dissent in the name of a higher, literary principle, as it is about the wish for release from internal division. In this case, however, the establishment of peace is challenged by those who, gripped by 'vernal extasies, / And passion's feverish dreams' (ll. 23–4), would 'enervate and defile' (l. 30) the restorative labour of the Apollonian bard.[24] It may be, as Carl Ketcham conjectures, that Wordsworth has Lord Byron in mind, whose recently published *Don Juan*, Canto 1, had directly lampooned Wordsworth.[25] But Wordsworth might also have wished to single out Byron for his ambivalent response to the defeat of Napoleon and for his support of radical political causes. Tellingly, in the poem's concluding stanzas Wordsworth invokes as model for the post-Peterloo bard the ancient Greek poet Alcaeus who supported the nobles in the civil war in Mytilene, and whose 'fierce vindictive song' was the scourge of the leaders of the people, known as 'Tyrants' (ll. 37–41). Combining sympotic and lyrical impulses, Alcaeus, together with Horace, is thus presented as an exemplar of the 'deathless powers' (l. 25) of poesy, assessing and overcoming literary and political corruption through the adoption of a timeless, dispassionate perspective. In adopting this perspective, Wordsworth resumes the vatic tone adopted in his earlier post-war autumnal sonnet 'September, 1815'.[26] Composed shortly after the victory at Waterloo, the octave registers a sense of an oncoming period of austerity and of the likelihood of a forthcoming civil war, culminating with the advice to 'Prepare / Against the threatening Foe your trustiest shields' (ll. 7–8). In the sestet, the forewarning of conflict is countered by the image of a 'season potent to renew, / Mid frost and snow, the instinctive joys of song, – / And nobler cares than listless summer knew' (ll. 12–14). In these lines the threat of destruction is incorporated within a rhythmic seasonal cycle, one that allows conflict to be refigured as a 'potent' source of creative, moral and political renewal.

Currents of Disturbance

The desire to transform discordant themes is present too in *The River Duddon* sonnet sequence. As is well known, Wordsworth casts his sequence as a response to Coleridge's aborted long poem 'The Brook', a work intended to rival Cowper's *Task* in providing 'equal room and freedom for description, incident, and impassioned reflections on men, nature, and society' while yet supplying 'in itself a natural connection to the parts, and unity to the whole'. Recalling the plan for 'The Recluse', Coleridge states that his own essay on 'men, nature, and society' was to have taken for its subject 'a stream, traced from its source in the hills [to the sea]'.[27] In the postscript to *The River Duddon* Wordsworth freely acknowledges his borrowing of this unifying motif, but states that his work differs from 'The Brook' on account of 'the restriction which the frame of the Sonnet imposed upon me, narrowing unavoidably the range of thought, and precluding, though not without its advantages, many graces to which a freer movement of verse would naturally have led'.[28] By embracing formal restrictions Wordsworth is able, as Daniel Robinson explains, to partially fulfil the promise of 'his and Coleridge's shared vision'.[29] But in revisiting these, as yet, unrealised works, through the medium of the loco-descriptive river poem, Wordsworth also, necessarily, recalls the genre's elegiac aspects. Thus, as much as *The River Duddon* seeks to make good on the youthful poet's promise to complete a work addressing 'men, nature, and society', the combination of formal 'narrowing' and thematic revisiting cannot help but place the sequence in relation to a greater and, seemingly, lost object. *The River Duddon*, I would suggest, is therefore couched, from the outset, as a work of melancholy.

But while it is fruitful to read *The River Duddon* as a fallen version of 'The Recluse', the publication of the sequence in the wake of Peterloo suggests a relationship not merely with a lost object, but with an impossible object. In Wordsworth's autumnal poems, as we have seen, the attempt to establish a realm of post-war harmony is jeopardised by the return of images of internal strife. Thus, as much as Wordsworth pursues the ideal of a peaceable society his poetry speaks repeatedly of the impossibility of establishing a society that is not always already at war with itself. Regarded in this light, Wordsworth's refusal to read St Peter's Field may be understood as a manifestation of perplexity at the blurring of distinctions between allies and enemies, citizens and soldiers, but also as a sign of the poet's unwillingness to register the work of *stasis* in determining that which is political and that which is unpolitical. Nevertheless, as the Duddon sonnets reveal, aspects of civil discord are manifest throughout the sequence, consuming not merely the city but also nature. For if, as Giorgio Agamben argues, 'civil war is a projection of the state of nature into the city' then the converse must also be true; that is, we should not be surprised to see descriptions of natural life (*zoē*) – the physical realm of rocks, rivers, earth and plants – marked by the effects of a dissolving *bios politikos*.[30] While this statement about the violent transformation of nature may seem counter-intuitive, it is important to remember that the pastoral tradition that Wordsworth recalls in his poetry is forged in a context of civil discord. In showing through the Duddon sequence how the significance of rivers is informed by the effects of war, Wordsworth positions himself in relation to Horace and Virgil, sharing, as we shall see, their anxieties about the politicisation of nature.[31]

The opening sonnet identifies three established and, by implication, overworked poetic precedents: Horace's spring of Bandusia (ll. 1–4); the Persian fountains that, in the wake of Sir William Jones' imitations of Nezami, had become a stock feature of literary orientalism (ll. 5–6), and the 'Alpine torrents' (ll. 7–8) that had featured in Wordsworth's earlier loco-descriptive poetry, as well as in Book 6 of the unpublished *Prelude*, and that Byron had since imitated to considerable acclaim in Canto III of *Childe Harold's Pilgrimage* and in *Manfred*.[32] Against these well-worn, exotic and populist precedents, dismissed through a series of verbal negations, the poet declares a wish to 'seek the birth-place of a native Stream' (l. 8) so that his verse may 'flow . . . pure, vigorous, free, and bright' (l. 13), unencumbered by generic expectations. Yet, despite the confident turn, the octave's accumulation of literary sources signals an understanding of the fraught relations between imitation and innovation and, further still, displays a shrewd awareness of the underlying violence of the pastoral tradition. Key to both insights is the significance of the opening allusion to Horace's Ode 3.13, a poem that seems to have held a lifelong fascination for Wordsworth.[33] Horace's verse takes the form of a dedicatory address to a *fons Bandusiae*, an obscure spring believed to be located in the grounds of Horace's Sabine estate.[34] As translators and commentators have pointed out, Horace is attempting in this poem to elevate a Roman fountain and, by extension, Roman verse to the distinguished position occupied by Greek springs and Greek pastoral poetry.[35] Thus the *fons Bandusiae* will emerge as a rival to Arethusa, Castalia and Hippocrene, and Ode 3.13 as a worthy successor to the fêted river songs of Theocritus and Callimachus. However, just as Horace's assertion of literary authority is qualified by its acknowledgement of Greek models of inspiration, in particular the modest 'holy fountain' in Callimachus' *Hymn to Apollo*,[36] so Wordsworth's evocation of native purity is sullied by its engagement with Horace. The priority of that 'rocky spring' may not be envied, but the sonnet must be forged within its 'shades' (ll. 1–2).

More pressing still, for both poets, is the problem of how to maintain the sense of the pastoral mode, with its associations of peace, obscurity and retirement. In stating that the Duddon and his poem about the Duddon is 'pure' Wordsworth displays his awareness of the contentious or mixed status of Horace's stream, which on the eve of a rustic festival is set to be stained by the blood of a sacrificial kid, a product of the 'wanton herd' (l. 8), whose 'budding horns' mark him out for 'Battles and love' (ll. 4–5).[37] While line 5 may be understood as a reference to benign battles of love (*et venerem et proelia*) the kid's status as a symbol of Callimachean eroticism is itself sacrificed to the ode's larger concern with literary authority. For, rather than dwelling on or indeed dismissing the ignoble taints of blood, sacrifice and war, the Horatian pastoral seeks to sublimate violence, thereby transforming itself into something greater than a Callimachean hymn to rural delights. In Erwin Panofsky's sense, Ode 3.13 demonstrates precisely the aim of pastoral to 'resolve' instances of individual suffering through incorporation within larger structures of artistic harmony.[38] Thus, though blood may spoil the waters, the stream's consecration as one of the 'famous fountains' (l. 13) ensures that no lasting harm is done.

While Horace, like Callimachus, demonstrates the ability of art to triumph over destruction by portraying the blood of the sacrificial kid as, at worst, a temporary sullying of the sacred spring, and of the poem itself as capable of encompassing the bifurcated themes of love and war, the elevation of the humble brook in pastoral lyric is brought about as a reaction to the bellicose legacy of the epic tradition. In George Chapman's translation of *Iliad* Book 21, for example, Achilles battles with enemies in the whirling currents of the Xanthus:

> The siluer-gulphed deepe
> Receiu'd them with a mightie crie: the billowes vast and steepe,
> Ror'd at their armours; which the shores, did round about resound:
> This way, and that, they swum, and shriekt; as in the gulphs they drownd.[39]

Blinded by fury, Achilles escalates the slaughter, prompting the river, in the shape of a man, to protest against the accumulation of bodies that choke its currents with 'mortalitie'.[40] But still Achilles fights on, accelerating the combat to a struggle between man and river, thereby revealing how 'simple natural life' is politicised as 'bare life' through exposure to death.[41]

Echoing the concerns of his classical antecedents, Wordsworth's sonnet sequence offers glimpses of a post-war world, of that which remains after the apocalyptic struggle of man, nature and society. In Sonnet 8, for example, a series of Keatsian rhetorical questions, seemingly addressed to the ghost of an ancient warrior – 'What aspect bore the Man who rove or fled . . . to this dark dell?', 'who first in this pellucid Current slaked his thirst?', 'Was the Intruder nurs'd / In hideous usages, and rites accurs'd, / That thinned the living and disturbed the dead?' (ll. 1–8) – is answered by silence: 'the earth, the air is mute', only the 'murmuring' stream provides a 'soft record' of a capacity to 'heal and to restore, / To soothe and cleanse, not madden and pollute!' (9–14). And in Sonnet 23, otherwise known as 'Sheep-Washing', the sequence returns to the relations between violence and purity addressed by Horace, only here, instead of receiving a slaughtered kid, the Duddon's 'laving currents' perform 'prelusive rites' (l. 3) so that the dales-men may shear their sheep. Moreover, should the 'Duddon's spotless breast receive / Unwelcome mixtures' of 'uncouth noise' (ll. 9–10), from 'barking dogs', boyish 'clamour' and fearful 'bleatings' (ll. 7–8), 'the pastoral river will forgive / Such wrong' (ll. 10–11). The 'stains' produced by such 'sports' are 'fugitive' and nature will be sustained in 'quiet equipoise' (ll. 13–14). Alert to the potential for furore encoded in the etymology of 'noise', Wordsworth in both poems presents the river as a form of sound baffle, a means of dampening the potential for tumult inherent in the pastoral mode.

In Sonnet 13, 'Open Prospect', however, the soothing influence of the river in 'Sheep-Washing' is curtailed by a 'dread swell of sound' that cuts through the 'stiff lance-like shoots of pollard ash' (ll. 6–7). Rather than muffling the sounds of war, the river is itself a source of discord, emitting 'angry' notes (l. 11) that the nearby households must drown out by means of 'mantling ale' and laughter (ll. 12–13). Still, in this poem, the turn in line 9 towards the social realm cannot wholly conceal the echoes of pre-pastoral violence encoded in the octave's allusion to *Aeneid*, III, lines 24–82. Specifically, the 'lance-like shoots' recall the densely packed myrtles, 'rough with many a spear' (l. 32), which Aeneas, seeking to establish a homeland in Thrace, uses to build a canopy for a sacrificial altar.[42] In Wordsworth's translation of Virgil's poem the harvesting of the green shoots reveals 'a dire portent, . . . wond'rous to be told!' (l. 36):

> No sooner was the shatter'd root laid bare
> Of the first Tree I struggled to uptear,
> Than from the fibres drops of blood distill'd,
> Whose blackness stain'd the ground. (ll. 37–40)

Aeneas tries a second time to tear the stalks from the earth and is met again by the sight of blood seeping from the torn bark. A third attempt elicits a 'mournful groan' (l. 56) and a warning to the hero to desist from his labours. The voice belongs to Polydorus, a victim of Achilles in the war against the Trojans, whose sword-pierced body, transformed into sanguineous 'myrtle lances' (l. 54), testifies to the co-implication of pastoral retirement and the reciprocal activity of death and wounding. For if rivers, plants, earth and air serve as indelible registers of human suffering must the *patria* itself be implicated? Is there no sacred space on which violence does not encroach?

Elsewhere, in *The River Duddon* volume, the Hobessian notion of nature at war with itself is manifested in 'The Brownie's Cell', which with its evocations of battle-wrought stars, 'winds combating with woods' and 'Lands delug'd by unbridled floods' (ll. 61–70), evokes the account of discordant nature as an auger of civil strife presented by Virgil in *Georgics* I: in advance of Caesar's assassination the sun is hid in 'dusky gloom'; Etna shoots out 'balls of flame and molten rocks'; the Alps rock with 'unwonted terrors'; the Eridanus, king of rivers, washes away whole forests, sweeping cattle and stalls alike across the plains; the sky is marked by lightning and 'blazing comets'.[43] A time will come when the farmer, tilling the soil with 'crooked plough', will uncover 'javelins eaten up with rusty mould, or with his heavy hoe shall strike on empty helms, and marvel at the giant bones in the upturned graves', but for now the 'crooked pruning-hooks are forged into stiff swords' and the world is convulsed by the thirst for annihilation.[44] The best that can be hoped for, as Virgil anticipates in *Eclogues* I, is a pastoral zone rescued from conflict: 'Happy old man! Here, amid familiar streams and sacred springs, you shall court the cooling shade' (ll. 46–58); but for every farmer who lives to till the soil, another must die so that the soil may be nourished, and thus there is no sacred spring that is not defiled by blood.[45]

In Sonnet 28 Wordsworth seeks to correct this assumption. The inspiration for the verse comes from the site of a disused Quaker burial ground, known locally as the Sepulchre, situated on the east bank of the Duddon about a mile above Ulpha Bridge. Amidst these 'retired domains', the poem records, there is no evidence of 'lance opposed to lance' (ll. 1–2) and, notably in light of the bleeding soil alluded to in Sonnets 8 and 13, no account of turf stained 'purple from the veins / Of heroes fall'n, or struggling to advance' (ll. 3–4). The ground, that is, bears no trace of epic fight or, more pointedly, of 'power usurp'd' (l. 13). 'Yet', the sestet confirms, the 'blank earth' shelters the remains of 'the loyal and the brave' who, though 'neglected and forlorn', receive the 'tribute' of 'passing Winds' and the 'praise' of torrents, 'inspiring scorn / Of power usurp'd . . . / And glad acknowledgment of lawful sway' (ll. 6–14). Composed between March and December 1819, the sonnet may be read as a pointedly anti-conspiratorial gesture, using Virgilian meditations on pastoral exceptionalism and the outcome of 'doubtful combat' (l. 5) to inform a reactionary judgement of the current state of affairs. For if, like St Peter's Field, the earth is now unmarked, it serves, nevertheless, as confirmation of a power greater and more enduring than the human capacity for revolt. Still, the objects of this praise remain unregistered, and the voices of the winds and of the river are strictly inarticulate, suggesting that pacific heroes must remain exiles from signification.

The characteristic pattern of affirmation via negation is sustained at the sequence's close. In Sonnet 31 the Duddon is released from the picturesque hold of 'flower-enamelled lands', 'blooming thickets' and 'rocky bands' allowing the river to flow in 'radiant progress' towards the Irish Sea (ll. 1–4). Following a densely plotted series of negated verbs – 'Not hurled . . . Lingering no more . . . nor . . . held' – in line 5 the heavily accented '*now*' signals the Duddon's possession of the tidal flats, allowing it to sweep in 'unfettered' majesty over 'smooth flat sands' (ll. 5–6). The river is presented from hereon in terms of the natural sublime, its grandeur unsullied by transient picturesque forms, by baroque rhetorical constructions, or by fears of mortality.[46] The octave, composed in advance of the sestet between December 1818 and March 1819, makes comparison between the Duddon and the 'sovereign Thames' (l. 12). United in 'Stately mien' (l. 12), the concluding lines depict the latter river 'Spreading his bosom under Kentish downs, / With freighted Commerce or triumphant War' (l. 14).[47] As the penultimate sonnet makes clear, the 'Majestic Duddon' may be 'allied' (Sonnet 31, l. 12) to the 'sovereign Thames' but is ultimately immunised from the oppositional logic that defines the capital river's supremacy. Thus, in Sonnet 32, the octave composed during the same period as the previous sonnet's sestet, confirms that 'no cannon thunders to the gale', and 'no haughty pendants cast / A crimson splendour' upon the waves (ll. 1–2); and in like manner, in the sestet, written in advance of the octave between December 1818 and March 1819, the 'Wanderer' (l. 7) and the 'Poet' (l. 9), taking the river's progress towards the sea as their model, resign the 'strange vicissitudes' (l. 6) of mortal life, 'Prepared, in peace of heart, in calm of mind / And soul' to 'mingle with Eternity!' (ll. 13–14). Peace, therefore, is presented at the close of *The River Duddon* as a release from the alternation between opposing or contrasting things; specifically, from the constitutional violence – 'Commerce' *or* 'War' – in which the *polis* is forged. Of significance here is the fact that the lines most preoccupied with conflict – the sestet of 31 and the octave of 32 – were both written after the violent events in Manchester. In its original form, as Benjamin Kim has argued, Sonnet 31 provided a much neater and far less worldly ending to the sequence.[48] The revised sestet of 31 therefore introduced a disjunctive element that the octave of 31 was designed to resolve, as if in recognition of the impossibility of preventing the alliance of warlike and pacific rivers.[49]

As the final sonnet in the sequence confirms, the attempt to pacify antagonism can succeed only by acknowledging and upholding a mode of life that, by virtue of its release from death, is no longer subject to politicisation. Looking back on his journey, the poet of Sonnet 33 sees 'what was, and is, and will abide; / Still glides the Stream and shall for ever glide; / The Form remains, the Function never dies' (ll. 4–6). In the continuity of being through past, present and future tenses, in the paradoxical logic of 'Still glides', and in the assertion of life living on, not as bare life, but as eternal Platonic Form, Wordsworth releases the stream and the literary work in which the stream is enshrined, from the exclusionary/inclusionary logic of the *polis*. From another perspective, however, the attempt to protect nature from death merely replaces one form of co-optation – the political – with another, namely, the religious. For just as the peaceable fount is retroactively produced through the violent suspension of the political, so that 'life' which lives on is made conditional on the inclusive exclusion of death through 'faith's transcendent dower' (l. 13). In line 9 the distinction between the acceptance of mortality and the acknowledgement of that 'something', which 'from our hands have power / To live, and act, and serve the future hour' (ll. 10–11) is, accordingly, signified through a protracted pause: 'We Men, who in our morn of youth defied / The elements must vanish; – be it so!' (ll. 8–9). The terminal clause that enables the poem to accept the necessity of non-existence, and that serves also to enable progression beyond the potentially fatal pause, is reminiscent of the '*now* expands' clause of Sonnet 31 and, in like manner, signals the poem's commitment to the upholding of internal division as a key element in the furtherance of life. By marking a reciprocal relation between nullity and activity, the clause thus paves the way for the iambic insistence of the transient verbs in line 10, which seek fulfilment in a deferred object, 'the future hour' (l. 10) in which 'We feel that we are greater than we know' (l. 14). In much the same way as the eternal life of the soldier is predicted on the sacrifice of self in a call to arms, so that which 'was, and is' is rescued from oblivion through service to that which 'will abide' (l.4). To adapt Steven Miller's analysis, Wordsworth's pacific poem can therefore be read as a defence of the 'dignity of war-and-death against the incursion of violence worse than death'.[50] For it is precisely because war 'imposes and upholds death' as 'both sacrifice and limit' that life is protected from annulment,[51] whether that annulment is conceived as the effect of the death drive or, in the sense outlined above, as a consequence of the submission to the divinely indeterminate.[52]

Outflow

In its original form, as the alternative title page makes clear, the Duddon sonnets were intended to be bound with '*Vaudracour and Julia; Peter Bell; The Waggoner; A Thanksgiving Ode and Miscellaneous Pieces*', thus forming the third volume of Wordsworth's collected *Poems*. Importantly, the poet's collected works were to have concluded with a poem derived from Wordsworth's experience of familial estrangement as a result of the outbreak of the war against France – *Vaudracour and Julia* – and with a set of poems – the 'Thanksgiving Ode' (18 January 1816) and related works – intended to mark the cessation of that period of estrangement. As I have argued elsewhere, Wordsworth's most notorious public poem turns out, after all, to have originated in personal loss and, in its concern with the passage from corporeal to incorporeal being, to be coeval with the central concerns of the 'Ode: Intimations of Immortality', that had concluded the second volume of the *Poems*.[53] A reader of Wordsworth's three-volume *Poems* would therefore have read *The River Duddon* as a conduit between two expressive odes, with the second ode enfolding the concerns of the first ode within a broader account of personal and national rejuvenation. The fact that the 'Thanksgiving Ode' was advertised as 'a sequel to the Sonnets, dedicated to Liberty' underscores the sense in which the three-volume *Poems* should be considered the most overtly political of Wordsworth's collected works.[54]

The 'Thanksgiving Ode' shares with the final sonnet in the Duddon sequence a sense of the transience of natural phenomena and a corresponding wish to valorise those works that are dedicated to God. Thus, Wordsworth claims that the 'current of this matin song' lies 'deeper . . . Than aught dependent on the fickle skies' (ll. 53–5); however, in this poem the fluvial imagery is not developed further.[55]

As is well known, following publication the ode was lambasted for its seemingly callous treatment of the dead and wounded. Shelley, Byron and Hunt all roundly denounced the verse for proposing that the slaughter of Waterloo had been divinely sanctioned. Yet, when read in sequence, the poems Wordsworth composed in the aftermath of the battle offer a range of perspectives and, in 'Elegiac Verses', a poem composed shortly after the ode, there is an attempt to address the human costs of war. Ventriloquising the 'plaintive' tones of a heavenly spirit, the poet seeks, while taking account of 'Unpitied havoc' and 'Victims unlamented' (l. 14), to 'wash away' the 'stains' of a 'perturbèd earth' (ll. 1–4). The spirit accordingly sprinkles 'soft celestial dews / Thy lost maternal heart to reinfuse!' and, 'Scattering this far-fetched moisture from my wings', cleanses the 'secret springs . . . stained so oft with human gore' (ll. 23–6).[56] Like Horace's Bandusia, mortal stains are temporary; through divine intervention blood is turned to water and the sacred river is rejuvenated. In the following poem, 'Ode. Composed in January 1816', an epigraph from Horace's ode to Censorinus reaffirms the lasting worth of poetry, while the verse itself envisions a post-war era of bucolic calm and 'festive beauty' (l. 28).[57] Wordsworth's fantasia portrays a peaceable realm in which warriors, with 'crimson banners proudly streaming, / And upright weapons innocently gleaming' (ll. 45–6) are attended by white-robed maidens. The vision recedes, but the poem goes on to imagine unfading tributes of the 'silent art' (l. 81), 'expressive records of a glorious strife . . . Trophies on which the morning sun may shine, / As changeful ages flow' (ll. 94–8). Thus, while conflict belongs to the turbulent course of history, art resides with eternity. But greater still than the tributes provided by sculpture are the transcendent records of elevated writing. Thus the ode concludes with a hymn of praise to the 'Pierian sisters' and, in particular, to Mnemosyne, for too long an exile from 'consecrated stream and grove' (l. 102), and a hope that 'I, or some more favoured Bard' (l. 115) may, from 'some spotless fountain' (l. 111), write verse that will secure a lasting memory of Britain's martial triumphs.

The *Thanksgiving* volume, and the third volume of *Poems*, ends therefore with a hope that Wordsworth will be remembered as a national poet. Drawing again on Horace, the final ode in this sequence confers on Wordsworth's works as a whole the right to versify in times of peace and war. More pointedly, when read in 1820, in the months following the culminating event in a lengthy period of political unrest, this purported concluding volume would have been read, by some, as a re-sacralising of the fount and as a re-inscription of nature in the name of the *polis*.

Notes

1. *The Letters of Mary Wordsworth, 1800–1855*, ed. Mary Elizabeth Burton (Oxford: Clarendon Press, 1955), pp. 55–6.
2. Ibid. p. 56.
3. Dorothy Wordsworth, *Journal of a Tour on the Continent 1820*; *The Journals of Dorothy Wordsworth*, ed. Ernest De Selincourt, 3 vols (London: Macmillan, 1941), vol. 3, p. 29.
4. William Wordsworth, *Sonnet Series and Itinerary Poems, 1820–1845*, ed. Geoffrey Jackson (Ithaca: Cornell University Press, 2004), p. 361.
5. *The Letters of William and Dorothy Wordsworth: The Middle Years, 1806–1820*, ed. Ernest De Selincourt, rev. Mary Moorman and Alan G. Hill, 2 vols (Oxford: Clarendon Press, 1970), vol. 2, p. 558.
6. Ibid. p. 657.
7. For further discussion of battlefield tourism, with a particular focus on Waterloo, see Philip Shaw, *Waterloo and the Romantic Imagination* (Basingstoke: Palgrave Macmillan, 2002), chapter 2.
8. *Peterloo Massacre, Containing a Faithful Narrative of the Events Which Preceded, Accompanied and Followed the Fatal Sixteenth of August 1819 . . . Edited by an Observer* (Manchester, 1819), p. 124. Anne Jones of Windmill Street informed the inquest that she had seen 'the cavalry cutting and slashing men on the way to the hustings. After getting to the hustings, they turned their horses round, and rode over the people in all directions, still cutting and slashing. . . . One of the special constables came into my house, and with great triumph exclaimed, "This is Waterloo for you, – This is Waterloo"', p. 178.
9. *The Letters of Mary Wordsworth*, p. 55.
10. Ibid.
11. Archibald Prentice, *Historical Sketches and Personal Recollections of Manchester Intended to Illustrate the Progress of Public Opinion From 1792–1832* (London, 1851), p. 159.
12. Book 6, l. 558, William Wordsworth, *The Thirteen-Book Prelude*, ed. Mark L. Reed (Ithaca: Cornell University Press, 1991), p. 190.
13. Samuel Bamford, *Passages in the Life of a Radical* (Oxford: Oxford University Press, 1984), p. 152.

14. Quotations from *Peter Bell*, l. 27, William Wordsworth, *Peter Bell*, ed. John E. Jordan (Ithaca: Cornell University Press, 1985), p. 46.
15. William Wordsworth, *The River Duddon, A Series of Sonnets: Vaudracour and Julia and other Poems. To which is Annexed, A Topographical Description of the Country of the Lakes, in the North of England* (London, 1820), preliminary matter.
16. Ibid. endpapers.
17. For further discussion of this 'most fugitive' publication see Eric C. Walker, *Marriage, Writing and Romanticism: Wordsworth and Austen After War* (Stanford: Stanford University Press, 2009), pp. 66–7 (66), and Eric C. Walker, 'Wordsworth's "Third Volume" and the Collected Editions, 1815–20', *Papers of the Bibliographical Society of America* 80 (1986), pp. 437–53.
18. Jerome J. McGann, *The Beauty of Inflections: Literary Investigations in Historical Method and Theory* (Oxford: Clarendon Press, 1985), p. 61. Significant critical responses to McGann's original 1979 article 'Keats and the Historical Method in Literary Criticism' include Paul H. Fry's 'History, Existence, and "To Autumn"', in *Studies in Romanticism* 25:2 (Summer 1986), pp. 211–19, and Nicholas Roe, 'Keats's Commonwealth', in *Keats and History*, ed. Nicholas Roe (Cambridge: Cambridge University Press, 1995). See also the essays in this volume by Vincent Newey, Michael O'Neill and Theresa M. Kelley.
19. Marjorie Levinson, *Wordsworth's Great Period Poems: Four Essays* (Cambridge: Cambridge University Press, 1986), p. 48.
20. James Chandler makes brief mention of Wordsworth's response to Peterloo in *England in 1819: The Politics of Literary Culture and the Case of Romantic Historicism* (Chicago and London: The University of Chicago Press, 1998), p. 10. More recently Brian R. Bates has pointed out that the dramatic shift from negative to positive appraisals of Wordsworth's poetry in the wake of Peterloo corresponds with George Canning's bold proclamation that 'November 1819 and March 1820 effectively belonged to different "epochs" in the nation's history'. See *Wordsworth's Poetic Collections, Supplementary Writing and Parodic Reception* (London and New York: Routledge, 2012), pp. 143–4.
21. Text taken from William Wordsworth, *Shorter Poems, 1807–1820*, ed. Carl H. Ketcham (Ithaca: Cornell University Press, 1989), pp. 283–4.
22. See Roe, 'Keats's Commonwealth', pp. 207–9.
23. Wordsworth, *The River Duddon*, p. 249.
24. 'Upon the Same Occasion', l. 30. Text taken from Wordsworth, *Shorter Poems*, pp. 284–6.
25. In Canto 1 of *Don Juan* Byron attacks Wordsworth as a 'shabby' civil servant (stanza 6), as 'unintelligible' (stanzas 4, 90 and 221) and as

'crazed beyond all hope' (stanza 205). *Lord Byron: The Major Works*, ed. Jerome J. McGann (Oxford: Oxford University Press, 1986), pp. 373–879. For Ketcham's comments on the allusion to Byron see Wordsworth, *Shorter Poems*, p. 550. Wordsworth's critique of Byron is sustained in another poem from the Duddon volume, 'The Pilgrim's Dream; Or, the Star and the Glow-Worm'. See Jalal Uddin Khan, 'The Allegories of "The Pilgrim's Dream; Or, the Star and the Glow-Worm"', *Studies in Philology* 94: 4 (Autumn 1997), pp. 508–22.

26. Wordsworth, *Shorter Poems*, p. 175.
27. Samuel Taylor Coleridge, *The Collected Coleridge: Biographia Literaria*, ed. James Engell and W. Jackson Bate, 2 vols (Princeton: Princeton University Press, 1983), vol. 2, pp. 195–6. For discussion of the influence of 'the Warton school' on the Duddon sonnets see David Fairer, *Organising Poetry: The Coleridge Circle, 1790–1798* (Oxford: Oxford University Press, 2009), chapter 4, and A. Harris Fairbanks, '"Dear Native Brook": Coleridge, Bowles, and Thomas Warton, the Younger', *The Wordsworth Circle* 6:4 (1975), pp. 313–15.
28. Wordsworth, *Sonnet Series and Itinerary Poems*, p. 76.
29. Daniel Robinson, '*The River Duddon* and Wordsworth, Sonneteer', in *The Oxford Handbook of William Wordsworth*, ed. Richard Gravil and Daniel Robinson (Oxford: Oxford University Press, 2015), pp. 289–308 (295).
30. Giorgio Agamben, *Stasis: Civil War as a Political Paradigm*, trans. Nicholas Heron (Edinburgh: Edinburgh University Press, 2015), p. 41.
31. For further analysis of the politicisation of 'simple natural life' see Giorgio Agamben, *Homo Sacer: Sovereign Power and Bare Life*, trans. Daniel Heller-Roazen (Stanford: Stanford University Press, 1995), pp. 1–8.
32. All subsequent quotations from the Duddon sonnets will be taken from Wordsworth, *Sonnet Series and Itinerary Poems*. This reference: p. 56.
33. Wordsworth's allusions to Ode 3.13 are numerous. See: *The Dog: An Idyllium* (1786); *An Evening Walk*, ll. 72–85; his translation of 1794; 'To Liberty' (1820), ll. 91–110; 'Musings Near Aquapendente' (1837), ll. 256–7. For discussion of Wordsworth's translation of Horace's ode see Bruce Edward Graver, *Wordsworth's Translations from Latin Poetry* (Chapel Hill: University of North Carolina Press, 1983), pp. 53–4. See also Edward W. Clancey, *Wordsworth's Classical Undersong: Education, Rhetoric and Poetic Truth* (Basingstoke: Macmillan, 2000), pp. 56–8.
34. Latin quotations taken from Horace, *The Odes*, ed. Kenneth Quinn (Basingstoke: Macmillan, 1980), p. 75.

35. For an excellent reading of this poem see Dan Curley, 'The Alcaic Kid (Horace, "Carm." 3.13)', *The Classical World* 97:2 (winter 2004), pp. 137–54.
36. Callimachus, *Hymn to Apollo*, l. 110, *The Hymns*, trans. Susan A. Stephens (Oxford: Oxford University Press, 2015), p. 81.
37. Quotations taken from Wordsworth, '[Ode] (from Horace)', *Early Poems and Fragments, 1785–1797*, ed. Carol Landon and Jarred R. Curtis (Ithaca: Cornell University Press, 1997), p. 769. In *An Evening Walk* (1793) Wordsworth makes clear his wish to supplant Horace's 'ruthless minister of death' (l. 74) with a 'more benignant sacrifice' (l. 78). *An Evening Walk*, ed. James Averill (Ithaca: Cornell University Press, 1984), p. 41.
38. Erwin Panofsky, *Meaning in the Visual Arts* (New York: Doubleday, 1995), p. 300. The connections between war and pastoral are explored by Kate McLoughlin in *Authoring War: The Literary Representation of War from the* Iliad *to Iraq* (Cambridge: Cambridge University Press, 2011), pp. 97–106.
39. *The Iliads of Homer prince of poets· Neuer before in any languag truely translated. With a co[m]ment vppon some of his chiefe places; donne according to the Greeke by Geo: Chapman* (London, 1611), p. 287. Wordsworth's library holds at least two early modern editions of Chapman's translation. See Chester L. Shaver and Alice C. Shaver, *Wordsworth's Library: A Catalogue* (New York and London: Garland, 1979), p. 126.
40. *The Iliads of Homer*, p. 291.
41. Agamben, *Homo Sacer*, p. 88.
42. Quotations taken from Wordsworth's translation in *Translations of Chaucer and Virgil*, ed. Bruce Graver (Ithaca: Cornell University Press, 1998), p. 248. Wordsworth's account of the bleeding and speaking tree owes much to Dante, Tasso and Spenser.
43. Virgil, *Eclogues*, *Georgics*, *Aeneid I–VI*, trans. H. Rushton Fairclough (Cambridge, MA: Harvard University Press, 1960), p. 113.
44. Ibid. p. 115.
45. Ibid. p. 7.
46. On the accenting of '*now*' as an effort to overcome the vitiating effects of time, see Paul de Man, 'Time and History in Wordsworth', *Romanticism and Contemporary Criticism: The Gauss Seminar and Other Papers*, ed. Kevin Newmark (Baltimore and London: Johns Hopkins University Press, 1993), pp. 74–94 (91).
47. The octave of 31 and the sestet of 32 originally formed one sonnet. See Wordsworth, *Sonnet Series and Itinerary Poems*, p. 109.

48. Benjamin Kim, 'Generating a National Sublime: Wordsworth's *The River Duddon* and *The Guide to the Lakes*', *Studies in Romanticism* 45:1 (spring 2005), pp. 49–76 (65–7).
49. See also Kim's observations on the martial significance of flood imagery in *Regarding the Convention of Cintra* (1809) and the conclusion of the Duddon sonnets. Ibid. pp. 63–4.
50. Steven Miller, *War After Death: On Violence and Its Limits* (New York: Fordham University Press, 2014), p. 4.
51. Ibid.
52. In opposition to Miller's somewhat gloomy prognosis, in *Means Without End* Agamben outlines a conception of the 'happy life' as 'an absolutely profane "sufficient life" that has reached the perfection of its own power and its own communicability – a life over which sovereignty and right no longer have any hold'. Giorgio Agamben, *Means Without End: Notes on Politics*, trans. Vincenzo Binetti and Cesare Casarino (Minneapolis: University of Minnesota Press, 2000), pp. 114–15.
53. See Philip Shaw, 'Wordsworth, Waterloo and Sacrifice', in *Sacrifice and Modern War Literature*, ed. Alex Houen and Jan-Melissa Schramm (Oxford: Oxford University Press, 2018), pp. 20–33, and Philip Shaw, 'Commemorating Waterloo: Wordsworth, Southey, and the "Muses' Page of State"', *Romanticism* 1:1 (1995), pp. 50–67.
54. Wordsworth, *Shorter Poems*, p. 536. The three-volume edition of *Poems* was quickly superseded in July 1820 by a new four-volume edition, *The Miscellaneous Poems of William Wordsworth*, which absorbed *The River Duddon* poems, adopting the classification system of the 1815 *Poems*. For further discussion of these volumes see Walker, *Marriage, Writing and Romanticism*, pp. 66–7, 73–83, 185–6, and Bates, *Wordsworth's Poetic Collections*, pp. 141–60.
55. Quotations from *Shorter Poems*, pp. 177–89.
56. Ibid. pp. 200–1.
57. Ibid. pp. 201–6.

Chapter 12

Shelley's Poetry and Suffering

Michael Scrivener

The intellectually rich debate of the past four decades about *The Mask of Anarchy*'s meaning – non-violent, insurrectionist, Godwinian, aestheticised fantasy, socialist, anarchist, communitarian, ambivalent, oratorical, interventionist, future-oriented, unpublishable – indicates how important the poem remains for so many of us. Meanwhile, historians since E. P. Thompson's ground-breaking narrative of Peterloo in *The Making of the English Working Class* continue to write about the Manchester massacre. In *Radical Shelley* I related *The Mask of Anarchy* to Peterloo and the popular depictions of the massacre, and twenty years later I introduced and edited a collection of essays in the *Romantic Circles Praxis* journal that dealt with the *Mask* and similarly political poems through the frame of Theodor Adorno's conception of autonomous and committed art.[1] *The Mask of Anarchy*, Shelley's longest political poem directed to a popular audience, responds complexly to violent injustice, but it is not unique in his oeuvre, so much of which addresses politics and injustice.

I am claiming that Shelley, under the pressure of the English political situation that had reached a crisis in 1819–20, was thinking through poetry – by metaphors, myths, associations and symbolic connections – for alternatives to ordinary politics; he was exploring what constituted political meanings in terms of how the mind and human nature functioned in a conflicted historical world and how they might function in a more ideal imagining. His poetic thinking led him to rely ever more on figures of the feminine and the maternal where alternative resolutions seemed most promising. Simply, feminine-centred and maternal myths promise to avoid the inevitable conflicts and injustice of patriarchal structures. Although his ostensible focus was socio-political, the poetic process, which he describes as 'inspired' and 'not subject to the control of the active powers of the mind',[2] drew upon psychological energies deriving from Oedipal and other unconscious conflicts, desires and anxieties. The fullest development of this project was reached in *Prometheus Unbound* and *The Mask of Anarchy*. Using the feminine and maternal for imagining revolution becomes parodic with *Oedipus Tyrannus*, the farcical satire on the Queen Caroline Affair. His later politically themed poetry – like *Hellas*, *Charles the First* and *Triumph of Life*, written when the prospects for radical politics were declining – does not draw much upon the feminine and maternal for essential ideas about emancipatory possibilities, thus suggesting a connection between the poetry of revolution and conceptions of the feminine.[3]

As a self-fashioned prophet of human emancipation, Shelley put suffering at the centre of his work. The repentant Prometheus who has repudiated his curse of Jupiter declares that 'I wish no living thing to suffer pain' (I, 305), thus providing a motto for the Shelleyan project of ideal revolution. Also, his character the Maniac in *Julian and Maddalo* expresses the process of empathy with suffering: '*Me* – who am as a nerve o'er which do creep / The else unfelt oppressions of this earth' (449–50). For the eighteenth-century 'man of feeling', sympathetic identification with the pain of others constituted a self-contained cultural discussion in literature and philosophy, but for Shelley empathy is a starting point in order to get towards socio-political justice. In the first act of *Prometheus Unbound*, the Furies inflict mental pain on the hero by forcing him to recognise not just the pervasiveness of wrong and misery but the failures of Christianity and the French Revolution to diminish injustice and suffering; the desperate implication is that social evil has no remedy, that efforts to improve society only make it worse. Prometheus' mental pain, which is described in images of physical suffering (cold, burning, cutting, and assorted visual and aural torments – I, 20–45), seems just like the experience of someone in extreme physical torment: 'Ah me, alas, pain, pain ever, forever!' (I, 23, 30, 635). He resorts to a literalism that simply gives an abstract name to his feeling, and he deploys a speech act that iambically imitates a howl of agony: ah me, alas! Discussing how the experience of extreme physical pain 'shatters' language, Elaine Scarry describes the 'inexpressibility' of physical pain: we have no words.[4] A similarly inexpressible moment is when Beatrice Cenci is violated by her father: 'O, world! O, life! O, day! O, misery!' (III, i, 32). Her coherent world is breaking down so that language cannot restore her sense of moral structure; rather, she has to act – perform a reality-altering deed – in order to repair her identity: 'If I try to speak / I shall go mad. Aye, something must be done; / What, yet I know not . . . something which shall make / The thing that I have suffered but a shadow / In the dread lightning which avenges it' (III, i, 85–9). In his first reaction to hearing about the Peterloo massacre, Shelley quotes these very lines in a letter to Charles Ollier, his publisher.[5] Ineffability, according to Ian Haywood, is a fundamental rhetorical trope in the description of atrocity and spectacular violence.[6]

I started with Prometheus' motto about suffering and the sympathetic mental pain of the Maniac in *Julian and Maddalo*, a poem that stages a debate on rival perspectives on social suffering between (more or less) Shelleyan and Byronic characters. Actual physical suffering is distanced and mediated, because the most miserable character, the Maniac, although expressing some of Shelley's own darkest feelings, is the object of the poem's dialogic discourse. Physical and mental suffering are distinct, but Shelley's poetry uses the physical to represent the mental. The language of the physical in *Prometheus Unbound* expresses the mental analogously, as the Preface explains (207). The reader understands that Prometheus' torments are both like and unlike physical torture, especially as Prometheus as a mythological character is both like and unlike a person; rather, his character condenses literary sufferers, such as the Greek Prometheus and the biblical Jesus. The suffering in both *The Mask of Anarchy* and *The Cenci* is predominantly physical, but severe physical pain, notoriously difficult to describe accurately, provokes the metaphorical language of mental anguish. That Shelley, writing to his publisher, thinks immediately of Beatrice Cenci's words when he is articulating his response to Peterloo shows that he experiences Peterloo, as many others did as well, as a kind of sexual violation by sadistic masculine power. The popular prints visually emphasised the special victimisation of children and women by the soldiers at St Peter's Field. The extremely popular Hone–Cruikshank depictions of Peterloo, on which I commented in *Radical Shelley*, make the swords and bayonets not just destructive but also phallic.[7] According to Mary Fairclough in her recent monograph, *The Romantic Crowd*, the popular press understood that the soldiers in Manchester went out of their way to target women.[8] Even the establishment press, in John Gardner's account of Peterloo, expressed widespread sympathy for the victims of the violence; the rhetorical task for radical writers was not so much creating sympathy as using it,[9] as Shelley did to promote his visionary politics.

Even before Peterloo *Julian and Maddalo* depicts the suffering of the Maniac as deriving from an unhappy sexual relationship. Kelvin Everest reads the Maniac as 'a poet frustrated by the failure to achieve an audience'.[10] It is distinctively Shelleyan to see a poet in need of an audience as symptomatic of socio-political injustice, for the true poet, in Shelley's perspective, is a prophet whose words have social power. As a failed poet and a failed lover – the failure in the one implies a failure in the other – the helpless but expressive Maniac is like Freud's melancholic who does not work through the grief over his loss, but he takes pleasure by tormenting himself, which is a displaced substitute for the lover he really wishes to punish.[11] The Maniac imagines at one point in his monologue that he will castrate himself to rectify the injury he thinks he has done to his beloved by his 'polluted' embraces (422–6), a disturbing image taken at face value, even more disturbing when seen as displaced aggression against the woman. He will imitate the action of a 'maniac monk' (424), alluding perhaps to the castrated Abelard, tragic lover of Héloïse. Alexander Pope's *Eloisa to Abelard* (1717), one of the most popular poems in the eighteenth century, provided the subtitle to one of Shelley's favourite novels, Rousseau's *Julie; or, the Nouvelle Héloïse* (1761). As victims of romantic tragedy, Abelard and St Preux suffer like the Maniac, separated from their lovers, unable to rectify what amounts to abandonment. Shelley's writing has some vivid depictions of the experience of being deeply wounded by being abandoned. The *Alastor* poet never recovers from his desertion by the visionary maiden, nor does the 'Sensitive-plant' completely recover from the departure of its maternal 'Lady' from the garden.[12] One of Shelley's figures of abandonment, who enjoys the restoration of his loved object, which he had seemed to have lost permanently, is Prometheus. Freud memorably represents the effort to master the trauma of being abandoned in the '*fort*'/'*da*' essay about his grandson in *Beyond the Pleasure Principle*; his grandson's game of tossing and retrieving a toy repetitively works through his feeling of being left behind by his mother.[13] Shelley assumed people – not just infants and children – had a natural *right* to be loved, that love was fundamental for being human, that without it, as he wrote in *On Love*, one was a 'living sepulchre' (504). Similarly, a poet who was a true poet had a right to be appreciated and read, recognised and honoured. *Julian and Maddalo's* Maniac is a neglected poet, as is the *Alastor* poet; indeed, the neglected poet is a trope in Shelley's work, not just an occasional episode. Shelley's poetry uses the abandonment anxiety we all have to illustrate the grief of the neglected poet-prophet, and he draws upon this anxiety as well when he depicts a loving society. If the true poet is a prophet who experiences divinity, intimations of the future, and the deep structure of social existence, then disregarding the poets has socio-political consequences. The inspired poets who are the 'unacknowledged legislators of the World' create not from their own will and 'spirit' but from 'the spirit of the age' (535). If such a prophetic poet is not read as he should be read, society deprives itself of a renovating resource, upon which humane advances in socio-political justice depend.

As critics such as Charles Robinson have remarked, *Julian and Maddalo*'s Maniac is part of Shelley's plan to write a poem on Torquato Tasso in reply to Byron's *Lament of Tasso* (1817).[14] Perhaps Byron's use of the word 'maniac' – 'the long and maniac cry / Of minds and bodies in captivity' (ll. 65–6) and 'The maniac and his tyrant' (l. 369)[15] – shaped Shelley's conception of his own Maniac. One observes that the word 'maniac' was used occasionally in Shelley's oeuvre; fifteen instances are recorded in the concordance.[16] According to the *OED*, maniac for the early nineteenth century has grimly sinister meanings connected with witches, evil spirits, madness requiring restraint, and 'uncontrolled, excited, or aggressive behaviour'.[17] The Gothic connotations of the word fit *Julian and Maddalo* for the most part, but the difficult instance of the word is in *The Mask of Anarchy* and its 'maniac maid', who plays a central role in the poem.

The maniac maid instigates the insurrection, which leads to the defeat of 'Anarchy' and the triumph of a popular revolt, the nature of which is articulated by the maternal voice of the earth. The turn to the feminine here has attracted attention. To account for this turn, one explanation I have already offered is the pressure exerted by the historical moment of 1819–20 when England's popular protest movements were the most active, perhaps approaching a level that could be considered revolutionary. This pressure acted as a stimulus for Shelley to think through with rigour and inventiveness the nature of revolution. As he did so, the figure of woman emerged as central, perhaps because, as Samuel Gladden has written, revolution is always the feminine antithesis to masculine hegemony, which needs to be overthrown; 'in patriarchal societies, authority is always masculine, and alternatives to authority must, by their very oppositional status, be feminine'.[18] Or, as Anne Janowitz has stated, the feminine was the most effective way for Shelley to articulate his communitarian vision, which negated the individualist Romanticism he was leaving behind, at least for this poem. Whereas Romantic woman typically represented nature in relation to a masculine imagination, and the literal in relation to a richly symbolic sign, here the maniac maid and the maternal earth ('a voluble peasant' and 'traditional wise woman') enable and exercise agency.[19]

The nature of the agency exercised by 'Hope', the maniac maid, is what I want to examine now. The eight lines she speaks that introduce the description of her actions are the only lines she utters:

> My father Time is weak and grey
> With waiting for a better day;
> See how idiot-like he stands,
> Fumbling with his palsied hands!
>
> He has had child after child
> And the dust of death is piled
> Over every one but me –
> Misery, oh, Misery! (90–8)

The hostility to the father is extraordinary, his physical ailments mocked, his passive non-resistance and patience rendered contemptible. Ineffectual, possibly syphilitic,[20] unable to sustain children, this father is a peculiar figure against which to rebel because, for one thing, as the allegorical figure of 'Time', he is not something that could be overcome in any ordinary sense. He is, however, somewhat like the authoritarian patriarchs Count Cenci and Jupiter in being old and sexually aberrant; although not rapists like them, 'father Time' produces death rather than life in a parody of healthy reproduction. The temporality of hoping entails a strategy for deferral of fulfilment and gratification; the present moment is unbearable, so one invents a future moment of satisfaction in fantasy. The relevance here of Walter Benjamin's critique of a belief in 'progress' and inevitable social improvement should be apparent. Hope's revulsion to the 'waiting for a better day' that never comes reminds one of Benjamin's rejection of a concept of history with no space for a messianic moment when the course of events can be turned suddenly in an entirely new direction. Opposing a concept of historicist and inevitable progress for which one waits, he develops a conception of the 'now-time', *Jetztzeit*, messianic time, the time of fulfilment.[21]

A male writer's imagining a daughter rebelling against the father entails less guilt than would a son's aggression against the father, and the weakness of 'father Time' anticipates the ultimate weakness of Anarchy and the assorted masculine authority figures who are forcefully removed from power. When Hope 'lay[s] down in the street / Right before the horses' feet' (98–9), as a daughter she can play the role of would-be martyr without raising the masculine issues of avoiding honourable combat. The act of hoping is not itself a violent deed entailing guilt, so the feminising of Hope accentuates its innocence. Indeed, in Western visual culture Hope is invariably represented as a woman, usually a young woman. Shelley's making Hope a woman is hardly novel; what is novel is the political role that she is playing. Demogorgon's final words in *Prometheus Unbound* provide a way to understand what the maniac maid is doing in *The Mask of Anarchy*: 'to hope, till Hope creates / From its own wreck the thing it contemplates' (IV, 373–4). Creating and contemplating are innocently fashioning something that is far from innocent, a violent 'wreck'. By making the wreck self-reflexive – 'its own wreck' – Shelley suggests that hope sustains itself with its own redundant energies. Somehow the violence directed against the self is not ultimately destructive but rather creative, as something emerges that did not exist before. Is this birth of the hoped-for-thing an immaculate conception? Or is it a clever way to represent in a disguised way a dangerous, violent and forbidden fantasy of tyrannicide? The fantasy animating these lines might be: I hope the Bad Father – the evil ruler – dies and leaves us alone. The infinitive form of hope, which parallels the other infinitives in Demogorgon's 'spell' to overthrow a hypothetical counter-revolution – to suffer, forgive, defy, love, bear – gives weight to agency, the essential necessity of acting and doing rather than waiting passively. These infinitives are a mixed group of actions, to be sure, with only 'defy' unequivocally assertive and traditionally masculine. The other infinitives could fit comfortably in a list of Christian virtues compatible with the injunction to turn the other cheek in the face of aggression. Shelley is developing his idea of non-violent resistance by drawing upon the Christian idea of pacifism but also shaping it in some ways not congruent with nineteenth-century English Christianity.

The maniac maid seems ready to become a martyr, a future Saint Hope, but a strange process averts her violent death and effects instead a glorious victory. A prosaic plot summary would be something like this: hopeful resistance to tyranny gives rise to a process of popular enlightenment, which leads to the downfall of the tyrants. The actual poetry is unsurprisingly richer than a summary can suggest. After Hope interposes her body in front of 'Murder, Fraud and Anarchy', the poetry resembles the 'Ode to the West Wind', a poem Shelley wrote shortly after finishing *The Mask of Anarchy*. As natural processes of seasonal change in the 'Ode' analogise social transformation, something similar happens in this section of the *Mask* dominated by the maniac maid. When the forces of Anarchy are about to achieve their victory, the maniac maid intervenes with her body and her voice (86–101), as there emerges a 'Shape' between Hope and her oppressors: it starts as a seemingly innocent object of nature – a misty light and image that turns into a 'frail' water 'vapour' – but it grows into storm clouds, looking like a warrior 'in mail', resembling a 'Viper'. Vapour into viper, something barely visible becomes something formidable and menacing, just as the seasonal phenomena in 'Ode to the West Wind' harness the powers of earth, wind and sea to fuel the transformative and prophetic energy of poetic 'fire'. The Shape then becomes a figure for poetry, associated with a favourite symbol of inspiration, the Morning Star (Venus), functioning as an influence over 'the heads of men' as 'Thoughts sprung' wherever she – the Shape – stepped. Like Queen Mab or the Witch of Atlas, the Shape allegorises the process of inspired consciousness, the mysterious process by which individual minds participate in what Shelley called the 'One Mind' (508).

The eleven stanzas (86–129) in which the maniac maid Hope acts, speaks and inspires function as a pivot for the entire poem. As the *Mask* was written after the first three acts of *Prometheus Unbound*, Hope follows the examples of Prometheus and Asia in her defiant act of non-violent resistance, her courageous and perilous leap of faith.

She breaks out of the confining normality of passive waiting and seizes the moment, which is the *Jetztzeit* she wrests away from historicist temporality. Her actions precipitate the messianic moment. Although I acknowledge the critical scepticism about Shelley's feminism and recognise how his writing can be read as 'colonising' the feminine rather than granting it autonomy,[22] I am reading the maniac maid in ways that highlight her heroic agency. After Gladden and Janowitz I see the gendered Hope as both structurally necessary and ideologically coherent in a poem that imagines a revolutionary transformation of an authoritarian masculine state. Because women in the actual history of the time were outside of political power, Shelley could use the feminine to signify a revolutionary subject who had nothing to lose but her chains. If he were tempted to do otherwise, there were additional Oedipal motives I have already mentioned that might have swayed him, who no doubt experienced the compositional 'choice' as an inspired necessity. Whether Shelley the historical person was a feminist is another question entirely, but the text that he has written is readable in a feminist way: a female character exercises a powerful will, has a voice, acts when no one else does, and displays daring courage. In his other political poetry, he also uses female characters: the fairy Queen Mab, Laon's sister/lover/comrade Cythna, and of course Asia. Shelley cannot imagine a visionary politics without also integrating what he considers a Wollstonecraftian dimension. Even in poems without prominent political intentions, such as *The Witch of Atlas* and *Epipsychidion*, the female character is much more than an object of masculine longing but is a subject through whom Shelley works out some of his most essential ideas.

Although Hope herself does not physically vanquish the oppressors, she enjoys with quiet serenity the sight of their violent removal (126–34). Her superiority to the masculine tyrants she has defeated could not be given more prominence than by her calm emotional demeanour; her own consciousness has not been contaminated by the evil powers with which she had to contend. Hope is not even mentioned in the stanza describing the violence:

> And Anarchy, the ghastly birth,
> Lay dead earth upon the earth –
> The Horse of Death tameless as wind
> Fled, and with his hoofs did grind
> To dust, the murderers thronged behind. (130–5)

The masculine allegorical figure who defeats Anarchy and his murderers enjoys his work enough to 'grind' his victims, thus inserting sadistic pleasure into the poem while imagining the defeat of the oppressors – and doing so without guilt. Hope did not commit any violence, although her non-violent resistance eventuated in it. In *Prometheus Unbound* it is Demogorgon, not Prometheus or Asia, who acts violently, preserving the moral purity of the ideal characters – a moral purity denied to the character of Beatrice Cenci, who participates in retaliation, violence and deception. In *Oedipus Tyrannus* the depicted revolutionary violence is comical, even gleefully carnivalesque, as Iona Taurina – the Queen Caroline figure – rides the Minotaur – the John Bull figure – to hunt for political enemies; the sexual humour and the satirical irony dissolve any guilt or ambivalence.[23]

When Shelley stages revolutionary violence, he has located this most dangerous of represented events within narratives that provide explanatory justification. Who would not applaud the destruction of 'Murder', 'Fraud' and 'Anarchy'? The poem names actual political antagonists – Castlereagh, Eldon, Sidmouth – but they are never represented as physically harmed. *The Cenci* does indeed describe the revenge killing of Count Cenci, but the play provides ample extenuating circumstances; few patriarchs are as unrepentantly loathsome as this character. In the associational logic of the loyalist mentality, the promotion of even the most moderate political reform in a democratic direction gave rise to images of mob violence and revolutionary conspiracy. In the 1794 Treason Trials the prosecution argued that the reform societies advocating for parliamentary reform were in fact treasonous, according to 'constructive treason' theory, because the extra-parliamentary activities would lead eventually to killing the king.[24] As even the most temperate plan for reform possessed nevertheless a revolutionary subtext in the eyes of the state's supporters, then Shelley has no choice but to work with violent scenarios. Although in fact there were few acts of revolutionary violence in late Georgian England – and the violence of those few riots and insurrections was directed against property, rarely persons – anxiety about revolutionary violence forcefully shaped political thinking.[25] The historian Robert Poole has described the reform marches at Manchester's St Peter's Field as orderly, disciplined, non-violent, culturally traditional and festive, not overtly menacing;[26]

and after Peterloo there seem to have been no retaliatory acts of violence directed against the perpetrators of the massacre. The problem of English political violence was state violence against its citizens. However, the French Revolution was indeed violent in an extraordinary way that Simon Schama represents vividly and that Slavoj Žižek justifies politically.[27] Shelley's stated position on the moral problem of violence in the French Revolution is not far from Žižek's in that he does not expect the 'trampled slave' to 'suddenly become liberal-minded, forbearing and independent', so that unsurprisingly there was excessive and unnecessary revolutionary violence.[28] He articulated this view, which he never seems to have changed, in the Preface to *The Revolt of Islam*, but in the poetry he keeps returning to scenes of violence that function in a variety of ways.

Gothic fiction in which an evil aristocrat typically torments a young woman from the middle classes gratified the taste of a broad reading public, including Shelley. The stylised violence of the Gothic, which Shelley enjoyed as writer and reader of the genre, played out the class resentment against the aristocracy. Shelley shared with the reading public an anti-aristocratic antipathy that was personal for him, as he loathed his baronet father Sir Timothy, but his own Oedipal struggle alone was not responsible for his poetry's many scenarios in which a patriarch and a child – not always a son – struggle violently; rather, such conflicts were cultural tropes. The situation seems to be one in which Shelley's Oedipal battle maps onto a broader social psychodynamics of anti-aristocratic hatred. The tyrant Othman has Laon and Cythna burnt at the stake – after he has raped Cythna; the tyrant Cenci rapes Beatrice, who is then tortured and executed by the Inquisition; the tyrant Jupiter's torturing of Prometheus is the initial premise of the drama, and of course masculine violence inflicted upon innocent victims is redundant in *The Mask of Anarchy*.

After the apocalyptic Horse of Death tramples Anarchy and his cohorts, there is now a space cleared for the maternal 'voice' of 'earth', which constitutes the last two-thirds of the poem. I concur with Janowitz that the 'wise' earth mother gets to articulate the political heart of the poem. About her long speech I have three points to make: (1) the poem, when it recommends non-violent resistance, asks the 'people' to do almost exactly what they already have done in Manchester when the troops attacked them and they did not retaliate; (2) the most prominent affect in the depiction of Peterloo is shame, deriving from the reality that English troops have killed *English* people (not Indians, Irish, West Indians); (3) despite the objections of Susan Wolfson to the political seriousness of the speech – and the poem in general[29] – the speech and the rest of the poem have entered international radical culture, for good or ill.

It is curious how many times and in what different ways the Peterloo massacre is represented in the poem: the subtitle ('*the Massacre at Manchester*'); when Hope lays down before the attacking forces of Anarchy (98–9); the image of the 'multitude' and Hope 'ankle-deep in blood' (126–8); the refrain about lions rising in unvanquishable number at the beginning (151–5) and end (368–72) of earth mother's speech; the prohibiting of revenge after the 'Tyrant's crew' slaughters them (190–6); the invocation for a 'great' (262), 'vast Assembly' (295) that allows the 'tyrants' to exercise their violence without the crowd retaliating (303–26, 340–7). As we now know from historians, the Manchester assembly was orderly, disciplined and non-violent. If Shelley has gotten credit for inventing the tactic of non-violent resistance, some credit should go to the Midlands' reformers who conducted a peaceful protest. The distinctive political feature of Shelley's poem is not non-violent resistance as such but calling for a *repetition* of Peterloo, for as many Peterloos as necessary until the established order is toppled. The poem is an unusual mixture of pacifism, warrior virtues of courage, strength and fortitude, republican Stoicism, and maternal protection and care.

The poem assumes that numerous Peterloos would produce widespread 'shame' (348) and thus effectively delegitimate the tyrannical regime, turning the soldiers against the ruling class (348–59), uniting public opinion against aristocratic despotism and effecting a (relatively) non-violent revolution. Would the shame of the violence operate the same way if the victims were Irish Catholics, Indian Hindus and Muslims, West Indian enslaved Africans? The English nationalism, which the poem takes for granted and does not unsettle, has not been addressed in the critical commentary. Not that Shelley was unaware of the ideological shortcomings of nationalism, for his cosmopolitanism is clear in other writings, including *Oedipus Tyrannus*, where the guilt of 'Purganax' (Castlereagh), who orchestrated the 1798 suppression of the United Irishmen Rebellion, is satirically represented (II, ii, 78–81).[30] Nevertheless in *The Mask of Anarchy* English nationalism goes unchallenged.

Another aspect of the poem's evocation of shame is the explicit and excessive language of violence describing how the soldiers will slaughter the innocent marchers.

> Let the fixed bayonet
> Gleam with sharp desire to wet
> Its bright point in English blood
> Looking keen as one for blood. (311–14)

These lines make prominent sadistic, violent pleasure, as though the cold metal of the weapon were warm but punishing flesh. Another stanza also comes from the world of heightened fantasy:

> And if the tyrants dare
> Let them ride among you there,
> Slash, and stab, and maim, and hew,–
> What they like, that let them do. (140–4)

The repeated insistence that the violated people refrain from retaliating, and that he uses four separate verbs, all monosyllabic like quick thrusts of a bayonet, suggests two things. The gesture of self-control barely conceals a fantasy of revenge, and retribution arrives anyway with the sadistic pleasure of shaming the soldiers, especially in the eyes of 'Every woman' (352). The affective regime of the poem concentrates aggressive violence ultimately on the 'tyrants' not the people who are protesting peacefully. The redirecting of violent fantasies is commonly understood in psychoanalytic literature, notably in Melanie Klein's writing.[31] The shame, then, is a shrewd political strategy that has been effective in specific situations – Gandhi's India, Martin Luther King Jr.'s American South – and an indispensable component in a psychological process of redirecting and containing aggression.

Susan Wolfson's reading of *The Mask of Anarchy* challenges many things about the poem, but not the nationalism. Some of her objections to the poem are ethical as she illustrates how Shelley self-servingly had incomplete understanding of what he hoped to accomplish with the poem. He must have known the poem was not going to have any immediate political effect because he was in Italy at the time of Peterloo, and he sent the poem to Leigh Hunt, someone in England he knew would not publish it. The bad faith of the poem is evident from the unclosed frame of a dream vision, as if the whole poetic effort were just a self-satisfying dream; the poem is a fantasy about political agency, as Shelley is seeking 'merely aesthetic self-satisfaction' (726). Wolfson sets the bar high for what constitutes good political poetry and by her criteria the *Mask* falls short, but flawed as it is, the poem has become part of radical culture, perhaps undeservingly so, perhaps not. When Shelley made the effort, he could, in London or Italy, get his radical texts published – in 1815 by way of the Spenceans' *Theological Inquirer*, in 1820 the quickly suppressed *Oedipus Tyrannus* – so Wolfson's hard questions are appropriate. If Shelley seems inconsistent and ambivalent about politics, something Wolfson brings out effectively, nevertheless *The Mask of Anarchy* has become one of the great political poems, contributing to the project of non-violent resistance and working-class radicalism.[32] The largely ethical issues Wolfson raises might have troubled Shelley himself because his philosophy valued self-knowledge. In *The Triumph of Life*, the character of Rousseau addresses the narrator about those who have been defeated by 'Life': that they 'did not know themselves', and they 'Could not repress the mutiny within' (212–13).

As nothing is simple in Shelley's work, even self-knowledge is sometimes problematic, as it is in *The Cenci*, when Orsino complains of Beatrice and her family for their 'trick' of analysing 'their own and other minds' because such 'self-anatomy' teaches 'the will / Dangerous secrets' (II, ii, 108–11). The self-knowledge that Orsino gains from his love of Beatrice is not morally virtuous in this extremely dark play, also a work of 1819, obviously connected with the political turmoil in England that *The Mask of Anarchy* addresses explicitly. Beatrice is a blameless rape victim, but her morally problematic actions afterwards generate in the reader what Shelley calls in the Preface a 'casuistry' to justify her actions, which appal us nevertheless (142). Shelley deprives the reader of the enjoyment of sympathising unambivalently with an innocent victim. The sexualising of political oppression, which makes rape the *ne plus ultra* of sadistic domination, turns Beatrice's situation into an allegory for England in 1819, and that this sexualising resonated with the political culture is apparent in the popular discourse about Peterloo. The psychoanalytic scenario, which I sketched out in *Radical Shelley*,[33] is the fantasy about the bad aristocratic father who castrates and rapes the children who place their hope in a good mother. Beatrice actually has no access to a good mother, so she desperately invents a good father the play mockingly withholds, but *The Mask of Anarchy* has the good mother who delivers the poem's long speech and in Romanticism in general the good mother is of course nature, at least from the time of Rousseau (the actual Rousseau, not Shelley's character). The myth of nature's plenitude and the bad aristocratic father's hoarding of nature's wealth also undergirds various socialistic efforts in the nineteenth century.

The most intricate treatment and working through of the Oedipal conflict is *Prometheus Unbound*, where Jupiter parallels Count Cenci the rapist in his own rape of Thetis (III, i, 19–51). Thinking the 'fatal child' from his union with Thetis will guarantee his reign, Jupiter suffers defeat because out of Demogorgon's realm comes not the hoped-for son of Thetis but Demogorgon himself, something more powerful than Jupiter. With Demogorgon overthrowing Jupiter, Shelley protects Prometheus from the power struggle so as not to perpetuate a future Oedipal struggle in which a son would overthrow Prometheus. The only children Prometheus and Asia will produce in the utopian world are images and aesthetic objects: they will 'make / Strange combinations out of common things / Like human babes in their brief innocence' (III, iii, 31–3). They will not have children with whom they might conflict; rather, they will *be* children. This and many other inversions unsettle the usual structural determinations, so that Prometheus' heroic action is not to act but to feel and to withdraw from action; Asia's heroism consists of her responsiveness to dreams and images, which lead her ultimately to the cave of Demogorgon, where she plays the role of the traditional epic and quest-romance hero, interrogating the underworld source of wisdom. One line of inversions in the post-Jupiter world is created by negations: 'thrones were kingless' and man is 'Sceptreless', 'uncircumscribed', 'unclassed, tribeless, and nationless' (III, iv, 131, 194–5). The symbols of the old order are now unreadable in the utopian future, 'no more remembered', 'not o'erthrown, but unregarded now' (III, iv, 164–79). The path out of Oedipal violence is mapped in the second act where Asia and Panthea dialogically recall dreams, trace their images, make associations, follow their intuitive sensations; they practice psychoanalysis, in other words.[34]

Even in the climactic conclusion of the third act of *Prometheus Unbound* the triumphant victory over oppression still leaves 'chance and death and mutability' (III, iv, 201) untransformed, so that while unnecessary suffering can be eliminated, a certain level of ordinary suffering is not available to alteration. For an objective correlative of suffering that is subject to change Shelley used acts of physical violence – rape, torture, murder – the worlds of *The Cenci* and *The Mask of Anarchy*. The helplessness and anguish of *Julian and Maddalo*'s Maniac establish a kind of suffering for which Shelley will produce a dramatic contrast in *The Cenci*, where Beatrice only seems to have options and room to exercise her will; she will achieve a state of radical disillusionment before the Inquisition dispatches her. At least Beatrice tried to act against her oppression. Finally, with another 'maniac' – the maniac maid Hope – Shelley finds a vehicle for acting effectively in the imagined social world of a dream allegory, releasing a figurative process that enables the earth mother to articulate a socio-political vision of justice and equality.

Notes

1. E. P. Thompson, *The Making of the English Working Class* (New York: Vintage, 1963). Michael Scrivener, *Radical Shelley: The Philosophical Anarchism and Utopian Thought of Percy Bysshe Shelley* (Princeton: Princeton University Press, 1982); *Reading Shelley's Interventionist Poetry, 1819–20*, ed. Michael Scrivener, Romantic Circles Praxis Series, May 2001 <http://www.rc.umd.edu/praxis/interventionist/toc.html> (last accessed 8 June 2017).
2. *Shelley's Poetry and Prose*, ed. Donald H. Reiman and Neil Fraistat (New York: W. W. Norton, 2002), p. 534. All quotations of Shelley unless otherwise designated are from this edition, references to which will appear hereafter parenthetically in the text.
3. For a psychoanalytic treatment of Shelley from a Jungian perspective, see Christine Gallant, *Shelley's Ambivalence* (New York: St. Martin's Press, 1989). My own approach, when I draw upon psychoanalysis, is Freudian.
4. Elaine Scarry, *The Body in Pain: The Making and Unmaking of the World* (Oxford: Oxford University Press, 1985), pp. 3–11.
5. *The Letters of Percy Bysshe Shelley*, ed. F. L. Jones, 2 vols (Oxford: Clarendon Press), vol. 2, p. 117.
6. Ian Haywood, *Bloody Romanticism: Spectacular Violence and the Politics of Representation, 1776–1832* (Basingstoke: Palgrave Macmillan, 2006), p. 8.
7. Scrivener, *Radical Shelley*, pp. 202–7.

8. Mary Fairclough, *The Romantic Crowd: Sympathy, Controversy, and Print Culture* (Cambridge: Cambridge University Press, 2013), p. 153.
9. John Gardner, *Poetry and Popular Protest: Peterloo, Cato Street and the Queen Caroline Controversy* (New York: Palgrave Macmillan, 2011), p. 86.
10. Kelvin Everest, 'Shelley's Doubles: An Approach to *Julian and Maddalo*', in Reiman and Fraistat, *Shelley's Poetry and Prose*, p. 680.
11. See Freud's 'Mourning and Melancholia' in *The Freud Reader*, ed. Peter Gay (New York: W. W. Norton, 1989), pp. 584–9.
12. See Richard Caldwell's psychoanalytic 'The Sensitive Plant as Original Fantasy', *Studies in Romanticism* 15 (1976), pp. 221–52. He takes an object-relations perspective.
13. Gay, *The Freud Reader*, pp. 597–601.
14. Charles Robinson, *Shelley and Byron: The Snake and the Eagle Wreathed in Fight* (Baltimore: Johns Hopkins University Press, 1976), pp. 81–104.
15. *Byron: Poetical Works*, ed. Frederick Page (Oxford: Oxford University Press, 1969), pp. 367, 369.
16. F. S. Ellis, *A Lexical Concordance to the Poetical Works of Percy Bysshe Shelley* (New York: Burt Franklin, 1968), p. 433.
17. *Oxford English Dictionary*, s.v. maniac, adj. and n. (Oxford: Oxford University Press, 1989) <http://www.oed.com/view/Entry/113462> (last accessed 31 May 2017).
18. Samuel Gladden, 'Shelley's Agenda Writ Large: Reconsidering *Oedipus Tyrannus; or, Swellfoot the Tyrant*, in Scrivener's *Reading Shelley's Interventionist Poetry*, n. 3.
19. Anne Janowitz, *Lyric and Labour in the Romantic Tradition* (Cambridge: Cambridge University Press, 1998), pp. 98–105.
20. Nora Crook and Derek Guiton, *Shelley's Venomed Melody* (Cambridge: Cambridge University Press, 1986), describe extensively Shelley's anxiety about syphilis and the many ways this anxiety gets into the writing.
21. Walter Benjamin, *Illuminations*, ed. and intro. H. Arendt, trans. H. Zohn (New York: Schocken Books, 1968), pp. 253–64.
22. One can find this critique in Barbara Gelpi, *Shelley's Goddess: Maternity, Language, Subjectivity* (New York: Oxford University Press, 1992).
23. *Shelley: Poetical Works*, ed. G. M. Matthews (Oxford: Oxford University Press, 1969), pp. 408–9.
24. Michael Scrivener, *Seditious Allegories: John Thelwall and Jacobin Writing* (University Park: Pennsylvania State University Press, 2001), pp. 168–78.
25. Haywood, *Bloody Romanticism*, p. 183.

26. Robert Poole, 'The March to Peterloo: Politics and Festivity in Late Georgian England', *Past and Present* 192 (2006), pp. 109–54.
27. Simon Schama, *Citizens: A Chronicle of the French Revolution* (New York: Random House, 1989), and Slavoj Žižek, *Robespierre: Virtue and Terror* (London: Verso, 2007).
28. Matthews, *Shelley: Poetical Works*, p. 33.
29. Susan J. Wolfson, 'Poetic Form and Political Reform: *The Mask of Anarchy* and 'England in 1819', in Reiman and Fraistat, *Shelley's Poetry and Prose*, pp. 722–35.
30. For Shelley's cosmopolitanism, see Michael Scrivener, *The Cosmopolitan Ideal in the Age of Revolution and Reaction, 1776–1832* (London: Pickering and Chatto, 2007), pp. 203–14.
31. See Melanie Klein, *Envy and Gratitude, and Other Works, 1946–1963* (London: Hogarth Press, 1975).
32. See Art Young, *Shelley and Nonviolence* (The Hague: Mouton, 1975); Paul Foot, *Red Shelley* (London: Sidgwick and Jackson, 1980); Michael Demson,'"Let a great Assembly be": Percy Shelley's "The Mask of Anarchy" and the Organization of Labor in New York City, 1910–30', *European Romantic Review* 22:5 (2011), pp. 641–65; Michael Demson and Summer McClinton (illus.), *Masks of Anarchy: The History of a Radical Poem from Percy Shelley to the Triangle Factory Fire* (London: Verso, 2013).
33. Scrivener, *Radical Shelley,* pp. 203–6.
34. A study that brings together psychoanalysis and Romanticism is Joel Faflak's, *Romantic Psychoanalysis. The Burden of the Mystery* (Albany: State University of New York Press, 2008).

Index

Note: Page numbers is *italics* indicate illustrations and page numbers followed by n indicate end-of-chapter notes.

EU representative:
Easy Access System Europe
Mustamäe tee 50, 10621 Tallinn, Estonia
Gpsr.requests@easproject.com

www.ingramcontent.com/pod-product-compliance
Lightning Source LLC
Chambersburg PA
CBHW070619100726
47907CB00007B/1793

* 9 7 8 1 4 7 4 4 2 8 5 7 6 *